COLD WAR R̶U̶I̶N̶S̶

MW01074602

COLD WAR RUINS

*Transpacific Critique of American Justice
and Japanese War Crimes*

LISA YONEYAMA

DUKE UNIVERSITY PRESS DURHAM AND LONDON 2016

© 2016 Duke University Press
All rights reserved
Designed by Heather Hensley
Typeset in Whitman by Westchester Book Group

Library of Congress Cataloging-in-Publication Data
Names: Yoneyama, Lisa, [date] author.
Title: Cold War ruins : TranspacificcritiqueofAmericanjusticea   nd
Japa nese war crimes / Lisa Yoneyama.
Description: Durham : Duke University Press, 2016. |
Includes bibliographical references and index.
Identifiers: LCCN 2016002411| ISBN 9780822361503
(hardcover : alk. paper) | ISBN 9780822361695 (pbk. : alk. paper)
ISBN 9780822374114 (e-book)
Subjects: LCSH: World War, 1939–1945—Atrocities—Japan. |
Reparations for historical injustices—Japan. | Cold war. |
Nationalism and feminism. | Decolonization. | Transnationalism.
Classification: LCC D804.J3 Y59 2016 | DDC 940.54/050952–dc23
LC record available at http://lccn.loc.gov/2016002411

Cover art: *Punish the Responsible—For Peace* by Kang
Duk-Kyoung. This picture is provided by the House of Sharing
and the Museum of Sexual Slavery by Japanese Military.

CONTENTS

Since the early nineties we have been witnessing renewed calls for historical justice, which are unparalleled in their intensity and scope.[1] In different parts of Asia, the Pacific Islands, and North America, redress demands at the turn of the new century have gained increasing visibility and urgency. Primarily if not exclusively concerned with the losses wrought by Japan's military and colonial aggression, this resurgence in calls for historical justice has not only added new stories to the inventory of wartime suffering. It has revealed that previously concluded postbelligerency adjudications, war indemnities settlements, and various state-to-state normalizations have rendered many instances of violence unredressable, or only incrementally redressed. In others words, the post-1990s redress efforts have been a major force in illuminating the gross oversights of the administration of transitional justice in the war's immediate aftermath. Much of the pathos uniting the collectivities of redress activism across various borders is spurred by the sense of belatedness and the indignation it renders. Why so late? Why after almost half a century? Why failure?

Cold War Ruins: Transpacific Critique of American Justice and Japanese War Crimes takes on this question of belatedness. It asks, in what ways must we deem the initial moment of transitional justice a failure, what are the geohistorical circumstances, international protocols and cultural forces that left certain injuries to certain bodies unredressed, and what implications might the belated attempts to address these initial shortcomings have on broader cultural politics and the production of knowledge? More than an examination of individual case histories, *Cold War Ruins* examines the post-1990s redress pursuits as a culture, that is, a complex social formation that is also embodied, an ideological matrix of juridico-political processes (which include backlashes, controversies, and their political unconscious), and powerful historical imaginaries marshaled across different borders, geographical, social, and otherwise.

Theories of violence and justice have come under new scrutiny as part of the broader reorganization of knowledge in the social and human sciences. The renewal reflects intensifying concerns for coextensive yet seemingly bipolarized historical developments. On one hand, we have witnessed the rise of new internationalism and increasing concerns about the human security paradigm. International feminist jurisprudence and the intensifying quest for redress, reparations, and reconciliation are both part of that process. On the other hand, the precariat and other new social movements have regalvanized under intensifying neoliberalization and in the face of the failing juridico-political premises of modernity. Paralleling these processes is the proliferation of weapons of mass destruction that have been simultaneously banalized and (re)spectacularized, the (re)assertion of sovereign power as we have witnessed in the latest U.S. wars, and the expansion of spaces of social death such as refugee and migrant camps, prisons and the so-called low-intensity conflict zones. What this seeming bipolarization shows is the mounting desire to universally condemn certain kinds of violence through exposure and focalization and, at the same time, the escalation of violence's invisibility in a myriad of microspaces. *Cold War Ruins* attempts to place the post-1990s redress culture and its genealogy within the late-capitalist, late-colonial, turn-of-the-century geography to explore the predicaments and possibilities of historical justice. In this context, the redress demands addressing Japanese war crimes, in particular, have raised important questions regarding the legibility of violence, the concept of the human, sovereignty, the economy of forgiveness, aporia of transnational critique, and perhaps most significantly, judicialization of the political.

As I hope to show, the post-1990s rearticulation of historical justice—or what I call "transborder redress culture"—has in one way or another interrogated the institutional and epistemic structures that have come to take hold of the world after World War II. It has exposed the scaffolds of transitional justice introduced at the war's end, which have long set the parameters of what can be known as egregious violence, as well as whose violence on which bodies can be addressed and redressed. *Cold War Ruins* scrutinizes this critical divide between the legibility and the illegibility of violence as an integral part of the post–World War II, Cold War knowledge formation. And this formation, it argues, cannot be grasped fully without observing the geopolitical shifts and continuities across the transwar period. This historical conjuncture saw the Allies not only liberating the areas formerly occupied by and colonized by the Japanese empire, but also the United States' ascendance to the military supremacy in what might be termed the Cold War "empire for liberty."[2] Having liberated much of Asia and the Pacific Islands from Japanese imperial violence, the United States simultaneously forged anticommunist networks linking the military-security-academic, free market client states, especially in North and Southeast Asia.[3] The ability to decisively affect the postbelligerency drawing of lines between the aggrieved and the aggressors, the redressable and the unredressable, the forgiven and the unforgiven—this prerogative constituted an integral part of what enabled this transwar, transpacific development. Transborder redress culture at the turn of the new century and the politics it has animated, I suggest, should be read as a trace of the deeply conjoined, enduring interimperial complex of historical violence that was disavowed in the initial phase of transitional justice, yet which was then protracted into our late-colonial, late-capitalist world.

How do we reckon with the myriad instances of violence that the two empires have occluded or made invisible, and hence unredressable? How might we rethink the idea of "justice" in order to highlight the transwar continuity and the transferability of violence between the two imperial powers? And most crucially, what are the transborder agencies, local mediations, and the remainders of justice within and beyond the U.S.-Japan binary that have animated redress in the 1990s, and in what ways do they unsettle or not unsettle knowledge concerning violence and the violence of counterviolence? To begin such inquiries, *Cold War Ruins* foregrounds transpacific critique as a critical methodology with which we might scrutinize the seemingly intractable Cold War formations and their lasting material and discursive effects.

While there are various contexts in which the idea of the transpacific can be deployed, I situate *Cold War Ruins* in the genealogy of transpacific critique that has emerged at the interstices of Asian studies, American studies, and Asian American studies—or more broadly, area studies, ethnic studies, and postcolonial studies. I do so to illuminate the predicaments that such disciplinary divides have concealed through their management of knowledge.[4] The term "transpacific" and its associations with geopolitics bear imprints of the existing nexus of knowledge and power. Taken literally, it can suggest mere movements across the ocean. It may be read as a concept affinal to the "Pacific Rim," or more recently the "Transpacific Partnership (TPP)," in the cartography of transnational capitalism, which has long vacated the people and histories of the Pacific Islands. The "transpacific" also marks the predicaments of the settler colonial present that need to be further articulated in the Pacific Islander–Asian American political and intellectual exchanges.[5] Bearing these and other problematic associations in mind, I propose a dissonant reading of the transpacific as an alternative to the Cold War geography, which emerged out of transwar, interimperial, and transnational entanglements. Eschewing reification of the "Asia-Pacific" as yet another area studies' militarized geopolitical category, and pushing against the conventional periodization and perceptions of violence and justice, the book advances what might be called a conjunctive cultural critique of the transpacific in order to elucidate the still-present Cold War frame of knowledge that, despite some adjustments and transvaluations, continues to stabilize international protocols, cultural assumptions, and normalized categories associated with our identities, histories, and boundaries.[6] At a minimum, such a methodology points to the limits of our political and positivist certitude and urges us to consider why we need to unlearn some of the most familiar terms with which we make demands for a just world.

The term "World War II" is used to indicate the historiographical universalism with which we understand the globalized midcentury belligerencies treated in this book as a single war fought between the tripartite Axis powers and the Allied powers. In addition, "the Asia-Pacific War" is used to highlight the multiple and complex nature of militarized conflicts between 1931 and 1945.[7] "The Asia-Pacific War" is a Japanese neologism proposed in the eighties with the intention of displacing earlier nomenclature and its normative periodization. The Greater East Asia War, U.S.-Japan War, Pacific War, Second Sino-Japanese War, and even Fifteen Year War—all fell into a binary discourse of civilization by casting the war as fought either exclusively between the West and the rest or among discrete and internally coherent nation-state universals. The periodization of World War II in the Pacific theater conventionally begins with the Japanese attack on Pearl Harbor and ends with the atomic bombing of Hiroshima and Nagasaki. Crucial to the book's discussion on historical justice, the neologism's spatial conjoining of the Pacific theater and the battlefields in Asia was also intended to shift the meaning of Japan's defeat: the earlier namings, with the exception of the Fifteen Year War and the Sino-Japanese War, suggested that Japan was defeated primarily by American military and technological supremacy, whereas "the Asia-Pacific War" pronounces an awareness that Japan lost multiple wars—that is, not only military but, if only briefly, colonial and capitalist wars—to resistance against Japanese imperial domination at multiple locations. As well, the new coinage sheds light on Japanese military aggression not only in mainland China but in such places as Indonesia, which had formerly been marginalized in World War II historiography due to their complex and not-so-linear histories of colonial occupation and decolonization.[8] While any naming necessarily demarcates its limits, I have adopted "the Asia-Pacific War" in the current study, as I did in my previous work, to signal that which has fallen out of the universalism and binarism of former designations.

The use of uppercase for the term "state," is meant to highlight its ontology as a sovereign polity, thus underscoring the entity's exceptional ability to decide on behalf of or regardless of the members' collective will, whether to kill, let live, apologize or punish. I will use lowercase (e.g., state-to-state agreements) when referring to countries or existing governments, although in practice, the two are obviously often indistinguishable.

Finally, I use the term "Cold War" to refer to the U.S.-Soviet confrontation, its globality, and the term's universalistic imaginary, as well as the Western hemispheric periodization of history. In contrast, I use "cold war" to signal the diverse regional manifestations of the seemingly parallel ideological confrontations. This differentiation is more than geographical. The use of uppercase is meant to suggest that while many of the regional cold wars were fought as hot wars and in other violent forms, their histories have been eclipsed by the reification of the globality of the U.S.-Soviet Cold War. Accordingly, I use "post–Cold War" or "Cold War hiatus" when referring to the period after the formal collapse of the Soviet Union and the unification of Germany. While the prefix, "post," signifies that the condition it refers to has not concluded but continues through modification, amendments, and/or intensification, the lowercase underscores that despite the formal declaration of the end of the Cold War in the West, and despite its undeniably far-reaching epistemic and institutional impacts on other parts of the world, such universal periodization does not automatically apply to the West's rest.[9]

Japanese, Korean, and Chinese names are in most cases rendered with surname first, followed by the given name, when the named individual resides or has resided primarily in East Asia. Korean proper nouns are written in modified McCune-Reischauer style. Romanization for Chinese proper nouns follows modified Pinyin style. Japanese romanization follows modified Hepburn style. Exceptions are made for proper nouns for which there are standard renderings in English (e.g., Chiang Kai-shek, Park Chung Hee, Kyoto, Ryukyu), or when the individual customarily uses another spelling.

Transpacific Cold War Formations
and the Question of (Un)Redressability

Imperialism cannot be overcome by another imperialism, nor can it be brought to justice by one.
Takeuchi Yoshimi, "Kindai no chōkoku"

Justice, insofar as it is not only a juridical or political concept, opens up for *l'avenir* the transformation, the recasting or refounding of law and politics.... Justice as the experience of absolute alterity is unpresentable, but it is the chance of the event and the condition of history.
Jacques Derrida, "Force of Law: The 'Mystical Foundation of Authority' "

What returns to us in the wake of the scene of world order governed by restored hegemony is a political logic that we are all too familiar with and which develops in the very heart of democracies: that of enlightened despotism.
Jacques Rancière, "Overlegitimation"

One of the twentieth century's cultural responses to wars, military aggression, and other egregious violations of human lives and the international order has been the administration of transitional justice. The military tribunals, state apologies, corporate reparations, and more recently, truth and reconciliation commissions (TRCs), all intended for both international and domestic audiences, have offered different modalities for redressing past injustices.[1] With regard to World War II, the Nuremberg Military Trials are most commonly known to have set new conventions for prosecuting such heinous acts as genocide and abuse of war prisoners under the judicial concepts of war crimes and crimes against humanity. On the Asia-Pacific front, the International Military Tribunal for the Far East (1946–1948; IMTFE or Tokyo War Crimes Trial, hereafter), a counterpart to the Nuremberg Trials, adjudicated on Japanese "crimes against peace" of conspiring to wage a war of aggression (Class A). Prosecution of "conventional war crimes" and "crimes against humanity" included military atrocities, civilian massacres, and abuses against POWs and other internees (Class B and C). Numerous local war crimes trials also took place independent of the IMTFE at various locales where Japanese troops had surrendered.

Reparations for Japanese aggression and war crimes—including civilian forced labor, the maltreatment of Allied POWs, and other war-related damages between 1941 and 1945—have been regarded as officially but arguably prematurely and insufficiently resolved by the multilateral San Francisco Peace Treaty of 1951 (official name, Treaty of Peace with Japan), which was signed by forty-nine nations, who thereby relinquished rights to further reparations.[2] The Southeast Asian nations that suffered immeasurable losses from Japan's military invasion and aggression in war—including Burma, the Philippines, Indonesia, and South Vietnam—four postcolonial states that achieved at least nominal independence shortly before or after the end of World War II—did not or only reluctantly agreed to sign the San Francisco Peace Treaty; but each obliged Japan to offer formal state reparations through treaties that came into force during the 1950s.[3] The San Francisco Peace Treaty and other normalization treaties and official agreements signed bilaterally over the Cold War decades—between Japan and Cambodia (1950), the Republic of China (1952, nullified after 1972), the Republic of Korea (1965), Singapore (1967), U.S.-Micronesia (1969), the People's Republic of China (1972), and more—are considered to have resolved the basic terms of reparations, at least at the state-to-state level, through economic aid, supplies, services, and other forms.

The architecture of postwar settlement, which was arranged during the early-to-middle years of the Cold War, has to this day been steadfastly upheld by the signatory governments. This is not to say that the initial terms of settlement were uncritically accepted. Numerous important archival studies have shown that the Allied nations were far from unanimous in supporting the United States' leniency toward Japan and its interest in rebuilding Japan as the major bulwark against Communism in the region. The Soviet Union, Australia, and the Republic of China, among others, questioned U.S. dominance and maneuvering over the IMTFE. Representatives of many Asian nations, especially the Philippines, resented concessions forced upon the less powerful, newly developing postindependence states with the signing of the San Francisco Peace Treaty.[4] While several European countries made reparations cases for the assets they had held in China but were lost due to the Japanese military invasion, the two emerging regimes representing the people of China, the Republic of China (1912–) and the People's Republic of China (1949–), which had been at war against Japan, were excluded from the treaty; their reparations had to be settled through the subsequent bilateral negotiations and agreements.[5] Strong opposition within Japan saw the San Francisco Peace Treaty as one-sided in its intensification of the Cold War and proclaimed in its stead a nonalignment position through the "four peace principles" of "no rearmament, no post-treaty U.S. military forces in Japan, an overall as opposed to separate peace, and permanent neutrality in the Cold War."[6] South Korea's negotiations with Japan over terms of the 1965 Basic Treaty were distinctive and particularly contentious because its status as a former Japanese colony (1910–1945) ineluctably brought international attention to the question of colonial restitution. Moreover, because many of the reparations were aimed predominantly at stimulating industrialization and economic development, corruption and plutocracy involving state leaders and multinational corporations prevented a large portion of the already compromised war indemnity from reaching individual victims.[7] Contentions and contradictions from the earlier postwar settlement thus remained an undercurrent for radical politics in many Asian nations, especially during the 1960s anti–Vietnam War protest and prodemocracy, antidictatorial movements in the successive decades.

Still, it was not until the 1990s that calls for redress took on a renewed and intensified international visibility and extensiveness. Demands for new and additional reparations in recent decades have involved multiple public venues and found different forms of expression in juridical, administrative, and legislative channels. Since 1999 the demands for redress, apologies, and reparations from the Japanese government and corporations have explicitly and vigorously involved the U.S. courts, American legislatures, and community politics. They have also incited many major public controversies through various cultural media such as museums, film, fiction, historians' debates, and Internet activism. What is the significance of such contestations over previously concluded adjudication and reparations? What distinguishes redress activism that emerged during the post–Cold War years from earlier ones, and why do the differences matter? In what ways do the post-1990s developments challenge or not challenge prevailing memories and understandings about the war and its aftermath?

Settling accounts of wars involves more than calculating the losses and damages brought on by the defeated regime's aggression. Reckoning with the costs of hostility, postwar settlements also performatively define the war's meaning for the postbelligerence world. They offer answers to questions about the war's origin; how it was fought; by, with, and against whom; according to what periodization; for what purposes; and ultimately for whose and what justice. In observing post–Cold War attempts to "redress Cold War redress," so to speak, it is important to note that to challenge previously agreed upon terms of settlement is more than an act of correcting initial miscalculations. It calls into question the very cultural assumptions, intellectual premises, and relations of power, according to which history and its meanings have been narrated and accepted as truth. The resilience of the earlier adjudication and reparations arrangements notwithstanding, the post–Cold War moment in Asia and the Pacific appears to have brought forth significant changes to the ways in which the war and its trajectories have previously been known—or not known—to us. The culture of redress at the new century's turn thus calls our attention to the fact that the discourse on historical justice is inseparable from how we understand the region's modernity, liberalism, history of colonialism, nationalism, and decolonization.

The upsurge in yearning for justice concerning the Asia-Pacific War is by no means an isolated phenomenon. The decade following the collapse of the Soviet Union was a period of adjustment on a global scale of political-economic alignments, sense of belonging, and the epistemic foundations of the post–World War II order. Not only did the rebirth of Germany in 1989 necessitate new terms of reconciliation. The post–Cold War adjustment furthermore led to revaluating the master narrative of World War II memories and the postwar national histories it authenticated. The 1995 milestone commemoration of the Vel d'Hiv Jewish roundup, followed by the famous prosecution of the Vichy regime's high official Maurice Papon, on charges of crimes against humanity, ushered in a full reassessment of the French state's accountability with regard to the pan-European Nazi Holocaust, challenging the post–World War II narrative of the French "resistance." Because Papon was also known for his role as police prefect in Algeria (1949–1958), and as the Paris police chief who ordered the 1961 roundup of over five thousand Algerians and other migrants which resulted in an estimated two hundred civilian deaths, the French reassessment of its accountability simultaneously evoked memories of the Algerian War and the legacy of colonialism. Not only could World War II no longer be remembered through the binary of resisters versus collaborators. Much like the post–Cold War politics of re-membering Hiroshima's atom bombing which I had also observed, the shift in the French discourse on historical justice marks a certain postcolonial condition in which any challenge to the orthodoxy of World War II remembering cannot but conjure up memories of colonial violence and challenges to present political and economic asymmetries rooted in the past. At the same time, as the transnational feminist scholar Fatima El-Tayeb reminds us: the "connection between colonial and metropolitan violence that Papon personified" is "persistently suppressed in European discourse."[8] The post-1990s redress culture focusing on the Asia-Pacific War cannot be grasped apart from such a global milieu and its critique.

To capture the hemispheric reach of the political and epistemic shifts that seem to have taken place largely during the 1990s, I name that historicized historical moment the "post–Cold War." Such a nomenclature immediately proves strained when considering how U.S. foreign policy experts seem vexed when they ponder whether the post–Cold War era of unipolar U.S. dominance might have been short lived and, when they confront the possibility that the Cold War might have returned when faced with the obviously resurgent Chinese military and economic might.[9] The term, moreover, reflects a geographical provincialism. To denote the period after the 1989 fall of the Berlin Wall as the "end" of the Cold War pertains only to the Western Hemisphere's temporality. The division of Korea into two political regimes persists as a regional cold war reality which remains as a legacy of the Korean War, the "hot" civil war. With respect to postwar settlement and normalization, Russia and North Korea remain two countries that have not signed full-fledged peace treaties with Japan. What appears to be history's telos, then, might be more appropriately understood as a structural cessation, a moment of rupture in the way we live through the continuing post–World War II/Cold War order. Rather than formal dissipation of the binary antagonism, the 1990s Cold War hiatus might best be posited as an epistemic rupture. It is at this critical juncture that the earlier unfulfilled, interrupted, or aborted attempts at transitional justice have resurfaced and become remobilized.

The twentieth century's reparations and adjudication efforts were in large measure a global Cold War enterprise, in the sense that they were pursued by States as primary agents with their territorially bound nationalist historical sensibilities, which were at the same time regimented by the U.S.- or Soviet-led East and West blocs. In contrast, redress and reparations demands at the twenty-first century's end increasingly attend to more than the injury brought on by one nation against another. They have increasingly foregrounded losses that have been left unaddressed by their victims' peripheral status within the national community, previously marginalized by imperial policies, during the war, or in the process of decolonization. More often than not, those who assert their rights to reparations have had to struggle against their own governments and official policies while relying on subnational and supranational spaces where alternative discursive parameters have allowed such juridico-historical claims to be heard. The emergent redress efforts have thus begun to seek not an international but transnational historical justice.

Furthermore, while state apparatuses necessarily present reparations demands and settlements as reflective of the collective will of a nation-state, understandings about historical justice have not been shared or pursued uniformly within national borders. Deep schisms run through not only national communities on the question of historical accountability, victimization, and loss. In so many cases the primary agent-subjects of post–Cold War redress culture have also been gendered and racialized minorities, colonial and transcolonial subjects, migrants and diasporic peoples, so-called collaborators, and the economically and politically disfranchised—namely subjects ambiguously or multiply positioned by their national and ideological affiliations who have had often precarious relations to the national polity and its free market.[10] Memories of war and its aftermaths remembered by the newly politicized subjects of the postnineties redress culture have thus increasingly become transborder. Even in the early eighties, as I have observed in earlier works, presentiments of change began to unleash previously untold stories of loss, violence, betrayal, unlikely alliances, alternative and fluid identities, and even hopes, which have long been suppressed or marginalized within the national and global historical narratives that have dominated most of the post–World War II decades.[11] This shift has critical ramifications on the politics of knowledge production, the book's primary concern.

To put it differently, the post-1990s redress culture highlights the inability of the State to fully represent its own subjects. It newly articulates the idea that the rights to reparations neither originate in nor are protected by the State. The State-centered argument that the reparation issues pertaining to Japan's war of aggression were resolved at least legally by postwar arrangements, mentioned above, has been the foremost obstacle to virtually all ongoing legal battles for new or additional reparations from the Japanese government and corporations. This globally sustained official position has preempted judicial solutions. Increasingly, activism that seeks to obtain belated reparations for the violence long forgotten by Cold War historiography has advanced the juridical argument that, even in those cases where standing international treaties have relinquished the government's rights to reparations, such state-to-state settlements do not preclude individuals' legal rights to compensation.[12] The interpretive schism in juridical views reflects the intellectual and ideological contestation over the State-mediated reparations and other conventions of international order that have contained claims of historical justice in previous decades. At the same time, transnational, post-Statist redress has become an integral part of the turn-of-the-century global political economy and its judicialization. In the global judicialization process, the transnational capital, often armored with powerful corporate legal teams, can also extend its reach over state sovereignty. Paralleling such developments, some of the new redress demands have been pushed into the privatized realm of moral accountability.[13]

Cold War Ruins concerns just such critical and not-so-uniform historical sensibilities, transnationality, and the emergent knowledge that the post-1990s redress culture has elicited as its own condition of possibility. The efforts to repair the wounds of past violence and the manner in which such reparations are sought are intimately tied to questions of society's vision for its future, how it envisages this future within the broader landscape of collective alliances, and what political subjects will be integral to this process. *Cold War Ruins* argues therefore that redress and the broader discourse on violence and justice of which it is a part are inseparable from the (re)constitution of self, sociality, and history. To the extent that the post-1990s discourse on historical justice disturbs the normativity of modern nation-states and their authentic belonging, the heated public debates and the memories of violence within redress culture have necessarily been transnational. Here, transnationality means much more than mere movements across nation-state borders or exchanges among multiple national actors and locations. It comprises insurgent memories, counterknowledges, and inauthentic identities that have been regimented by the discourse and institutions centering on nation-states. Transnationality, in other words, points to the presence of excess in the hegemonic post–World War II/Cold War epistemic and material formations.[14]

Not surprisingly, therefore, many postnineties redress cases and the memories of violence they evoke have instigated intense cultural struggles— or what some have called "culture wars"—over the question of what constitutes the authentic contours of national, gender, racial, and other important organizing categories. It goes without saying that "culture wars" does not refer to a Huntington-like clash between two or more discrete and mutually exclusive cultural entities or value systems. While they are symptoms of old and new colonial-modern contradictions of capitalism, they cannot be reductively considered surrogate class wars. Rather, "culture wars" symptomatically manifests the contradictions of capitalist colonial modernity in which capital's transgressive nature and disregard for normative identities imperils the State's function to discipline and regulate surplus populations—in other words, the State's desire to protect "the sanctity of 'community,' 'family,' and 'nation,'" to borrow from the sociologist Roderick A. Ferguson.[15]

Specifically, the book situates the failure of transitional justice at the threshold of U.S. Cold War ascendancy and the Japanese empire's collapse. It argues that the post-1990s redress culture centering on the discourse on Japanese imperial violence contains profound critiques of the way the transpacific arrangement of Cold War justice has set the parameters of what can be known as violence and whose violence, on which bodies, can be addressed and redressed. As will be discussed in the following pages, the redress culture since the end of the Cold War cannot be understood adequately unless we take into consideration the *longue durée* of violence as the anthropologist Allen Feldman has done provocatively in another context.[16] Moreover, recent works in American Cold War studies have stressed that U.S. foreign policies during these decades not only aimed to contain the Communist advance; crucially for our context, they also undercut anticolonial and other struggles for a radically transformed world order that was to come. This post–World War II containment of decolonization, as Randall Williams has shown with immense insight, is inseparable from the then emerging international human rights protocols. The secret intimacy Williams exposed between the Declaration of Universal Human Rights and containment of anticolonial struggles and aspirations is one that also haunts many ongoing projects for historical justice.[17]

It is my contention that redress demands of the past two decades can and should be understood as part of a continuing struggle over still powerful political, legal, and intellectual Cold War formations. As a Cold War trace, the Asia-Pacific redress culture conjures up the specter of the postwar arrangements that came into existence during the early Cold War years, while signaling the possibilities of moving beyond its recalcitrant legacies. More than a study of individual war reparations cases, *Cold War Ruins* explores the ways in which some of the central redress debates have been figured through their traversals across Asia and the Pacific Islands, with each constituting critical sites of transborder memories, newly politicized political subjects, and transpacific critiques of the foundational collusion of law, geopolitics, and historical knowledge.

Repoliticizing Justice

Cold War Ruins makes five general observations with respect to the intimate relations among justice, violence, and the sovereign. Primarily, the book argues that the project for historical justice in the Asia-Pacific region needs to be situated within the longue durée of decolonization. As I hope to demonstrate, redress and adjudication cases emerging in the post–Cold War years cannot be grasped adequately without acknowledging the long history of political and social engagements with the post–World War II institutional architectures of transitional justice. It is through various oppositional challenges to the structure of Cold War neocolonial ordering that a certain loss came to be perceived *as* a loss deserving redress. This decolonizing approach will allow us to see that the pursuit of historical justice and redress could not have begun without the unrelenting history of social activism, even in its apparent failures and historical invisibility. Such earlier moments of justice—whether failed, accomplished, interrupted, or partial—have all contributed to shaping the institutional structure and culture of postnineties redress.

Central to the book's decolonizing approach is the idea that the universalism of rights, liberty, justice, and the concept of the human they underwrite are enmeshed in a geohistorical politics of knowledge. The cultural theorist Lisa Lowe, among others, identifies what she calls the "economy of affirmation and forgetting" in the Euro-American political philosophy's formalization of modern humanism.[18] As Lowe succinctly puts it: "Colonial labor relations on the plantations in the Americas were the conditions of possibility for European philosophy to think the universality of human freedom, however much freedom for colonized people was precisely foreclosed within that philosophy" (193). This economy of "affirmation and forgetting" further lends itself to the uneven geographical imaginary which maps out the modern world into those cultural spaces that are assumed to have progressed into embracing modern humanism and those that have not.[19] It is also against and through this association of geography and culture that the viability of human rights practices is measured and explained. The critical legal scholar Leti Volpp questions, for instance, the asymmetrical ways in which the international women's human rights regime, while blaming religious culture for violence against Muslim women, does not similarly link the Christian far right's violations against sexual minorities and the exercise of reproductive rights to particular cultural beliefs and practices.[20] Violations and violence against women that take place in the United States, moreover, are hardly considered a human rights issue. While constituting subjects of good will who can act through their empathetic identification with the suffering of others, the women's human rights regime nevertheless tends to locate women in need of rescue as victimized exclusively by patriarchal culture, religion, or the polity to which they belong, while leaving the human rights law and practice unmarked by their cultural, racial, national, and geographical affiliations. The discourse on gender justice and the universal humanism of which it is a part center abstracted individuals as normatively free and modern subjects through such dialectics.

The critique of asymmetries as seen above exposes the epistemic violence of the universalist human rights discourse and the way it institutes the intimate relation between power/law and knowledge. It unveils that the unevenness of the human rights regime may not stem from the differential *application* of human rights law, as often assumed, but its discursive logic and assumptions. To be sure, the idea that human rights originated in the West made cultural relativists suspicious of its application to the other parts of the world. But the problem of unevenness derives from not only the provincial origin of human rights discourse, but also the assumptions of its universal applicability and translatability. Such universalism makes it possible to blame factors deemed particular to specific geohistorical and cultural locations for the failure of human rights enforcement. The common assumption is that, if indeed it were applied in a truly universal manner without the encumbrance of—mostly non-Western—cultural impediments and mistranslations, international human rights law can do only good. The global telos of human rights, then, leads to the pernicious, historically and geographically rooted asymmetries between universalism and particularism, such as the one we have known for some time as Orientalism. Critical reflections on the universalist extension and enforcement of human rights as a regime necessarily beg the question of knowledge production. We need to ask, which and whose sufferings are known to us as human rights violations, and for whom and for which suffering is human rights justice practiced? Who has the power to represent them legitimately? Redress activism that exploits the hegemonic power of universal human rights discourse must thus negotiate between, on the one hand, the global visibility and authenticity the discourse renders to the vulnerable and the victimized and, on the other hand, the geohistorically rooted contradictions of modern humanism and its universalism.

Second, *Cold War Ruins* considers the predicaments of instrumentalized justice and their implications on the practice and subject of redress, apology, and reparations. In large part inspired by the TRC in post-Apartheid South Africa and the two international military tribunals in the former Yugoslavia and Rwanda, much has been written over the last twenty years about various cases of TRCs, war crimes courts, restitutions, and other forms of transitional justice for postdictatorial, postconflict societies. The pursuit of justice is often advocated to mollify unsettled sentiments and volatile memories of traumatic pasts that might lead to future conflicts, disorder, and cycles of vengeance. While some are more cautious than others about the premature foreclosure such pursuits could bring to overcoming the past, scholars of transitional justice tend to see their merits for ushering in reconciliation, harmony, and normalcy.[21] In contrast, Jacques Derrida famously warned against the global exportation and proliferation of an "industry of forgiveness" that utilized a Judeo-Christian formula to produce an institutionalized language of reconciliation.[22] State-sponsored reconciliation, according to his view, instrumentalizes forgiveness in exchange for legitimating the sovereign State and the suprastate institutions that oversee the process of reconciliation and amnesty.

Insofar as redress is pursued as a politics of recognition and State-mediated redistribution, apologies, compensations, and even forgiveness for historical injustices become converted into objects of equitable exchange within institutionalized spheres.[23] One is not hard put to find instances in which justice was easily instrumentalized in given political, juridical, and other spheres. During the immediate post-9/11 months, when the U.S.-led war machine acted as the sovereign subject of justice to save Afghani women from the Muslim fundamentalists' abuse of women's rights, the Feminist Majority Foundation also became the subjects of war and bolstered the home front through the discourse of gender justice.[24] The U.S. Feminist Majority's assimilation to the state policy was possible because its agenda fit the latter's liberal language of equality, freedom, individual rights, and parity. Historical dispossession, however, is not the same as inequity and unfairness in a given collective whole. The quest for historical justice must then be theorized at least provisionally as that which is heterogeneous and unassimilable to the institutional, often State-centered language of distribution, equity, and just decisions.

Borrowing from Emmanuel Levinas, Derrida aligned the notion of justice with absolute alterity—the Other and the Future (*l'avenir*, "to come").[25] Justice conceived as an alterity to existing law, rules, and rights becomes an aporia, or a kind of "undecidability" that is different from simply oscillating between different options. For Derrida, justice is realized in the moment this aporia deconstructs the political and judicial. The experience of justice must then be sought in aporia itself. In fact, we have always possessed our own familiar images of justice that are at once within and outside the existing realm of law and politics. Popular superheroes and heroines must always present themselves as anonymous and superhuman because the justice they embody, like Walter Benjamin's divine violence, is not meant to be assimilable to secular politics, law, language, or the existing social apparatuses and identities. The figures of modern superheroes and heroines who appear against the backdrop of monopoly capitalism and malfunctioning representative democracy generate small catastrophes in various places as they expose injustices that cannot be heard within given corrupt political systems or legal procedures. Usually our superheroes and heroines live ordinary bourgeois lives. Masked and anonymous, they sometimes appear to be among our neighbors and friends, yet their identities are never fully disclosed. True heroes and heroines of justice must thus suspend their worldly affiliations and desires. They are forever placed in a state of suspension between their otherworldly, superhuman power (read justice as absolute alterity) and their secular desires toward specific significant others (read justice's assimilation to the existing process of politicization, instrumentalization, and institutionalization).

The true subject of justice is thus left in a state of suspension. The superheroes and heroines have not always occupied the position of justice's sovereign but have stood by its side, remaining no more than its "ally."[26] However, the fact that the experience of justice must remain beyond law, as Derrida would have it, is not tantamount to their nonaction. It does not mean to opt out of the existing realm of politics, law, and human rights regimes. For justice's otherness—as either the aborted or that which is "to come"—can only be known as a threshold at a moment when one confronts the limits of a given language of adjudication, reconciliation, and representations. The subject of our transborder redress culture, then, must first subject itself to the available juridical, legislative, and other processes to be reckoned as a legitimate speaking subject; but in doing so, whether in victory or defeat, it also exposes what is left of justice that defies the instrumentalization and the assimilation into the hegemonic order of knowledge.

In Derrida's words, "Justice as the experience of absolute alterity is unpresentable, but it is the chance of the event and the condition of history."[27]

Transitional justice, moreover, has tended to focus on how to manage disturbing pasts and to secure the globalized system of liberal economy. My investigation will attend to what Allen Feldman saw as "post-violence reason" specific to post–World War II/Cold War transitional justice and the problematic ways it has shaped the knowledge about the history prior to, during, and after the Asia-Pacific War. Feldman problematized the ways in which the spectacularization and moralization of the medico-therapeutic ideas of "trauma," prevailing at the post-Apartheid South African TRC, generated the sense of a clean break between the past and present. By defining "post-violence reason" as deriving from "a moment in which reason divides itself in two, exiling its double through convenient periodization" while producing moral oppositions between the two periods, Feldman provocatively asks: "If traumatic intrusion presumes a non-traumatized prior self that was not disfigured, how is the imputed homeostatic concept of the state of self and society prior to traumatic intrusion reconciled with what we know of colonial and postcolonial histories, the *longue durée* of structural violence of racial, gender, sexual, and ethnic inequities, the historical norm and routine of Walter Benjamin's state of emergency?"[28]

This leads to the third major observation I wish to make in *Cold War Ruins* with regards to why and how justice needs to be urgently repoliticized and dejudicialized. The global rush toward juridical forms of redress and reconciliation may well be seen as a symptom of the pervasive retraction in liberal societies of the political that takes the form of parapolitics. The Marxist critic Slavoj Žižek saw parapolitics as "the attempt to de-antagonize politics by formulating the clear rules to be obeyed so that the agonistic procedure of litigation does not explode into politics proper."[29] In relation to the disavowal of "the proper logic of political antagonism" in the modern history of political thought, Žižek indicated that the apparatuses of the liberal public sphere, such as law, often depoliticize conflicts by translating them into recognizable forms of divergent interests and representative groups competing over the supposedly even terrain of an open forum. "The political struggle proper," as Žižek put it, is "never simply a rational debate between multiple interests but, simultaneously, the struggle for one's voice to be heard and recognized as the voice of a legitimate partner."[30] For Žižek, depoliticization commences at the moment of recognition and legitimation. Even more illuminatingly, Jacques Rancière saw in France during the period leading up to the first Gulf War "a proliferation of legislative activity:

the creation or development of rights and norms."[31] He summarizes the process as follows: "To the extent that the law comes to blanket every situation and every possible dispute, it is more and more identified with a system of guarantees that are first of all guarantees of power" (253). In France and subsequently in the spectacular global alliance against the Iraqi invasion of Kuwait, law functioned to fulfill purposes other than justice in the sense of Kantian morality. The sovereign States, international law, and power were mobilized, as Rancière observed, according to the long-standing European way of mapping others onto colonial spatial knowledge to realize the desire of the superpower and to reconsolidate the world order prior to Iraq's "criminal" disruption. I suggest that the "happy identification between justice and equilibrium" (255) and juridico-political realism Rancière found in eighties France is what needs to be problematized in any administering of postconflict transitional justice. To the extent that transitional justice concerns management of the destabilizing elements in postviolence societies, whether international or domestic, the concept also expects reintegration of the violence-torn society without disturbing the structure existing prior to the upheaval. In exploring the Asia-Pacific War redress culture, we need to remain suspicious of whether such judicialization of justice might indeed reflect the overall incapacitation of effective political movements in the existing public spheres.

Insofar as the practice of redress and reparations inherently holds out as its telos some form of closure, settlement, and sublation, the official acknowledgment of and accounting for past wrongs within a given institutional venue could risk relegitimizing the very establishments that offer reparations and apologies. Law's liberal premise moreover individualizes the issues. While attending to the need to restore presupposed wholeness to the injured bodies, it falls short of addressing the enduring regime of unredressability—Feldman's "*longue durée* of structural violence of racial, gender, sexual, and ethnic inequities"—that is indexed by the very presence of justice as trace. The notion of transitional justice, furthermore, tends to presuppose that once the societies have established liberal organizations and formal democracy they are no longer in transition. What might be a productive way to confront the predicament of transitional justice? Here, I turn once again to Rancière who offers important correctives to the logical critique of the metaphysics of modern politics, which is radically unsettling in and of itself yet tends to be unworkable for transformative politics unless situated in a specific geohistorical context. Commenting on scholarship that considers modernity's operative terms increasingly through the concepts of states of exception and bio/necropower, Rancière questions the absenting of arguments for politicization in such analyses.[32] He amends Giorgio Agamben's provocation of the intimacy between sovereignty and life in modern politics by pointing to a way of countering what he sees as the "ontological trap" to which the biopolitical theory of the pure logics of state of exception might lead (301). Without undermining the radical core of Agamben's critique, I highlight Rancière's reminder that the metaphysical line drawn between bare life and qualified life is not inevitable or universal, but one that is *politically* constituted (and thus can be reconstituted). As Rancière puts it, "Political predicates are open predicates: they open up a dispute" (303).[33]

Post–Cold War redress culture, as I hope to show throughout the book, can and ought to be seen as an integral part of the politicization of justice that "open[s] up a dispute" on the terrain of knowledge. In other words, post–Cold War redress engages in another politicization of the struggle over not only the demarcation itself between the redressable and unredressable but the very premises upon which such a line is made possible. And these premises, I suggest, need to be sought first and foremost in the geohistorical specificities of the enduring Cold War knowledge formations. This methodology, above all, will enable us to discern the makeup of the il/legibility of violence—to not only expose, but to undo the way borders are drawn between those subjects of modern humanity deserving of proper redress and those whose racial, sexual, gender, colonial, and other civilizational attributes make them inviolable and disposable, thus keeping violations against them invisible and unredressable in the realm of law and humanity. By repoliticizing the terms of redress through *and* beyond "the struggle for one's voice to be heard and recognized as the voice of a legitimate partner," in Žižek's phrasing, the testimonials at the TRCs, courts of law, and other sites of post–Cold War redress can potentially reintroduce proper antagonism over the hard-fought questions of structural inequity, values, ethicality, and ways of being.[34] Put differently, the redress activism concerning the Asia-Pacific War can be productively viewed as a process of repoliticization that begins to challenge what Feldman saw as the problematic "boundary line between violence and post-violence."[35] Seen in this way, the post-1990s redress culture then begins to call into question the triumphalism and automatism undergirding any notion of transitional justice.

Fourth, by shedding light on Cold War knowledge production about the Asia-Pacific, *Cold War Ruins* places the inquiry in relation to the question of why and how U.S. war crimes, even when perceived as such, remain unredressable.[36] In what way does the unredressability of American injustice need to be understood conjunctively as a problem inseparable from the failure to bring thoroughgoing justice to Japanese war crimes? One common answer to this question has been that transitional justice in the aftermath of World War II was no more than "victor's justice."[37] *Cold War Ruins* extends and complicates this acknowledgment by considering the oversight's broader and longer ramifications within the American transpacific imaginary. During the U.S. military invasion and occupation of Iraq, I argued that the reason why so many U.S. war crimes, especially those in Asia, remain unredressed might be found in what can be most appropriately called the American imperialist myth of "liberation and rehabilitation." According to this myth, the losses and damages brought on by U.S. military violence are deemed "prepaid debts" incurred by those liberated by American intervention. This myth, which presents both violence and liberation as "gifts for the liberated," has serious implications for the redressability of U.S. military violence.[38] The injured and violated bodies of the liberated, I wrote at the time, do not seem to require redress according to this discourse of indebtedness, for their liberation has already served as the payment/reparation that supposedly precedes the violence inflicted upon them. This economy of debt, I further suggest, is what sustains the regime of unredressability pertaining especially to colonial injustices.[39]

This brings me to the final general observation I wish to make in this book. Though with varying degrees, the growing critical literature on justice, redress, and reconciliation shows that there are competing notions of justice that cannot be subsumed uniformly under one overarching project. The U.S. decision to attack Afghanistan revealed how the equal-rights feminists' idea of gender justice could be instrumentalized to support the U.S. military empire, even as it helped mobilize powerful support to end certain violence against some women. This instance revealed that universalistic gender justice is not necessarily compatible with the idea of historical justice specific to particular geopolitical wrongs. The conundrum of justice also appeared when "comfort women" redress found its articulation in the global discourse on women's rights. When the United Nations and other nongovernmental organizations began to press for an end to the impunity of gender and sexual violence against women in war and other military conflicts, they brought immediate international visibility to the wartime history of the Japanese military comfort system and created pressure on the Japanese government. Yet in that process other equally important questions asked by many feminists in Korea, the Philippines, Guam, Hong Kong, Okinawa, and elsewhere in Japan about the lasting colonial legacy and the state violence in the sexualized transpacific military-political-economy have been muted. Moreover, while the U.S. legislators' increasing involvement in the wartime "comfort women" issue can effectively discipline Japanese revisionist ventures, the same righteousness may inadvertently fuel the American claim to stand in as the world's adjudicator.

How are we to approach the multivalence inherent in the discourse of justice? Vigilance toward the coevality of justice is required to grasp productively the language and practice of redress that at times appears univocal with respect to ultimate objectives, while at other times setting off contradictory and even contentious visions and politics. Yet, if the idea of coevality points to the condition of cotemporaneity with a difference, merely acknowledging the simultaneous diversity of competing claims to justice will not do. These seeming antinomies, instead, call for critically situated historical thinking—that is, an ability to perceive different appeals for and failures of justice as incommensurable and yet interlinked as they have unfolded on a global scale within specific historical moments. The myriad calls for justice and their competing assertions should not and cannot be reduced to a universal global history, or sacrificed in the name of the progress of a uniform civilization and humanity. What we are asked to do, then, is to deploy what might be called a conjunctive cultural critique in order to discern the deeply entangled geohistories of violence and their shared yet localized genealogies.[40] They remain hidden in the familiar frame of knowledge with which we speak of justice.

The Cold War Frame of America's "Good War"

The United States would not stand for irresponsible meddling in Japanese industrial recovery through some "frivolous" reparations programme while she was paying out $500,000,000 a year to get Japan on her feet again.
—George Kennan, June 3, 1948, quoted by John Price in *Orienting Canada*

Most Americans can't locate Indonesia on the map. This fact is puzzling to Indonesians, since for the past sixty years the fate of their nation has been directly tied to U.S. foreign policy.
—Barack Obama, *The Audacity of Hope*

Echoing the postnationalist turn in American studies, scholarship on Cold War U.S. politics and culture has increasingly become attentive to the intimate interplay between the international and the domestic.[41] Especially pertinent to our concern for redress's longue durée is the Cold War competition over racial and colonial discourse. With regard to domestic race relations, the U.S. historians Derrick Bell, Mary Dudziak, and Thomas Borstelmann, among others, have demonstrated that Cold War confrontations made the thoroughgoing realization of civil rights and the desegregation of African Americans imperative. Rather than viewing U.S. history as the fulfillment of the great American promise of liberty and equality embedded in the unfolding national essence of the republic, these scholars have shown that national security interests in the Cold War rivalry against the Soviet Union and the demand for the United States to improve its image in the eyes of the Third World and other international audiences led U.S. policy makers to cultivate and exploit racially tolerant self-portraits. This in turn produced a number of significant institutional changes, including racial desegregation and the extension of civil rights and eligibility for naturalization to racial minorities and immigrants. By exploring the Cold War dialectics between U.S. foreign policies and their often contradictory ramifications on American culture and politics, much of this scholarship has illuminated, in Christian G. Appy's apt phrasing, that "the Cold War was, as much as anything else, a competition over discourse."[42]

If domestically, the image of racial harmony and equality was crucial, the disavowal of formal colonialism was equally critical in the international arena for winning the Cold War "competition over discourse." The American historian Jonathan Nashel put this dimension of the Cold War most succinctly: "two of the most vexing foreign policy problems facing the United States during the Cold War: how to ensure that the newly independent countries of the third world became integrated into a capitalist network of market relations, and conversely, how to prevent these desperately poor countries from becoming communist."[43] In her analysis of the interplay between U.S. foreign policies over the Middle East and American popular cultural production, the American studies scholar Melani McAlister focuses on the 1951 term "benevolent supremacy," coined by the right-wing politician Charles Hilliard, to understand U.S. efforts to present itself as an alternative to formal colonialism in its Middle East policy.[44] As McAlister put it, the term captured "a broadly diffused construction of the United States as a 'World Leader' that refused to behave like a colonial power" (82–83). This American self-portrait became crucial in securing its position in the Middle East. Stressing the consensual nature of American Cold War hegemony in the Middle East, she stated, "The operative terms were the American refusal of empire, the right of 'free peoples' to choose their destinies, and the consensual partnership between U.S. power and a subordinated third world nationalism" (82).

Remarkably, recent Cold War studies that stress the productive power of international performativity and the geopolitical importance of the rhetoric of racial and colonial justice tend to overlook the transwar continuities. They pay little attention to the fact that the United States had been engaged in a similar "competition over discourse" during the war against Japan. This oversight may simply be a technical one; after all, for U.S. foreign affairs the Cold War did not start officially before 1945. And yet, this overall indifference to the racialized and anticolonial dimension of the Asia-Pacific War, of which the U.S. war against Japan was but one phase, and to how the discursive transformation during the transwar years made the postwar Americanization of racial justice possible, raises many important questions about history, the meaning of the war(s), and Japan's significance in the production of U.S. Cold War knowledge. The Cold War Americanization of racial justice, as I will briefly consider below, would not have been as effective, if even possible, without the discursive production of the U.S. relation with the enemy of color that had earlier championed the rhetoric of racial justice. If we take into account that U.S. blueprints for the post-cease-fire world had already begun to be drawn up during the war years, we begin to realize the extent to which the U.S. ascendancy to power in the postwar world critically hinged on the Americanization of justice as it sought to settle memories of the U.S. war against Japan. It is therefore imperative that we consider the implications of not reckoning with this earlier moment of "competition over discourse" for world justice and the stakes such a critique might have in the discussion of post-1990s redress culture.

Historical studies have shown that during World War II the United States' repudiation of the powerful rhetoric of racial emancipation, which Japan had advocated before and during the war, became a military strategic imperative. In analyzing the 1940s recruitment of Japanese American soldiers from the internment camps, T. Fujitani compellingly demonstrated the extent to which American officials paid attention to the implications the war against Japan would have on issues of race and colonialism.[45] Colleen Lye likewise pointed to Pearl Buck's keen wartime awareness that racism was "the Achilles' heel of U.S. military strategy against Japan." Buck feared and publicly declared that the United States was losing the global war of propaganda vis-à-vis Japan due to American white supremacy and racism.[46] According to Lye, Buck's concern not to lose the "hearts and minds" of nations of color in the war against Japan was by no means isolated. Moreover, as Gerald Horne revealed in his unconventional historiography, Japan's propaganda for racial and colonial emancipation gained special verisimilitude, particularly in areas under British colonial rule.[47] What these historical accounts indicate is that the United States had been competing with Japan's own imperial modernity and its universalist assertion of racial equality and liberation from European colonialism *prior to* the Cold War campaign against the Soviet Union. To be sure, the American claim to racial freedom, democracy, and equality has a much longer and complex history: crucially, it was advanced *domestically* by relentless activism for racial justice within and against State violence and law. But the credibility of such assertions *internationally* had to be won initially during the Asia-Pacific War as a response to its racialized enemy in an explicitly racialized war. Still, most American Cold War studies do not attend to the Cold War's prehistory, during which Japan had manipulated an anticolonial and antiracist discourse in the interests of furthering its own imperial aspirations against its Euro-American counterparts. Such studies tend to locate the exploitation of the U.S. rhetoric of liberation and racial justice at a much later stage—that is, in the Cold War confrontation. The transwar significance of Japanese imperial practices in the making of Cold War America is largely lost in such accounts.

This indifference, I suggest, stems in large part from the master narrative that regards World War II as a "good war" and the powerful American political unconscious it undergirds about modernity and its belatedness in Asia. The "good war" narrative, disseminated in the Cold War years as a postvictory reprocessing of wartime propaganda, remembers that the United States fought the just war against the evil of fascism to liberate the Jews and other Europeans from the terror of Nazism. On the Pacific front, the United States fought against Japan to rightly defend "American soil" and to rescue Asia and the Pacific from Japanese aggression. Significantly, the "surprise attack" narrative on Pearl Harbor that remains the mainstay of America's just-war narrative conveniently erases the fact that Hawai'i was an American colony at the time. Such an elision disavows the history that the Japanese attack on the U.S. colonial military outpost was an instantiation of Japan's own liberal just-war propaganda for racial and anticolonial emancipation. Refiguring these and other histories, the "good war" narrative produced during the Cold War years remembers that the United States fought a just war for the liberation of the people of Asia and the Pacific region, including the Japanese themselves, from Japan's barbaric militarism and racial backwardness. Because this narrative has so powerfully shaped understandings about the U.S. war against Japan and its aftermath, the wartime "competition over discourse" between the two countries on the issue of racial and colonial justice has easily gone unnoticed, along with what this elision meant for the postwar American self-portraiture.

Even more important for our current discussion, therefore, the "good war" narrative is not limited in its coverage to only the period of belligerency, but extends to American conduct in the war's afterlife. The narrative recounts that Japan before the war was a nation lagging in its modern development, and that it had failed to cultivate its latent potential to embrace liberal ideals until it was vanquished and then reborn under U.S. "benevolent supremacy." As I will discuss further in chapter 1, area studies' anthropological knowledge about Japan produced during the transwar decade gave academic credibility to this dimension of the "good war" narrative. In the "good war" narrative, Japan was to be racially rehabilitated as a biopolitical space of American governmentality.[48] With regard to the U.S. disavowal of formal colonialism and white supremacy in the Cold War "competition over discourse," which was aimed at an audience made up primarily of postcolonial nation-states and domestic minorities, the fact that the defeated and rehabilitated enemy was a nonwhite, non-Western nation took on special significance in a way that was unfathomable on the Atlantic front. Presenting the United States as a magnanimous victor, the "good war" master narrative lent truthfulness to the image of the United States as the benefactor of equality, freedom, and democracy to nations of color in its Cold War rivalry. Again, perceptions of how, by whom, and for what purposes the war was fought have had grave implications for how to envisage historical justice.

To this day, the Cold War narrative of the "good war" and the credibility it conferred on America's "benevolent supremacy" in the war's aftermath continue to find use value. Shortly after the U.S. military's seizure of Baghdad in April 2003, the *Rocky Mountain News* featured an article on a lecture by Beate Sirota Gordon. Entitled, "Japan's Women Could be Model in Postwar Iraq," the article read, "Japanese women who lived through the reconstruction of their country after World War II could help the United States rebuild Iraq and Afghanistan, says the woman who helped Gen. Douglas MacArthur write the Japanese Constitution." At the age of twenty-two, during the U.S. occupation of Japan (1945–1952), Gordon had joined the committee that drafted the Japanese Constitution and worked specifically on the women's rights clause. According to the newspaper's account, Gordon maintained that Japanese women who "had no rights" prior to the new Constitution are successful in "politics and business" today. As "a colored people," Gordon reportedly noted, they could "bolster U.S. credibility with Iraqis and Afghans" by demonstrating that the U.S. military occupation "did not run their islands into a colony."[49] During the occupation Gordon served as an interpreter for the Supreme Commander for the Allied Powers (SCAP). She was fluent in Japanese since she had been raised in Japan prior to the war's outbreak. She was a daughter of an accomplished Ukrainian Jewish pianist who had fled from Russia to Austria, and then to Japan in the 1920s. It is not clear whether U.S. policy makers at the time consciously intended to utilize Gordon for the management of postcolonial space. But the significance of her narrative, as well as the timeliness of its public resurgence, should be located in the discursive force the "good war" narrative continues to exert in making and justifying America's new racialized wars. This story encapsulates the lasting performative effects of the Americanization of racial and gender justice that gained particular exigency during the U.S. occupation of Japan. Chapter 2 considers how the representation of Japanese women's enfranchisement under the U.S.-led Allied occupation became a paradigmatic "frame of war" that continues to shape the American notion of just war.[50] As Gordon's interview illuminates, the discourse on women's liberation from Japanese patriarchy was an essential enabling element of the transpacific Cold War complicity in suppressing a different reordering of the decolonizing world.

Yet for such a Cold War discourse of American racial and gender justice to gain authenticity and historical verisimilitude, it also had to strategically write out another important past: the history of Japanese colonialism and U.S. advancement into the postcolonial space that emerged after the Japanese empire's collapse. If Japan was reconstituted as the site of the "successful" American project of liberation, rehabilitation, and integration, such a depiction omitted all but the metropolitan core of the vast prewar Japanese empire. As social anthropologist Heonik Kwon aptly put it, for most of the new nation-states that emerged in the postcolonial space, "the onset of the cold war meant entering an epoch of 'unbridled reality' characterized by vicious civil wars and other exceptional forms of political violence" (6).[51] Fierce insurgencies and armed resistance to the old and new occupying forces as well as the outbreak of civil war continued to fill the region Japan had vacated. For instance, the Republic of Indonesia proclaimed its independence in 1945 but it was not until 1949 that it received UN recognition. For the Democratic Republic of Vietnam, nine years passed between the 1945 proclamation of independence and the 1954 Geneva Accords. In China the armed conflict between the Nationalist and Communist Parties resumed immediately following Japan's surrender and did not conclude until the establishment of the People's Republic of China in 1949. And the People's Republic of Korea was established as a transitional regime as early as September 1945 and drafted a radically democratic constitution but was immediately engulfed by the conflicts that developed into the Korean War.[52] That the Korean War is remembered in the United States and Canada only as a "forgotten war" suggests the degree to which the memories of violent trajectories of postcolonial Asian nations in the immediate aftermath of World War II have been marginalized in the dominant North American geographical imaginary.[53]

This absenting of knowledge about Asia's necrohistories is especially illuminating when considered in relationship to an anthology on violence put together by two U.S.-based anthropologists. *Violence in War and Peace: Anthology* is a compilation of cultural critiques on violence of various forms, symbolic and physical, manifest and latent. In part responding to the post-9/11 milieu, *Violence in War and Peace* makes an important intervention by urging the discipline to self-consciously foreground questions of structural violence, histories of imperialism, and such political upheavals as war, anti-colonial insurgencies, and revolution. Curiously, while the anthology covers vastly different geopolitical spaces, there are no contributions among its over fifty articles that consider violence in Asia, excepting one on South Asia.[54] In other words, the areas that appeared as postcolonies in the aftermath of Japan's defeat have been perceived for the most part as unproductive sites for anthropologically theorizing "violence in war and peace." It is certainly possible that the editors' limited scholarly network did not permit them to consider anthropological observations on violence in this region. Since anthropological studies of Asia often ask historical questions, it is also possible that they were considered less central to the discipline. Yet, given that the representation of others in the discipline of anthropology is always already a statement about the anthropologists' own cultural and ideological assumptions, and when considering that most officially recognized twentieth-century U.S. wars were fought in North and Southeast Asia, this excision is too conspicuous to be dismissed as simply a technical matter or a lack of scholarly expertise. This absence, in my view, expresses and reflects the power of the American geohistorical imaginary of Asia in which the immediate U.S. military violence may be acknowledged but also disavowed.

Christina Klein's observations on American middlebrow culture may be helpful in understanding the historical context behind this lacuna in American anthropological knowledge.[55] In contrast to previous scholarship that emphasized the "containment" side of Cold War policies, Klein underscored the working of "integration" as an equally important U.S. Cold War project. Arguing that the idea of "containment" alone could not have mobilized the majority of Americans, Klein demonstrated that musicals, films, travel writings, and other popular texts contributed to the image of the early Cold War American presence in Asia cleansed of violence and brute force. The image of cooperation, intimacy, familial metaphors, and sentimentalism, as well as the inclusionary view of multiethnicity disseminated through these texts, made it possible for the middlebrow American to imagine Asia as integrated into Cold War America through the cultural tropes of "voluntary affiliation" (146) and positive incentives for consensus building. We could further read Klein's discussion alongside Aimé Césaire's historicized remark on the Cold War "Yankee risk." Césaire famously described the emerging U.S. hegemony in the post–World War II decolonizing world as the "American domination—the only domination from which one never recovers."[56] The "positive incentives" of the American material glamour and the romanticized visions of freedom and democracy disseminated through official venues and popular culture seized many people's "hearts and minds." At the same time, it is equally important not to forget that Cold War America could in fact mobilize territories in postwar Asia and the Pacific Islands without concern for consensus or integration. What became insulated from the American imaginary of a harmoniously integrated world were the struggles for and the brutal suppression of the hopes and ideals for alternative sociality, justice, and polity in the postwar, decolonizing world.

The United States has thus ascended to hegemonic power across Asia and the Pacific region through its ability to define the terms of military, racial, and gender justice in the post–World War II transitional moment. That same process also dialectically helped secure the memories and meanings of the U.S. war in the region, even as the United States and its postwar allies prepared for the new war of the American century, namely, the Cold War. The post-1990s shift in the location of redress activism, from Asia and the Pacific Islands to U.S. juridical and legislative venues, is best viewed as an instance of the Americanization of justice. This process, however, is by no means new. The Japanese postwar settlement, as I have been arguing, has always been an *American* concern.[57] As much as I am invested in the practical resolution of redress issues in Japan, *Cold War Ruins* equally explores the decisive impacts the postwar settlements in Asia have had on culture, knowledge, social identities, and global imaginaries in the United States. As Setsu Shigematsu and Keith L. Camacho remind us in their pathbreaking anthology on the transpacific militarized cultures and histories, "the United States [has] defined its national interests not along the borders of the continental United States but in Asia and the Pacific."[58] The U.S. Cold War intervention on the postwar settlement for Japan left an equally serious imprint, even in its disavowal, on American understandings of the war and its place in the world.

Most urgently, as the inter- and intra-Asia scholarship attuned to anticolonial, antiracist critique has informed us, postwar settlements during the decades following the formal cease-fire successfully managed the terms of Japanese reparations in ways that served the purpose of containing the region's attempts at thoroughgoing decolonization.[59] The book's following chapters will make clear how profoundly Cold War America was and remains—in its enduring transpacific epistemological and institutional legacies—implicated in this process. A geohistorically situated critique of violence and justice, as I hope to show, will reveal the Cold War complicity of the United States and Japan and its indelible traces and wounds on the region's political and intellectual landscape. But neither the earlier formation of Cold War America nor the Americanization of post-1990s redress and reparations is reducible to a single nation or its past state policy. In exploring the transpacific traversals of redress discourse, Cold War Ruins hopes to demonstrate how America as a multifarious presence has shaped and will continue to shape the discursive parameters that govern what we can know and say about the history of violence and the meaning of justice. The postnineties, post–Cold War redress culture ought to be read in its relationships to such power/ knowledge matrices to which the initial postwar settlement was integral.

Decolonization and Redress's Longue Durée

The post-1990s sensibility and sociality Cold War Ruins examines are in many respects new and specific to their own geohistorical milieu. Yet the recent redress culture and its underlying critique of the Cold War institutional and knowledge formations have several earlier emergences and trajectories. In the remaining pages I will briefly delineate this genealogy by focusing on two key arenas of knowledge production and contestation: the histories and memories of Japan's wartime military comfort system and the diverse and conflictual intellectual challenges to the Tokyo War Crimes Trial (IMTFE).

A quick glance at the genealogy of inter- and intra-Asia redress discourse on Japan's military sex slavery, or the "military comfort women issue" (jūgun ianfu mondai), will reveal how it emerged out of the decades-long trajectories of institutional and intellectual challenges to the region's Cold War edifice. The issue gained international publicity in 1991 when Kim Hak-sun became the first Korean woman to publicly testify on the history of the wartime Japanese comfort system. While the wartime military comfort system had sometimes appeared in postwar memoirs, fiction, and other representations, it was not until the 1990s that a solid consensus emerged around characterizing the system as the coercive trafficking of women into sex slavery—in other words, as a violation against women's human rights. This epistemic shift was a constitutive part of the 1990s consolidation of the international protocols that have come to stipulate wartime gender and sexual violence as war crimes. The timely reception of Kim Hak-sun's testimony by wide-ranging sections of the international community was enabled to a great extent by this nineties global milieu. At the same time, however, the manifold significance of the "military comfort women issue" cannot be grasped without calling attention to the longue durée of redress activism and the deeper critique of post–World War II, Cold War epistemic and institutional formations that preceded and provoked the re-remembering of the Japanese military's egregious violations against women in the occupied territories.

Prior to this well-publicized moment, however, Yun Chŏng-ok, professor at Ewha Women's University, had already organized the Korean Council for Women Drafted for Military Sexual Slavery by Japan (Korean Council, hereafter) and initiated regular survivors' street rallies in front of the Japanese Consulate General in Seoul. Kang Duk-Kyoung (Kang Tŏk-kyŏng), the author of the book's cover art, "Punish the Responsible—For Peace," was a regular rally participant. Yun had also conducted research in the late eighties on surviving women. The Korean Council and others gave support to many survivors who wished to testify to the wretched condition of the Japanese military comfort system.[60] The Korean Council's redress activism over many years initiated a series of responses in Japan: national newspapers reported on historian Yoshimi Yoshiaki's archival findings that pointed to direct military involvement in the comfort system; and a number of high-ranking Japanese government officials, including then prime minister Miyazawa Kiichi, offered formal apologies to the South as well as North Korean governments. In response to the increasing number of testimonies, then Cabinet Secretariat Kōno Yōhei issued an official press statement in 1993. This was the watershed year when nearly four decades of rule by the pro–United States Liberal Democratic Party (LDP), which had been continuous since 1955, came to a close. In the statement Kōno admitted to the "coercive" nature of the wartime recruitment of women into the military comfort system and offered "apologies and remorse." The 1993 Kōno statement was no doubt part of post–Cold War realpolitikal adjustment within the bounds of the post–World War II interstate system. Serious flaws notwithstanding, the Kōno statement remains the single official position upheld even by successive revisionist cabinets and prime ministers. It should also be noted that the Kōno statement promptly made a significant impact domestically on public education; immediately following the release of the statement, all seven government-approved textbooks uniformly included descriptions of the history of Japan's wartime military comfort system. In response, conservatives, militarists, and the far-right historical revisionists began to form a united front against this national consensus, which was emerging in the post–Cold War milieu. The Kōno statement eventually led to the establishment of the Asian Women's Fund (Josei No Tame No Ajia Heiwa Kokumin Kikin, 1994–2007). The Korean Council, however, immediately objected to the operation of the Asian Women's Fund, arguing that its nonjuridical, moral solution would deter the Japanese state from facing its accountability. The Korean Council's and its supporters' insistence on reparation in the name of the law and the State continues to pose multivalent challenges to the immunity of the previously agreed upon state-to-state normalization treaties.

At the same time, South Korea's "comfort women" redress activism, though hardly uniform, has engaged a wide spectrum of issues concerning the region's postwar decolonization as well as post- and neocolonial formations. As Chungmoo Choi and C. Sarah Soh have shown, in denouncing the Japanese government's obstinate evasion of state accountability, the activism also interrogated South Korea's patriarchal and heteronormative ideals of proper femininity that had long marginalized the survivors of the comfort system and their histories.[61] Memories of Japan's wartime military sex enslavement have also simultaneously problematized the uneven decolonization and the postcolonial continuity of violence. The more the extent and conspicuousness of the violence perpetrated by the wartime comfort system became exposed, the more serious the initial failure of the U.S.-Allied prosecution of these crimes against women began to appear.[62] Such reflections on the earlier postwar moment further resonated with the interrogation of the continuing neocolonial U.S. military presence in the region over the past six decades. From certain feminist perspectives, especially those aligned with Korean and Korean American transnational feminist critiques, the history of Japan's military comfort system prefigured the military camp town and other continuing structures of violence against women that have been sustained around U.S. bases throughout the region.[63] Redress activism concerning the military comfort system also emerged as an integral part of the interrogation of the antidemocratic legacies of Japanese colonial modernity in Asia. Elements of the colonial regime—for example, police state apparatuses, military forces, and heteronormative, patriarchal social policies—had been put to renewed use by the postindependent, cold war surveillance state. When the late president Roh Moo-Hyun's regime (2003–2008) began to formally address the need for the Japanese government to offer state reparations and an apology to the former "comfort women," it also echoed the growing critical reflection on the earlier regimes' insufficient dismantling of Japanese colonial legacies, which had been an effect of Cold War constraints.

Inter-Asian "comfort women" redress activism initiated by Yun and others can also be traced back to the 1970s campaign against sex tours, which was led by feminist activists in South Korea, the Philippines, and Japan. This genealogy shows that the "comfort women" redress discourse is not only concerned to critique violence against women, but has addressed the problem of sexual and gendered violence as a constitutive part of postwar transpacific capitalist relations. The antisex tour movement of the seventies did not limit its campaign solely to the commercial practice of individual Japanese men buying women, but theorized the Japanese men's sex tours as an instantiation of the sexualized Japanese colonial relation and its neocolonial incarnation. In other words, the transnational feminist anti–sex tour activism censured the sexualized and classed condition of uneven inter-Asia economic development under the Cold War.[64] This and other transnational feminist networks became instrumental in organizing the 2000 Women's International War Crimes Tribunal on Japan's Military Sexual Slavery, or Women's Tribunal in short, a people's court that charged state leaders for wartime crimes against women (chapter 3).[65]

Even earlier, Japan's wartime military comfort system came to the fore in negotiations for colonial reparations on the eve of the signing of the 1965 ROK-Japan Basic Treaty. The educational pamphlet issued by a group of Maoist-Leninist intellectuals at the Korea Research Institute (Chōsen Kenkyūsho) made an impassioned plea to halt the treaty's signing.[66] They saw it as leading to further entrenchment of the Cold War geopolitics that had placed Japan one-sidedly with the United States through the San Francisco Peace Treaty and U.S.-Japan Security Treaty, both of which had come into force during the previous decade. Resonating with the PRC position at that time, these intellectuals problematized the ways in which the U.S.-

led Cold War political economy had been grafted onto the region's prewar Japanese colonial order and global capitalism. In their analyses, the Cold War architecture and colonial mentality as a legacy of Japanese imperialism were the two paramount impediments standing in the way of forging solidarities among the Chinese, Korean, and Japanese working people. What is most relevant to our discussion here is that this group of intellectuals and activists sought to rectify these wrongs by intervening in the question of how to narrate the past—that is, by focalizing on the production of historical knowledge. Censuring the historical memory prevailing in postwar Japan as "thieves' memories" (100) inherited by "thieves' offspring" (104), they recounted, in addition to the issue of military comfort system, the uneven processes of industrialization, the repression of progressive movements, and other historical sacrifices the working Korean people had to bear under Japanese colonial rule. The pamphlet concluded: "the deeds of Japanese imperialism ought to be met with some form of apology as well as reparations" (60–61). To date, this is considered one of the first explicit Japanese articulations of the concept of colonial restitution.

More recently, Itagaki Ryūta, a historical anthropologist of Korea, revisited the concept of colonial restitution in a recently published two-part essay (2005–2008). As early as the latter half of the forties, when the South Korean interim government under the Rhee Syngman regime (established in 1948) internationally insisted on participating in the San Francisco Peace Treaty, postcolonial Korean intellectuals began formulating the idea of colonial reparations from Japan as that which is "special in nature and different from the notion of war indemnity [negotiated between the victorious and the vanquished]."[67] Ultimately, South Korea was excluded from the signing of the peace treaty due to the two oppositional forces that objected to South Korean participation: Japan, which insisted that Korea had not been at war with Japan and also feared that Koreans in occupied Japan, the majority of whom were described as Communists, might gain privileges as subjects of a victorious nation; and the United Kingdom, which raised concerns that redressing Koreans for Japanese colonialism might have ramifications for its own colonies and which hoped to prevent the issue of colonial restitution from entering the stage of the peace treaty. Although it is far beyond the current study's scope, Itagaki's research alerts us to the importance of considering the British colonial legacies as well as the history of Anglo-Japanese interimperial alliances in shaping the postwar, postcolonial settlement in Asia. More immediately, his study identifies the way in which war reparations have in effect eclipsed colonial redress, paving the way for the

United States and its allies to act with impunity in their joint continuation of de facto colonization and neocolonization of much of Asia and the Pacific region. These and other new investigations into Japanese redress issues have recently begun to situate the shortcomings of postwar settlements ever more explicitly in relation to the overlapping and ongoing global processes of colonialism and racism.

The genealogy of "military comfort women" redress activism in Korea and Japan thus encapsulates the convergence of the multiple trajectories of critical thinking that have been calling into question Cold War institutional and epistemic structures, of which the postwar settlement was an integral part. *Cold War Ruins* considers the consensus, contentions, and negotiations over the meanings and memories of the "military comfort women" across national and other borders as paradigmatic of post-1990s redress culture. The Cold War order's obfuscation of violence and the way it selectively addressed and redressed egregious violations during the Japanese war of aggression must then be grasped and revisited in its relationship to the way the emergent transformative possibilities were contained, precisely at the moment when it seemed that transitional justice might be attained. Crucially, the belated ways in which this particular historical injury came to be known *as* injury cannot but point to the lasting presence of the deeply entrenched, transnationally interlocking biopolitical normativities of capitalist colonial-modernity. Put differently, in interrogating the Cold War terms of transitional justice over half a century ago, post-1990s redress culture opens up an opportunity to critically remember earlier visions of reparations in relationship to the question of colonial extortion and the long deferral of decolonization. To paraphrase the sociologist Nakano Toshio, to query postwar Asia is to critique the continuation of colonialism and imperial geographies into the post–Cold War.[68]

Rethinking "Victor's Justice"

Along with the "military comfort women issue," another important earlier trajectory of criticism that aided the post-1990s renewed redress culture was critical assessment of the IMTFE, or the Tokyo War Crimes Trial. While scholars differ in their assessment of the degree to which U.S. occupation policy planning for Japan remained consistent over the transwar years, experts who have examined the archival record have generally concluded that U.S. decision makers recognized the utility of retaining Emperor Hirohito for the purpose of rebuilding an anticommunist postwar Japan during the war years, and that he was exempted from postwar prosecution for this reason.[69] Historians also agree that U.S. Cold War policy over northeast Asia initiated a decisive turn (e.g., NSC13/2, October 1948) during the IMTFE deliberations, a shift that was immediately followed by the 1949 "loss of China" to the Chinese Communist Party and the 1950 outbreak of the Korean War. Occupation policy toward Japan also became more explicitly antidemocratic and antilabor, culminating in General Douglas MacArthur's crackdown on the February 1, 1947, General Strike and the subsequent purging of the members and supporters of Japan's Communist Party from public offices. The U.S. occupation also remilitarized Japan through the introduction of the National Police Reserve in 1950, which was soon reorganized to form the Japan Self-Defense Forces. Paralleling the series of key decisions to remake Japan into a robust pro–United States, anticommunist regime open to free market capitalism, occupation authorities influenced the course of the IMTFE through exemption of a number of central figures from the trial, above all Kishi Nobusuke.[70] The cover-up of the Japanese Army Unit 731's biological experiments in northeast China also took place in this context.[71] Kishi, who was initially arrested on suspicion of A-class war crimes but was later released without trial, served as a high-ranking bureaucrat in Manchuria during the Asia-Pacific War. His powerful prewar transnational network of industrialists, financiers, and far-right nationalists in the region remained influential into the Cold War years. After the occupation Kishi led the pro–United States Liberal Democratic Party and as a prime minister signed the controversial 1960 United States–Japan Security Treaty. The latter formalized the military subordination of Japan, with the burden overwhelmingly carried by Okinawa, to American military and political hegemony and semi-extraterritoriality. Situated against this historical backdrop, the IMTFE and its legacy might well be assessed as showcases for the "Victor's Exoneration" of the vanquished—as much as an instance of "Victor's Justice" that overlooked war crimes committed by the Allied powers, which ultimately served to establish the Cold War U.S.-Japan alliance over far-reaching domains that included geopolitics, military cooperation, and the sharing of technology and science. The Tokyo War Crimes Trial, regardless of internal dissents and contradictions, commenced the culture of impunity that would serve U.S. geopolitical interests in the Cold War Asia-Pacific.

During the eighties important critiques of the IMTFE emerged. They concerned the IMTFE's Euro-American centrism and its laxity in prosecution of "crimes against humanity." The historians Arai Shinichi, Awaya Kentarō, and Utsumi Aiko, among others, pointed out the unevenness of the trial's attention to the different Japanese war crimes in the Asia-Pacific War. While some atrocities such as the Rape of Nanjing, which had been exposed early on by the Western media, were questioned as war crimes, the trial overall failed to interrogate many Japanese aggressions against the people of Asia and the Pacific Islands as crimes against humanity, including the military enslavement of women from this region. In an effort to redress the IMTFE's oversights, some of these scholars advocated the establishment of an "Asian People's Tribunal," an international people's court that would reopen cases that had not been addressed adequately in the trial.[72] According to this view, the IMTFE punished and executed Japanese political and military leaders for disturbing the peace and order reserved for white European and U.S. domination and for violating their colonial entitlements, properties, and privileges, while disregarding the humanity of people who remained under their colonial control.[73] The trial's unwillingness to fully interrogate Japanese atrocities against tens of millions of people in Asia and the Pacific as "crimes against humanity" was thus understood to demonstrate the elisions and exclusions produced by the West-centric notion of "humanity," as well as the trial's geohistorical perceptions, which were rooted in colonialism. The West-centric idea of civilization, the U.S. Cold War presence, and the selective, uneven, and racialized notion of "humanity"—these are the three primary elements that progressive redress activists and critics have emphasized whenever they have critiqued the IMTFE's legacy.[74]

The earlier leftist criticism of the Tokyo War Crimes Trial is rapidly being eclipsed by Japan's far-right historical revisionists who also criticize IMTFE, but for different reasons (chapter 3). Of late, partly in order to thwart the conservative revisionists' challenges, some liberal historians have attempted to redeem the trial's legacy. This line of argument underscores that, despite the Cold War compromise and marginalization of socialist countries, the IMTFE's prosecution in fact managed to record Japanese war crimes, including civilian massacres, sexual violence against women, and other human rights violations, more than has previously been understood.[75] It appreciates the IMTFE's universal significance and its contributions, paralleling the Nuremberg Trials, to the postwar advancement of new international legal protocols. The Nuremberg Trials' legal precedents, for instance, are deemed to have provided impetus for the subsequent development of the international criminal justice system. Such an assimilationist move, however, risks obscuring the previous anticolonial critique of the IMTFE that has tried to articulate the limits of West-centrism in international law and its colonial-civilizational discourse. It also preempts potentially transformative efforts to connect the currently unfolding critical assessment of international law with the earlier critique of the IMTFE.

In light of the post-9/11 discussions on international law and sovereignty, which some critical legal scholars have reanimated, as well as the vigilant call by these scholars to reflect on what it means to adjudicate wars, the positive reappraisal of the Tokyo Trial's accomplishment as measured against the international protocols set by the Nuremberg Trials seems to require careful reconsideration. Danilo Zolo, among others, problematized the uneven application of the twentieth-century international doctrine that universally illegalized all wars waged against international peace and order.[76] Warning against what the international law scholar Antonio Cassese called "a 'Nuremberg syndrome' by which international criminal jurisdiction perpetuates the model of the 'justice of the victors'" (6), Zolo noted that neither the United States nor any of the other victorious major powers in World War II or their allies has been formally charged according to international law with the "supreme international crime" of waging a war of aggression, even when indisputable evidence has been present. At the same time, *jus in bello* has hardly been applied to prosecute aggression in colonial wars or the killing of political partisans (i.e., Carl Schmitt's "irregular enemies") during counterinsurgencies. Moreover, international criminal jurisdiction based on the model of the "justice of the victors" has serious ramifications that go beyond the adjudication of war crimes. By instating the victorious as overseers and protectors of besieged sovereignties, the latter of which are expected to transition from criminally belligerent status to those who act in accordance with the norm of the peaceful global order, "victor's justice" could legitimize prolonged occupations after cease-fire.

When reflecting on the Tokyo War Crimes Trial's historical meaning and its ramifications on broader configurations of knowledge about modernity and colonialism in Asia and the Pacific, we must then at the least consider the IMTFE and the Nuremberg Trials—the two military tribunals Zolo identifies, following Carl Schmitt, as "the real origin of international criminal jurisdiction" (23)—by situating them critically in the genealogy of the illegalization of war and the accompanying geopolitical predicaments we currently face. In his observations of the planetary epistemic shift that took place at the end of World War II in the way nations, territories, and wars have been perceived and governed, Schmitt famously pointed out that the 1945 London Charter, which set the protocols for the Nuremberg Trials, marked the demise of the European system of war.[77] According to Schmitt, the idea of *justus hostis*, or "just enemy," had undergirded the European system of war and served to mitigate the war's escalation into *bellum justus*, the ultimate aim of which is to annihilate the absolute evil. The largely American effort to eliminate wars by illegalizing them—which was unevenly but continuously pursued during the interwar years punctuated especially by the two important developments of the 1924 Geneva protocol and the 1928 Kellogg-Briand Pact—came to fruition when the new legal concept of "crime against peace" was adjudicated at the Nuremberg Trials. Politicized and judicialized, wars thereafter are fought as bellum justus until total victory is achieved over a completely vanquished enemy; for only at that point could the war's political justness be legitimated.[78] In contrast, Achille Mbembe foregrounded the militarized history of slavery, conquest, and colonialism to point out that the "war of annihilation" was not a new phenomenon, but in fact a *constitutive* part of the genealogy of the European system of war.[79] Important to our inquiry, therefore, is a need to understand that Schmitt saw the total and annihilating character of wars as alien to modern Europe and that he perceived its *newness* in the post–World War II, Cold War international milieu, which coincided with the era of decolonization. Seen in this light, the international doctrine that criminalizes war against peace—what Carl Schmitt saw as the post–World War II *nomos* of the earth—can be regarded as a new postcolonial global apparatus of abstracting an absolute evil (e.g., Communists, anarchists, the anticolonial revolutionaries, terrorists, the axis of evil, etc.) which then must be vanquished to safeguard Anglo-American-centered international security and the status quo. The "Nuremberg syndrome" and its critique thus lay bare the problem of the uneven application of international law as much as what the law has enabled and sustained.

In the aftermath of the Iraq War, Sun Ge, a cultural critic who has written extensively on East Asian modernity, warned against the danger that uncritical celebration of the Tokyo War Crimes Trials may pose to China:

> Now more than ever, the historical narrative with which we Chinese understand the IMTFE as proof of victory in the war of resistance against Japan, or as justice that adjudicated Japanese militarism must be met with skepticism. To be sure, this skepticism by no means suggests exoneration of Japanese militarism for its crimes or lending support to the Japanese right wing's "anti-Americanism." Nor does it mean to deny the Trial's historical feat. Our skepticism ultimately needs to be directed at the hegemonic politics of America that forcibly claims to speak as the

representative of civilization, our Manichean modes of thinking, and the idea of "unitary civilization" that Takeuchi Yoshimi problematized half a century ago. The Manichean thinking and the idea of unitary civilization dictate the way we understand the Iraq War today. They continue to leave us external to the movement of history.[80]

Sun's reflection alludes precisely to the problem of bellum justus observed by Zolo and others which we currently face. At the same time, when she notes how the current U.S. unilateralism "continue[s] to leave us external to the movement of history," Sun's criticism also unveils the incommensurability between the transitional justice the United States had choreographed at the Tokyo War Crimes Trial and the Chinese people's exasperations during the war of resistance against Japan. Sun thus succinctly captured the inter- and intra-Asian sensibilities that have long underpinned redress culture's critical genealogy.

Sun's above passage referred to the Japanese philosopher Takeuchi Yoshimi and his essay, published in 1959, concerning the famous wartime roundtable symposium titled "Overcoming Modernity." This reference perhaps requires further qualification. The symposium, which took place in 1942, gathered together thirteen prominent intellectuals who largely shared an antimaterialist, romanticist politics, and who came from a wide range of fields, including literature, art, history, and philosophy. Though the participants' views were far from uniform, today the symposium is generally understood to have given the outbreak of the U.S.-Japan War intellectual endorsement by lending it universalistic historical significance. It characterized the war largely as an epoch-making moment in world history and as an unprecedented attempt by a non-Western nation to overcome the normativity, representativeness, and contradictions of modernity that had originated in the West. Takeuchi reflected on the roundtable's suggestion of a duality in what came to be named the Greater East Asia War: a war of invasion into China, on one hand, and a war against the Western imperial presence in Asia on the other. Takeuchi then concluded that "imperialism cannot be overcome by another imperialism, nor can it be brought to justice by one."[81]

This oft-cited line, which I have invoked for this chapter's epigraph, condenses Takeuchi's indictment of Japanese imperialism as well as his critique of those intellectuals who gave theoretical and moral legitimation to the war as a challenge to Western imperialism. Though hardly mentioned by his critics, immediately following this statement Takeuchi went on to note that in order to adjudicate imperialism one requires such "universal values" as "liberty, justice, and humanity as exemplified at the Tokyo War Crimes Trial" (306). From the vantage point of hindsight we can see how such an appraisal of the Tokyo War Crimes Trial ignores the gross exceptionalization of millions of people who were precluded from the category of humanity entitled to liberty and justice. To leave this oversight unproblematized begs the question of how the "universal values" Takeuchi found in the IMTFE's adjudication of Japanese war crimes also came to proffer U.S. military, political, and economic expansion since the war's end with ethico-juridical justification. When read along with the more recent critiques of the new imperialisms that increasingly extend their power through supranational networks and in the universalist language of human rights and humanitarian justice, a carefully situated reconsideration of Takeuchi's indictment takes on ever greater urgency.[82]

The notion of transitional justice concerns management of destabilizing elements in postviolence societies, whether international or domestic. The concept also expects reintegration of violence-torn elements of the society, but without disturbing structures existing prior to the upheaval. Transitional justice tends to presuppose that societies that have attained liberal organizations and formal democracy are no longer in transition. From this perspective, the postwar transitional justice administered for the Asia-Pacific War can indeed be seen as a "success": it more or less ushered in a stable world order that is likely to continue into the future. Postwar transitional justice and the generous terms of reconciliation apparently precluded vengeance, while the former enemy was integrated, tamed, and rehabilitated into a prosperous, free, and peace-loving ally. Yet, if indeed "every society is in transition," as the political philosopher Elizabeth Kiss reminds us, so is every world order restored in the war's aftermath.[83] Any idea of a successful transitional justice must then embrace a critical awareness of Cold War legacies in the region, thus ultimately challenging the dialectics of redressable and unredressable as integral to the (in)justices sustained by post–World War II neocoloniality and the structures of American dominance. *Cold War Ruins* is one modest attempt to consider the intellectual ramifications such challenges might bring to assumptions about modernity in the Asia-Pacific region and the latter's inseparable ties to the United States.

Cold War Ruins is divided into two parts. Part I, "Space of Occupation," contains two chapters, each devoted to a distinct geographical location and/or target population that came under the U.S. occupation in the aftermath of the dissolution of Japanese empire.

Chapter 1 considers the neocolonial condition of Okinawa in America's long "Pacific Century."[84] Situated at the geopolitical threshold of East Asia and the northwest Pacific, Okinawa became an increasingly important subject of knowledge in anthropology and area studies during the transwar 1940s. After the Allied powers' victory, Okinawa was both liberated from Japanese imperial rule and occupied by the United States until 1972. It has remained a crucial geopolitical site in the Cold War geography of what Eleanor Lattimore once noted as "security imperialism."[85] The chapter closely reads the Okinawan writer Ōshiro Tatsuhiro's novella, *Kakuteru pātī* (*The Cocktail Party*, 1967), alongside the disciplinary self-scrutiny of area studies and cultural anthropology since the 1990s. These critiques reveal how Okinawa's "liberated yet occupied" condition was produced by and then helped sustain the transpacific entanglements of Japanese and U.S. military-security concerns. Okinawa's liminality—produced out of the interimperial war, multiply overlapping colonialisms, the suspension of indigenous sovereignty, and continuing militarization resulting from the U.S.-Japan alliance—cannot be accounted for either within the postwar international conventions or the Cold War frame of war. The chapter hopes to show that Okinawa's liminality has been integral to the Cold War regime of unredressability and yet enabling of alternative politicizations of historical knowledge and justice.

Attending further to the midcentury as the emergent moment of the transpacific Cold War formations, chapter 2 analyzes the representation of Japanese women's enfranchisement in Japan's mainland under U.S. military occupation. Following the military victory in Asia and the Pacific, the United States became the supreme overseer of the region's progress, democracy, and modernization. The notion that the American occupation brought gender justice to racialized women of the vanquished enemy empire was integral to the process. The chapter examines the U.S. media's coverage of women's emancipation in Japan under General Douglas MacArthur's mandate. I will ask, in what ways did media representations and their discursive strategies help resolve for the American audience the contradiction that Japanese women gained rights, freedom, and equality but under the illiberal condition of foreign occupation? What are the implications of showcasing Japanese women's enfranchisement internationally, even as the disfranchisement and continuing dispossession of former Japanese colonial subjects were left unacknowledged? By interrogating the rhetoric of liberation that the United States has circulated not only to Japanese women and their American watchers but throughout the postwar decolonizing world, the chapter traces the connections of America's *jus ad bellum* to the universalizing idea of gender justice.

Part II, "Transnational Memory Borders," explores the post–Cold War transborder redress culture by investigating the multiple publics' contestations over the ongoing issues of apologies, redress, and reparations.

Chapter 3 observes the latest manifestations of transpacific Cold War entanglements in the "military comfort women" issue. I will focus on Japan's historical revisionism and its inability to perceive the Japanese military and colonial injustices. By attending to the racial and sexual dimensions of the revisionists' narratives and the "culture wars" they have incited, the chapter considers several issues that the revisionists, wittingly or unwittingly, bring together as interrelated: textbooks controversy, state-sponsored apologies, the transnational feminist redress politics that resulted in the aforementioned Women's Tribunal, China's cold war leniency policy and expressions of contrition by former Japanese POWs (Chūkiren), and the aberrant feature in Japan's Constitution that renounces the sovereign right to wage war. Rather than simply a sensationalist politics pursued by reactionary extremists, I consider the current revisionism a discourse historically structured by the political unconscious of Japan's "client state" status in postwar U.S.-Japan relations.

If the above chapter highlights the latest manifestations of transpacific Cold War entanglements outside the North American geographical parameter, the next two chapters will discuss the way Asia-Pacific War memories leave indelible Cold War imprints on U.S. domestic cultural politics. Chapter 4 examines the new phase in the Americanization of justice by observing Asian/American engagements in the transborder redress culture at the new century's turn. I will focus on the increasing involvement of Asian/Americans and Pacific Islanders in American legislative and juridical redress cases over the past two decades (e.g., House Resolution 121, the California Code of Civil Procedure [§354.6], etc.) to consider the new meanings they confer on questions of unredressability. By demonstrating the not-so-uniform ways in which Asians and Asian Americans have become mobilized into redress culture within the U.S. public sphere, the chapter hopes to illuminate the contradictory effects their involvement produces on the discourse on American justice, militarism, race, and nationalism.

I will conclude the book with a final consideration of the perils and possibilities of a transnational critique of historical justice but by revisiting the immediate milieu of the end of the Cold War in the United States. Chapter 5 scrutinizes the American Cold War memories of the Asia-Pacific War that figured prominently in what came to be called "the Smithsonian *Enola Gay* controversy"—that is, the impassioned dissension that spread across the United States over the Smithsonian Air and Space Museum's planned exhibit to commemorate the fiftieth anniversary of the end of World War II. The chapter examines academic discussions and media coverage that move across the national borders of the United States and Japan to elucidate what has fallen out of that process. Simultaneously a testament to the 1990s cultural wars, the controversy illuminated that the transnationalization of historical representations and their critiques can result in a kind of "warping" of politics. That is, when a critique travels from one location to another, it often inadvertently results in allying with intellectual and political positions that are at odds with those it endorsed in the original contexts. The predicaments of warped politics the chapter observes increasingly plague the ongoing transnational and transpacific citations, representations, and coalitions among the subaltern voices and calls for historical justice. By distinguishing critical transnationalism from transnational ventriloquism, the chapter addresses the possibilities of transpacific critique, which may prove vital to intensifying struggles in Asia and the Pacific Islands over the meaning of American exceptionalism, militarized security, justice, and decolonization.

PART I

Space of Occupation

ONE

Liminal Justice
Okinawa

To atone for your country and to demand redress for my daughter are one and the same....What I try to condemn, ultimately, is not merely an American crime but the cocktail party in and of itself.

Ōshiro Tatsuhiro, *Kakuteru pātī* [The Cocktail Party]

A disjointed or dis-adjusted time without which there would be neither history, nor event, nor promise of justice.

Jacques Derrida, *Specters of Marx*

In spring 2010, just less than a year after having led the Democratic Party of Japan (DPJ) to its historic landslide victory in the Lower House election, Prime Minister Hatoyama Yukio abruptly resigned from office. Previously during the campaign for the 2009 election Hatoyama had visited Okinawa and pledged to local voters that in the event of victory his party would completely remove base facilities at the Marine Corps Air Station Futenma (MCAS Futenma). The area surrounding the Futenma Air Station has been plagued by the histories of land appropriation, fatal accidents caused by high-risk military exercises, extreme noise, and other health and environmental hazards. Futenma became singled out as the paramount representation of Okinawa's base-related problems, especially following the 1995 sensational rape incident involving a twelve-year-old girl by three American servicemen. A year later the two governments agreed to relocate the naval station in Futenma to other U.S. bases. The plan would shift the Futenma facilities, partly to Guam and partly to the already existing base in Okinawa, Camp Schwab, which is in the Henoko District of Nago City. The Henoko plan came as a disappointment to those who aspired to a total removal of the military bases from the islands. It also raised serious environmental concerns and incited protests because the plan would involve extensive offshore reclamation.[1]

The U.S. military seizure of Okinawa began with its land invasion during the final months of the Asia-Pacific War. During the 1950s the U.S. Army continued the land requisition with forcible measures relying on "bayonets and bulldozers" and converted most of the seized areas into airfields, a naval port, military stockpiles, boot camps, and various other facilities accommodating U.S. troops and their attendants. The U.S. State Department and the military had not necessarily agreed on the monetary worth of maintaining U.S. possession of Okinawa, and there were different understandings over time. Nonetheless, it was not until 1972 that the United States ended its total occupation and Okinawa became a prefecture in Japanese sovereign territory. This "Reversion to the Mainland" (*hondo fukki*) marked a significant turning point in the de jure status of Okinawa. But it did little to change the island's militarized condition. Today the U.S. military occupies about 20 percent of Okinawa's main island and 40 percent of its airspace. Because of the U.S. military presence, Okinawa has been implicated in virtually all major American wars since World War II—in Korea, Vietnam, the Persian Gulf, and most recently Iraq and Afghanistan.[2]

Hatoyama's attempt to respond to local demands for lessening Okinawa's inordinate burden in accommodating U.S. bases in part resonated with his own broader political vision. He had advocated the establishment of what he called the East Asian Community in which Japan would seek to lessen U.S. influence over the region and instead cultivate closer fraternal ties with other Asian countries, including the PRC, through the establishment of an integrated currency and regional peace security arrangements. Investigative journalists clarified that political maneuvering in Tokyo and Washington had led to the spectacular failure of the Democratic Party's attempt to secure the U.S. government's consent to remove the American troops.[3] Several preceding incidents also fueled pressure for the politician to step down, including his family's inappropriate political donations. But the public media, at least at the time, attributed the dissolution of his short-lived cabinet not so much to the monetary scandal as to his inability to keep his promise of relocating the U.S. base facilities.

I open this chapter with the relatively recent political upheaval involving Okinawa, Japan, and the United States for several reasons. For one, this political episode exposed more spectacularly than ever the United States' and Japan's continuing joint expropriation of Okinawa.[4] The predicament demonstrated by the Hatoyama cabinet's downfall reflects the structure of the transpacific complicity between the United States and Japan and the historical sedimentations evident in Okinawa's current militarized condition. Though the degrees of commitment may have varied, since its takeover of Okinawa the U.S. government has consistently regarded it as a key strategic outpost for its military command over Asia and the Pacific Islands. The Liberal Democratic Party (LDP), Japan's pro–United States anticommunist party that came into power in 1955 and has ruled ever since except for a brief interruption in the 1990s and again between 2009 and 2012, has sustained Okinawa's status quo by its unwavering embrace of the U.S.-Japan Security Treaty (first signed in 1960, and automatically renewed since the second signing in 1970). Under the Status of Forces Agreement (SOFA) of the Security Treaty the United States maintains virtual extraterritorial use of the Okinawan land it seized during the initial phase of the occupation. The extraterritorial nature of SOFA also prevents U.S. military personnel accused of crimes from being handed over to Japanese police until there is an indictment, severely compromising the ability of Japanese police and local officials to gather evidence and build their cases.[5]

Okinawa's political representatives have repeatedly requested Tokyo to implement measures to alleviate problems associated with the U.S. military's presence. Some civic groups have insisted that it is not enough for the U.S. military to leave Okinawa, only to move somewhere else in the Pacific or elsewhere. At a minimum, local legislators have requested the central government to lighten Okinawa's burden of accommodating U.S. troops in Japan—over 70 percent (as of 2014) of whom are stationed on Okinawa—by distributing them more evenly across other Japanese prefectures. Yet successive LDP-led cabinets have largely remained reluctant to respond, except by increasing financial support and compensation to locals and thereby further locking the local economy into a center-periphery dependency. To be sure, the U.S. government has not necessarily demanded the constant physical presence of U.S. troops in Okinawa; it nonetheless insists that all bases in Okinawa must remain available for American military use at any and all times. In response, the Japanese government continues to guarantee the U.S. government's privileged access to bases in Okinawa and their military use by honoring the SOFA. In this way, the Japanese government has been faithful to what Gavan McCormack aptly named "client-statism." This refers to the asymmetrical interstate relations in which the lesser country (i.e., Japan) willingly subordinates itself to seek the protection of the patron state (i.e., the United States) by succumbing to the latter's needs.[6] With regard to Japan, however much individual Japanese mainlanders may have expressed sympathy for Okinawa's plight, they have for the most part acquiesced to the status quo. By largely containing the U.S. military presence to this peripheral island, and to a lesser degree a few other locations, the Japanese central government has managed to quell whatever discomfort or resentment mainland Japanese may harbor about transpacific "client-statism" and its obligatory political subordination. The 2010 diplomatic debacle over Futenma, then, is yet another instance that has brought international attention to the predicaments besetting Okinawa, which have originated in the U.S.-Japan Cold War alliance. It showcased the tenacity of the transnational forces committed to containing any destabilizing elements that might threaten post–World War II arrangements.

How are we to address and redress, if at all, the transpacific triad sustaining Okinawa's dilemma? I will begin with a brief historiographical exploration of Cold War Okinawa as a space of at least three overlapping liminalities—epistemically within academic discourse, legally with regard to its sovereignty and territorial belonging, and materially as a space of violence in a supposedly postviolence world. Okinawa's liminality, above all, is characterized by its ambiguous post–World War II, Cold War condition as a "liberated yet occupied" space under U.S. occupation. At the same time, in the transition from wartime to Cold War geopolitical and military mapping, Okinawa was located at the intersections of the "American Lake" and the "Far East/northeast Asia." The chapter then introduces *Kakuteru pātī* (*The Cocktail Party*, 1969), an award winning novella by Ōshiro Tatsuhiro, who is one of Okinawa's most prolific and renowned authors.[7] I will read Ōshiro's story alongside the metadisciplinary self-interrogation of Cold War area studies in anthropology and Asian studies. The critique of knowledge production we find in both *The Cocktail Party*, published at the Cold War's height, and the postnineties, post–Cold War self-reflections from within the academic disciplines, will reveal the problematic ways in which Okinawa came to be studied and represented on the cusp of the midcentury Pax Americana. By placing the geohistorical insights of Ōshiro's text in dialogue with more recent academic reflections on the ways in which area studies and American anthropological knowledge have been militarized, the chapter hopes to identify critical analytics with which we might grasp the complex sedimentation of violent histories in Asia and the Pacific Islands since the war's end.

Ultimately, my reading encourages us to understand *The Cocktail Party* as a hermeneutics critical of Cold War formations, both transpacific and transnational. *The Cocktail Party* reveals that the instrumentalization of knowledge about Okinawa's culture and history was integral to the justification and establishment of the United States' sovereign presence across the post–World War II Pacific. Importantly, Ōshiro's story exposes the limits of the modern categories according to which we habitually understand and present history and memories of violence. Okinawa's Cold War liminality as "liberated yet occupied" blurs the binary lines that supposedly demarcate and indicate the mutual exclusivity of liberal and illiberal, democracy and autocracy, peace and war, life and death, free and unfree, and amity and enmity. Such a perspective, which is critically attuned to Okinawa's liminal condition, introduces an alternative articulation of historical justice that compels us to move beyond the debilitating post–World War II, Cold War legacy. It may well incite us toward different historical sensibilities that help discern alternative spatial imaginations and temporalities, making it possible to envisage a different justice in Okinawa, and by extension, a different decolonized world.

Before we begin, however, it is important to note a curious remainder of the 2010 political drama. The debacle over the Futenma base relocation did not conclude with the prime minister's resignation, but unfolded with a stunning discursive turn. At his inaugural press conference (June 4, 2010) the DPJ leader Kan Naoto, who immediately succeeded Hatoyama as prime minister, was asked his political visions for the Futenma issue. To the reporters' astonishment, the new prime minister replied abruptly and without hesitation that he had been gaining insights into Okinawa's history from a nonfiction novel, *Ryukyu Disposition, a Novel* (*Shōsetsu Ryūkyū Shobun*). The historical novel Kan referred to is our author Ōshiro's magnum opus, which was written around the same time as *The Cocktail Party*. If the latter thematized the postwar Okinawa under U.S. military occupation, *Ryukyu Disposition, a Novel* portrayed the end of the nineteenth-century annexation of the Ryukyu Kingdom by the then emerging and expanding Japanese modern colonial empire.

The nomenclature the "Ryukyu Disposition" refers to a series of administrative measures the Meiji State undertook to encroach upon the region. The process, which ultimately concluded with the 1879 incorporation of Ryukyu into the Japanese body politic as Okinawa prefecture, involved the overthrow of the Ryukyu monarchy, followed by enlistment of the Okinawan royal family into the ranks of the modern Japanese aristocracy, and attempts to integrate the Ryukyu region by severing the multidimensional ties the kingdom had maintained over many centuries with the Chinese and other neighboring states. *Ryukyu Disposition, a Novel* first appeared in 1959 as a yearlong series in the local daily newspaper, *Ryūkyū Shimpō*. Kōdansha later published the novel in a single volume in 1968.[8] The novel centers on Matsuda Michiyuki, a high-ranking bureaucrat in the Meiji government who was appointed to an administrative position that mandated the entire annexation process between 1875 and 1879. According to Ōshiro, Matsuda left a colossal archive made up of official and unofficial documents, compilations of journals, diaries, and his own essays related to the disposition, all of which then became the basis for fictionalization. For average Japanese mainland readers, Ōshiro's monumental novel was not necessarily the most well-known literary piece within his enormous body of works. The prime minister's startling mention of it during his national press conference brought the novel unexpectedly back into the spotlight. Given the heightened media attention on the Futenma relocation issue, the novel was republished soon after the press conference and became available in a paperback edition.[9]

Historically, the Ryukyu Disposition marked the beginning of Okinawa's colonial modernity. Following annexation the population of Okinawa as well as those who migrated to mainland Japan as industrial and service laborers were subjected to various modern technologies of nationalization and normalization in schools and factories, including strict imposition of the standardized Japanese language, a disciplinary work ethic and heteronorms conducive to industrial capitalism, and a lifestyle and conventions of etiquette that were deemed appropriate for the modern and civilized "first class" nation that Japan was then striving to become.[10] Yet in Japan's mainland such knowledge about Okinawa's modernity has been for the most part overshadowed by cultural memories of the Battle of Okinawa and the U.S. military-colonial settlement that ensued. Popular media representations have unfailingly portrayed Okinawan residents during the war as martyrs who tragically sacrificed their lives for the defeated nation. To be sure, the audience in mainland Japan has been exposed to news of the pernicious U.S. military presence in Okinawa and the series of failed governmental measures. Today, in the liberal multicultural milieu, the overt racism many Okinawans have experienced in the mainland has also become part of popular knowledge. Yet rarely does the Ryukyu Disposition figure as a decisive historical juncture in the asymmetrical relationship between mainland Japan and Okinawa. Okinawa's two histories before and after World War II are divorced from one another and do not seem to occupy the same space. The 2010 disquiet around Ōshiro's historical fiction must be read against this dominant discursive configuration.

If anything, the publics' bewilderment with the citation of the nineteenth-century historical episode in deliberations on Okinawa in the twenty-first century betrayed the widely accepted epistemic injunction against making explicit associations between the U.S. military settlement in Okinawa and Japanese colonial annexation. This sense of bafflement signaled the discursive habit of ignoring the entanglement of transpacific geohistories before and after 1945.[11] What this episode brought to light, then, was the way in which "transwar connectivity"—that is, the *ability* to make connections, to perceive affinities and convergences of geohistorical elements that have worked together to constitute mid-twentieth-century violence—has been repressed, if not entirely denied, in the production of knowledge about Okinawa. And yet, the dissensus over Futenma could not help but summon the specter of Japan's colonial empire. If there was indeed a ghost haunting the discursive perimeters of Okinawa's American base issues at the time, it was there to mark that very epistemic repression. Whatever the politician himself may have intended, the evocation of nineteenth-century Okinawan history was utterly unexpected for the media and the public at large. It caught people by surprise across the Okinawa-mainland divide, sounded awkward, and left the impression that the politician had made an erroneous statement that was grossly irrelevant to the realpolitiks of his immediate situation.

Yet in the very untimeliness of this failed speech, a stupefying time that was "out of joint," lay provocations for historical justice and its politicization.[12] In order to meet the exigency of the moment, something else from the past had to be remembered, something that did not immediately belong to the present. Part of what I wish to explore in the following pages is "catachrony," or temporal discombobulation, and its effects on knowledge. What significance lies in the sense of temporal disjointedness which the politician's apparently confused, inept public statement stirred up, if only for a moment? What are the ways in which an act of "remembering the wrong things at a wrong moment" might generate an unlearning that critically unsettles the way we believe we know our history? If, as sociologist Avery F. Gordon observed, the idea of spectrality does not only remind us of the instability, uncertainty, and imperfection of positivist knowledge but also newly articulates "a something to be done," this catachrony in which the social critique based on the ontology of U.S. military presence in Okinawa became haunted by memories of nineteenth-century Japanese colonialism was precisely such an emergent moment.[13] Its spectrality took the different publics by surprise, albeit momentarily, but it deeply and surely unsettled the convention of knowing the past and urged a way to remember otherwise.

Okinawa's Liminalities in America's Long "Pacific Century"

Inquiries into the possible continuum, complicity, and compatibility between the ways in which the United States and Japan have dominated the twentieth-century Asia-Pacific region have been marginal, if not entirely absent, to post–World War II mainstream knowledge production. Only colonial and postcolonial studies scholars have insisted on the transwar continuities of, for instance, prewar Japanese colonial education, law enforcement, corporate practices, and other modern institutions and ideologies in postcolonial state apparatuses.[14] Here I propose a related but different kind of transwar inquiry. It looks at transpacific relations by primarily focusing on the interimperial connections of Japanese and American hegemonies and the effects of the disavowal of these links. What are the implications of not seeing the continuity between the prewar and postwar, or not seeing the simultaneous complicity between the United States and Japan prior to and after 1945? What does it mean to set a clean epistemic break at the moment of cease-fire?

Keenly attuned to the situation of the Korean peninsula during the interregnum years immediately following liberation from Japanese colonial rule, the social anthropologist Heonik Kwon challenges the mainstream Euro-American historiography that defines the Cold War globally as a period of "long peace." By rejecting the predominant characterization of the Cold War as an "imaginary war" fought as "a balance-of-power affair," Kwon insists that the globality of the Cold War needs to be situated in the specificity of cold wars that were fought "in large parts of the postcolonial world as a civil war or other forms of organized violence."[15] In the southern part of "liberated" Korea, as exemplified by the long-silenced plight of Jeju Island, the localized anticommunist counterinsurgencies unfolded fiercely under the occupying U.S. military command, leading up to the outbreak of the Korean War. Kwon's understanding that the Cold War was coextensive with postcoloniality resonates with the observation put forth by North American Cold War studies since the 1990s, but with a different accent. In contrast to Kwon, who observes deaths and destruction in the intense local conflicts of the decolonizing areas, much recent American studies scholarship—which likewise notes the simultaneity of the deepening Cold War and the accelerating decolonization process during the post–World War II decades—tends to emphasize the attempted biopolitical inclusion of the newly independent nations into either camp in the Cold War rivalry. In theory, the U.S. Cold War governmentality relied on a new technology of governance that targets life and the bodies without territorial possession or coercive force. Yet, as Kwon reminds us, in many areas formerly under Japanese imperial rule, the Allied occupation was often synonymous with continuing states of emergencies as manifested in civil wars, counterinsurgencies, militarized seizures, and politicides under martial law. The discursive convention of setting a temporal benchmark at 1945 as the origin of historical progress, peace, and prosperity, which is represented in binary contrast with pre-1945 dispossession, exceptional violence, and underdevelopment, rests on selective spatial knowledge and belies the important realities of other new imperial geographies of the post–World War II world.

In the wake of the Japanese empire's collapse and on the threshold of the Cold War's awakening, an extensive area Japan had formerly occupied transitioned into a space in which violence coexisted alongside the ideology of the prosperous liberal world.[16] Okinawa, too, belonged to such liminal spaces where the prewar Japanese colonial infrastructures often converged with and helped facilitate Cold War violence. At the same time, Okinawa's liminality was legally defined through the suspension of sovereignty. Immediately following the war, Okinawa was severed from the defeated Japanese empire and came under U.S. rule with two provisions: one, the United States recognized Japan's "residual sovereignty" over Okinawa, thereby containing the idea of indigenous as well as local sovereignty; and two, the United States would maintain control over Okinawa until its eventual approval as a UN trusteeship under U.S. authority.[17] The historian Toriyama Atsushi points out that the two concepts "residual sovereignty" and "pending" trusteeship were emplotted with the intent of prolonging the U.S. occupation by deferring Okinawa's independence. Commenting on John Foster Dulles's famous statement on "residual sovereignty" (September 8, 1951), in which Dulles laid out the terms of the postwar U.S. control of Okinawa, Toriyama notes: "The US required Japanese 'residual sovereignty' in order to head off any threat to the stability of its 'exclusive strategic management' of Okinawa by demands for self-determination from the inhabitants."[18] In other words, the notion of "the residual" was a highly ambiguous concept that theoretically framed the liminality of Okinawa under U.S. military rule. It denoted that while in principle Japan's imperial sovereignty over Okinawa had formally ended, Japanese sovereignty would remain as a lingering remnant so as to preempt the possibility that Okinawans might insist on their independence to oust the foreign occupiers. Dulles's statement betrays that such a possibility existed. Crucially, the idea that Japan held "residual sovereignty" enabled the United States to disavow the colonial nature of its relation with Okinawa.[19] It helped rationalize the United States' de facto sovereign control of the islands without contradicting its claims to be the champion of the free and liberated post–World War II world. Coupled with the indefinitely postponed prospective of UN trusteeship, the notion of "residual sovereignty" wrought by U.S. Cold War policy preempted any Okinawan indigenous claim to independence and autonomy. No longer formally colonized but not yet sovereign, Okinawa's liminal status under U.S. occupation signaled at once the postwar continuation of colonial relations and its disavowal.

In the following, I wish to explore the analytic with which we might critically address and redress Cold War violence in the postcolonial space as a continuation of Japanese imperial violence. The epistemic demarcation that perceives the pre- to postwar transition as a clear severance from the (Japanese) time of supposedly illiberal violence to a peaceful world of (American) life and liberty has rendered illegible both the transwar continuity and the transferability of violence between the new and the old military and imperial powers. In what way can we understand the violence of hot wars and Kwon's "civil war or other forms of organized violence," which are coextensive with injuries under the Cold War even as they are inflicted in the name of conviviality, aid, and friendship? What are the ways in which we can cast light even further on the failure of transitional justice by perceiving violence and injustice as constitutive parts of the Cold War empire's liberal and biopolitical governmentality?

Disarticulating Empires: The Cocktail Party

Although *Ryukyu Disposition, a Novel* unexpectedly gained national attention in the midst of the 2010 political debacle, the writer Ōshiro Tatsuhiro had been more prominently known for *The Cocktail Party*, his award-winning novella thematizing the U.S. military presence in 1960s Okinawa. Considering that the two works were in production at roughly the same time, there is some geopolitical irony in the contrasting appraisals the two novels have received over two different sets of historical circumstances, one in the late sixties and the other in the early twenty-first century. Ōshiro recalls that *Ryukyu Disposition, A Novel* was so unpopular that the local daily newspaper canceled the original newspaper series in which it was published. In contrast, *The Cocktail Party*, which came out in 1967, won Japan's prestigious Akutagawa literary prize. Of course, extratextual conditions do not dictate aesthetic judgments. Still, it would be crass to ignore that behind the contrasting appraisal of the two novels lay an intensifying call for Okinawa's "reversion" to Japan and the internationally escalating protest against the U.S. wars in S.E. Asia. Since *The Cocktail Party* Ōshiro has become known as the first Japanese author indigenous to Okinawa to win the prize.

Because of the story's representativeness and its author, *The Cocktail Party* has received much scholarly and critical attention. Literary critics have noted that *The Cocktail Party* should be approached as a multivalent text insofar as Ōshiro adopts an ambivalent position toward history.[20] While the text invites multiple interpretations, one of its most striking qualities is its depiction of the multiple temporalities and geopolitical investments competing over Okinawa. Diegetically, the text revolves around the rape of the protagonist's daughter by an American serviceman and the struggles to bring justice to this case of military sexual violence. Set in Okinawa as it entered into the third decade of the U.S. occupation and on the cusp of "Mainland Reversion," the story depicts the contradictions brought on by what Chalmers Johnson aptly called the American "empire of bases."[21] At the same time, it poignantly illuminates the subaltern condition, one in which the voices that speak out for Okinawan indigeneity have been at once enabled and yet muted by the discursive regime of Cold War geopolitics.

Deeply entrenched in the male-centered, unabashedly patriarchal imaginary, the four central characters in *The Cocktail Party* are portrayed through the following national figurations: the Okinawan protagonist who fought in mainland China as a Japanese soldier during World War II and who will learn in the story's latter half that his daughter was raped by an American serviceman, Robert Harris; Miller, who is later revealed to be a member of the U.S. Counter-Intelligence Corps; Ogawa, a journalist from mainland Japan who the protagonist suspects has been involved in civil rights struggles for historically stigmatized communities in Japan; and Sun, who is known to have fled mainland China after the Communist takeover and later reveals that his wife had been raped by Japanese soldiers during the second Sino-Japanese War. Readers are introduced to them through scenes at a convivial evening gathering hosted by Miller. By then the four characters had already developed a close friendship through the private Chinese language tutorials Sun had volunteered to offer. Their relationships had grown so intimate that even Ogawa and the protagonist were included among the exclusive guests to Miller's luxurious residence within the otherwise forbidden U.S. military compound. And yet, when the protagonist attempts to bring the American who raped his daughter to justice, neither Sun nor Miller is willing to help. Ogawa emerges as the sole figure who expresses sympathy and support though he is virtually powerless in Okinawa, which is under U.S. jurisdiction.

The Cocktail Party is starkly divided into two temporal segments, before and after the narrator's discovery of his daughter's rape. The story opens in the first person narrative, with the protagonist describing his apprehension as he trespasses the U.S. military compound on his way to attend the Millers' cocktail party. He muses over how the uncontested privilege of the occupying forces not only segregates but subordinates the local residents in their own native place. Similar to other colonial spaces, the U.S. occupation in Okinawa suspended the rights of the occupied but placed them under protective surveillance. Contrary to the narrator's initial anxieties over the space of American privilege, however, Miller's cocktail party turns out to be an amicable occasion, though not entirely devoid of underlying tensions. The story is then abruptly ruptured as it moves into its second half. When the narrator returns home after the intoxicating gathering of "international friendship," he discovers that his daughter has been raped by an American soldier named Robert Harris. The narrative pointedly shifts from the almost idyllic, self-indulging pace of the first person narrative to a transcendent and condemnatory third person who addresses the protagonist through the reproachful second person form, "you (*omae*)."

The Cocktail Party thus deploys "rape" as a central metaphor for illustrating the militarized and colonial injustice of late sixties Okinawa under U.S. governance. Critics have identified in Ōshiro's story the familiar link between national allegories and the patriarchal subordination of women.[22] The heteropatriarchal national allegory often relies on tropes of rape to address political subjugation, territorial dispossession, and abjection. The story thus appears to reiterate the familiar anticolonial nationalist investment of possessive racialized masculinity and nationalism in the objectification, ownership, and disciplinization of the native woman. Even while *The Cocktail Party* does not render the daughter as filial or subservient but depicts her as robust, defiant, and determined to bring the matter to public justice, she remains voiceless and spoken for by the protagonist only as a juridical subject-object. To be sure, while the subjugation of women and femininity in the symbolic reduction of rape needs to be fully problematized, such a single-axis gender critique of rape and patriarchal nationalism may risk prematurely writing off the story's complex engagement with Cold War formations and the potentially unraveling work that it can do. As the literary critics Miyagi Kimiko and Shinjō Ikuo observed, militarized sexual violence in Okinawa cannot be grasped fully through the conventional binary gender theory that lacks perspectives on the intersectionality of powers.[23]

The story's second half opens by juxtaposing the protagonist's two diametrically opposed yet coextensive realities during the same evening: the convivial international gathering inside the U.S. military family compound and the institutional reality of the unpunishable crime against his daughter. The previously myopic "I," which had been immersed in the rhetoric of international friendship, becomes interpellated by a transcendent, omniscient narrator and transforms into a vocative and self-objectifying "You" who has achieved a demystified state of clear consciousness about Okinawa's material reality. Now awakened, the protagonist tries to convince his daughter to fight in the courts for justice. Seen in this way, it appears as though the story resolves the crisis—or, for that matter, Okinawa's subordination as metaphorized by the daughter's rape—through the modernist notions of the enlightened self, the critique of false consciousness, and the rule of law.

The striking cotemporality of the U.S.-Ryukyu friendship on the one hand, and violence on the other, lays bare the coevalness found in any carceral space that operates between biopolitical management (that is, an incitement to life and coprosperity for the Okinawan people under siege) and the sovereign power of the occupying force to unilaterally render the daughter's rape unredressable and unpunishable (that is, the condition of bare life and social death). In this context, the story's apparent faith in modern reason and juridical institutions is cautiously guarded. At the story's end, the protagonist projects his hopes for a different Okinawa onto his daughter's willingness to testify publicly in court. It is important, however, to recognize that in the narrated scene in which the daughter rehearses the crime scene to the police, she is investigated not as a victim but as an accused. This is because after having raped the daughter, Robert Harris went on to press a criminal charge against her for the injury she had inflicted on him when resisting rape. Drawing a stark contrast in the manner in which the two cases would be handled, the story unveils the asymmetrical duplicity of justice in the military-colonial regime: the case against the daughter will be subjected to full scrutiny by the U.S. military police and its Criminal Investigation Division, while her case against Robert Harris will be filed in the Okinawan district court, which actually has no formal jurisdiction over American personnel. In her eventual military court appearance, the daughter would be summoned to testify as a perpetrator and defendant. Ironically, therefore, it is only because of the criminal charges brought against the daughter that the original American violence is brought to light and recorded in the occupiers' archive.

This is yet another asymmetry of violence and justice that the text insinuates: the subaltern can only succeed in making the original violence visible when it reveals its wounds through the act of counterviolence. Even more illuminatingly, the story closes with the protagonist's prediction that despite his faith in her resilience and robustness, his daughter's two separate court cases will end in defeat. The concluding pages of the story are thus profoundly suggestive of how violence and justice might look differently in threshold places such as those under military-colonial siege like Okinawa. In such places the immanence of violence is made invisible in the name of militarized security. Yet, as we will see below, the story makes equally clear that formal juridical defeat does not mean there is no remainder to justice.

Throughout *The Cocktail Party*, moreover, we find abundant references to the relationship between an empire and decolonized (as well as potentially decolonizable) nation-states. The story opens with a scene in which the protagonist receives Miller's invitation letter to his cocktail party. In this seemingly innocuous opening passage, the protagonist pays special attention to the latter's unconventional visual rendering of the idiom "cocktail party." Having noted the arbitrariness, he then playfully decomposes the term "cocktail" into "cock" and "tail" and muses over the different choice of the Chinese ideographs for the two phonemes. Though it might easily go unnoticed, I find that this passage intimates an allegory of empire suggested by the proverbial phrase: "Better to be a cock's head than a bull's tail."[24] The ancient Chinese maxim preaches the merits of maintaining sovereign status, even as a lesser nation, over becoming an appendage to a powerful empire. In other words, *The Cocktail Party* announces at the outset its self-conscious engagement with a particular historical outlook, a perspective that regards world history spatially—as a process of territorial possession, annexation, decolonization, and recolonization.

The suggestiveness of the apparently insignificant reference to the Chinese proverb becomes clearer when we turn our attention to another nationalized figure, "Lincoln," a euphoric character cast as a jovial "Mexican American." Ōshiro's story observes the articulation and disarticulation of empires through this figure and draws an analogy between the U.S. annexation of Mexican, or formerly Spanish, territory, and the Japanese takeover of Okinawa. It goes without saying that the name "Lincoln" carries ample historical import in its common association with the official American history of emancipation, racial integration, and liberalism—that is, those elements upholding U.S. exceptionalism. But the story does not introduce the figure of the Mexican American to celebrate the racial inclusiveness of American liberalism and thus parts with the common move to contrast American tolerance with Japan's racial exclusionism. Though some may still be tempted to do so, once we see the story's problematization of the collusion between Japanese and U.S. military imperialisms, it becomes clear that this remarkable acknowledgment of diversity among the occupying Americans is underpinned by the following historical perception: that both Japan and the United States, as empires, emerged into modernity out of a parallel mid-nineteenth-century history of military expansion, annexation of territories, and their colonization. The protagonist's wartime mobilization as a Japanese imperial soldier also suggests that the Japanese empire was as multiracial and multiethnic as the American empire claims to be.[25] The figure of "Lincoln" in Okinawa therefore represents the story's critical stance toward the homogenizing myths of nationalist epistemology.

At the same time, the story abandons the historical analogies it highlights between the two empires by drawing a sharp contrast between the Okinawan protagonist and the "Mexican American." This distinction stems from the asymmetry not only between the occupied and the occupier but between the two states to which they belong respectively. The Okinawan protagonist is perplexed by Lincoln's excessively jovial demeanor. To him, Lincoln's generous attitude toward his colleagues, presumably predominantly white American military elites, drastically differs from his own relationship to Japanese and other non-Okinawan associates. Especially bewildering to the protagonist is Lincoln's exultation about his biracial heritage. Lincoln is boastful that he was born to a mother of Mexican descent as a result of "international amity," a phrase reminiscent of one commonly deployed by U.S. forces in Okinawa (*Kakuteru pātī*, 176). The juxtapositioning of the two racial formations in their respective imperial contexts also brings into relief that despite the analogous histories of Japanese and U.S. colonial expansion and territorial annexation, the different ways in which the two nation-states are positioned in the global power configuration and vis-à-vis each other can result in an entirely different historical awareness for those ethnonationalized peoples who have been incorporated as minoritized populations. Unlike the "Mexican American," the indigenous Okinawans in Ōshiro's story are those who have been relegated to the fate of not even "the bull's tail" or "cock's head," but "the cock's tail," a subordinated part of a country that is already subjugated to a more powerful external force. By doing so, *The Cocktail Party* hints at the limits of analogical thinking with which we approach geohistories of violence and injustice. I will return to this point.

The task of deconstructing the Cold War knowledge formation thus requires the story to rehash and self-reference the actually existing nationalist formations that it seeks to undo. Through the heavy deployment of nationalist allegories, *The Cocktail Party* simultaneously perceives the nation-state as a powerful category of knowledge and affective attachments. In doing so, the novella self-consciously engages with U.S. Cold War knowledge politics. In one of the friendly conversations at Miller's party, the protagonist is joined by several U.S. military officers who make playful references to gross historical generalizations about whether Okinawa's cultural roots lie in Japan or China:

> "[Speaking of the nineteenth century notion of Okinawan independence] I have evidence that proves its viability into the twentieth century as well. Have you all read Dr. George Kerr's *Okinawa: The History of an Island People?*"
>
> Quite a chatterer, I thought. The local Americans in Okinawa have learned from Kerr's book, and those who own public relations media have been writing about how the Shimazu clan exploited the Ryukyus ever since it invaded the islands in the seventeenth century, and how discriminatory the Japanese bureaucratic government's treatment of Okinawa Prefecture has been since Meiji.
>
> "That book was . . . ," I started, but then hesitated. I didn't quite have the audacity to ask if it was written to justify U.S. foreign policies. (154–55, my translation)

Okinawa: The History of an Island People was published in 1958 by George H. Kerr, a former American diplomat and U.S. Navy expert on Formosa during the Asia-Pacific War. Undertaken as part of the Scientific Investigation of the Ryukyu Islands (SIRI, 1951–1954), this project was sponsored by the National Research Council–Pacific Science Board (NRC-PSB) under the auspices of the Department of the Army. Kerr's work later came to be regarded as a canonical anthropological study of Okinawa's vanishing culture. It was translated into Japanese and paved the way for the establishment of post–World War II Okinawa studies. The novel's bold evocation of Kerr's book is a discerning critique of the ethnohistorical knowledge produced by anthropologists and their liberal endorsement and appreciation of "cultural differences." But before moving on to explore Kerr's and other anthropological studies of Okinawa and the Pacific Islands in the next section, I wish to briefly call attention to a self-imposed silence in the quoted passage.

Apparently, the process whereby the protagonist acquires an undeceived, demystified state of clear consciousness about occupied Okinawa is paralleled by his increasing ability to break silences. In the above passage, when invited to share his view of George Kerr's work at the Millers' party, the protagonist was unable to voice his view that "it was written to justify U.S. foreign policy." And yet, a dramatic shift occurs in the story's latter half. Having learned not only that Robert Harris had raped his daughter, but also that a criminal charge had been lodged against her for the injury she had inflicted on him, the protagonist seeks help from three male figures. In Miller's living room, the very same space where the American gathering had previously taken place, the protagonist ascertains that Miller is unwilling to lend him support. Instead, the American intelligence officer attempts to resume the cocktail party conversation:

> "What century did contacts begin between Okinawa and China?" Miller questioned you abruptly.
>
> "Are you interested in that issue that much?" Your parlance suddenly but clearly stiffened.
>
> "What?" Slightly taken a back, Miller nonetheless continued. "I do not dislike history to begin with. I thought I might use this opportunity to study the history of cultural exchange."
>
> "I'd suggest you not do that."
>
> Miller: Eh? Why? (291, my translation)

In depicting the protagonist's awakening from his deluded self and acquiescence, *The Cocktail Party* at the same time exposes the futility of a certain way of knowing history. For the protagonist the American infatuation with Kerr's Ryukyuan history only amounts to an instrumentalized politics of memory whereby historical knowledge is used to legitimate the U.S. presence. In this sense, Ōshiro's *The Cocktail Party* presciently intuited a problem well before the academic articulation and problematization of the institutionalization of knowledge in Cold War area studies. Moreover, the story's readers are reminded from time to time that most of the conversations among the four male figures are conducted in Chinese, unless otherwise noted. The choice of Mandarin as the lingua franca of 1960s Okinawa carries special significance. It goes without saying that this linguistic choice underscores the U.S. preoccupation with China's regional civil war/cold war: the United States regarded Okinawa as a key strategic site in the military containment of Communism on the Far Eastern cold war/Cold War front. The American investment in spoken Chinese is furthermore contrasted to the affinities that might center on sinographs. That the protagonist makes special note of the "irony" that he had learned to speak Chinese from "Miller, an American," then, suggests the troubling reality of Cold War East Asia in which hardly any international relationship with China could be negotiated without the mediation of American presence.

Because the story draws a palpable connection between the protagonist's breaking his silence and the debunking of ethnohistorical knowledge, it is tempting to understand this abandonment of self-imposed quietude as a gesture toward reclaiming indigenous agency and the sovereign self who can speak out on its own behalf. And yet, even though the protagonist's rejection of Miller's discourse in the quoted passage is unmistakably a sign of upheaval, the text does not allow a reading that locates such agency simply in breaking silence. In fact, the story contains several similar instances of self-imposed muteness, not all of which are broken. This becomes evident when we contrast the direct confrontation with Miller to another stance of silence, one which the protagonist adopts toward Ogawa. Ogawa turns out to be the only individual/nation that comes to the protagonist's aid in pursuit of Robert Harris. Given the precariousness of Japanese sovereignty due to the semiextraterritorial status the 1960 U.S.-Japan Security Treaty had granted American military forces in Japan, Ogawa's influence is similarly if not more compromised than the Okinawan protagonist's. Nevertheless the latter must rely on the mainland Japanese character in order to counter the U.S. occupation. In the following passage, the protagonist chooses not to reveal to Ogawa his memory of Japanese military atrocities in wartime Okinawa.

> [Previously, at the time of the party, Ogawa had said] "In Kuo Mo-jo's novel, *Waves*, there is a scene of a mother who in the midst of the Sino-Japanese War hears the roar of the enemy's—that is, the Japanese—planes, and strangles her own screaming child to death."
>
> You replied this much at that time: "In the Battle of Okinawa as well."
> And now you recall what you had tried to say but couldn't.
>
> "Sometimes the Japanese soldiers did such things. The Japanese soldiers bayoneted Okinawan infants inside the bomb shelters they were sharing."
>
> Yet, again, you could not utter those words in the presence of Ogawa, who might have ties to those soldiers. (213, my translation)

It is difficult to overlook the resonance between the fervor of the "Reversion to the Mainland" movement that swept across Okinawa at the time the novella was written and the way it depicts the alliance between Ogawa and the protagonist. Less obvious is the story's observations on what had to be foreclosed for the "Reversion" discourse to acquire coherence. Memories of Japanese military violence in China and Okinawa are simultaneously elicited in the above passage, yet the latter remains the inarticulate, subaltern historical knowledge which, precisely in its unspeakability, enables the fragile alliance between Okinawa and mainland Japan.

Here, silence is not tantamount to absenting, but enabling agency. The cooperative relationship between Ogawa and the protagonist can only be forged through the suspension of testimonial truth about Okinawa's suffering at the hands of the Japanese military. The story thus assigns agency to the Okinawan protagonist not in his act of breaking silence, but in his complicity in the secreting of history. Yet from our present vantage point, we also know that this pact of silence has remained precarious. The protagonist's choice not to speak of Japanese imperial violence in Okinawa stands as an ominous prognosis of what would come after the island's reversion to the "homeland." In the 1990s post–Cold War milieu, moreover, the breach of silence unleashed the cached memories of "collective suicide/self-determination [*shūdan jiketsu*]" into the public spheres.[26] During the Battle of Okinawa, the Japanese army in its desperate retreat from the U.S. land attack ordered local residents not to surrender to the invading forces, but to choose death with honor. The enforcement of such military discipline sometimes led to extreme situations in which people assisted members of their beloved families in killing themselves.[27] These and other similarly heartrending memories of Japanese imperial violence in Okinawa have more often than not exposed and unsettled the asymmetrical ties between Okinawa and mainland Japan.

Sovereignty in the Imperial Interstices

As the Cold War of the so-called Eastern and Western blocs came to a close, scholars in various disciplines began to critically assess the ways in which U.S. national security interests and foreign affairs concerns, since at least the mid-twentieth century, have shaped research on other places, cultures, and people. This self-reflective investigation has been multifarious and far-reaching across various disciplines. In American literature the process involved questioning the previously dominant New Criticism and the ideological work it performed in its treatment of literary works as transhistorical objects of formal aesthetic appreciation. Asian studies scholars in the United States likewise participated in self-critique to explore the way Cold War interests have figured knowledge about Asia. It should be noted, even at the height of the Cold War, some Asian studies historians and political scientists critiqued the escalating U.S. involvement in S.E. Asia. Led by the Committee of Concerned Asian Scholars, this reflective movement was perhaps the first to acknowledge how profoundly U.S. geopolitical concerns have shaped the region.[28] The historian Bruce Cumings, among others, has summarily reflected that area studies was developed as an apparatus of Cold War knowledge production and was exported to anticommunist allies throughout the world with the financial backing of U.S.-based capital.[29] Area studies specialists in various disciplines received their academic training according to assumptions about the boundaries and authenticities of national and subnational languages, cultures, territories, and histories. Largely interested in the normative development of nation-states and statehood, area studies scholars primarily produced studies of entities that were already constituted as, or were becoming, nation-states.[30] Area studies–trained anthropologists, in particular, aided the American geopolitical investment in the postindependence nation-state building by observing people and their lives and rendering them into discretely identifiable and spatially fixed ethnonational categories.[31] As a result, Cold War area studies marginalized concerns about the history of empires, interregional and transnational movements, or cross-hemispheric diasporic cultural forms.

Area studies' close association with U.S. Cold War policies and the problematic pedagogy about the non-American others it underwrote has been so well documented since the 1990s that another detailed reiteration is unnecessary. Still, for the purpose of assessing the key role area studies played in the U.S. governance of the post–World War II decolonizing world, it is well worth briefly considering so-called modernization theory and its performance. This powerful American social science paradigm dating from the 1950s and '60s provided area studies specialists in North America and elsewhere with a technology of knowledge that gave validity to the belief in U.S. supremacy. It offered and prescribed for the postwar free world an ideal type of modernization modeled on the "American way of life" and the U.S. history of capitalist modernity and industrialization, as well as the American rights-based political system of liberal democracy. Area studies specialists investigated social organizations, kinship systems, religious beliefs, interpersonal behavior, and other social practices among targeted populations to identify indigenous elements that would teleologically lead them onto the next stage of universal history and help achieve a modernity paralleling that of the United States. These elements would of course vary according to the areas or nations under investigation. But they were thought to be *functionally equivalent* cross-culturally, and it was these elements that would enable comparisons among the people studied.[32] While these "functional equivalents" could potentially lead the observed societies on the path toward modernization, inherent cultural and other differences might impede such progress. The technology of cross-cultural comparison identified the impediments to modernization in so-called feudal remnants or those elements that came to be defined as "traditional" in binaristic contrast to the normative modern. Although with some variation, modernization theory generally offered a powerful temporal and spatial epistemological framework that made it possible to map out different areas of the world as potentially integrated entities that were more or less poised to "take off" into a common history.

What is especially noteworthy for our present inquiry, however, is that area studies' interest in Asia and the Pacific initially emerged out of military security concerns at a time when the region was transitioning from wartime belligerency to postwar peace and liberation. Institutionally, the Association for Asian Studies, the single professional association covering all aspects of research on Asia, was established in 1956 as an extension of the Far Eastern Association, which had originated in 1943. Area studies in general, but especially research on Asia and the Pacific Islands, along with such closely associated disciplines as American anthropology, began to take its present form as an academic aid to U.S. military operations during World War II. The Japanese empire's extension into the Pacific during the first half of the twentieth century posed an especially urgent problem for U.S. wartime intelligence. This was especially true for Micronesia, the area previously known as Oceania. After Germany's defeat in World War I, its possessions in the Pacific—including the Marianas, the Carolines, and the Marshalls— were relegated to Japan under the mandate system, a new form of global territorial governance introduced by the League of Nations. Cold War area studies' entanglements with the wartime need for intelligence gathering is nowhere more in evidence than in the increasing investment in knowledge production about the Pacific region during the transwar decade.[33]

Rexmond C. Cochrane's developmental narrative on the institutional history of the National Research Council's Pacific Science Board gives us further insights into the wartime origin of Cold War area studies.[34] The Pacific region was perceived, according to Cochrane, as a "vast area which previously had been closed to American scientists" (487) because of Japan's imperial mandate over the region for more than two decades prior to the outbreak of the U.S.-Japan war. The demands of military intelligence mobilized scientists and helped advance scientific studies of the Pacific region in the 1940s transwar decade. "In June 1942," Cochrane writes, "the National Research Council, the American Council of Learned Societies, the Social Science Research Council and the Smithsonian set up what was to become the Ethnogeographic Board, to act as a clearing house in assembling for future invasion forces everything that was known of Oceania. All during the military advance up the island chain, the Board provided a continuous stream of strategic intelligence reports" (486–87). Thus according to Cochrane's narrative, the Pacific region, which the American academic community had regarded as "*terra incognita*" (487) at the beginning of the war against Japan, emerged as a bountiful frontier for the sciences "as a result of the responsibilities thrust upon it by the war" (487).

The Harvard anthropologist and linguist Alfred M. Tozzer's research on Okinawa vividly illustrates the strategic instrumentalization of ethnohistorical knowledge suggested in *The Cocktail Party*. Tozzer worked for the Office of Strategic Services in Honolulu and prepared a study on the strategic importance of "the people of the Loo Choo Islands" and their descendants in Hawaiʻi, the Japanese mandate Micronesia, the Philippines, and even Latin America.[35] Defining the Okinawans as Japan's "[e]asily [i]dentifiable" "minority group" with a different "racial composition" (5), Tozzer stressed the importance of attending to the heterogeneity of the enemy population. On the basis of his findings in Hawaiʻi, Tozzer highlighted the Okinawan antipathy toward mainland Japanese because of the long history of exploitation and discrimination. "Since Pearl Harbor," he reported, "there often appears among the Hawaiian Okinawas [sic] a feeling of elation at their status today and the stress is placed in the theory that they are *not* Japanese and never have been; hence, they should have no blame placed upon them for what the Japanese are now doing" (5–6). Tozzer found the "Operative Usefulness of the Okinawas [sic]" in the cultivation of racial cleavages among the enemy population:

> Both open and black propaganda would have many points to attack, not the least of which would be to stress a loyalty to the memory of their own rulers, their centuries of associations with struggling China, and their oppression by the Japanese, governmentally, socially and economically. . . . Psychological Warfare in its various aspects might well be brought to bear upon the cleavage outlined here between the two Japanese groups,

each with its own physical type, its own history, its dynasties, its mores and attitudes. The Okinawa [sic] himself might well prove useful in this movement as an agent and in the civil and military administration at home, in his own islands, in the Mandates and in the Philippines. (6–7)

In order to enhance the "operative usefulness," therefore, not only Okinawa's race and culture but its history needed to be distinguished from that of Japan. Tozzer thus unabashedly and optimistically highlighted the importance of making the people in and from Okinawa possess a sense of sovereignty clearly distinguished from that of the Japanese. This could be encouraged, Tozzer recommended, by making the former aware of the "cleft" between the two and the unjust discrimination of the Okinawans by the Japanese.

Tozzer furthermore anticipated the eventual American military occupation and administration of the areas where significant concentrations of Okinawan people would be found. His report discussed the postbelligerency usefulness of Okinawans "in Areas Occupied by American Forces" and made the following recommendation to the Civil Affairs Command of the navy: "Different attitudes and reactions could well be expected and *a knowledge of the Okinawan history might be used* among the more intelligent members of the population to gain their confidence and respect. Cooperation greater than that of the Naichijin [mainland Japanese] might well be looked for. Their abilities along certain lines might also be utilized so that these people could play an important role and one quite different from that of the Japanese proper in any plans for reconstruction" (emphasis added).[36] Tozzer believed that the anthropological knowledge about the Okinawan difference could be utilized for the navy's postbelligerency "work of rehabilitation."[37] Meanwhile, anxieties about the vacuum of U.S. power and knowledge in the regions occupied by the Japanese empire lingered on after the cease-fire. Cochrane's narrative captures how the keenly perceived need for postwar intelligence work in the Pacific region facilitated the continuing joint operation of the military and academia. Promptly responding to the navy's request for the much-needed information in Micronesia, the National Research Council established the Pacific Science Board (NRC-PSB) in 1946. The United States Navy began a series of nuclear tests in the Bikini Atoll in the Marshall Islands in the same year. The PSB conference, which gathered scholars from widely ranging fields including anthropology, zoology, earth sciences, oceanography, meteorology, public health, and medicine, was coorganized by George Peter Murdock, the prominent

Yale anthropologist known for the establishment of the Human Relations Area Files (HRAF) and research on the functional universality of the "nuclear family" across different cultures. But during the final year of the U.S.-Japan War Murdock had also served in the U.S. Navy and coprepared a series called *Civil Affairs Handbook* for the U.S. Navy Department, covering areas ranging from the Marshall Islands and Mariana Islands to Okinawa (all prepared in 1944). He remained in Okinawa after the war as a member of the U.S. occupation forces.[38]

To put it differently, area studies knowledge concerning the Pacific region was formed with an explicit awareness that the United States was entering the space Japan had vacated. Consequently, Cold War area studies did not emerge in an epistemic vacuum but in negotiation with the existing edifice of Japanese imperial ethnology and history. The cultural historian Tomiyama Ichirō argues that Japanese ethnology's postwar development also contributed to the U.S. occupation policy that aimed to detach Okinawa from Japan. The geopolitics of Japan's expanding empire designated parts of "Oceania" with its own imperial nomenclature, such that the region came to be called the "South Seas" (*nanyō*), a frontier viewed through the lens of tropical fantasies and considered rich in natural resources. Prior to 1945 Japanese ethnologists had conducted extensive research throughout their colonies and other occupied territories, including Okinawa and Micronesia. Postwar area studies under U.S. global Cold War policies thus had to negotiate with the legacy of Japan's colonial studies. Yet as Tomiyama observes, this negotiation was not unidirectional, but a mutually constitutive process. As they witnessed the postdefeat breakup of the Japanese empire, a group of Japanese ethnologists began to question the prewar discourse on "Okinawa" as "an odd variety" of Japanese mainland culture, and they wondered if they had overlooked indications that the Ryukyu Islands had always exhibited a distinctly unique and wholly independent culture.[39] The inauguration of postwar Okinawan studies by U.S. area studies scholars thus coincided with Japanese ethnologists' intellectual divestment from Okinawa and other parts of the Pacific Japan had formerly occupied. This epistemic decolonization of Okinawa within Japanese postimperial ethnology further validated the establishment of "Okinawa" as an object of study within U.S. area studies *independent of* Japan. In this process, as Tomiyama artfully puts it, Okinawa came to serve as a "boot camp" (17)—that is, a site for "training" emerging Cold War area studies specialists who would later be dispatched to different parts of the decolonizing world.

Considering the complexly intersecting histories and geopolitical investments of the militarized knowledge produced during the transwar decade,
the immense insight with which Ōshiro embedded Kerr's work deftly in
the text through the "Culture Talk" of the U.S. military elites and the Okinawan protagonist is remarkable.[40] The supposed racial and cultural ambi-
guity of Okinawa vis-à-vis Japan—that is, its doubleness from having been
constructed as racially and culturally different, yet destined for assimilation
into Japan's imperial modernity—made it possible for American anthropologists to posit "Ryukyuans" as Japan's interior exteriority. The idea of
Okinawa's independence under American tutelage then served as the telos
of postwar Pacific research under U.S. foreign policy initiatives.[41] This discursive configuration, however, had grave ramifications for the production
of knowledge concerning Okinawa's sovereignty. *The Cocktail Party* observes
this process through the sardonic reference to Kerr's study—precisely by
suggesting that Okinawa's indigeneity and self-determination could not be
talked about without pushing it into one positivist category or another, into
one imperial affinity or another. Not unlike Gayatri Chakravorty Spivak's
subaltern figure of the woman who becomes displaced as the reified "third-
world woman," only to disappear in "a violent shuttling" between competing representations of tradition and modernity, the matter of Okinawan
sovereignty became obfuscated in the violent subaltern space between the
two imperial archives.[42] Representations of Okinawa's ethnohistorical difference could not easily escape the alignment with the positionality already
mapped out within the given geopolitical discourse (e.g., pro– or anti–
United States, protected or dominated by China, greater or lesser cultural
affinity with Japan, etc.), while such shuttling required suppression of the
multifaceted dimensions of Okinawa's past and present.

This impossible condition, moreover, has shaped assessments of the author himself. In his critique of writers indigenous to Okinawa, the literary
critic and historian Namihira Tsuneo observes that literary assessments
oblivious of Okinawa's complex geopolitical position have tended to catego-
rize Ōshiro's writings—especially those that perceive Okinawa's modernity
as ambivalently yet integrally constitutive of Japan's imperial modernity—
as "pro-Japanese" and dismiss them as unidimensionally speaking on behalf
of Japanese state policies.[43] Namihira observes that writers indigenous to
Okinawa frequently thematized how in the initial postwar years the U.S.
military was welcomed as a "liberating army" (133) that relieved them
from the devastations of war. Ōshiro, too, recalled the openness people felt

toward the American forces in Okinawa. Referencing the author's autobiographical commentary, Namihira further points out that for Ōshiro the initial euphoria soon dissipated as it became increasingly clear that the supposed liberator, the United States, would stay on as a new occupier. Namihira painstakingly demonstrates how Ōshiro's position, rather than conforming to any given stance, is far more complex and ambivalent than commonly understood. When he reflected on the collection of his novellas that were republished in 2001, Ōshiro seems to have been keenly aware of this predicament. He repeatedly underscored how Okinawa's intimacies with the two empires are often lost in representations of its modern history: "The reality was far too complicated to have only one of its corners cut out [as representative]."[44] That Okinawa's modernization was as much an integral part of Japanese colonization as its liberation was part of the American invasion constitutes the "complicated" reality Ōshiro observed. And yet, this transpacific conjunction, complexity, and complicity have constantly been repudiated through the binary of imperial rivalry and the discourse of the Cold War nation-states. Only through a geohistorically informed, locally situated reading such as Namihira's, then, can we begin to see that the entirety of *The Cocktail Party* is devoted to uncovering the risks one must take whenever enunciating anything definitive about Okinawa's history, integrity, and identity.[45]

The foregoing discussion critically implicates our present inquiry on historical justice. Insofar as Okinawa has been geohistorically and epistemically located at the edge of the two empires (or more precisely three, to highlight the historical proximities to China), any demand for justice also risks being heard as an announcement of alliance with a given, already formed political position, whether in terms of national belonging or political platform. A critical look at the postwar relationship between Okinawa and the Japanese mainland also urges us to be vigilant about similar questions concerning for whom, for what purpose, and in whose interests Okinawa's predicaments are spoken for. During the "Reversion to Homeland" movement, many liberals, socialists, and pacifists in mainland Japan joined the antioccupation movement in Okinawa. Yet when Japanese mainland intellectuals and activists spoke for the rage and torment of Okinawa, the issue of Japanese colonialism and the racial subordination of "Okinawans" was obliterated by the uncritically identitarian call for solidarity under the common denominator of "*sokoku*" (homeland) against U.S. imperialism.[46] In the next section I will examine the ways in which *The Cocktail Party* disarticulates the Cold War epistemology and its deployment of ethnonational categories to expose their debilitating consequences for the possibility of bringing justice.

Liminal Justice

Besides positing Okinawa as a "liberated yet occupied" liminal space, *The Cocktail Party* also portrays it as an intersection where contradictory memories of violence and visions of justice meet and collide. It represents Okinawa as a space of U.S. military occupation as much as a borderland of transnational memories of the region's manifold experiences of mid-twentieth-century violence. Critics have positively appraised Ōshiro's novella for its courageous confrontation with the difficult history of Okinawa's participation in Japan's war of aggression.[47] The text remembers different instances of wartime injuries through the nationally marked characters. Sun, the expatriate from mainland China, unambiguously evokes memories of Chinese civilian victimization at the hands of the Japanese military. The war in China mobilized people of Okinawa as imperial subjects despite their subjection to Japan's civilizational racism. Thus when the Japanese figure, Ogawa, refers to the Japanese civilian bombing over Chinese cities during the second Sino-Japanese War, the Okinawan protagonist must bear the burden of responsibility for Japan's aggressive war even as he harbors other ghastly memories from the other side of violence in the same war—namely, the story of Japanese soldiers killing children in Okinawa during the ground battle against the invading U.S. forces. At the same time, to the extent that the ethnohistorical categories are tainted by strategic investments—as we saw in the gamelike search for Okinawa's cultural roots at Miller's party—the story seems to imply that "history," in so far as it remains part of the Cold War epistemology, almost always falls short of providing the occupied and the colonized with effective means by which to bring about changes.

The Cocktail Party recalls and renders historical losses in a far more complex and interconnected manner than do nationalistic and Manichean representations of war and colonialism. Sun, the Chinese expatriate, deserves special attention in this respect. Though more sympathetic than Miller and showing a clear gesture of support by speaking to Robert Harris, Sun ultimately refuses to participate in the protagonist's struggle. To recall, besides demanding that Harris appear as a plaintiff-witness in the American military court where his daughter will be prosecuted for the injury she caused, the protagonist wishes to charge Harris in the Okinawan juridical system for the crime of rape. By refusing to help, Sun practically sides with the American occupier.

Given the multivalent quality of *The Cocktail Party*, Sun's reticence, too, can have a variety of meanings. His solitary status as a refugee places him equally distant from the immediate realities of Japan, Okinawa, the United States, or even his place of origin, China. He remains allied with Miller and insists that their friendship, mutual leniency, and forgiveness must not be abandoned, if only superficially. He believes that the facade of amity is necessary for survival even while he is fully aware of its dissimulative nature. As a result, this figure comes across as an opportunistic, noncommittal individualist who refuses any form of politicization. Sun accepts the position of "a third-country national" (*daisankokujin*) in the following manner: "Unfortunately, I do not have the right to speak up in local politics. My status may appear secure to you because I have an occupation here and the right to domicile, in addition to being outside the bounds of politics; but such rights of mine are precarious. I must remain even more careful than you of what I say" (*Kakuteru pātī*, 200, my translation). One possible reading of Sun's reticence is to understand it as the diasporic subject's ineptness at becoming involved in the struggles of the "here and now." Sun's precarious status earns the protagonist's sympathetic understanding. Yet, insofar as he remains an émigré fettered by the memories of his originary belonging, he may not effectively cultivate a new sociality or forge a transformative political alliance at his present location. Alternatively, to the extent that *The Cocktail Party* is a critique of the post–World War II, Cold War formations at various levels, Sun's "neutral third-party" stance, though manifestly aligned with the Chinese Nationalist Party, could be read as an allegory for the then emerging Third World Nonaligned Movement. Like Sun, if refuge were to be taken in the delicately managed balance of powers, this third position could not be an effective challenge but would remain an enabling supplement to the global Cold War.

While there are certainly a number of different ways we can interpret his averseness, I wish to call special attention to the curious inconsistency in Sun's attitudes toward his experiences of past and present violence. Throughout, Sun prioritizes the maintenance of mutual generosity and international harmony at the expense of testimonial truths. He almost obsessively adheres to the idea of reciprocal leniency. Although eager to avoid disturbances, Sun nonetheless irresistibly and abruptly reveals to the protagonist that his wife had been raped by Japanese soldiers in the wartime Chongqing suburbs. His overall composure notwithstanding, Sun cannot but chastise both the Oki-

victims who should have had the opportunity to reckon on their own terms the irreparable losses they had suffered under Japanese aggression. Not unlike the problematic "provocation of amnesty" in post-Apartheid South Africa, the two warring regimes' provocation of leniency prematurely foreclosed the possibility of redress and, if at all, reconciliation.[52] Read within such a geohistorical context, Sun's investment in Chiang's terms of leniency and forgiveness may well be understood as the trauma deriving from the primal scene of historical repression. The way Sun oscillates between measured explanation of the Chinese people's impossible effort at "forgetting enmity and striving for amity" and his compulsive eyewitness accounting of the Japanese assault symptomatically indexes the conundrum of justice rooted in the regional cold war (*Kakuteru pātī*, 223). In this postindependent space the popular imperative for justice was suspended in the interests of ensuring the newly emerging nation-states' survival and geopolitics.

The narrative thrust of *The Cocktail Party* ultimately brings us to a face-off between the Okinawan protagonist and Sun. Since Sun is a refugee as a result of the Japanese invasion and the Chinese civil war/cold war, his survival in Okinawa depends on its status quo, which is its occupied condition under the United States' transpacific Cold War hegemony. Thus when the Okinawan protagonist tries to confront the U.S. intelligence officer, it is Sun who, albeit superficially, objects to the unraveling of the quadrangular alliance. Disregarding Sun's plea, the protagonist insists on terminating the friendship of "disguised equilibrium [*itsuwari no antei*]" (222) and sets himself up against both Sun and Miller. He then declares: "You were the one who enlightened me, Mr. Sun. To atone for your country and to demand redress for my daughter are *one and the same*. . . . What I try to condemn, ultimately, is not merely an American crime but the cocktail party in and of itself" (223, my translation and italics). This passage, which I have used as this chapter's epigraph, condenses the historical sensibility that *The Cocktail Party* painstakingly delineates. Of course, it is possible to interpret the "false pretenses" and "disguise" of friendship under the banner of U.S.-Ryukyuan international amity as a mere ideological distortion of the exploitative material reality. Yet the story's ample references to the inextricably tangled violent histories forbid us to overlook the overdetermined composition of the situation. More than an ideological exposé, the protagonist's challenge to the "disguised equilibrium" is aimed at unraveling the institutional and epistemic configuration of biopolitical complicity and amnesia in its entirety—"the cocktail party in and of itself"—that has sustained Okinawa's militarized-colonial status quo.

It should be underscored, however, that this sensibility could not have been attained without Sun's provocation. Sun's complex and precarious character epitomizes not only the continuity of violence from the Sino-Japanese War to China's civil war, but also the way in which the regional cold war has led to the unredressability of the Chinese people's suffering— even as his presence in Okinawa is entirely dependent upon U.S. supremacy in the Cold War. Sun is thus a catachronic figure haunted by multiple histories of violence whose disjointed temporalities ineluctably expose transwar connectivities and transpacific complicities. In fact, all four key figures of *The Cocktail Party* engage in catachrony in one way or another. They each remember things that do not immediately belong to the primal scenes. For instance, in the U.S. military brigade, Ogawa and the protagonist recall a novel about the Japanese bombing of China as they search for a missing American child. There the protagonist also recollects the murder of Okinawan infants by Japanese soldiers, although this memory remains ultimately unspoken. Meanwhile, Miller and other U.S. intelligence officers bring back discussions of the Ryukyus' sixteenth-century ties to China in their "Culture Talk." A nexus of transnational memories, "liberated yet occupied" Okinawa is a space where discrepant times and locations are conjured up and intersect. It is a liminal space where catachrony is immanent and commanding, obliging the protagonist to assert that the injury the Japanese military inflicted on the Chinese people cannot be divorced from the violence of the U.S. occupation of Okinawa. Yet these are two instances that practically and empirically belong to disparate historical and geographical contexts. Radically diverting from notions of redress that are available in our conventional thinking and existing institutional venues, the story suggests that one historical loss cannot be addressed and redressed without implicating other histories of violence and dispossession.

With this particular sensibility in mind, we can also perceive the marked distinction the story draws between the Okinawan protagonist's and Ogawa's attitudes toward history and justice. If the protagonist finds connections between Japanese war crimes and Cold War injustice in U.S.-occupied Okinawa, Ogawa emphasizes the structural analogies—hence the severance—between the Chongqing suburbs under Japanese occupation and Okinawa under the U.S. occupation. Thus when Sun discloses his experience of Japanese wartime atrocities in China and refuses to render wholesale support, Ogawa advises the protagonist not to be discouraged by Sun's personal experience, insisting that each instance of injustice must be dealt with separately, as if each suffering is structurally equivalent in its own context with no mutual connection ("*are wa are, kore wa kore* [212]"). The story thus contrasts two distinctive ways of confronting the past: one that perceives histories of violence and subordination as intersected so that justice must also be sought relationally; the other that views such histories as comparable and analogous yet discrete and disconnected. It should be clear by now that the difference the story draws between the Okinawan and Japanese positions has important ramifications for envisioning alliances and solidarity. Ogawa's is a position that understands the possibility of a universal alliance among those who occupy the pure and exclusive position of the oppressed within the given binary of domination and subordination, victimizers and the victims. In contrast, the protagonist's is a position that insists on the intersecting genealogies and colluding relations and position-alities across different histories of violence and injustice. To realize justice in the liminal space of Okinawa, according to the latter view, is not enough to simply reverse the positions in each separate binary relation. Other dissimilar yet interconnected instances of injustice elsewhere, in other times, must also be undone.

On Statelessness

World War II's end marked a disruption in the world organized by the nineteenth-century colonial empires. While it inaugurated the beginning of a new world order, much within modern-colonial relations remained intact even as nation-states, which are the normative primary units of international law and relations, arose out of the formerly colonized areas. This chapter has placed Okinawa in this larger geohistorical milieu. Yet Okinawa's transformation into a space of the "liberated yet occupied," a liminal condition in Cold War postcoloniality, was certainly not unique. The historical singularity of each locality notwithstanding, it is my hope that the critical epistemology I have tried to capture in this chapter can be read provocatively as applicable to other similarly liminal sites.

In the past two decades American studies scholars have increasingly turned their attention to the history of the United States as a colonial and military empire. *Cultures of United States Imperialism* (1993), edited by the two American literature scholars Amy Kaplan and Donald E. Pease, was a landmark volume of the era that collectively addressed the complex issues arising from the disavowal of the history of imperialism that shaped the United States as an empire. In her American Studies Association (ASA) presidential address, delivered in 1998, Janice Radway addressed the issues

d in the Kaplan and Pease volume and propounded that the American
ies' "presumption that American culture is exceptional in some way
that it is dominated by consensus" has been and can further be challenged by studies that call into question the notion of an "America" that is
tied to a geopolitically bounded physical territory.[53] Together, these works
productively scrutinized the geophysical delimitation of "America." In an
earlier version of this chapter I placed Ōshiro's story and the critique of
Cold War area studies in relation to such fervent discussions on the absence
of empire in American studies.[54] As my central research concern increasingly came to focus on the Cold War epistemology and its problematic effects
on ideas of justice and violence, I became redrawn to the multiple significa-
tions of The Cocktail Party, but especially the Chinese refugee figure, Sun.
What has driven my inquiry is the conjunction between this figure and the
protagonist in their shared unease in belonging—in other words, in their
in-between-ness, liminality and survival.

The analysis of the story's final showdown between the protagonist and
Sun would not be complete without commenting on how these two figures
share a type of statelessness. Far from identical, they nonetheless each find
themselves in precarious conditions: one is a refugee while for the other
indigenous sovereignty is under siege. The protagonist, like his daughter
and other local Okinawans in the story, has no recourse to law, while Sun,
a practitioner of the occupier's law, feels he has no standing in local politics. Thus when the protagonist faces up to Sun, stating, "to atone for your
country and to demand redress for my daughter are one and the same," it is
certainly possible to see that what he acknowledges is the mutually shared
predicament of statelessness and that redress would mean redemption of
the rights, privileges, and protection enjoyed by those belonging to a State.
If, however, we attend carefully (as I have tried to do) to the way the story
interrogates the distinctions and binaries foundational to modern political
categories (e.g., liberation and occupation, free and unfree, amity and enmity, etc.), it becomes apparent that Sun's and the protagonist's affinity for
justice is far from the recuperation of institutional normalcy. Instead, the
two figures render ironic the very notion of the State as the guarantor of
rights, justice, and well-being.

To grasp the full implications of such statelessness, it would be helpful to
turn to Giorgio Agamben's radical critique of Western political philosophy
and his exposé of the secret intimacies among sovereignty, violence, law,
and human rights in modern biopolitics. In his critique of Hannah Arendt's
famous formulation of refugees as people turned rightless with the decline

of nation-states, Agamben wrote paradoxically: "That there is no autonomous space within the political order of the nation-state for something like the pure man in itself is evident at the very least from the fact that, even in the best cases, the status of the refugee has always been considered a temporary condition that ought to lead either to naturalization or to repatriation. A permanent statute for *the human in itself* is inconceivable for the law of the nation-state" (emphasis added).[55] For Agamben, therefore, it is the modern nation-state that bans the possibilities of life as such, a natural life that is capable of existing in itself without having rights and prerogatives inscribed on to it. Elsewhere Agamben has written that at the heart of modern democratic nation-states is "not man as a free and conscious political subject but, above all, man's bare life, the simple birth that as such is, in the passage from subject [of monarchical regime] to citizen, invested with the principle of sovereignty"[56] In other words, in the biopolitical sphere of national-social democracy it is no longer the executive power alone but citizens vested with rights and the power of representation who decide to kill and manage life on behalf of the nation's survival. What Agamben is after, then, is a politics of pure life, "truly thinking a politics freed from the form of the State" (*Homo Sacer*, 109), in which people, too, are divested—perilously, for sure—of the state-given power to decide which life is worthy or unworthy for rights, prolonging, and belonging.

It would be useful in this light to return to Ōshiro's autobiographical commentary on the "liberated yet occupied" Okinawa. "Upon returning to [postwar] Okinawa under the American occupation," Ōshiro reminisced, "what I found was, ironically, freedom. It was a freedom of speaking liberally in uchināguchi (the Okinawan vernacular) and a freedom of having been liberated from the constrictions of 'the State' ['kokka' no seiyaku]."[57] The statelessness Ōshiro found in Okinawa was liberty from the constrictions imposed by Japanese rule, which first and foremost judged the indigenous languages and local customs to be unfit for normative modernity. It is "ironic," indeed, when considering that Ōshiro's observations of liberty for the indigenous way of life were initially realized in the POW camps that the U.S. army set up in Okinawa, where most of the local residents who had surrendered were interned. One might even go so far as to say that it was in this exceptional space under siege that the Ryukyuan as an internally homogenous category was reborn. "Constrictions" lifted by the U.S. occupation, then, must have concerned more than Japan's repressive state policies. More radically, the freedom Ōshiro perceived in Okinawa's stateless condition was an effect of the nation-states' divestment from the people of rights and rogatives as the sovereign power (that is, the political rights the State tows in the people), including the right to determine the lines of distinc-1 between life and death. In finding an affinity between the precarious refugee figure and occupied Okinawa, the justice that is called for is the possibility of "the human in itself," beyond existing juridico-political categories. In Ōshiro's liminal Okinawa we are confronted with the unspeakable wretchedness of statelessness but also the paradoxically enlivening ban on the State's inscription of the sovereign in areas where violence, law, and the social have come dangerously together. Seen in this way, we may view Okinawa's famous antiwar slogan, "nothing is more precious than life in itself [nuchi du takara]," as suggesting much more than a condemnation of war per se as an act of taking life. Equally powerfully, it is possible to receive it as an expression of not so much postnationalism as poststatism, a declaration of independence for "truly thinking a politics freed from the form of the State." While Ōshiro's writing needs to be situated specifically in occupied Okinawa at the Cold War's height, this book's following chapters seek out, in different times and locations, calls for redress that similarly appreciate the predicaments of the State as the privileged guarantor of freedom, rights, justice, and well-being. Such different analytics and sensibilities are mutually incommensurable yet derived from the intersecting genealogies of the transwar, transpacific Cold War formations.

Ōshiro's story painfully reminds us of just how difficult it is to attain a complex historical understanding of Okinawa's status as both "liberated and occupied" and to gauge the extent of the failure of transitional justice at war's end. Yet Okinawa's very liminality, as I have described it in this chapter, was a condition that also invited a different notion of justice that compels us to undo the Cold War stranglehold that continues to dictate our perception of the world. As a limit concept, the idea of justice we find in Ōshiro's occupied Okinawa may not be easily translated into existing institutional languages. At the same time, precisely because it pushes against the boundaries of the possible, it also leads us to a radically different way of addressing and redressing not only the initial moment of failed justice but its afterlife.

TWO

Liberation under Siege

Japanese Women

The most important emancipator of Japanese women was General Douglas MacArthur, who made women's suffrage occupation policy. The liberators of Afghan women wore U.S. battle dress.

George F. Will, "Another Pose of Rectitude," *Newsweek*, September 2, 2002

Victor's justice, besides giving the victorious the power to decide whose and which incidents of war violence either constitute international crimes or receive immunity, further extends the power of legitimation into the postbelligerency occupation. In this transitional space the law of war remains to govern the threshold between subjects and nonsubjects in the newly emerging regime. Okinawa's Cold War (post)coloniality initially originated in what was then the conventional practice of foreign occupation whereby the victorious could legitimately exercise full sovereignty over the territory and people it vanquished. This chapter continues to examine transpacific knowledge production but by focalizing on another part of the Japanese empire occupied by the Allied powers: namely, the Japanese mainland itself. The U.S. occupation of the Okinawan islands did not end formally until 1972, and many of its militarized infrastructures have virtually remained intact up to the present day under the U.S.-Japan Security Treaty Status of Forces Agreements. The Allied occupation of Japan's mainland on the other hand formally concluded as early as 1952. The chapter considers this asymmetry and its implications. In sharp contrast to knowledge about Okinawa's coloniality, which was over-shadowed by the prolonged U.S. occupation, information about mainland Japan was widely disseminated as it was undergoing various reforms initi-ated by the Supreme Commander for the Allied Powers (SCAP). According to this knowledge, Japan was on a steady and rapid path toward becoming a peaceful, democratic, and economically liberal sovereign entity and was hence fully deserving of international recognition and reintegration into the comity of advanced nations. As we will see in the following pages, the American image of the occupation of Japan, in which the U.S. biopoliti-cal governmentality appeared to be successfully rehabilitating a racially de-praved former enemy, helped shape Cold War understandings of the lasting effects of the Asia-Pacific War as well as postwar American justice.

The memory of the "successful" Allied occupation of Japan has been so deeply engrained at the level of the American political unconscious that it continues to haunt the way the United States fights its wars even into the twenty-first century. About six months prior to the United States–led inva-sion of Iraq, a *New York Times* article headlined "U.S. Has a Plan to Occupy Iraq, Officials Report" informed the American public that the Bush ad-ministration was drafting a plan for postwar Iraq "modeled on the postwar occupation of Japan."[1] The occupation of Japan's mainland (1945–1952), however, was not the only instance of past U.S. military involvements to be invoked. Divergent memories of past American wars fought against dif-ferent enemies at different times and places resurfaced throughout differ-ent phases of the national emergency that followed the 9/11 incidents. By September 2003, less than six months after the completion of "Operation Iraqi Liberation" (later renamed "Operation Iraqi Freedom") that began in March of the same year, White House reporters were noting that the Bush administration was viewing the Iraqi situation as closer to that of post-war Germany than Japan. By then militant opposition against the occupy-ing U.S. forces appeared much more formidable than the administration had initially led the public to expect. During his October 2003 visit to the Philip-pines, President George W. Bush spoke to the Philippine Congress and bra-zenly suggested that the 1898 Spanish-American War ought to be recalled as a model for the postwar rebuilding of Iraq. In challenging such selective amnesia and the distortion of history, the American literature scholar Amy Kaplan cited Mark Twain to point out that "what Bush called liberation, Twain decried as a bloody campaign against the Philippine struggle for in-dependence, a campaign that would usher in five decades of occupation by the United States."[2] Before and during the 2004 presidential election, the seemingly endless attacks against U.S. troops, roadside bombings, hostage abductions, and the obscurity of intelligence ineluctably evoked memories of the Vietnam War quagmire and the perils of guerilla warfare.

The distinctiveness that marks evoking the memory of occupied Japan, then, lay in its (un)timeliness. The analogy Washington officials drew between the U.S. occupation of Japan and postwar plans for occupying Iraq was being publicized precisely at the moment when the United States was threatening to resort to war, even as millions of people throughout the world were vigilantly protesting its illegality. It remains crucial that remembering the occupation of Japan as a "success" *prior to* the beginning of war proved effective in preparing the public, both domestic and international, for the preemptive military attack the U.S. government was about to launch against Iraq. This anachronism, which enabled the American public to foresee the "success" of the postwar U.S. occupation of Iraq antecedent to the war itself, is arguably one instantiation of the discursive power the dominant memory of the U.S.-Japan War and its aftermath can exert on America's jus ad bellum. This dominant memory not only remembers the U.S. war against Japan as a "good war" that liberated the people of Asia and the Pacific, including the Japanese themselves, from Japan's military fanaticism, cultic imperial worship, and feudalism—all of which helped define the normativity of U.S. modernity and democracy through *their* otherness. It also remembers that those liberated by the United States were reformed into free and advanced citizens of the postwar democratic world. Insisting that the war's mission was rescue and rehabilitation, this memory shapes and feeds the American myth that allows people to at once anticipate and explain that the enemy can be freed and reformed through U.S. military interventions and territorial takeovers.[3] The ability to anticipate Iraq's successful postwar recovery while planning its destruction stemmed precisely from the compelling power of this myth—a myth that allows for the simultaneous enunciation of violence and recovery.

At the core of this American myth and the "just war" it endorses is the "woman question" and the universal idea of gender justice. In the midst of mounting difficulties and increasing violence in post–cease-fire Iraq, the Bush administration continued to draw parallels between its "war on terror" and the World War II missions that led to the demise of totalitarian regimes and "women's freedom."[4] In his effort to counter the European and other nations' challenges to U.S. "unilateralism," George F. Will defended the Bush administration's abrogation of the Kyoto environmental protocol and the United Nation's Convention on the Elimination of All Forms of Discrimination against Women, among other policies, by claiming that American democracy is so "uniquely well developed" that it surpasses the standards of international supervision. For proof of such uniqueness, Will reminded us that "the most important emancipator of Japanese women was Gen. Douglas MacArthur, who made women's suffrage occupation policy. The liberators of Afghan women wore U.S. battle dress."[5] The knowledge that "Japanese women" gained constitutional rights in this occupied space at the borders of the U.S. empire is thus integral to American exceptionalism.[6] If, as Kaplan astutely put it, the Bush administration confuses occupation with liberation in its justification of the U.S. military presence in Iraq, the persistence and verisimilitude of such confusion have hinged on American popular memories of midcentury Japanese women's liberation under occupation.

"Japanese women" embodied and enacted both the changes wrought by the U.S.-led occupation and the renewal of the national polity at large. I have argued elsewhere that the transformation of the Japanese national polity from a wartime belligerent nation to a postwar demilitarized and peaceful one was a decisively gendered process.[7] Japan's postwar Constitution—drafted during the occupation and promulgated in 1946—relinquished the country's sovereign right to wage war. In some political circles this shift has long been associated with the emasculating trauma of the nation's defeat and foreign occupation, an issue I will take up in the next chapter. The same Constitution also punctuated the gendered shift in the national polity by SCAP's granting of suffrage to female subjects in occupied Japan—and in so doing established their formal citizenship and nationality status as "Japanese women." The transformation of the defeated nation's political character bore special significance for the occupiers. As the political scientist Susan Pharr once noted, Americans viewed Japanese women's increasing presence in the formal political arena as an eloquent demonstration of the extent to which occupation reforms were "improving women's status" overall.[8] The occupation forces, particularly those of the United States, regarded Japanese women's suffrage and women's visibility in the national election as a barometer with which to measure the overall improvement of life under occupation. Japanese women's political liberation thus showcased the success of occupation policy to the international community. Yet, if publicizing Japanese women's liberation and their improved status was central to U.S. postwar/Cold War propaganda at that time, and if indeed the issue of gender justice and other democratizing projects helped justify the U.S. occupation of Japan, how has this discourse remained so powerfully effective nearly sixty years later? In what way has Japanese women's enfranchisement lent material credibility to midcentury American exceptionalism and the then emerging image of the United States as the champion of gender justice? How have various representations of Japanese women's liberation come to proffer such overwhelming faith in the possibility of the vanquished enemy's rehabilitation? If U.S. geopolitics have indeed relied, as the American studies scholar Melani McAlister succinctly summarized, on the "construction of the United States as a 'World Leader' that refused to behave like a colonial power,"[9] midcentury Japan, where racialized women were liberated by U.S. foreign policy, stands out as a key strategic site in the American Cold War geopolitical imaginary. There we find the formative moment in which such a construction began to gain authenticity through the production of knowledge about "the other women."

In the following I attempt to address the past's productive power over the present historical moment, by analyzing the ways in which the American public at midcentury came to be informed about Japanese women's enfranchisement and improvements in their legal and other social statuses. I trace the problematic association between the American claim to gender justice in occupied Japan and U.S. exceptionalism by investigating U.S. media coverage of the occupation of Japan. Focusing on the emergent moment of postwar knowledge production, I examine the critical juncture at which memories of America's mid-twentieth-century imperial project of democratization and reform of the former enemy in Asia came to be shaped and then became effective in abetting the expansion of U.S. military, political, economic, and juridical borders. While a number of excellent studies of the American occupation of Japan have scrupulously documented the processes whereby the reforms emanating out of Washington and SCAP became instituted through active Japanese collaboration, resulting in numerous unintended consequences and contradictions, there has been virtually no sustained analysis of the ways in which the occupation was presented and conveyed to the American public.[10] The American media's portrayals of Japanese women were no less unstable and inconsistent than the complex realities of occupied Japan. This chapter's chief objective, then, lies less in re-presenting occupied Japan than in examining the enduring ideological implications of the process whereby knowledge about Japanese women's "liberation" was produced through its travels from the fringe of the American empire to the mainland.

In articulating how certain stories of Japanese women's liberation acquired remarkable consistency and dominance, the chapter seeks to problematize the subjugation of other stories that contradicted and yet were constitutive of that very same trajectory of knowledge. Primarily, I discuss how U.S. media representations of Japanese women under occupation helped center and naturalize the American audience as the subject of rescue, liberal democracy, and gender justice, while simultaneously marginalizing other subjects and the competing desires for radical social justice and transformation. Japan under U.S.-led Allied occupation—a state of exception wherein Japanese women were unfree yet granted political rights by the Supreme Commander for the Allied Powers (SCAP) General Douglas MacArthur— has existed as an outside that is simultaneously an inside, a liminal border that helps define the mainland United States as the principal space for freedom and rights-bearing subjects, including American women. My aim is to demonstrate how the cultural logic that posits the United States and its allies as the site of democratic rights and freedom has been inseparably linked to the feminist universalism that characterizes American gender justice—or what I call "Cold War feminism."[11] Through an examination of U.S. representations of Japanese women under occupation and the memories (and repression) they have spawned, the chapter reveals how the U.S. discourse on the rights and democratization of Japanese women established a normative Cold War subject of liberation in this transitional space, even as it proceeded to marginalize and subordinate a number of other diverse transformative modalities, social identities, and aspirations.

From "Women Warriors" to the "Unhappiest Women in the World"

The U.S. ascendancy to Cold War superpower in Asia and the Pacific relied to a great extent on a much popularized image of history which emphasized that the region's true modernity began only after the U.S. victory in war against Japan. To be sure, the notion that 1945 marked a clean break in the region's historical progress was as important to U.S. Cold War knowledge production as it was the material reality for people in Asia and the Pacific Islands who were at long last liberated from Japanese colonial rule and military occupation. For the American public at large, however, this shift was presented largely as the formal demilitarization and democratization of Japan, but highlighted by the breathtaking transformation of the status of Japanese women. In this section I will explore the dramatic way in which the image of women in Japan changed during the transwar years from ferocious and perverse "women warriors" to "the unhappiest women in the world"—that is, the rights-less, chattel-like victims of Japanese society waiting to be saved.

Reflecting the broader perceptions that the war's end was approaching, the July 1944 *Saturday Evening Post* featured an article entitled "The Unhappiest Women in the World."[12] The author was a European woman who had apparently gained authoritative knowledge of Japanese women when she accompanied her Polish minister husband on a visit to Japan. After having lived in Japan for three years, she explained to her readers that she had come to discover that "the graceful, smiling Japanese women were the unhappiest [she] had ever known." Japanese women were "intended as either the servant or pretty toy of men" who demand "unquestioning obedience." They are "not regarded as a person" according to Japanese law and "marriage is her only career unless she becomes a geisha." In Japan, the author went on to observe, even the empress was a "frightened, timid, little" being who was "unable to break through the wall of her own shyness and sense of inferiority." The article then concluded, "The Japanese wife has very few pleasures" regardless of wealth or class; "the only pleasure to which a Japanese wife can look forward is the satisfaction of becoming a mother-in-law," whose abuse of her daughters-in-law was "another case of the legalized traditional sadism of the Japanese."[13] The author of this article seems oblivious that she, too, was no less an appendage to her husband's travel to Japan even as she deplored Japanese women's total subjugation to their men. Such representational asymmetry and occlusion reveal more about the writer's ideological position than the women who were the objects of her observation.

Yet what concerns me here is neither the accuracy of the article's representation of Japanese gender relations nor the white female author's racial and gender subjectivity. I wish to underscore instead the abrupt timing of the article's appearance. Abrupt, because media coverage since the beginning of the war had for the most part represented Japanese women not as the timid little "unhappiest women," but as "women warriors." A quick survey of *New York Times* articles that dealt with Japanese women from around the time of the U.S.-Japan War's outbreak to the occupation reveals that the media was concerned less with Japanese women's inferiority and traditional submissiveness than with their modern progressiveness and eccentricity. An article published on the eve of the Pearl Harbor attack introduced the modern transformation of Japanese women since the 1920s emergence of the "modern girl" and their active presence as industrial and white-collar workers as well as consumers. The article went on to note that since the

1930s national emergency, women were gaining increasing importance as they had come to fill in for men sent overseas for military service.[14] Beginning with Japan's all out military attack on China and continuing into the period of the U.S.-Japan War, American news reports repeatedly emphasized the mobilization of Japanese women into unconventional gender roles under wartime state policy. Less than three months into the war with Japan, a news report noted that the government urged Japanese women to wear gender-neutral traditional trousers for war-related activities.[15]

An article that solicited wartime U.S. women volunteers, "Women of Japan Called Fanatical," described former ambassador to Japan Joseph C. Grew's speech at a Red Cross Nurses' Aide Rally. Grew had told the mass audience of mainly American women how Japanese women were "supporting their men with that same fanatical loyalty and valor" and that "in Japan, women, too are made of strong stuff."[16] Alongside reports on Japanese women's mobilization into the nation's war effort there were occasional yet consistent references to Japanese women warriors who were willing to "take up arms." Between 1942 and 1944, media images of Japanese women were coupled with the fear of women "in uniform," of even dangerously armed women and those "killed in action."[17] Considering that Japanese women were not officially mobilized as combatants until 1945, it is reasonable to conclude that rather than reflecting any actual policy for mobilizing women, such a portrayal of Japanese "women warriors" was aimed, like the report on Grew's speech, to inspire and mobilize American women for the U.S. war effort.[18] At the same time, the gender transgressive "women warriors" image effectively suggested that Americans were at war with an "unconventional" enemy that confounded the boundary between the battlefield and home, one that needed to be met with unconventional military strategies.[19]

Once situated within such a transwar trajectory, we then begin to see how the July 1944 *Saturday Evening Post* article "Unhappiest Women in the World" marks a clear shift from the earlier portrayals of Japanese women as ferocious patriots and even combatants. This shift emerged with the onset of a discourse that attempted to make differentiations within the ranks of an enemy that had until then been portrayed as racially uniform and ideologically monolithic. A similar argument distinguishing the virtuous yet self-deprecating Japanese women from evil, tyrannical Japanese men can also be found in "Slave Women of Japan," published in a 1943 issue of the popular magazine *Women's Home Companion*. It detailed that despite the fact that "millions of women have entered industry, managed farms single-handedly and made the major sacrifices in the spectacular decline of Japan's standard of living," they "have gained little or no public recognition." The article predicted that "Japan's women may begin to assert themselves" as a result of the indispensable work they do for the war-torn society and went on to conclude: "Japan would be a far better nation if this should happen. The Japanese men and the Japanese women appear to come from different races—the men being brutal and fanatical, while the women appear kind and reasonable."[20]

In his seminal study of the profound ways in which racism shaped the U.S.-Japan War on both sides of the Pacific, the historian John Dower pointed out that while the evils of European enemies were confined to particular individuals and groups such as Hitler, Mussolini, or the Nazis, prewar and wartime anti-Japanese racism collectively vilified the Japanese as a whole and represented them as "swarms" of faceless insects or "hordes" of subhumans.[21] Yet, while effective in stirring bellicose sentiments, such totalizing representations of the enemy would prove impractical, if not useless, in building relations beyond hostility. To ensure stability in the relationship between the victor and the defeated, the occupier and the occupied, the elements of evil had to be separated out discursively. The prewar to postwar transformation of Japanese nationhood was gendered in part because of the need to deploy women as differentiated from Japanese men, who were singularly made to bear the burden of evil. A similar differentiation among the former enemy "race" was made as well along the ethnonational boundary, as we have observed through the transwar development of anthropology and area studies knowledge focusing on Okinawa.

What the above exploration of American news reports and editorial comments during the transwar years suggests is that representations of Japanese women as victims of the male dominant military state began to increasingly appear as Washington policy makers anticipated Japan's near defeat. Once transformed from fanatic women warriors participating in the holy war to unhappiest women enslaved by brutal men, the gender binary that defined the latter continued to frame postwar reports on the democratization of Japan. As a *Life* magazine article published half a year after the start of the occupation put it: "The U.S. can properly take credit for giving a higher degree of freedom to the Japanese schools, press, radio, theater. . . . The Japs are doing some things for themselves. Women are voting for the first time. If they can shake off their status as dolls and chattels, Japanese women may become an effective brake on militarism."[22] The occupation authorities encouraged and sometimes actively propagated the view of Japanese women as homogeneously enslaved by Japanese men and traditional gender norms.

In this process, "Japanese women" were discursively constituted as passive victims in need of rescue and outside intervention. They were once objects of male-dominant militarism and the devastations of war, who were then liberated as a result of the postdefeat foreign occupation. As we shall see, this gender binary—of positing women as a uniform entity universally victimized by patriarchy and male dominance regardless of race, sexuality, class, colonialism, religion, and other relations—facilitated the representation of Japanese women as subject-objects of American liberation and recipients of Cold War liberal feminist tutelage.

Liberation under Occupation

The memory of the successful occupation of Japan was elicited prior to commencement of hostility against Iraq. A few months before the launch of "Operation Iraqi Freedom," the political elites' effort to shore up a casus belli for the United States remembered General Douglas MacArthur as "the most important emancipator of Japanese women." Although Douglas MacArthur is known to have not been particularly keen on women's equal rights or other kinds of feminism, as we have seen the U.S. media presented Japanese women's liberation and enfranchisement as primarily his accomplishments. MacArthur, who directed the occupation of Japan as Supreme Commander for the Allied Powers until relieved of his duty in April 1951, listed the enfranchisement of women at the top of his so-called Five Great Reforms. As early as October 12, 1945, the *New York Times* outlined the "Five Great Reforms" and SCAP's plans to liberalize the Japanese Constitution. Under the headline that fully captured the paradoxical situation, "Democratic Rule Ordered in Japan," the article highlighted that MacArthur had directed the Japanese premier Shidehara Kijūrō to "Give Women [the] Vote and Encourage Labor Unions."[23] Two days later, another article announced that in response to SCAP directives the Japanese cabinet had voted to amend the Japanese election law to grant women suffrage. It once again underscored women's enfranchisement in its headline, "Japanese Cabinet for Women's Vote."[24]

U.S. newspaper and magazine articles reflected Washington's and SCAP's overall propaganda policy to accentuate women's liberation as one of the primary indices of the occupation's "success." They reported extensively on Japanese women's enfranchisement and the overall improvement in their legal status, as well as the surprisingly high female voter turnout in the first postwar general election of 1946, which resulted in the election of a number of female candidates. A few examples may suffice to illustrate how these events were reported to the American audience. A *Newsweek* foreign affairs column introduced the liberation of Japanese women under the title "Free Butterfly": "The humble, plodding little female for untold centuries has trotted quietly along in the footsteps of the lordly Japanese male. But last week Japanese women made history on their own account. Of the 2,500-odd Diet candidates who applied for certification in the April 10 general elections, 75 were women."[25] Following the report on the April election, the *New York Times* also ran several articles on the changing status of women under the occupation. They emphasized that the women voter turnout far exceeded expectations, while in some regions women voters surpassed male voters in number.[26] Still another article, titled "New Laws to Free Japanese Women," reported on the occupation's initiatives to reform the Japanese civil code to end the "ancient custom" of primogeniture and to make women "the equal economic partners of their husbands."[27]

The various representations of the early phase of occupation facilitated the transwar shift in the American image of Japanese women. A *Senior Scholastic* article, "The Rising Sun of Japan," argued that Japan's future "depends largely on the present—how successful we are today in reeducating the Japanese people toward a democratic and peaceful way of life" and noted as the first sign of success that "women were permitted to vote for the first time and they turned out in large numbers."[28] The article included a photo of a Japanese female police officer choking a fellow male officer by the neck. The caption read "Under Allied occupation, Japanese police have opened their ranks to women. Police women learn art of judo." The enthusiastic reporting of the legal reform that enabled Japanese women to join the ranks of police officers is not only further evidence of the high visibility of Japanese women in media reports coming out of the occupation; it marks sudden amnesia about the fear of wartime Japanese women warriors.[29] Likewise deploying the image of a woman police officer to convey Japanese women's new legal status, the *Christian Science Monitor* featured an article titled "New World for Japanese Women," which commented: "The little woman who has for generations been walking a respectful two steps behind honorable husband is stepping out in front today." Opening with such a familiar narrative of oppression, the article introduced the activities of Lieutenant Ethel B. Weed, the low-ranking yet central figure in promoting gender reforms through the SCAP Civil Information and Education (CI&E) Office. It emphasized the compatibility of U.S. occupation policies with Japanese women's progress: "After centuries of suppression and subservient obedience, [Japanese women] suddenly find themselves not only enjoying equal rights with men, but given great political and social privilege. Those who planned the strategy of our occupation gave great consideration to the women of Japan and counted confidently on their co-operation. Granting equal rights and suffrage to Japanese women was one of the first steps of the occupation."[30] The "unhappiest women in the world," having previously reincarnated from "women warriors," thus became discursively reconstituted as the liberated subjects of the occupation. As a highly visible sign of a newly freed and rehabilitated Japan, they were at once made to vindicate and welcome the transpacific, Cold War U.S. governmentality for the American audience.

News about Japanese women's acquisition of civil rights was also accompanied by the representations of the Japanese who heartily welcomed U.S. troops. The postwar amity was often visually disseminated to the American audience through the image of the bodily intimacy of Japanese women and white male soldiers. For instance, the aforementioned *New York Times* article, "Japanese Cabinet for Women's Vote" included two photos, each pairing a smiling white male solider with an Asian woman with an even merrier smile. One was captioned "Bob Johnson, Reading Mass., is assisted by geisha girl, Miss Gama, in the selection of a new record for their next dance"; the other, "Corp. Orvel Stone, Randolph, Wiss., waltzing with geisha girl, Teru Shiduse, in the Japanese capital." The same set of images reappeared in the military services section of the October 22 issue of *Newsweek*, along with several other similar photos that were captioned "Servicemen in Tokyo are teaching geisha girls a few things about American jive and dancing."[31]

These heterosexed interracial images are striking when contrasted to the iconic two-shot photo image of MacArthur and Hirohito (see figure 2.1). In this famous, well-circulated image, the gap in the two men's height and physicality was stunning, its shattering visual effect allegedly giving many Japanese a vivid impression of their newly subordinate status to the United States. In contrast, the above images of fraternization not only underplayed the height differences between Japanese women and American servicemen. They also differed from the MacArthur-Hirohito image in that the couples do not face the camera, but each other. This gendered unevenness in the interracial representations seems to imply that, unlike their male counterparts, Japan's "New Women" liberated by the U.S. occupation policy not only might embrace white men, as well as the United States and the international community that these men signified, but also might be capable

FIGURE 2.1 The two-shot photo of General Douglas MacArthur standing next to Emperor Hirohito was taken on September 27, 1945 in Tokyo and was published in Japanese newspapers two days later. MacArthur's informal demeanor in contrast to Hirohito's aristocratic uptightness is said to have impressed upon many viewers that His Majesty was overshadowed by the General. (U.S. Army Signal Corps/Getty Images.)

of literally *facing up* to them, or standing *shoulder to shoulder* with them. At the same time, these articles and photos together inscribed the Japanese women who are about to receive full citizenship from MacArthur as "geisha girls." Needless to say, "geisha girls" have little to do with actual geishas or women workers in erotic exchange. Rather, they are figures born out of the nineteenth-century Western fantasy about the submissive yet licentious "Oriental women" that has continued to persist into the twentieth and twenty-first centuries. In evoking "geisha," these texts insinuate that the newly enfranchised Japanese women will remain objectified as those "geisha girls" of the possessive Western male fantasy. Moreover, propaganda concerning the U.S.-led emancipation of Japanese women was constantly plagued with anxiety about the licentious sexuality of "Oriental women." The image of the newborn, rehabilitated Japan as visually illustrated through the interracial bodily proximity between Japanese women and white American men elicited the fear of miscegenation as much as it accentuated the virtues of liberation as the occupiers' benevolent gift. The knowledge produced by news reports on the historic first vote ever cast by Japanese women was supplemented by ample warnings against the "promiscuous relationships" between U.S. occupation troops stationed in Japan and native women.[32]

Not all U.S. media reports represented Japanese women's liberation as a simple top-down achievement. A series of articles by Lindesay Parrott, who served as Tokyo bureau chief for the *New York Times* during the transwar decade, observed how the colonial space of occupation had instituted revolutionary changes in the status of Japanese women. Parrott's article "Out of Feudalism: Japan's Women" begins with a familiar lead about oppressed Japanese women: "The dawn has slowly begun to break in the Land of the Rising Sun for Japan's most depressed class—the patient, plodding Japanese women. For uncounted generations the Japanese woman has tramped along the muddy roads three paces behind her lord and master. For centuries there has been dinned into her little ears 'obedience and modesty are essential virtues of the Japanese woman.'" At the same time, through an interview with the "veteran feminist" Fusae Ichikawa, Parrott introduced the long history of the prewar Japanese women's suffrage movement and the presence of Japanese feminists who sought equal rights.[33] In her interview with Parrott, Ichikawa apparently suggested that Japanese women would have sooner or later gained suffrage without the occupation, primarily as a result of their active participation in the war effort. A year later, in a *New York Times Magazine* article reporting on the 1946 election, Parrott pointed to three professions—police officer, labor activist, and politician—as representative of the new career paths the occupation reforms had introduced to Japanese women; but he also warned against a simple generalization and stereotyping of them: "The Japanese woman never was either such a fool or such a chattel as some have represented her to be. . . . I know quite intimately a small village down in the Chiba Prefecture. I have heard these women talk. There is no question that they are 'illiterate,' if one takes the standard of literacy to be a knowledge of Chinese characters. . . . Nevertheless, I always found them 'smart'—precisely as a New England farm woman might be called 'smart.'"[34]

Representations drawing such parallels between women in Japan and the United States were not many. The above article betrays that the representation of Japanese women's liberation could not help but serve as a mirror bringing women's issues back home. Ultimately, however, Parrott's narrative did not reject the liberal feminism promoted by SCAP. It reauthenticated occupation policy by labeling prewar and wartime Japan as "feudal," as well as by presenting women's suffrage and other constitutional rights as gains that Japanese women themselves had aspired to, yet could not achieve without MacArthur's intervention. More than anything, closely paralleling Cold War modernization theory, the sympathetic portrayal of intimacy between women in Chiba and those in New England underscored the transpacific compatibility of American and Japanese modernity insofar as the latter did not divert from the path of democratization introduced by the U.S. occupation policy.

Cold War Feminism

Scholarship on the American occupation of Japan invariably notes that U.S. Cold War geopolitical interests powerfully dictated Allied policy over Japan.[35] Shortly before the Chinese Communist Party's 1949 victory in the civil war against the Nationalist Party, Washington's policy for the region took a decisive turn. The so-called post-1947 Reverse Course—in which occupation authorities instituted a series of reactionary measures to contain the spread of radical democracy, including the "red purge," remilitarization, the armed suppression of Korean ethnic schools, the release of A-class war criminals, and a ban on the general strike—reflected this shift. The Korean War broke out shortly after.

In this period we begin to notice a remarkable contraction in the U.S. media's coverage of Japanese women's political participation. It reported on debates over the civil code reforms, albeit sparsely, but virtually ignored women's prominence in the 1947 Upper House election. Though not specifically pertaining to women's issues, a May 1947 Newsweek column poignantly suggests how the production of knowledge about Japan's democratization during the occupation years was intimately linked to the ideological regimentation of American readers: "Democracy was more than skin deep in Japan. . . . One Japanese asked an American: 'When were you last on strike?' The American replied that he had never been on strike in his life. The bewildered Japanese remarked: 'But then how can you be democratic?' This Japanese misconception [of democracy] is, to a considerable extent, based on the actions of American officials, in allowing the return to Japan or release from prison of Japanese Communists at the end of the war. The Americans failed entirely to foresee the Japanese misinterpretation of this action."[36] Disciplinization of radical democratic aspirations among the Japanese was inextricable from the production of normative American democracy in the Cold War United States. An article in the *Commonweal* defended the occupation's overall plan to democratize Japan, but ended up suggesting the superiority of antilabor, anticommunist American-style democracy and explained radical democratic movements in Japan as the effect of political immaturity: "Japanese have been *guilty of excesses in the name of democracy*. Laborers have seized factories under the guise of being democrats. Mass demonstrations, openly led by communists, were becoming more and more unruly. . . . These excesses, however, are the exception to and not the rule. They are excesses of *a newly liberated people*, taking the first wobbly, uncertain steps toward establishment of freedom and equality" (emphasis added).[37]

It may be worthwhile noting that such disciplinization and normalization of what counted as legitimate social dissent for a properly democratized nation—that is, nondirect, nonviolent, deliberative process for political consensus through formal, institutionalized venues—also affected academic knowledge production about Japan's past. In the aftermath of the anti–Vietnam War era, American historiography on modern Japan began to shift its attention to the possible indigenous forms of grassroots antiauthoritarian, pro-democratic practices that included militant labor strife, egalitarianism, anarcho-feminism, proletarianism, and antimonarchical activism.[38] Once we situate American perceptions of Japanese democracy in the midcentury formation of knowledge about the "liberation" and "democratization" of the Japanese people under the U.S. occupation, it is possible to appreciate the school of Japanese history that revisited political militancy and social struggles in modern Japan as a correction to the earlier Cold War historiography. Ascertaining that "democracy was more than skin deep" in occupied Japan, the latter obviated the diverging aspirations present at the time for a just world, and their former historical trajectories. Chapter 3 will examine how the post-1990s Japanese conservative revisionism, by advocating antimaterialist representations of the nation's past, continues to supplement the midcentury American Cold War knowledge about Japan.

Paralleling the general Cold War retraction of democratic radicalism within the United States and at its outposts, the "Reverse Course" in media representations of Japanese women depoliticized and desocialized understandings of gender relations, liberation, and democracy.[39] Here we begin to identify what might be best termed "Cold War feminism."[40] Cold War feminism can be thought of as a variant of liberal feminism. It valorizes equality between the two sexes, autonomy, free choice, individual spontaneity and subjectivity while it is conspicuously silent on social and economic structural issues. Insisting on a pure notion of gender dissociated from race, class, colonial, and other social relations, it advocates equality between men and women in formal democracy as well as the dissolution of gender inequities and barriers within given, often nationalized, public spheres. Cold War feminism regards gender justice as a matter that can be addressed without considering intersecting relations of power. At least in occupied Japan, Cold War feminism's idea of liberation and democratization confiscated the language with which to address the multiply interlocking social and economic subordination of women, which has been rooted in the colonial-modern history of militarized capitalism and racialized nationalism.

The autobiographical accounts by Beate Sirota Gordon, a SCAP staff member and interpreter who took part in the committee to draft the postwar Japanese Constitution, eloquently demonstrate how Cold War feminism underpinned Japanese women's liberation as it was promoted under occupation. Popularly dubbed as "the only woman in the room" to "inscribe the equality between the sexes in the Japanese Constitution,"[41] Gordon widely circulated her firsthand testimonials of how she advocated the inclusion of clauses into the Constitution that would democratize women's status in Japan. Gordon contributed especially to drafting Article 24, which stipulates that marriage should be based on mutual consent and individual choice and that equality between husband and wife in marriage should be protected.[42] Because she understood from her childhood experience that "Japanese women were historically treated like chattel; they were property to be bought and sold on a whim," Gordon was especially impassioned about ensuring women's freedom in entering into marriage.[43] Japanese women thus received as "the gift from Beate" not social and economic rights but the right to freely choose an equal partner in a heterosexual marriage.

By framing stories of Japanese women's liberation within binary gender relations, the American media's Cold War feminism overshadowed other feminist desires to intervene on multiple fronts of sociality. An *Independent Woman* article by Gertrude Penrose reveals this shift most eloquently. The piece gave an account of the activities of Dorris Cochrane, a liaison officer for the State Department who had visited Japan to help promote

women's issues for SCAP's CI&E section: "From the beginning of the occupation, Miss Cochrane stated, General MacArthur encouraged the women's
emancipation movement, and the Civil Information and Education section
[to] set up a program to show the women of Japan how women in other
countries organize and further their causes by democratic processes." The
article attempted to show how Cochrane's visits to various villages and
towns successfully mobilized and inspired many women and that Japanese
women were the most "earnest and energetic follower-uppers" of American
women's guidance. At the same time, by emphasizing that Japanese women
themselves felt that the major obstacle to their participation in public affairs
was "the traditional attitude of Japanese men toward women," the report
intimated that women's liberation meant for them the improvement of personal relationships between women and men, as well as their spontaneous
participation in self-governing, women-only community organizations.[44]
Similarly, the New York Times article that contained Weed's perfunctory
comment on the three-year anniversary of women's suffrage in Japan was
reticent about securing the newly instituted women's political rights and
legal status, instead dwelling primarily on the occupation's efforts in "building confidence" to increase women's leadership and participation in various
cultural and other organizations.[45] Such representations stand in particular
contrast to Parrott's aforementioned article, in which he had introduced a
Japanese labor activist—a woman who had devoted herself to organizing
coal mine workers, about one-third of whom were former Korean colonial
subjects—as an instance of women's liberation and democratization. By
the time the occupation drew to a close, Cold War feminism had appropriated the meanings of liberation and democratization for Japanese women.
It recast the ultimate goal of the democratization of women as no more
than having the aim of achieving equality and freedom in conjugal relations
within an imagined bourgeois domesticity.

Crucially, during the postwar and Cold War years women in the United
States, no less than their Japanese counterparts, became contained within
the bourgeois, heteronormative family. The postwar U.S. government's official policies explicitly and implicitly encouraged women to withdraw from
jobs they had acquired as a result of the wartime male labor shortage.[46]
Elaine Tyler May, among others, has elucidated the unambiguous linkages
between the Cold War ideology of Communist containment and discursive
practices that aimed at the regulation and disciplinization of gender and
sexuality within the parameters of bourgeois domesticity.[47] Yet the Cold
War rivalry required that the containment process be pursued without dis-

turbing the image of the United States as the prime patron of liberation, democratic rights, and equality. Mary Dudziak, Penny Von Eschen, and Christina Klein, among others, have shown how the United States' championing of the ideas of racial equality and tolerance in Cold War propaganda generated contradictions between "security and liberty" at home, and as a result both advanced and compromised civil rights pursuits.[48] Moreover, in her analysis of the ways in which the meanings and representations of the "Middle East" have shaped the United States in the latter half of the twentieth century, Melani McAlister has argued that in the early 1950s, desires for social transformation—unintendedly set loose by the United States through its counter-Soviet propaganda of independence and liberation—were contained discursively through the strategic deployment of heterosexualized, bourgeois gender relations. McAlister finds one instantiation of such containment in 1950s Hollywood films, where it is "the spunky, independent woman who nonetheless chooses to take up the subservient position in marriage."[49]

Cold War feminism's representation of Japanese women's liberation, then, was intimately tied to the disciplinization of American women. Transnational American studies scholars have observed analogous processes at work at various other U.S. imperial locations since the nineteenth century, whereby the discourse on racialized, colonial women helped constitute white, middle-class American women as the bearers of modernity and progress.[50] Each of those instances requires scrutiny of its relations to the differing global and national conditions specific to particular geohistorical moments. To understand the effects of popular knowledge about Japanese women's democratization under occupation, then, we need to take into account the mid-twentieth-century postcolonial context in which Third World independence and the disavowal of racial segregation had become imperative for U.S. foreign policies. Popular knowledge about Japanese women and their liberation was constitutively linked to the American drive for Cold War global hegemony and "the competition over discourse,"[51] in which the U.S. sought to demonstrate the authenticity of its claims over modernity, equality, rights, and democracy to potential allies. At the same time, the hopes and desires unleashed by such a rhetoric of emancipation and social transformation had to be kept at bay in the interests of managing global as well as domestic security. Likewise, the stories of Japanese women's liberation under the occupation were told in such a way that gender justice, normalized through a particular class and sexuality, contained and managed unruly concepts of women's liberation and autonomy. They also reveal that this process of containment required the presence of "Japanese women" who could securely center "American women" within Cold War global politics. In other words, the discursive containment of gender equality and sexual independence was racially mediated and made obscure through the figure of the rehabilitated enemy nation. A *New York Times* article on General Douglas MacArthur's wife illustrates just how integral the Japanese presence was to this process of Cold War gender containment. Headlined "M'Arthur's Wife Refused to Reign: By Choosing to Stay in Role of Head of Household She Won Applause of Japanese," the piece reported to its American readers that "Mrs. MacArthur has become a celebrity in this country by trying to avoid attention. As wife of the Supreme Commander, she could have reigned as a queen. She chose to remain a housewife. The Japanese applauded her decision. . . . General MacArthur loves a fight. But at the end of the day, when he goes home, from a war or from the office, the first thing he does is to embrace his wife. 'Hello, boss,' she always says."[52] Through its depiction of the passionate love and praise that "Japanese office girls and executives" lavished on MacArthur's wife, the article suggested that the respectable path for an American woman who might lead the Japanese, and by extension other postindependent nations of color toward democracy and liberation, was to choose to stay home to be an exemplar of the good wife and wise mother.

Yet, shortly before and after the end of the occupation, a dire prognosis began to fill the media that, despite the best efforts of the occupation authorities, Japanese women's liberation might be doomed to failure. Indeed, coverage emphasizing the vicious tenacity of sexist Japanese culture and tradition increased after the occupation's formal closure.[53] These stories predicted that with the departure of the occupation forces, the centuries-old Japanese tradition would compromise Japanese women's newly acquired freedom and legal rights. Two years after Japan recuperated its sovereignty, a *Time* magazine report on Japan introduced a photo image of a bathing-suit contest held in Tokyo, demonstrating the postwar consumer liberty for women. At the same time it elaborated on why "the principal problem still facing Japanese women is men."[54] A few months later, a *New York Times* article featured an interview with the daughter of Yoshida Shigeru, the prime minister of Japan between 1948 and 1954, who led Japan out of the occupation by staying the pro-U.S. course.[55] Allowing her to speak with the authority of a native informant, the newspaper quoted Yoshida's daughter as saying that Japanese women's new status "was as enthusiastically received as it was undigested . . . because you cannot change concepts so deeply imbedded in Japanese tradition. . . . . Japan is essentially a country for men and most men would prefer to keep the women at home." She predicted that it would take another generation to "create a new trend" as "Japan does not have a society in the Western sense."

In contrast to the article about MacArthur's American wife who "chose to remain a housewife," this narrative assumed that "old habits" and "Japanese tradition" were depriving Japanese women of their will and independence. Even when similarly subordinated to such heteropatriarchal male figures, the American woman's case was considered the outcome of spontaneous choice, whereas the Japanese woman's situation was regarded as stemming from the stranglehold imposed by a centuries-old sexist feudal tradition. As the critical race feminist scholar Leti Volpp has astutely noted, such an "asymmetrical ascription of culture" is not only allowed by the persistent assumption that non-Western cultures are inherently more sexist and anti-feminist than those considered mainstream in the United States. By obscuring the equally profound cultural limitations imposed on mainstream, white American women, it establishes them as subjects of free will, agency, and choice, while casting nonwhite, non-American women as in need of a rescue from their own culture.[56] In this sense, Japanese women came to exist as "the other woman" for women in Cold War containment discourse.[57] By contrasting Japanese women to white American women and by depicting the latter as subjects of free will who are not bound by tradition but who spontaneously choose heteronormative, bourgeois domesticity, U.S. media representations of Japanese women's liberation—or more precisely, its failure despite the U.S. occupation's institution of de jure gender equality—helped constitute white American bourgeois women as the authentic practitioners of Cold War American gender justice.

Genealogy of America's Gender Justice

The history of international law generally highlights the 1907 Hague Regulations and the 1949 Fourth Geneva Convention as the two benchmarks in the law of occupation. While the Hague Regulations began to articulate the occupying power's obligations to maintain the public order in occupied territories, the Geneva Convention inscribed the norms of occupation to include moral considerations for the people under occupation. Primarily reflecting the intensifying anticolonial independence struggles, according to the legal scholar Eyal Benvenisti, the Geneva Convention laid down a set of duties and obligations for the occupiers based on the principle of the inalienability of sovereignty, especially with respect to the welfare of the occupied populations. In contrast, Benvenisti argues that in the aftermath of World War II, the Allied powers treated Germany and to a lesser extent Japan through the earlier doctrine of *deballatio*, or total subjugation of the vanquished: "The Allies never treated the law of occupation as the source of their authority in Germany and Japan, nor did they consider their administrations bound by the Hague Regulations."[58] Recognition that the defeated states had so thoroughly collapsed that they had ceased to function lent justification to the law instituting changes the victors' occupying forces would initiate in the occupied areas. Although the Japanese government did not entirely cease to function, in accordance with the terms of unconditional surrender the Allied occupation was able "to implement— mainly through the Japanese government, serving as an intermediary— fundamental changes of Japan's laws and institutions, similar in scope to those effected in vanquished Germany" (92–93).[59] As we have seen, as early as 1942 the Washington policy makers had begun considering a plan for the retention of Japanese sovereignty to serve as an intermediary—a "puppet" regime—for postwar U.S. foreign policies.

According to Benvenisti, the doctrine [of deballatio] "has no place in contemporary international law, which has come to recognize the principle that sovereignty lies in a people, not in a political elite" (95). Nonetheless, Benvenisti also observes that, even as it extended considerations for the inalienable sovereignty of people subjected to occupation, the 1949 Geneva Convention simultaneously stipulated that the law of occupation gives the occupiers the power to repeal or suspend locally existing laws and to introduce new laws and criminal jurisdictions for the purposes of maintaining security and orderly government of the territory. Recent cases of occupation have involved the imposition of profound changes to local laws and institutions, the extension of the occupiers' jurisdiction over the occupied in the form of military tribunals adjudicating war crimes, and even regime change as an explicitly stated war objective, as in the case of Iraq. The series of postconflict developments at the turn of the new century—in Palestine, Bosnia, Kosovo, and Iraq—has led others to revisit the relationship between the law of wars and law of occupation.[60]

It is within this broader reconsideration of the politics of international law that scholars in recent years have observed how sovereignty is constituted through spaces of exception, such as refugee camps, imprisonment, detention centers, so-called low-intensity conflict zones, and occupied territories. The feminist political scientist Jenny Edkins, among others, has observed that during the Kosovo conflict NATO forces effectively demonstrated their sovereign power through the creation of refugee camps. Edkins drew from Giorgio Agamben, who theorized the intimacy between sovereign power and biopolitics in relationship to Nazi concentration camps. Both Nazi and NATO sovereignty, according to this view, were made possible through the establishment of spaces of indistinction. The camp emerges as a space where, through the temporary suspension of law and rights, the very distinction between a human reduced to the state of social death and a human qualified as a political being bestowed with rights and moral prerogatives is also suspended.[61] It is through generating such a threshold space of suspension and deciding on the exceptions that the sovereign emerges. For Edkins, in particular, the NATO forces, in the name of protecting the sovereignty of people under violence, acted as the sovereign through the establishment of camps that offered humanitarian aid but also policed the refugees fleeing from violence—even though, as Edkins makes clear, NATO might have been responsible for such violence in the first place.

Obviously, I refer to the above spatial theorization of sovereignty and its inseparable ties to power over death and life not to evoke historiographical similarities between the U.S. occupation and European camps. What I wish to highlight, instead, is the shared logical structure in which sovereignty asserts itself through a space of indistinction between freed and unfree, righted and rightless. Though in each and every instance the circumstances are distinct, the space of militarized occupation is not unlike Edkins's camps to the extent that they both constitute a lawful state of exception. Here social and political rights, as well as forms of belonging as imagined through citizenship, territory, nationality, or statehood, are temporarily confiscated. In this very sense, Japan under occupation was a site at which the United States could claim itself as sovereign by categorically suspending the existing rights of some while giving new rights to others. For the former colonial subjects of the Japanese empire (i.e., Taiwanese, Koreans, Okinawans, Micronesians, and so on), their already minimal and compromised rights and identities were suspended as they were made into nonsubjects of the U.S. occupation at least over Japan's mainland. As the cultural historian Tessa Morris-Suzuki points out, while SCAP continued to uphold the Japanese government's colonial policy that regarded Koreans and Taiwanese as Japanese nationals, "in practice, however, matters were much less clear-cut" than the official statements.[62] Regarded as neither "liberated people" nor "defeated people," former colonial subjects who remained in the Japanese mainland were temporarily reduced to a liminal state of social death until such time as their sovereignty would be recovered, at least theoretically, through their formal belonging as nationals to their respective postcolonial states. This suspension of the rights and identities of some occurred simultaneously with the unilateral granting of newly defined rights, agency, and subjectivities to the chosen (i.e., Japanese women, anticommunist nationalists, pro-monarchists, pro-American liberal industrialists and financiers, etc.). Japan under the U.S.-led Allied occupation was a legal borderland, a threshold space through which the new subjects of U.S. occupation policy and Cold War governmentality were produced out of the population under siege. The insistence on the United States as the grantor of constitutional rights to Japanese women obscures the occupation as a space of unfreedom, a place of nonrights, and thus masks the paradox of its simultaneous violence and benevolence. Memories of Japanese women's enfranchisement, then, remain critically vital to America's self-image, its militarized justness, and the political and moral supremacy the nation confers upon itself.

The new Constitution which was promulgated under the U.S. occupation guaranteed the equal treatment of all national subjects regardless of their differences, including gender. Accordingly, the civil code newly stipulated equal inheritance among male and female heirs, as well as obligations to support family dependents. Still, occupation reforms intended to secure women's rights and eliminate gender inequalities in law and other spheres of social life stopped short of achieving their full ideals. Occupation reformers' Orientalist assumptions about Japanese "reality" coupled with the tenacious maneuvering of conservative male bureaucrats, legislators, and legalists, disrupted the total dismantling of existing disparities entrenched in heteropatriarchal arrangements.[63] For instance, the Family Registry Law continues to this day to uphold the normative constitution of families and the modern nation through codes of marriage, monogamy, conjugality, and heterosexism. The Nationality Law also recognized only patrilineality in the transmission of nationality until its renunciation in 1985. Historians have generally charged the "Reverse Course" with primary responsibility for the short-circuited character of Japan's democratization under U.S. occupation. Some scholars have described how the Bureau of Women and Minors—the office established in 1947 by the Socialist Party government under the U.S. occupation to oversee women's issues—became ultimately "ineffective in resolving the problems of de facto gender inequality in employment and society" because Cold War SCAP policy not only deprived the office of the legal power of enforcement, but also alienated it from the majority of women's associations that sought more radical reforms.[64]

In closing, I return to the remarkable "timeliness" of the resurgence of Beate Sirota Gordon and her memories for the end of the Cold War international scene. To recall, as a SCAP staff member Gordon joined the committee that drafted the Japanese Constitution and worked on the women's rights clause. Gordon's stories about the crucial role she had allegedly played in drafting the Constitution under the SCAP directives came to be known widely to the public, especially from the mid-1990s. This was a period when the diverse predicaments that plague women in various locations throughout the world increasingly became rearticulated and addressed, in global and universalistic terms, as violations against women's human rights. Yet it was not until the recent invasion of Afghanistan and Iraq that Gordon's authoritative account of U.S. occupation policy over Japanese women gained renewed currency in the mainstream American media. Gordon emphasized on various occasions that Japanese women should be held up as an exemplar for other women of color in Afghanistan and Iraq since the Japanese case demonstrated that the U.S. military did not colonize but rather brought women's rights and freedom as gifts of the occupier.[65] Remarkably, the uncanniness of Gordon's remembering the midcentury occupation of Japan during twenty-first-century America's aggressive war did not resonate to many as "catachrony," a disjointed sense of time I discussed in chapter 1. The U.S. media instead eagerly reported on Gordon's story as if it were perfectly timely. By Gordon's remembering "the right thing at the right time," so to speak, the memories of Japanese women's acquisition of rights and freedom under the U.S. occupation stabilized and secured the otherwise unsettling proximity between sovereign violence and liberation. By the time she passed at the age of eighty-nine, Gordon had become a beloved icon of America's democratization of Japan. One of many obituaries in the United States described her as "an American to whom Japan remains indebted," once again extending the Cold War "figurative deployment of debt" discussed in the introduction.[66]

The postwar discursive construction of "Japanese women" as mere victims of male-dominated militarism and patriarchy, who became liberated and gained power as a result of the postwar occupation, has contributed to yet another problematically nationalized aspect of historical knowledge concerning Japan's past. As I have argued extensively in another context, the presumption that Japanese women's status became drastically transformed in the war's aftermath has contributed to a pervasive amnesia about Japanese women's active participation in colonialism and wars of aggression.[67] The recent redeployment of these Japanese women in support of the wars in

Iraq and Afghanistan suggests that this narrative has had another problematic memory effect. Remembering Japanese women exclusively as victims saved by MacArthur and his advisers, that is, remembering them according to the still-powerful narrative of America's Cold War gender justice, may well risk reenlisting them as agents in the current U.S. imperial imaginary of rescue and rehabilitation even as it promotes forgetfulness about their collusion in colonialism, racism, and war.

The hypervisibility of Japanese women's enfranchisement under the occupation was, to reiterate, achieved *in exchange with* the invisibility of the disenfranchisement and continued dispossession of the social and political rights of women and men from Japan's former colonies.[68] If Cold War feminism failed to acknowledge the victims of the Japanese military comfort system even as it brought "the Japanese women" onto the international stage of historical progress, the U.S. media was equally, if not even less unconcerned to report on the categorical political disenfranchisement of Korean and Taiwanese men residing in mainland Japan. While the pronouncement of Japanese women's acquisition of new rights earned the United States a positive image as the benefactor of equality, freedom, and democracy, knowledge about the disenfranchisement of Japan's former colonial subjects contradicted the Cold War self-portrait of America as an exceptionally multiethnic and multiracial nation. Naturally, the invisibility of Japan's postcolonial subjects under the occupation produced a serious gap in knowledge in Cold War area studies. Here it may be worthwhile underscoring that the problematic analogy introduced at the beginning of this chapter—in which Japan as the site of the "successful" American imperial project of occupation, reform, and rebuilding was regarded as a model for the occupation of Iraq—depended upon a very restricted perspective that focused only on the metropolitan core of the formerly vast prewar Japanese Empire. Crucially, the Japan/Iraq analogy forgets that fierce insurgencies and resistance to the new occupying forces, as well as the outbreak of civil wars, turned many other parts of Japan's former empire into necrospaces, at least in the initial phase of decolonization. Put differently, this tunnel vision underwrites the notion that the U.S. governance of the post–World War II, postcolonial world during the Cold War was predominantly promoted through positive biopolitical and consensual means, while forgetting that such a modality of governance was also in large part enabled by foreign occupation, military policing, counterinsurgency and other forms of necropolitical violence. The marginalization and silencing of the Japanese empire's "comfort women" within the postwar, postcolonial space were integral to this dialectics of remembering and forgetting.

While conveying to audiences back home that U.S. policies had liberated Japanese women by enfranchising them and by enforcing various reforms, representations of occupied Japan ultimately blamed the failure of democratization on Japanese racial and cultural differences. Such culturalist explanations obscured the material effects of both the U.S. Cold War containment policies and the Japanese conservative elites' collaborative maneuvers. The acquisition of formal rights and equality undeniably signaled "liberation," in the limited sense of democratic procedure, but it did not necessarily liberate women in other sites of power, particularly across the intersections of class, ethnonationality, colonial relations, and other biopolitical distinctions of race and sexuality. We must thus ask, for which women, along which fronts of power relations, and in what specific respects did the U.S. occupation bring liberation and progress? And crucially, where and who was "the other woman" who made it possible for Japanese women to become the authentic object and subject of U.S. Cold War gender justice? As memories of occupied Japan are invoked and mobilized to sanction U.S. wars and militarized occupations in the twenty-first century, it becomes even more urgent to cast a critical gaze on the past, and to dissect dialectically how stories about this midcentury imperial location were originally told and gained dominance. Cautioning against the seductive rhetoric of liberation and critically remembering Japanese women's enfranchisement in the context of the current war on terror lay bare the disciplinization and assimilation that the transpacific U.S. governmentality has demanded of its subjects. With such a critical analytic in mind, the next chapter will continue the investigation of the genealogy of American justice, but with special attention to its supplementary relationship to Japan's conservative nationalism at the turn of the new century.

PART II

Transnational Memory Borders

THREE

Sovereignty, Apology, Forgiveness
Revisionisms

"I want Japan to ask for forgiveness."
Ching-lin Yuen, testimony at the Women's International War Crimes Tribunal

How can one both make a biopower function and exercise the rights of war,
the rights of murder and the function of death, without becoming racist?
Michel Foucault, Society Must be Defended

Since its establishment in 1996 the Japan Society for History
Textbook Reform (Atarashii Kyōkasho o Tsukuru Kai, the Reform
Society or the Society hereafter) has vigorously campaigned
against historical works critical of Japan's colonial and military
expansion. It has challenged the state and other reparations
measures that have tried to respond to the ethical demands of
redress. The Reform Society unveiled the full tenets of its revisionism in 2001 when it published two middle school textbooks,
a history textbook that presented a romantically constructed
National History and a civics education textbook that valorized
modern heteropatriarchal family values. This chapter examines
the modalities of conservative historical revisionism, often also
labeled neonationalist revisionism, that have evolved around the
Textbook Reform Society and its network since the turn into the
new millennium. Japan's revisionism and the "military comfort
women issue" (*jūgun ianfu mondai*) to which it reacted—the two
key components of the post-1990s redress culture nationally and

transnationally—epitomize one of the latest manifestations of transpacific Cold War entanglements over the question of historical justice and (un)redressability.

Since the mid-1990s the Textbook Reform Society has brought together forces that are not necessarily harmonious, but which have shared an agenda similar enough to form a united front. The membership and the internal allegiance of the Reform Society and its partner organizations have fluctuated over the years. But for the most part they have managed to generate activism at a dense intersection of writers, artists, legislators, academics, former bureaucrats, retired corporate executives, and others who invariably characterize themselves as "conservatives." The primary venues for their activism have ranged from newspapers, journals, magazines, book collections, and TV talk shows to the blogosphere. At the same time, the Textbook Reform Society's network and its allies have infiltrated public institutions and the media—local assemblies, schools, public broadcasting, museums, talk events, and cinema screenings—by mobilizing political and media connections or sometimes by using real or threatened physical violence. Their activities furthermore extend beyond the national public sphere to target the international audience. A brief illustration of its organizational network is as follows: the Society has worked in collaboration with the Liberal Historical View Study Group (Jiyūshugi Shikan Kenkyūkai; the official English name is Association for Advancement of Unbiased View of History).[1] The study group began in 1995, originally as a grassroots history writing group. Among its many "national campaigns," the group launched publication of a best-selling four-volume book series that collected what were then lesser known historical anecdotes of modern Japan. The Society also partners with a policy study group of right-wing and far-right members of the Liberal Democratic Party called the Group of Concerned Diet Members for Japan's Future and History Education (Nihon no Zento to Rekishi Kyōkasho o Kangaeru Giin no Kai, formerly known as Wakate Giin no Kai; Concerned Diet Members, hereafter).[2] Together they argue that Japan's war atrocities and colonial exploitation should not be singled out, and that those who ceaselessly call attention to Japan's dishonorable pasts have marred the nation's image.

To be sure, while working in unison on various fronts, the central ideologues, the policy makers, and the network media sympathetic to the Textbook Reform Society's causes are far from homogeneous in their views. They do not necessarily share the same positions on sovereignty, the historical assessment of colonialism and war, or on the realpolitik of apologies and reparations. Nor do they agree on the nature and future of Japan's military alliance with the United States.[3] Nonetheless, it is possible to identify three fields that are consistently concatenated in the revisionist discourse. One obviously concerns how the nation's past is represented. The Reform Society's campaigns chastise historical materialism. Their main target had been the left-leaning Japan Teachers' Union until the union lost effective oppositional strategies. The neologism "self-flagellating history view" (*jigyaku shikan*) is perhaps the most effective among revisionism's operative slogans. It is a nebulous concept and is only vaguely understood in relation to the way Japan was represented one-sidedly at the Tokyo War Crimes Trial (IMTFE). Because of its amorphous nature the term can conjure up multiple affective attachments, while the speech act helps define what constitutes the "self" that has been flagellated and by whom. The unbridled use of this concept allowed the revisionists to discredit and expel any serious engagement with Japan's militarist and colonialist past. By 2014 the term officially entered the LDP's platform as a problem that the party had to conquer. As we will see in detail, the Textbook Reform Society and its allies have called for historical narratives that would restore pride and honor for the nation to counter the critical orthodoxy of postwar Japanese historiography.[4]

Revisionist discourse is furthermore remarkably consistent in its strident attack on queer feminist politics. The Reform Society and its allies publicly oppose the following three gender-related public measures: Gender Equality (or literally, Men and Women's Collaborative Participation, *danjo kyōdō sankaku*), the state-initiated administrative program run by the Gender Equality Bureau, which aims to promote the equal participation of men and women in the public and private sectors; the so-called gender-free curriculum that calls for an end to impositions of heteronormative gender distinctions; and sex education pedagogy that promotes knowledge about sexually transmitted diseases, unwanted pregnancy, and sexual violence.[5] There are significant differences among these administrative and educational programs with respect to their understandings of gender and the genealogy of feminist thought. Nonetheless revisionists categorically condemn these developments because they are viewed as undermining patriotism.[6] In the revisionist discourse these three strains in gender policies are integral to what they regard as the "self-flagellating view of history."

Nishio Kanji, the Textbook Reform Society's founding member and a scholar of German literature and philosophy, reflected on its trajectory in an essay published in 2005. In this intriguingly entitled essay, "Responsibility We Owe to History and the Ethnos: Pathology Common to the Gender Equality Project and the 'Military Comfort Women,'" he wrote: "About ten years ago when we became keen to establish the Reform Society, the starting point was the gender issue [*otoko to onna no mondai*]. Of course we were equally aware that the current history textbooks were atrocious because of their exclusive reliance on historical materialism. But the driving force behind the actual foundation of the Society was the issue of wartime sex."[7]

Likewise Fujioka Nobukatsu—an educational studies scholar, the Society's other key founding member, and the concurrent leader of the Liberal Historical View Study Group mentioned above—reminisced that mention of the "military comfort women" in Japanese school textbooks had triggered their revisionist campaign.[8] When the revisionist campaigns began, all seven history textbooks that had passed the Japanese government's inspection included descriptions of the wartime military comfort system. Reflecting on the state of history education at the time, one of the Concerned Diet Members reportedly told the media how appalled he was by the thought that "his daughter would be learning from such a textbook."[9] The Society and its affiliates have thus insisted that the history textbooks that teach Japanese military atrocities and colonialism work in tandem with progressive gender and sexuality curricula to produce an abject national identity, thereby preventing the Japanese from feeling love and pride for one another and their country.[10]

Finally, historical revisionism questions Japan's aberrant sovereignty status from international norms. It targets the so-called peace clause, Article 9, which relinquishes Japan's sovereign right to wage war. Historical revisionists ultimately aim to reform the postwar Constitution, arguing that the occupying Allied forces imposed it upon the Japanese people and that it does not accurately reflect the latter's general will.[11] The revisionists' patriarchal nationalism is thus underpinned by the desire to recover Japan's sovereignty internationally, but especially vis-à-vis the militarized relation with the United States. It seeks to correct any deviation from modern normative standards of national statehood that might have resulted from the recent history of demilitarization.[12]

In this way, since the late nineties Japan's revisionism has linked the "military comfort women issue," as well as contemporary gender and sexual debates, to the question of national sovereignty and history. Certainly it is not surprising that the revisionists' patriotic calls are deeply entangled with heteropatriarchal disciplinization. Feminist colonial and postcolonial studies have amply documented modern nationalism's inseparable ties to the management of gender and sexual differences. What is distinct about the gendered and sexualized dimensions of Japan's historical revisionism is that it reveals, among other conditions, the sedimentation of transpacific geo-historical contradictions.

Moreover, while the eruption of the history of military comfort system into the international scene was admittedly a primary factor, the anxiety associated with the imminent end of the Cold War on the transpacific front also contributed greatly to the rise of revisionism. The critic Satō Manabu was the first to articulate this connection to the Cold War's ending. As Satō sardonically put it, historical revisionism was driven by the ironic sense that the "self-flagellating predilection" in postwar Japanese history educa-tion would become further "exacerbated after the close of the Cold War."[13] Indeed, Fujioka unequivocally pointed to the collapse of "the leviathan So-viet Union" as the "decisive" moment that brought him to lead the crusade against "anti-Japanese history education." For Fujioka, the post–Cold War milieu appeared before him as a horrifying scene, "as if the leviathan's cardi-nal humor had been scattered all over the place."[14] Thus historical revision-ism was in large measure prompted by deep anxieties over the breakdown of the East-West confrontation and the uncertainty of defining the enemy after the dissolution of the ideologically bounded binary and its associated territorial imaginaries.

Rather than a sensationalist politics pursued by reactionary extremists, I regard revisionism as a historically structured discourse that needs to be taken seriously. The above brief overview demonstrates that historical revi-sionism concatenates a wide range of concerns simultaneously. Even when its target seems solely focused on the narrative of the history textbooks, the revisionist discourse implies the necessity of considering ostensibly unre-lated matters. What I offer in the following, then, is a symptomatic reading of this discourse. I will explore both the literal, denotative meanings as well as what is implicitly and unintendedly suggested in the revisionists' narra-tives by attending to their racial and sexual dimensions. In every field of intervention, masculinity seems to emerge as a salient concept, a contradic-tory and embattled signifier, deployed in important ways so as to determine the modalities of Japan's revisionism. I will, for instance, ask the following questions. How is masculinity imagined and contested—in the historical narrative on Japan's war and colonialism as it is directed against the femi-nist politics of redress centered on the wartime military comfort system; in the challenge to apologies and the expression of contrition for the nation's past wrongs; and in perceiving the Japanese Constitution as an aberration from modern notions of sovereignty? How have these urgent yet seemingly disparate concerns at the turn into the new millennium been sutured so seamlessly to the question of historical representation, and how does the idea of masculinity play into that process? Why must the normative idea of masculinity in revisionist discourse take the form that it does? In order to identify their political unconscious, I argue that the conservative revisionist narratives must be read in conjunction with other concurrent revisionist claims which aim to achieve often diametrically opposed political ends. The "comfort women" redress discourse, for example, equally insists on revising dominant Asia-Pacific War memories and the nearly half-a-century of forgetting of the violence of Japan's wartime military comfort system in official World War II historiography. The revisionist discourse's ideological matrices as elucidated through such an inquiry will hopefully guide us toward the disavowed history of violence, complicity, and other problematic legacies of transpacific Cold War formations, both epistemic and institutional.

The Narrative of Honor and National Pride

Revisionists insist that the Japanese ought to learn the "correct" National History. The primary motive for the establishment of the Society, Fujioka has recalled, was to promote education that would teach a Japanese history that would be "worthwhile boasting to the world."[15] Likewise in his dialogue with Kobayashi Yoshinori, a comic book writer known for his controversial works on patriotism, colonialism, sovereignty, and Japan's wartime military comfort system, Nishio concurred that if the Japanese had accurate knowledge about their history and traditional heritage comparable to that held by Europeans, "they could be unequivocally proud of being Japanese."[16] Revisionism's premise is this: once the Japanese are taught their unbiased history, their sense of national honor will be restored and they will then be able to walk shoulder to shoulder with people of other nations. The revisionist discourse, while primarily concerned with domestic public education, has always also involved a global politics of recognition and Japan's international reputation. As we will see below, this inevitable unease about the gaze of foreign others is an effect of the racialized transpacific modernity.

The Reform Society's first textbook, *The New History Textbook*, was published by Fusōsha in 2001, and from the outset multiple publics ravaged and strongly disapproved of it.[17] News that *The New History Textbook* had passed government inspection in the same year and that it had been listed among the books officially approved for classroom use triggered a nationwide "nonadoption" campaign. As a result, not one school adopted the Reform Society's textbook that year. Its circulation and adoption rate has been poor, even in more recent years when state guidelines have increasingly favored patriotic education. To help refute the misappropriation and misinformation of academic historians' work in *The New History Textbook*, the literary critic Komori Yōichi, the political scientist Sakamoto Yoshikazu, and the historian Yasumaru Yoshio copublished a Q&A manual. Besides identifying inadequate selections and clarifying historical facts, the Q&A astutely summarized the core problem of *The New History Textbook* as follows. According to these three prominent leftist critics, Fusōsha's textbook views Japan's military defeat and its subsequent democratization and demilitarization as still unhealed national "wounds."[18] They suggested that the textbook attributes historical agency solely to the General Headquarters of the Allied powers. Consequently, the portrayal of postwar democratization becomes not the result of the Japanese people's active choice or self-determination, but of coercion "under GHQ direction." *The New History Textbook*, they concluded, represents the postwar Japanese people as deprived of autonomy and "independence."[19]

The Akutagawa laureate Nosaka Akiyuki's "Amerika Hijiki" (1968) perhaps best captures the racialized Oedipal complex that often characterizes the postwar U.S.-Japan relationship.[20] The story centers on the encounter of two male characters in late sixties Japan: Toshio, the Japanese male protagonist who as a young child had experienced defeat in war and the Allied occupation, and Higgins, a white American male figure. Higgins and his spouse had once hosted Toshio's wife during her American "home stay." One day Toshio and his wife heard from Higgins that he and his wife would be coming to Japan. Toshio decides to let the Higgins couple stay at his house to return the favor they had previously extended to his wife. But his torment begins upon Higgins's arrival. Toshio compulsively remembers how as a small child he was frightened by "the towering bodies of the Allied troops" (48). He muses on his confused feelings toward Higgins and their relationship in the following way: "How is it that I feel I need to please him for all my worth? He is from a country that killed my dad and yet I harbor no ill feelings. Or rather, I even feel nostalgic" (48). Reflecting on how he seemingly cannot help but labor to entertain his guest, Toshio finds himself behaving like a "pimp." Nosaka surely evokes this sexual analogy to suggest postwar Japan's survival strategy in the region under Cold War U.S. hegemony. Since Toshio is cast as a "pimp" who earns his living by exchanging his women and other subordinates in return for his superior's favor, his relationship to Higgins allegorizes patriarchal strategies of survival under absolute rule. Furthermore, "Amerika hijiki" satirizes the disgust Toshio feels toward his wife, who appears overzealous about hosting their white American male guest. The story pokes fun at the reactionary male psyche, which is in fact similar to that directed at the postwar Japanese women who appeared "whimsically seduced by the victors."[21] The narration culminates in the spectacular failure of what Nosaka described as "weenie nationalism" (52). In this scene, Yotchan, a character who is known for his legendary giant penis, suddenly falls impotent at the sight of Higgins, leading Toshio to reflect: "Higgins will eventually leave. Even so, Americans will continue to occupy a huge part of me." The story concludes with Toshio's own diagnosis of his tormented self; he, like other Japanese men of his generation, is suffering from an "incurable American allergy" (54).

To a great extent, the diagnostics of historical revisionism can be located in this genealogy of the racialized trauma of Japan's military surrender and the loss of empire, which was followed by foreign occupation. Nosaka's "Amerika hijiki" unambiguously introduces the poignancy of death, loss, suffering and humiliation wrought by the wartime U.S. bombing of civilians and the occupation. At the same time, with an admixture of hilarity and anguish commonly found in the tragicomedy vernacular of Osaka, the story elucidates the futile—and indeed ironically "self-flagellating"—nature of psychic attempts to compensate for lost patriarchal authority. Q&A, too, identified a "rather comical example" in *The New History Textbook*. The authors compare ancient mausoleums from a world perspective and then boast that the ancient Japanese imperial mounds are comparable in their magnificence to the Egyptian pyramids. Komori, Sakamoto, and Yasumaru found that this illustrates the authors' "self-adoration" and interpreted this narcissistic patriotism as a compensatory reaction to their own lack of confidence. Indeed, it is tempting to see the international contest over the size of royal tombs as a reincarnation of Nosaka's competitive "weenie nationalism." At the same time, the "self-adoration" the Q&A authors identified in *The New History Textbook* is far too complex to be reduced to the nation's primary scene of loss or the phallic desire the original moment seems to have triggered.

In the revisionists' call for redemption as an honorable nation, I suggest that the racial ideology and the global politics of recognition disseminated through the dialectics of imperialism and nationalism since the nineteenth century have been as operative as the racialized postwar trauma in rendering verisimilitude and affective force. Conservative historical revisionism's far-reaching, often noxious effects need to be placed in relation to the longer historical trajectory of global racial ideology that has given shape to, and is internalized as, Asian masculinity.[22] Feminist critique in ethnic and colonial studies has long observed that resistance to symbolic castration and the material subjugation of men of color under racialized, colonial domination often takes the form of the recuperation of patriarchal and phallus-centric virility.[23] Nationalist patriarchal fantasy, as Frantz Fanon perhaps most acutely and presciently forewarned, even while he may be accused of replicating the very discourse he critiqued, links the deprivation of power, status, and function that many men experience as a result of colonialism, foreign occupation, and racial subordination to the dispossession of and loss of control over women.[24] Japan's conservative revisionists' anti-feminism is almost a caricature of Fanon's forewarnings about postcolonial masculinity. It is a *literal* intake of and reaction against the occupiers' transpacific colonial fantasy. We need to ask, then, on what grounds does the postnineties revisionists' assertion that the Japanese have lost their sense of national honor, love, and confidence gain credibility? What underlies their obsession to reclaim what they believe to be their proper masculinity? And to whom are these assertions addressed?

In the aforementioned 2005 essay, "Responsibility We Owe to History and the Ethnos," Nishio offers revealing allegations against what he has regarded as the "common pathology" in the state policy which promotes women's integration into state-corporate spheres, on the one hand, and the "military comfort women issue" on the other. Nishio opens his essay with an objection to sex education. He then moves on to critique gender-free education by way of a spectacular time warp:

> In a place rampant with the gender-free advocates' superstitious and unscientific denial of sexual difference, men and women . . . are "neutered" and treated as things. Might not the true cause of the "low birth rate" lie in the six decades of our nation's reality, namely our Constitution's Article Nine that has dispelled our martial spirit . . . ?
>
> To treat humans as gender neutral [*chūsei ni atsukau*] is to become obtuse with regard to the bashfulness [one should feel] toward certain conduct or speech between men and women. In *The Aaron War Prisoner Camp* Aida Yūji wrote that in the POW camp where an English woman abused the Japanese POWs as if they were her slaves, she would disrobe [in the presence of the Japanese soldiers] without any fear or hesitation. This is because she did not regard the Japanese soldiers as men. In contrast, according to Aida, if an English officer entered the room she would panic and show embarrassment. Humans do not feel any embarrassment when exposing their genital organs to dogs or cats. The Japanese soldiers were not treated as humans in the POW camps.

This demonstrates how inhuman it is to treat humans as gender neutral [*chūsei ni atsukau*]. (133–34)

This passage collocates the current low birth rate and the problem of the gender-free curriculum with the *ressentiment* associated with the history of Japanese male imprisonment, surrender, and demilitarization under foreign occupation. In order to be properly recognized as a human equivalent of the British officer, it suggests, men must possess an aggressive heterosexuality and militarized virility (i.e., "the martial spirit") in portion sufficient to sexually humiliate a woman. And yet Japanese men are prevented from receiving such recognition because Article 9 forbids the use of military force. Aida Yūji, a Renaissance historian and the author of *The Aaron War Prisoner Camp* (1962), was enlisted into the military in 1943 while he was a graduate student in history at Kyoto University. Upon surrender Aida was incarcerated in the British POW camp in Rangoon until his release in 1947. He published *The Aaron War Prisoner Camp* in 1962 as a memoir of his life as a POW. In it he observed the British soldiers, their families, and other colonial settlers associated with the POW camp in Burma. Aida theorized in the scene quoted by Nishio that the European tradition that sets a clear boundary between humans and animals allowed the British to view "Orientals" as existing outside the category of the human—as mere cattle. Since its republication in 1973 *The Aaron War Prison Camp* continues to be reprinted.

In fact, Nishio's paranoiac concatenation of the different emasculating moments betrays how the global racial politics of recognition has been an integral part of modern universal humanism.[25] Universal humanism offers the possibility of inclusion for the racialized who are often considered as lagging in progress toward full humanity. At the same time this inclusionary move sets off a politics of recognition and processes of identification and counteridentification. Nineteenth-century humanism's normative white heteropatriarchal virility (i.e., "the English officer") produces Asian masculinity's deviance as its foil. It may be worthwhile remembering in this context that Japan's nineteenth-century state policies to civilize and enlighten its subjects in the eyes of the West were inseparably linked to the disciplinization and regulation of extremely diverse gender, sexual, and kinship practices into a modern heteropatriarchal family system. The more complete the introjection of this civilizational ideal and the stronger the desire to identify with humanity's normatively racialized masculinity, the greater becomes the torment over the rift between one's being and the norm. And yet, such a subject is thoroughly besieged by the universalist humanist discourse and the global racial politics of recognition of which it is a part, to the extent that there is no room for counteridentification or disidentification. Consequently, in such a global racial dialectics, the subject of the narrative of honor and national pride must compulsively repudiate and direct his aggression toward those elements that might otherwise suggest the aberrant and queer character of his masculinity.

Importantly, the Textbook Reform Society and its allies do not universally denigrate or exclude women. Instead, the revisionist discourse fears and must repudiate the elements of women and men that do not conform to identitarian gender norms. The lack is projected as much on loss of control over Japanese women as the disappearing distinction between the two genders. Those active in the Reform Society and its network thus attack not only the programs and legislative incentives that aim to promote equal opportunity and pay for women and men. More vehemently they also target single and nonprocreative women as well as the "gender free" pedagogy that is critical of the normative heterosexualist distinctions between masculinity and femininity. The way the former head of the Textbook Reform Society, Yagi Hidetsugu, censured passage of the Basic Act for Gender-Equal Society illustrates this point well. In dialogue with the fellow LDP politician Yamatani Eriko, Yagi objected to such a law and lamented that he would "lose sexual desire if we continue to erase the gender difference between men and women."[26] Needless to say, Yagi's fear of sexual impotence derives from his own internalized heteronormativity. His racialized castration anxiety, however, is only exacerbated insofar as he remains interpellated by the normative discourse of heteropatriarchy in the global racial politics of recognition.

Women's Tribunal and NHK Censorship

In January 2001 NHK (Nihon Hōsō Kyōkai), Japan's only public broadcasting agency, aired a four-night series on the educational television channel (ETV). Titled *How Are Wars to be Adjudicated* [*Sensō o dō sabaku ka*], the NHK-ETV series aimed to explore the emerging international legal protocols for historical justice at the end of the twentieth century. Earlier, the French philosophy scholar and critic Ukai Satoshi had translated Jacques Derrida's essay "Le siècle et le pardon" (translated into English as "On Forgiveness"), which had originally appeared in *Le Monde des Débats* (1999). Inspired by Derrida's discussion of the aporia of postviolence justice and reconciliation, the NHK-ETV series set out to consider the significance of war crimes tribunals, truth and reconciliation commissions, state apologies and restitutions.

In concrete, the series focused on the major shift in the ways some of the most ghastly incidents of the twentieth century have come to be reevaluated and reckoned with, even taking up some of the most difficult cases. *How Are Wars to be Adjudicated* focused on the concept of "crimes against humanity" as its overarching theme and put together a lineup that considered the pan-European participation in the Nazi Holocaust, the French war in Algeria, mass rape in Bosnia-Herzegovina (part 1), the Japanese military's sexual enslavement of women in Asia and the Pacific Islands (part 2), sexual violence and torture in Guatemala (part 3), and South African Apartheid (part 4). I served as a studio commentator for parts 2 and 3 with the philosopher Takahashi Tetsuya, who personally invited me to be involved in the production, while Ukai appeared with Takahashi in parts 1 and 4. Part 2 of the programming, however, aired only after heavy censorship and excision. Later it was revealed that NHK's high-ranking administrators censored the program's content after having succumbed to pressures from several Concerned Diet Members, the revisionist LDP legislators' subgroup mentioned earlier. The incident has gained infamy as one of the most egregious censorship cases in the history of the modern Japanese media.

The program for part 2 was intended to cover the details of the Women's International War Crimes Tribunal on Japan's Military Sexual Slavery (Women's Tribunal hereafter), which convened in Tokyo in December 2000. The three primary conveners were the Korean Council for Women Drafted for Military Sexual Slavery by Japan (Korean Council), the Asian Centre for Women's Human Rights (ASCENT) of the Philippines, and the Violence against Women in War-Network, Japan (VAWW-NET). Made possible by this and other transnational networks of feminist organizations, the tribunal was modeled after the 1967 Russell Tribunal, a people's court in which world citizens responded to the call of two philosophers, Bertrand Russell and Jean-Paul Sartre, to prosecute the United States and its allies for violations of international law against people in S. E. Asia. Likewise, the Women's Tribunal borrowed the authority of the international community. Its primary objective was to consider Japan's wartime military comfort system as a form of sex slavery, to determine whether this system constituted a war crime in light of legal standings at the time, and if so, to determine who should be held accountable. The four-day tribunal reportedly brought together more than a thousand people. Sixty-four former "comfort women" testified as plaintiffs in front of the judges and prosecutors, accompanied by legal teams representing eight countries, including South and North Korea, China, the Philippines, Taiwan, Malaysia, the Netherlands, Indonesia, and East Timor (see figure 3.1).

FIGURE 3.1 Opening scene of the 2000 Women's International War Crimes Tribunal on Japan's Military Sexual Slavery. Credit: Video Juku, dir. *Breaking the History of Silence: The Women's International War Crimes Tribunal for the Trial of Japanese Military Sexual Slavery* (DVD. Tokyo: Video Juku; VAWW-NET Japan, 2006.)

The attempt to adjudicate wartime gender and sexual violence as war crimes resonated with the 1990s consolidation of international protocols and global feminists' advocacy of a women's human rights regime. The network of supranational organizations and legalists, centering on the United Nations, positively responded and strongly endorsed the action initiated by the three Asian nongovernmental organizations (NGOs). During the tribunal women who had survived the military comfort system were joined by other women who testified in a parallel public hearing sponsored by the affiliated members of the United Nations. The latter spoke to similar instances of sexual violence in subsequent wars, military conflicts, and political dissents. The international legal authorities, Patricia Viseur-Sellers and Gabrielle Kirk McDonald, who had been centrally involved in the former Yugoslavia's War Crimes Tribunal, were among the chief prosecutors and presiding judges. That the two presiding judges had also served in the recent postconflict military tribunal also attested to the strong UN investment in the expansion of the women's human rights regime in relation to international criminal justice.[27] At the same time, the chief prosecutor, Ustinia Dolgopol, announced the tribunal's distinctive position in her opening remarks when she explicitly named critical race theory as the tribunal's overarching legal approach.[28] While critical race theory draws on the women of color intellectual engagements specific to U.S. history, its focalization of race in theorizing the uneven juridical process resonated well with the intra- and inter-Asia feminist trajectories that have tried to shed light on the Japanese empire's racialized violence against women in the region. The tribunal thus attempted to critically examine the intersecting historical and structural asymmetries of race, class, and colonialism as important elements that constitute gendered and sexualized violations.

On a practical front, the tribunal mediated international opinions criticizing the Asian Women's Fund, a reparations program the Japanese government established in 1995 to fulfill "moral" responsibility for the surviving victims.[29] To recall, earlier in 1993 outgoing chief cabinet secretary Kōno Yōhei expressed the Japanese government's official stance and formally acknowledged that "the Japanese military at that time was, directly or indirectly, involved in the establishment and management of the comfort system and the transfer of comfort women." The statement admitted the coercive and abusive nature of the system and expressed "sincere apologies and remorse" to those who "suffered immeasurable pain and incurable physical and psychological wounds as comfort women" and pledged "never to repeat the same mistake by forever engraving such issues in our memories through the study and teaching of history."[30] Every successive regime, even those led by the hawkish prime minister Abe, has affirmed the Kōno statement as Japan's official position on the history of the military comfort system. In retrospect this momentary suspension of the pro-U.S. LDP hegemony clearly reflected the brief Cold War hiatus, which necessitated various national and international adjustments in Asia and the Pacific.

It was at this juncture that the state openly recognized the "military comfort women issue" as one of the most egregious oversights in previously agreed-upon postwar settlements. At the same time, the Kōno statement fell short of legally addressing the issue and instead only ambiguously referred to the government's commitment to seek "how best to express this sentiment [of apologies and remorse]." This was an indication that whatever adjustments might be made, they would not challenge the standing official position that settlements of the war had been concluded, at least among countries that had signed the multilateral San Francisco Peace Treaty and the other subsequent normalization treaties, including the 1965 treaty signed between South Korea and Japan (formally, Treaty on Basic Relations between Japan and the Republic of Korea). The Asian Women's Fund was thus established as an already compromised solution to the shortcomings of the earlier Cold War redress. Kōno's statement, as noted above, acknowledged the Japanese military's accountability. But it did so without contravening the official hardline. In other words, the Asian Women's Fund was a failed post–Cold War attempt at redressing the failure of Cold War transitional justice.

The Women's Fund offered individual monetary compensation, accompanied by a letter of apology and remorse signed by the prime minister, and was set up to support educational programs to disseminate knowledge about the history of the military comfort system. Yet many surviving victims rejected the payment from the Asian Women's Fund on the grounds that the Fund's moral atonement detracted the Japanese state from facing its legal accountability. They demanded reparation in the name of the state, rather than from the semigovernmental, semiprivate fund. The tribunal's organizers responded to these survivors' calls by establishing the following juridical terms of redress: without reckoning with past wrongs through law, there will be no end to the culture of impunity—and hence, no true reconciliation. To be sure, those who have had intimate contact with the survivors have argued that the transformative process of healing cannot be attained through geopolitical reconciliations alone, but must occur inter-subjectively.[31] Nonetheless, although hardly sufficient, the official and unequivocal acknowledgment of wrongs committed in the name of the Japanese state is necessary to begin to forthrightly answer the survivors' call for justice. This is despite the fact that more recent investigations of World War II history and memory in East Asia have increasingly disclosed the relevant states' past and present instrumentalization of the reparations and apology issue for their own geopolitical purposes.[32] Taken even more radically, insofar as the Asian Women's Fund was a redress effort attempted within the bounds of Cold War formations, the rejection of its rationale can be read as signaling the impossibility of justice without a thoroughgoing makeover of state-to-state reparations agreements, international protocols, military alliances, and other arrangements that have shaped the post-World War II Asia and the Pacific.

Importantly, the Asian Women's Fund did not "ask for forgiveness" of the survivors, a point I underscored during the studio recording for the NHK-ETV program. It offered unilateral apologies and presumed that its terms of apology would be automatically accepted.[33] In other words, the Japanese government not only failed to invite the victims into the economy of forgiveness, however fraught such a relation might in fact be. It also deprived the survivors of their sovereignty, their ability to decide whether to extend exceptional forgiveness to the perpetrators of the unforgivable act. More insidiously, however, as the anthropologist Chungmoo Choi noted some time ago, the Asian Women's Fund created a rift between those who accepted the reparations from the Fund and those who refused to do so.[34] Not only did the former become objects of criticism, threats, and even further marginalization; they also became a new subaltern, overshadowed and silenced by the same injurious discourses that rendered hypervisibility and authenticity to those who rejected the Fund's terms of reconciliation. This is yet another added injury and silencing inflicted by the Japanese government's shortsightedness and, ultimately, its inability to respond to the victims' aspiration for justice. For this new wound to be healed, however, an entirely different vision of justice, if not necessarily Choi's spiritual one, is in order.

Insofar as it took shape as a corrective to the IMTFE, the Women's Tribunal inevitably replicated the limits in the language and units of the international criminal justice system. Nonetheless, it unsettled the familiar terms of historical knowledge by exposing the failure of earlier war crimes adjudication. It revealed the Cold War shortcomings of the Tokyo War Crimes Trial (IMTFE) in several ways. First, the court prosecuted and found the deceased emperor Hirohito guilty in his capacity as supreme commander of Japan's imperial army for having violated laws existing at the time prohibiting slavery and forced prostitution. Second, the Women's Tribunal determined that while "primary" responsibility lay with Japan, the "initial" responsibility for suppressing knowledge of the wartime comfort system rested with the Allied powers who, despite the weight of available evidence, had left the issue uninterrogated. The court found that the initial failure to fully prosecute militarized sexual violence against women after the war's conclusion had led to a culture of impunity which left many similar cases of violence in subsequent decades unredressable. Third, by prosecuting military violence committed against women in the North and Southeast Asia as "crimes against humanity," the Women's Tribunal challenged the normative concept of "humanity," a category which many felt at the time of the Tokyo War Crimes Trial applied primarily to Japanese violations against the men and women of respectable class of their Western colonial-imperial counterparts. In these different ways, the Women's Tribunal critically provoked alternative ideas and categories, disrupting habitual ways in which we think of history and violence. The tribunal unleashed, as it were, knowledge about the paths not taken that might have led to a different present.

The Women's Tribunal did not possess the institutional power to enforce its judgment. But it was expected that its findings and adjudications would be widely disseminated in various material forms. Many observers noted that the "moral authority" of a people's court, which relied on the opinions of internationally recognized legal authorities and communities, could not be discounted. The tribunal surely represented the international juridical consensus on the women's human rights violations committed by Japan's military comfort system. But even though the tribunal addressed the crimes in existing legal terms, it lacked the secular power to enforce its decisions. To put it differently, precisely by virtue of its imaginary status, it offered a connection between justice and social transformation in ways the actually existing legal system or other state apparatuses could not dare to propose. In fact, I spoke most directly on this point during the studio recording. For the tribunal's findings to gain any significance, audiences had to realize that its justice could not be located in the present, in institutional realism or the status quo. Instead, its significance had to be sought in the future, as the yet unseen, born out of a transformed present. In other words, the Women's Tribunal's historical efficacy will depend on whether and how those who respond to the survivors' testimonial accounts become transnationally and nationally engaged so as to intervene critically in long-inherited institutions and knowledges.[35]

Given the surfeit of the revisionists' sophistries that ensued in the subsequent decade, and considering the interdictive power of public opinion that the tribunal could potentially have generated, it is regrettable that NHK failed to capitalize on the opportunity to report fully on the proceedings and judgment. The problem of censorship, as I have stressed, lies not so much in the secreting of information but its positive power to produce knowledge and truth.[36] The altered program not only deleted and distorted the vital facts of the tribunal. It also crafted another truth about the history of Japan's military comfort system that contradicted the knowledge put forward by the tribunal organizers and the former "comfort women" who had stood as witnesses. The conservative historian Hata Ikuhiko's interview, which was videotaped and intercalated into the program only three days prior to the broadcast, dominated the narrative.[37] This redacted the program as a whole so that it characterized the military comfort system exclusively as commercially run businesses. The disproportionate use of Hata's interview, in which he spoke at length on the fact that the Japanese war crimes had already been adjudicated at the time of the Tokyo War Crimes Trial, overshadowed the tribunal's legal scrupulousness and discredited it by giving the impression that those tried had been subjected to double jeopardy. The knowledge produced through censorship became authorized as truthful by virtue of airing as an NHK program.[38]

Suppression nonetheless invites discursive proliferation.[39] News of the unprecedented alteration of the ETV program triggered various actions against NHK. The first whistleblower was Sakagami Kaori, an award-winning documentary producer for the subcontracting company in charge of the second and third nights' programs.[40] Sakagami was also the first to surmise, rightly as it turned out, that NHK had committed "excessive self-censorship" in the face of direct and indirect political pressure. The Violence against Women in War-Network, Japan, immediately filed a lawsuit against NHK on charges that it had violated the principle of the public media's autonomy by succumbing to extraneous political interferences. I filed a formal complaint with BRC-BRO (Broadcast and Human Rights/Other Related Rights Organization) against NHK with the charge that the program that aired had violated the ethical principles of the production process. The organization formally arbitrates on cases involving abusive media representations.[41] The VAWW-NET lawsuit concluded in 2008, ultimately in NHK's favor.[42] The Supreme Court avoided mentioning Abe and other LDP politicians' involvement. Instead it ruled that NHK had not violated the law within the bounds of the media's liberty to exercise editorial rights. Nonetheless, from the testimonies, firsthand accounts, and exposés amassed over the course of an almost-decade-long lawsuit, activism, and investigative journalism, it became clear that the supporters of the Textbook Reform Society, their far-right affiliates, and the LDP politicians who belonged to the Group of Concerned Diet Members counseled NHK's top administrators against use of the public airwaves to broadcast the tribunal's details.

The NHK-ETV incident has come to be known as one of the most egregious cases of media censorship involving NHK. Yet infringement on the press's freedom was not this case's only distinguishing feature. The 2001 NHK-ETV incident lay bare the voluntary nature of the way the censorship occurred—through what Sakagami noted as the "excessive self-censorship." Moreover, it was not only NHK that willingly subjected itself to censorship. The journalist Saitō Takao, who has written extensively on Japan's neoliberalism, called attention to the Japanese media's general reticence to cover the tribunal. When allegations against NHK censorship became widely publicized, the Asahi newspaper, which had been reporting on the tribunal from its inception, was virtually the only daily national newspaper concerned enough to launch an original investigation. Subsequently, the burden of proof was exclusively placed on one Asahi reporter, Honda Masakazu, who had scooped the LDP politicians' interference. The censorship case also regressed into a sensationalized battle between the two media giants, NHK versus *Asahi*. Commenting on the Japanese news media's total failure to duly interrogate the NHK-ETV censorship, Saitō drew an analogy to the early twentieth-century case of suppression known as Hakkō Jiken. He warned that the general collapse of the news media in this earlier instance was a portent of the imminent approach of militarized fascism. More than NHK's self-censorship in and of itself, then, it is highly probable that this incident marked a critical historical watershed in terms of the established media's unwillingness to inquire into what exactly had been suppressed, and to take up the opportunity to properly consider both the significance and limitations of the tribunal. Confirming Saitō's prescient forewarning, some twelve years later, as of this writing the second Abe regime seems bent on an ever-accelerating headlong drive toward even further remilitarization.[43]

Apology and the (Un)Forgiven

While the revisionist discourse denigrates the policies and school curricula promoting women's rights and welfare as "anti-Japanese," it no less consistently reviles and targets men. Sometimes even more vehemently than toward women, the revisionism directs the attack on the statesmen, historians, public intellectuals, and peace activists who have exposed what they regard as the nation's dishonorable pasts. Kōno Yōhei, who in his capacity as the chief cabinet secretary officially acknowledged and apologized for the coercive nature of the Japanese military comfort system, was one such target. Several years after the issuing of the so-called Kōno statement, the Concerned Diet Members had subjected Kōno to group inquisition. Kobayashi Kōki, the vice secretary of the group at the time, questioned: "Do we really need to apologize so profusely about such a commonplace matter? You say we were the ones who were brutal but miseries always accompany war. It would be different if it was a time without prostitutes. But the streets were filled with them. It was common sense to attach such things to soldiers heading for wars. . . . Every country made them an accompaniment [of war]."[44] Kōno responded to this as follows:

> I am afraid I do not agree with such a view. You say it is "a commonplace matter." But I think that the commonplace matter must have been singularly decisive for each and every woman who encountered it. It could not be helped that a woman or two had to endure the miseries because of war—that is not the way I see it. Rather, it is a matter of women's dignity. . . . The inclination to argue [that such wretchedness

is commonplace and therefore natural] is not acceptable, I believe, in today's international society. . . . Mr. Kobayashi asks if we should apologize for such a commonplace matter. But I even doubt that it can indeed be regarded as commonplace."[45]

Kōno thus remained steadfast to the 1993 statement in the face of his own party members' relentless interrogation. Clearly, his statements were not intended to reject the State or militarism per se. The Kōno statement itself was also unwilling to challenge the Cold War architecture of postwar settlements and thus failed to acknowledge the shortfalls of the standing international protocols as well as the radical questionings of the post–World War II order such an admission would demand. In the above remarks, in particular, Kōno is so eager to impress upon his listeners the universality of women's human rights that he bypasses the colonial and racial dimensions of the military comfort system. Still, the above statement reflects a fundamental suspicion about the commonsense gendering and sexualization of modern militarism.[46]

If Kōno's response may be read as disidentification with the dominant norm of military sexuality and the maleness it interpellates, the freelance journalist Nishino Rumiko's work, *The Military Comfort Women: Testimonies of the Former Soldiers*, further testifies to the different ideas of sexuality and masculinity that compete over the meaning of the military comfort system.[47] Through numerous interviews and participant observation, Nishino collected rare testimonies of the former Japanese male soldiers' encounters with women detained at comfort stations. More often than not, the former imperial soldiers' accounts simulate the conservative revisionist discourse. They deny the military's direct involvement in—hence the state's official accountability for—the comfort station system's establishment and operation. Such testimonies tend to naturalize and universalize male soldiers' sexuality as inherently destructive and regard the comfort system as necessary for its management. Their accounts simultaneously refuse to see the comfort system as a space for the utilitarian and regimented exchange of militarized sexuality. Nishino's collection reveals how the individualistic outlook on history moralizes the asymmetrical relationship between the male soldiers and the "comfort women." Thus former soldiers justify the military comfort system by expressing "gratitude" toward individual women or by attributing moral meanings to the relationships, insisting that women were "never regarded as mere objects of sexual gratification" (48).

In contrast to the universalizing and essentializing views that understand militarized sex as a "necessary part of war" and the sexual subordination of

women as "the fate of humanity" (175), some former soldiers also introduced by Nishino insist that the military comfort system violated "women's
human dignity" and therefore should be treated as Japanese war crimes
(22). Reflecting on the ways in which women were forced into the military comfort system during Japan's war of invasion, some of these former
soldiers conclude that what transpired in the comfort system was "no different from rape" (153). Contrary to the rationale that the military established
the comfort station system to contain the soldiers' otherwise unruly sexuality, some insist that the younger soldiers *learned* to desire rape through their
experiences at the comfort station. A conversation Nishio recorded at a
roundtable discussion of six former soldiers is especially noteworthy. The
six invariably insist that their wartime conduct as soldiers constituted "war
crimes" against the Chinese people. They argue that the Japanese male
soldiers' aggressiveness was a product of social and political condition-
ing. The army's disciplinization demanded absolute obedience to higher
commands, punitive sanctions against any violations, and internalization of
racist perceptions toward enemy populations (158–79). Nishino's research
demonstrates how some former Japanese soldiers developed different understandings of militarism, war, and their own sexualization.[48]

Several former soldiers appearing in Nishino's research were in one way
or another related to the Association of Returnees from China (Chūgoku
Kikansha Renrakukai; Chūkiren, hereafter). Chūkiren was established in
1957 by a group of former Japanese POWs who repatriated from China. The
members were former soldiers who were involved in some of the most
deadly campaigns in northeast China. They were detained as POWs under
war crimes charges but were acquitted or received mitigated sentences before being repatriated under the leniency policy adopted by Zhou Enlai,
who was the Chinese Communist Party leader at the time. Zhou's leniency
policy famously sought not severe punishment, but so-called guilt reckoning (*ninzai*), a rational process whereby each individual Japanese POW was
expected to realize his own wartime sins. This officially sanctioned autore-
flection practice sought to transform the detainees' historical consciousness
so that they would come to understand the heinousness of their wartime
act. Yet the path toward reckoning with one's guilt had to be achieved not by
coercion or under corporeal punishment, but through volition.[49]

The philosophy of "guilt reckoning" posited that in order for the Japanese POWs to come to terms with their wartime inhumanity, their own
humanity as ordinary men had to be dialectically restored. More than one
thousand POWs detained at the two War Criminals Management Centers

at Fushun—where Aisin-Gioro Puyi, the last emperor of the Qing Dynasty was also detained—and Taiyuan were exempted from hard labor. Instead, under the care of the Chinese attendants who themselves had suffered at the hands of the Japanese troops, they were compelled to reflect daily on how they had dutifully carried out the military raids that resulted in mass killing, burning, torture, and rape in the villages they destroyed. As if to literally excise and exorcise the "demons" out of the Japanese soldiers whom many Chinese despised as "Oriental demons," the institutionalized microrituals of "self-reckoning" aimed, it was understood, to redeem the humanity of the savages. Chūkiren memoirs poignantly recall the arresting moments in which members came to grasp the entirely new meanings of their deeds during combat. For some these happened through daily encounters with instructors and guards at the management center. Having learned to see their "enemy" outside the "frame of war," according to many, they underwent a dissolution of their prior self. For some the transformative moment of desubjectivization came in the midst of the war crimes trials. At the Shenyang trial one former soldier faced a survivor who had witnessed one of the mopping-up campaigns he had commanded. He recalled that the moment he saw the old woman's unrestrained outrage, which utterly exceeded conventional juridical language and procedures in what should have been an orderly courtroom setting, he realized that no form of punishment or term of justice could repair what he had done.[50]

To be sure, the mass clemency policy was not without domestic opposition. During the Cultural Revolution those who had been in daily contact with the Japanese POWs at Fushun were prosecuted as antirevolutionary. As I noted in chapter 1, the leniency toward Japanese war crimes needs to be understood within the context of the newly born state's local cold war maneuvering. Prior to Zhou's clemency, the Chinese Nationalist Party leader Chiang Kai-shek, in anticipation of a return to civil war with the Communists, had already announced a similar policy to treat the surrendered Japanese soldiers with magnanimity in order to gain support of the Japanese militarists remaining in China. The leniency policy adopted by the two warring Chinese regimes as part of their war propaganda seems to have prematurely foreclosed the possibility, if any, of justice and reconciliation. The act of forgiving, moreover, institutes the exceptional power of the sovereign. We can return to Derrida's thoughts on history and justice to consider this point. The sovereign right to pardon is an exception within the juridico-political order that places the one who pardons (the king, the State) as legally above the law, hence absolute. It requires that the object of pardoning be postulated as unforgivable, except by the exceptional power of the sovereign. For the two Chinese cold war regimes rivaling for international recognition, the ability to grant amnesty to the Japanese POWs, therefore, was as important as the power to adjudicate and execute. This is the predicament Derrida provocatively pointed out when he critiqued the politics of amnesty and reconciliation in the aforementioned article "On Forgiveness."[51] "The right of grace," Derrida ascertained, "could not be exercised without injustice. *In fact*, one knows that it is always exercised in a conditional manner, in the function of an interpretation or a calculation on the part of the sovereign regarding what joins a particular interest (his own, those of his family, of those of a fraction of society) and the interests of the State"(46).

While the instrumentalized role it performed in cold war geopolitics cannot be minimized, the leniency policy did bear witness to a rare form of contrition and love held unequivocally by Chūkiren members ever since their repatriation. For more than half a century, literally until the moment of death for many, former Fushun POWs have continued to perform acts of penance and "guilt reckoning" through their public testimonies. They have tirelessly spoken and written on the Japanese military atrocities which they themselves had committed in China. They have also repented, apologized, and assigned themselves the impossible mission of seeking forgiveness for what they had already learned is unforgivable.[52] The outcome of the leniency policy has been dubbed a "miracle" to indicate the extraordinary nature of the transformation that took place in the Japanese POWs' psychic, political, and historical attitude. In 2002 Chūkiren disbanded its national-level organization and regrouped as the Fushun Miracle Inheritance Association (Fushun no Kiseki o Uketsugu Kai) under the new representation of a much younger generation peace activist, Kumagai Shin'ichirō, whose primary goal is to disseminate Chūkiren testimonies.[53] According to Chūkiren members and their interlocutors, the "miracle" stands for the way Zhou's leniency policy made the impossible possible: it enabled the Japanese demons to redeem their humanity and even paved the path to future reconciliation.

However, another interpretation is possible. Might not the extraordinariness of the event lie in the epiphany of unredressability, or pure unforgivability, rather than the possibility of reconciliation? To be sure, to the extent that the Chinese Communists and Nationalists both adopted the leniency policy with the aim of winning the war of propaganda and international legitimacy, they instrumentalized the relationship of the victims with the victimizers. Further, as Derrida observed, we need to attend to the risks of reconciliation for the one who was violated, that is, the one who is asked to forgive. Derrida wrote: "As soon as the victim 'understands' the criminal, as soon as she exchanges, speaks, agrees with him the scene of reconciliation has commenced, and with it this ordinary forgiveness which is anything but forgiveness. Even if I say 'I do not forgive you' to someone who asks my forgiveness, but whom I understand and who understands me, then a process of reconciliation has begun; the third has intervened. Yet, this is the end of pure forgiveness" (49).

The instrumentalization of leniency by the warring states notwithstanding, the largely unintended consequence of the policy ruptured the ordinary procedure of justice and reconciliation. The Chūkiren members' contrition was born out of their face-to-face encounter with the immensity and sheer irreparability of the loss they inflicted on their wartime enemy Other. In their self-learning, the Japanese were the unforgivable; the Japanese war crimes were beyond repair. To them, the clemency did not mean the victims had forgiven them; it meant simply that the Japanese violators were free to live as the *forever unforgiven*. Instead of demanding that the victim enter the horizon of reconciliation and the economy of forgiveness, the practice of self-reckoning has established a radical incommensurability—hence unconditional fraternity—between the violated and the violator. It created an enigma, Derrida's "insoluble," that would forever severe the Japanese POWs from the state propaganda's intended dialectics. "The ordinary forgiveness" of the cold war policy of leniency and clemency no doubt established the two Chinese regimes as competing sovereigns; and the mass clemency may indeed have introduced the Japanese into an economy of debt in the regional cold war's realpolitik. In contrast, the former POWs' "self-reckoning" to the unredressability of their crimes consequently placed the violators' relationship to the violated outside the existing language of justice, law, and sovereignty, beyond the dialectics of apology and forgiveness. If it sometimes seems that Chūkiren members' manner of testifying does not manifest a sufficient sense of remorse but appears even defiant, this is because these former Japanese soldiers are not offering atonement or asking for forgiveness from their immediate audience—or for that matter, any agent of justice who assumes the position of the sovereign by offering practical forgiveness. Their apology transcends our ordinary moral economy.

The censored NHK-ETV program originally included a video image of two Chūkiren members and their court testimonies at the Women's Tribunal.[54] Kaneko Yasuji and Kojima Takao, both eighty years old at the time, each offered accounts of how they committed rape while deployed in China and shared their views of how the military comfort system they frequented was an integral part of the violence that structured the soldiers' battlefield routines. Chūkiren members' "guilt reckoning" shared the necessary if not sufficient premise of reconciliation with the organizers of the Women's Tribunal: without a reckoning, there can be no reconciliation. The deleted testimonies were therefore an essential part of the tribunal's philosophy. The decision to excise the court scene was among the many passed down by the NHK's high-ranking administrators. Firsthand accounts of the production process noted that the head of the ETV division expressed strong "discomfort" toward the scene of the two former soldiers' testimonies.[55] The ring of LDP Diet members, the Textbook Reform Society, and their supporters thus relentlessly target and loathe the apologizing men. With regard to Chūkiren in particular, the Cold War language continues to label its members as the "brainwashed" who speak on behalf of the Chinese Communist Party. According to Kumagai, one of the testimonial collections, Sankō, which was published in 1957 and sold fifty thousand copies in the first twenty days after its publication, soon went out of print due to far-right pressures. It was not until the eighties that the book was republished in the new edition.[56] In the English sphere Chūkiren has not received the attention it deserves in literatures on forgiveness, in part because Zhou's leniency policy is often perceived cynically as an instrument of cold war realpolitik.[57] It is also conceivable that Chūkiren disturbs those who hold antipathy toward China because its members are deemed to be indebted to Zhou's gift of amnesty, which exists as an uneasy reminder of China's autonomy and absolute power. More fundamentally, however, the "discomfort" may well be a testament to the incommensurability which Chūkiren embodies. The extraordinary contrition with which its members remain perpetually unforgiven—irrespective of who has the right to forgive—is indeed beyond our intelligibility, and is hence radically inassimilable to the instrumentalized language of the politics of state apology or the secular economy of reconciliation.

Repressed History of the "Model Minority Nation"

Disavowed histories turned inward are internalized in—and as—Asian American male subjectivity.

—David Eng, *Racial Castration: Managing Masculinity in Asian America*

At the chapter's outset, we traced how the recent Japanese revisionist discourse emerged in the context of fluctuating post–Cold War transpacific relations, even as it is deeply rooted in the genealogy of the trauma of defeat and foreign occupation. The revisionist discourse moreover has garnered affective force through its conjuring of the dense history of global racial or sexual representations in Asia and across the Pacific. Analysis of Japan's revisionism, however, would not be complete without considering another important geohistorical context: the effects of the contradictory post–World War II arrangements that enabled Japan to become integrated into the transpacific Cold War order. Revisionists' own remembering of this piece of National History has been deeply conflicted. The literary critic David Eng's retheorization of hysteria as a psychic condition of multicultural assimilation helps clarify this important dimension of historical revisionism.

In *Racial Castration: Managing Masculinity in Asian America* (2001), Eng retheorized hysteria in relationship to the problem of Asian American assimilation.[58] Hysteria generally refers to a type of neurosis that manifests itself as aphasia, sexual impotence, withdrawal, and dystonia, among other symptoms. Placing these in relationship to larger ideological structures, Slavoj Žižek posited that the hysteric symptoms can be seen as "the testimony of a failed interpellation."[59] For instance, symptoms of hysteria, as exhibited in the case of Freud's Dora, attest to the incompleteness and inadequacy of the patriarchal injunction upon female subjects. Proposing that the condition of hysteria cannot be understood without accounting for the psyche's relations to not only sexual but also racial difference, Eng situates the Asian American literary texts' displays of "Asian American racial hysteria" within the treacherous paths of Asian interpellation, assimilation, and integration into the U.S. public spheres.[60]

Racial hysteria becomes more acute, according to Eng, at the moment the subjects embrace the interpellating normative ideologies under conditions in which, despite actual structural subjugation and marginalization, the subjects are theoretically welcomed into national membership.[61] The U.S. model minority myth expects Asian American male subjects to disavow the very racism that thrives on the myth, even as the laws of racialized (white) heteropatriarchy continue to challenge their fitness as ideal patriarchs (194). The figure of the Asian American model minority and its relative success *despite racism* have offered an alibi for structural racism and have underwritten the postracial ideology of what Avery Gordon called America's liberal racism.[62] Male hysteria, in other words, is a trace of that symbolic violence, an index that points to the repression required in exchange for selective inclusion and qualified integration. To be sure, the masculinity of domestically racialized minorities cannot be dealt with in the same way as the masculinity of those who occupy the majority position centered securely within a given national sphere. At the same time, as we have seen at the chapter's outset, the image of a sexually deviant Asian male was integral to not only U.S. domestic ideology of race and immigration but global civilizational discourse throughout the age of imperialism. Moreover, insofar as the power of the transpacific assimilationist discourse of normative American modernity has long instituted the law of geopolitical inclusion and exclusion for our subject, the analytics of hysteria in this particular sense are useful. We have seen symptoms of the revisionist discourse manifesting as aphasia (e.g., the inability to condemn U.S. nuclear and other foreign policies in international public settings), fear of impotence along with compensatory aggression (e.g., the violent attack against transgender pedagogy, the North Koreans and other racialized postcolonial minorities, and transnational feminist redress activism), and withdrawal (e.g., rejection of UN protocols, atavism, and refusal of diplomatic dialogues with neighboring countries).

What I find especially relevant to our context is Eng's insistence on linking hysteria to the question of memory. It is this dimension of racial hysteria that helps us understand the conservative revisionists' paradoxical remembering of the war between Japan and the United States. As Eng reminds us, Freud himself observed that hysteria "might perhaps be best understood as analogous to a kind of overinvolvement in history" (177). Hysterics, after all, are those who "suffer mainly from reminiscences" (183). To put it differently, symptoms of hysteria index the mnemonic violence a normalizing subject must exercise in the process of repudiating contradictory pasts. If hysteria suggests the absent presence of the past, which has been suppressed in the assimilation process, to what extent can we diagnose the discourse on wounded national honor and pride as a sign of psychic suffering resulting from the demands of transpacific integration during the Cold War? For Japan to be positioned as America's "model minority nation" in the post–World War II political, economic, and military formation meant that certain memories that are potentially unsettling to the relations between the two nations had to be kept at bay.[63] Or, more precisely, memories of certain pasts had to be reprogrammed in the production of Japan's National History so as not to threaten the U.S.-Japan Cold War alliance.

In this regard, no other instance more eloquently illustrates the presence of the repressed past than conferral of the imperial decoration, the Order of the Rising Sun, to United States Air Force officer Curtis LeMay. In 1964 the Japanese government awarded him the order to acknowledge his contribution to the postwar development of Japan's Air Self-Defense Force. Conferral of the imperial decoration on LeMay was a sovereign gesture to demonstrate Japan's power to determine and reward loyal subjects even beyond its own citizenry. At the same time, Japan's military integration into the transpacific Cold War alliance also obfuscated the exterminationist nature of civilian killings in the history of American aerial bombing. During the U.S.-Japan War LeMay had led the indiscriminate aerial bombing campaign against Japanese cities and devised use of napalm bombs as a new strategy to maximize the destructive efficacy of the air raids. Another instance of repressed or reprogrammed past can be found in the way the nationalized narrative of the atomic bombing of Hiroshima and Nagasaki almost never mentions the United States as the subject of aggression. Immediately following the war, the Japanese energy industry began to develop nuclear power plants with U.S. aid. Thoroughly integrated under America's "nuclear umbrella," the Japanese government has consistently refrained from officially questioning use of the two nuclear weapons in the international legal arena.[64] Likewise, although increasingly vocalized by some revisionists in recent years, the argument that the IMTFE was no more than "victors' justice"—because it unfairly punished the Japanese for war crimes while giving impunity to many inhumane violations committed by the Allied powers—has always loomed large, albeit in muted form, as the far right's heterodoxy against the region's official historiography.

Arguably, among the most carefully sequestered of national pasts in Japan's integration into U.S. Cold War supremacy were the racial and colonial dimensions of the Asia-Pacific War. Japan's jus ad bellum was officially made on the grounds of national survival against, and liberation of Asia from, the Western superpowers. It goes without saying that the claim that Japan was at war not for its self-interested expansionism but for the liberation of Asia carried little more than partial truth. Indeed, any mention of this dimension of the Asia-Pacific War requires special caution. The wartime statist propaganda was intended to win favorable support for Japan in its "competition over discourse" with the Euro-American superpowers for territorial and colonial resources. Japan's aggressive challenge to the region's Euro-American dominance ultimately wreaked ghastly consequences on people subordinated to the imperial rivalry. Most important for our current inquiry into the Cold War management of historical knowledge, it is imperative that we *not mislocate* the agency of decolonialization. Whether or not one recognizes the agency that ultimately rejected and discredited Japan's antiracist imperial rhetoric *in* the region's anticolonial, anti-imperial, and anti-State forces has great ramifications for how we assess the world order that ensued with Cold War transitional justice. At the same time, Japan's propaganda of "Asia for the Asiatics" threatened the United States and the other Western colonial powers to such an extent that these latter sought countermeasures.[65] It is then worthwhile critically asking to what extent Japan's universalistic rhetoric of racial and colonial emancipation before and during the war contradicted the United States' self-anointment as the supreme rescuer and liberator in the post–World War II world.

In fact, the revisionists risk going against the grain of the orthodoxy of the World War II narrative when it comes to matters relating to race and colonialism, whether in justifying the war as a war of liberation or insisting on the unfairness of the IMTFE. The following comment by the political philosopher Kang Sang-jung sheds light on what this heresy might mean for U.S.-Japan relations since the Cold War. Kang, who has spoken vocally against Japan's xenophobia and neonationalism for many years, commented on the way the United States is positioned in the discourse of the Reform Society's *New History Textbook* and Fujioka's Liberal Historical View Study Group: "[The revisionists are] waving the anti-American banner and harboring the desire to declare independence from the United States, and yet they cannot put this into words. They know intuitively that, if indeed such a view is openly professed, there is no possibility for survival given the dynamics of realpolitik. . . . For sure, theirs is a sort of bottom-up movement to redefine history, and yet there are areas that remain regulated. The American presence weighs heavily, preventing such a movement from becoming state policy."[66]

To the extent that any attempt to "redefine history" must necessarily question the post–World War II, Cold War epistemological and institutional structures of Pax Americana, the revisionist discourse inevitably overlaps with some of the most radical challenges posed by the post–Cold War redress culture. As I have been arguing, the attempts to redress Japanese war crimes at various locales have often exposed the premature foreclosure of the processes for attaining justice in the immediate postwar decades whenever they have been impeded by the unredressability inherited from the legal, diplomatic, and other scaffolds of transitional justice instituted during the Cold War. In other words, U.S. Cold War policies in the Asia-Pacific region virtually suspended the sovereignty of the people whose lives had been most devastated by the Japanese aggression, thus preempting the possibility that they might take justice into their own hands. As "a sort of bottom-up movement," the revisionist discourse inadvertently mirrors that which it impugns. The postnineties redress efforts and historical revisionism, therefore, are two sides of the same historical trajectory originating in the nomos of the transpacific Cold War order.

It is only too obvious, however, that an immense distance separates the two. For one, in sharp contrast to the Women's Tribunal and other comfort women redress activism in Asia and the Pacific, revisionists are equivocal in questioning U.S. hegemony in the region. Historical revisionism does not exhume Japan's prewar left radicalism and its reach across the empire, or the intra-Asian trajectories of anti-imperialism, antimonarchism, radical democracy, socialism, anarchism, anticapitalism, or militant feminism—all of which are important undercurrents to the present transborder redress culture but remain marginalized or at best provincialized in the standard Japanese national historiography. Most dissimilar, the revisionists do not question the Cold War historical epistemology and the way it has confiscated knowledge about the region's early twentieth-century history. Tellingly, they do not challenge the suppression of knowledge about Japan's prewar state as a multiracial colonial empire. This suppression has not only obfuscated the presence of Japan's colonial subjects and their postcolonial struggles; it has also made it difficult to see the simultaneity and entanglement of the Japanese empire and the U.S. empire. The stories the Reform Society and its allies counterpose to the orthodoxy of the World War II narrative is highly selective.

The revisionism's inability to fully challenge U.S. predominance in the region can then be seen as a symptom of the suppression of multiple pasts in the production of the Cold War historical epistemology. Much as the discourse on Asian Americans as the model minority contributed to American racial integration without undermining white supremacy and other dominant structures associated with it, the internationally disseminated image of Japan as the model minority nation, happily integrated and assimilated into the transpacific Cold War arrangement, served as a visible alibi for the global neoracial and neocolonial ordering of the post–World War II world. The role Japan was expected to perform as a model minority nation vis-à-vis other nonwhite nations of Asia and the Pacific was to demonstrate that the United States' presence in the region, however powerful, would be different from that of previous European and Japanese colonial rulers in that it would ostensibly promote harmony, consensus, cooperation, and integration among the area's independent countries. The revisions contained in the narrative of national pride are thus regulated, as Kang observed, by the "American presence." As one participant at a symposium organized by the Textbook Reform Society remarked, "the U.S.-Japan Security Treaty is Japan's lifeline."[67]

For the maintenance of the U.S.-led Asia-Pacific order and Japan's status as America's model minority nation within that arrangement, certain historical memories must remain cached. Most likely, then, "male hysteria" will continue to torment the manufacturers of the national pride narrative. If, as Eng observes of the Asian American male model minority in U.S. multicultural liberalism, hysterics indeed "exhume the disavowed, alternative, and buried stories of its sufferers" (177), symptomatic treatment will not suffice. Selective remembering only leads to further repression and reproduces a narcissistic subject. Ultimately, however, it is not the cure for "male hysteria" we are after. If hysteria is a precious index of violence and repudiated knowledge, as we have seen above, what is most urgent is pursuit of a critical analytic that will allow us to discern and transform the very structural conditions to which the index points. Throughout Asia and the Pacific Islands, the Cold War rendering of the World War II narrative has marginalized or reprogrammed numerous disavowed memories. The analytic of racial hysteria should rightly lead us toward undoing the Cold War knowledge that is the original suppression.

On Japan's Aberrant Sovereignty

War, after all, is as much a means of achieving sovereignty as a way of exercising the right to kill.
—Achille Mbembe, "Necropolitics"

No other term better captures postwar Japan's "independent yet dependent" relationship to the United States than the Asian studies scholar Gavan McCormack's characterization of Japan as America's "client state."[68] McCormack investigates the post–World War II trajectory of the paradoxical Japanese nationalism that insists on the Japanese nation's unique and exceptional status in Asia even as it participates in the maintenance of U.S. political and economic dominance. As he straightforwardly observes: "US insistence on Japan's national uniqueness and fundamental difference from Asia, and its implacable opposition to any moves towards Japanese involvement in an East Asian community, have been fundamental to US policy since the very outset of the occupation" (2). What has developed out of this relation over the past six decades, then, is "a [contradictory] formula combining obedience to the US with the construction of an exclusivist, proud, and pure Japanese history and identity." Revisionists' self-pitying narcissistic nationalism must be understood in this context. A progeny of prewar Japanese imperialism, it is no less a byproduct of expanding U.S. capital and the American military empire as well as the long postwar history in which the United States, as the world's new adjudicator, has deemed that Japan's wartime deeds do not require further redress as long as the Japanese nation remains the loyal procurator of U.S. Far Eastern policy. The revisionists remain conservative in the sense that they prefer not to perturb Japan's client-state status. As we have seen, the revisionist discourse disavows many memories that contradict integration under the U.S.-Japan security alliance and is tethered, as it is, to the issue of sovereignty under the Cold War order. I will conclude this chapter with the following observations on the third field of the revisionists' intervention—that is, ongoing attempts to rectify its aberrant sovereignty, or put differently, to "normalize" Japan.

The revisionists' desire for a "normal" Japan is expressed on several fronts. Historical revisionists generally do not deny the "regrettable" consequences of Japan's military endeavors, and in this regard they are in agreement with the government's repeated official statements. Rather, revisionists' objections are primarily directed at what they see as the unfair exceptionalization of Japan. According to their view, the Japanese military was no different from other imperialist armies; wars are universally brutal and other countries have been committing similar or even more egregious atrocities, such that the Japanese war crimes should not be treated as exceptionally horrendous; Japan's war crimes have been adjudicated, unjustly they often claim, and apologies and settlements have been offered many times over; colonial takeover was the game of the great powers in those days, and Japan was a law-abiding member of the international community up until World War II; and yet Japan is wrongly singled out by countries like China and Korea which, according to these revisionists, fan their dangerous nationalisms with anti-Japanese history lessons.[69] In many ways, the revisionists' outrageous assertions are inseparable from the "contradictory formula" for Japanese survival within the U.S. Cold War empire.

The 1999 legislation recognizing Hinomaru and "Kimigayo" as Japan's official national flag and national anthem, respectively, is an instance that illustrates this crusade for normal country status. Prior to these laws, there had been no Japanese counterparts to U.S. congressional resolutions officially recognizing the "Star Spangled Banner" and American flag. Antiwar and anticolonial activists in Japan continue to contest use of the rising-sun flag because of its associations with the history of military and colonial aggression. Most likely, the legislation aimed to give the flag new meaning precisely through its continued use. It thus anticipates the day when the flag can be transformed into a symbol of victory, possibly as part of a global alliance. Only a few years prior to the legislation, America was said to have finally overcome the so-called Vietnam War syndrome by achieving victory in the first Gulf War. The United States redeemed the American flag by fighting another war. The Hinomaru and "Kimigayo" legislation was a provision for a war in the imminent future. It was meant to carry the nation into a new "postwar," one that is envisioned as normal.[70]

But the revisionists' desire for a "normal" Japan is found most unambiguously in their complaints about Japan's postwar Constitution. As we have seen, they believe that in light of international law, the peace clause of Article 9 is aberrant. Some proponents of militant revisionism no longer seek limited ad hoc reinterpretations of the Constitution but its wholesale rewriting so as to permit Japan's sovereign right to wage war. In his essay "Japanese before and after August 15," Nishio called out to his audience as follows:[71] "The future remains unseen in the midst of a deed. To act is to decide, to wager. . . . Now, everyone, has the time not come for Japan to be asked once again to act as a sovereign? Everyone, please behold East Asian affairs. . . . The time for a true fight is upon us. Ladies and gentlemen, the era for deliberating on judgments is over. The time has come for us to take the future into our own hands" (57). It is easy to dismiss the above as the hyperbole of a zealot. This essay, in which Nishio advocated Japan's self-determination, opens with the author's memory of his mother, petrified in her lament, on the day of Japan's surrender. For Nishio this image iconically represents mourning for those prematurely lost to the defeated war. He then juxtaposes this fetishized female image to current feminist redress activism for the "military comfort women" and disparages the latter as a "disgrace to the dead." Elsewhere I drew an analogy between Nishio's call to act and the writer Mishima Yukio's act of self-determination, the martial suicide. As if to redeem the dead whose sacrifice was rendered meaningless by defeat, Nishio's decisionism, I suggested, could drive the nation into another war and possibly to the collective suicide that had never been.[72] It is important to understand, however, that the seemingly rogue politics of a death-driven extremist and his embrace of necropolitics in fact reflect no more than normal conditions under modern nation-states.

To grasp this point, one can turn to Michel Foucault, Giorgio Agamben, and others for their fundamental challenge to the premises of liberalism and modernity.[73] But even more illuminatingly, the philosopher

Achille Mbembe's analysis of life and death in the dialectics of sovereignty extends the above interventions to expose the historical "link between modernity and terror."[74] To further theorize modernity through the lens of necropolitics, Mbembe observed the development of the mechanism of waging war that is not permitted among the civilized nations of *Jus publicum Europaeum* and the deterritorialized state of war and violence in the late-colonial, late-capitalist global South.[75] Mbembe foregrounds the death worlds of "colonies, apartheid regime and slavery" as a precession to Nazism. This sweeping observation of Europe's other death worlds illuminates the intimate connection between death and the production of sovereign political subjects. Turning Hegel's modernity on its head, Mbembe states, it is death, not life—and the reason associated with modernity's biopolitics—that structures politics and sovereignty. "Within the Hegelian paradigm," writes Mbembe, "human death is essentially voluntary. It is the result of risks consciously assumed by the subject. According to Hegel, in these risks the 'animal' that constitutes the human subject's natural being is defeated." Mbembe continues:

> In other words, the human being truly *becomes a subject*—that is, separated from the animal—in the struggle and the work through which he or she confronts death (understood as the violence of negativity). It is through this confrontation with death that he or she is cast into the incessant movement of history. *Becoming subject therefore supposes upholding the work of death.* To uphold the work of death is precisely how Hegel defines the life of the Spirit. The life of the Spirit, he says, is not that life which is frightened of death, and spares itself destruction, but that life which assumes death and lives with it. . . . *Politics is therefore death that lives a human life. Such, too, is the definition of absolute knowledge and sovereignty: risking the entirety of one's life.* (13–14; second and third italics added)

Touching on the secret "conflation of reason and terror" (19) in the history of Western political philosophy, Mbembe thus challenges the convention, from Hegel to Marx, that regards violence and terror as that which is extraneous to modernity and reason. Death is integral to the reasoned modern-state forms that can be at once "the racist state, the murderous state, and the suicidal state" (17). Seen in light of some of these most radical attempts to rethink modern politics, it becomes evident that Nishio's decisionism and death drive, if not literally the same as Mishima's, are in fact more the norm than the exception within modern conditions of sovereignty. Thus the anormal is actually the limited sovereignty inscribed in Japan's Cold War Constitution. The state's drive toward war and death is indeed what is denied in Article 9, an injunction against the right to wage war, which is an aberrant form of sovereignty within modernity.

It is in this anormality of Article 9 that the cultural theorist Naoki Sakai finds hope.[76] Over the years Sakai has theorized that the post–World War II transpacific relation has been one in which Japan's cultural particularism and American nationalism's claim to modernity and universalism have been mutually cofiguring.[77] Within this structure, Japan's nationalism and sovereignty cannot constitute resistance to the United States or its exteriority. In his discussion of Japan's client-state status, McCormack noted that the "independent yet dependent" formula might be seen as "plainly contradictory. It makes little sense, as right-wing critic Nishibe Susumu puts it, to 'protect Japan's culture by becoming a 51st US state'" (89). Sakai re-visions and places this contradiction in a parallax. In the cofigured transpacific arrangement, Japan's cultural nationalism does not contradict the embrace of U.S. nationalism and its polity but is preserved and endorsed by it. Theoretically, then, Japanese rearmament should not threaten the U.S. military presence in the region. Article 9 is critical, according to Sakai, ironically because it has been a "stumbling block" to U.S. investment in Japan's remilitarization.[78]

The contradiction Article 9 poses to the American embrace of Japan's Cold War sovereignty is best epitomized by the history of the Japanese Self-Defense Forces. Initially introduced in 1950 as the National Police Reserve for the purpose of facilitating U.S. occupation policies, this de facto Japanese military force has triggered numerous deliberations on how it contradicts the Constitution, which has renounced the possession of "land, sea, and air forces and other war potential."[79] It is also worthwhile recalling that exactly four decades after the end of the occupation, when the political scientist Chalmers Johnson offered his realist assessment of the transpacific political economy in the immediate aftermath of the first Gulf War, Johnson was reenacting the occupiers' misgivings about disarmament. In his essay, "Japan in Search of a 'Normal' Role," Johnson offered various scenarios for post–Cold War adjustments to U.S.-Japan relations, including resolution of the Constitutional inconsistency regarding the status of the Self-Defense Forces. He concluded: "The problems surrounding Japan's search for a 'normal' role stem from the fact that Japan is not a normal country. It is an economic giant and a political pygmy. This distortion has been an unintended consequence of the strategy pursued by the United States during the Cold War. But the United States has also been warped by its Cold

War, superpower role—a role that it must now abandon. Recognition of this could serve as the basis for achieving normal roles for both nations."[80] A few years after the publication of this essay Johnson became one of the most adamant critics of the U.S. bases in Okinawa. In the film *Japan's Peace Constitution*, Johnson went as far as to say the current peace clause and the pledge never to wage war ought to be seen as the supreme form of apology and repentance the Japanese could possibly offer to the victims of their aggressive war.[81]

Through the postwar decades we find in such confused American responses to Japan's disarmament and rearmament what is akin to the colonizers' dilemma—that is, the fear of mutiny by natives who are overexcelling in what they were taught by the foreign occupiers, in this case, upholding the Peace Constitution. If, as we saw in chapter 2, the American media accused Japanese laborers under the U.S. occupation of "excesses in the name of democracy,"[82] Japan today is suffering from excess peace. Article 9 may indeed be the bug that may one day trigger a system-wide shut down. Instead of seeking normalization, therefore, the aberration of Japan's limited sovereignty can be preserved as a constant reminder of Japanese nationalism's complicity in enabling the U.S. Cold War liberal empire. Japan's Peace Constitution, which embodies the aberrant modern sovereignty, indeed bears the marker of defeat, war crimes, loss of empire, foreign occupation, and—as the revisionists' symptoms of male hysteria amply expose—Japan's client-state status. Rather than seek to "normalize" Japan, efforts to retain the transgressive and the abject may help denote the aberrant sovereignty's origin as an imperial artifact, one which can also haunt America's Cold War and post–Cold War "empire of bases" through critical remembering.

But what then happens to the revisionists' nationalism, and for that matter, American imperialism and Japan's independent dependence on it when the United States—Fujioka's other "leviathan"—can no longer be consigned exclusively to "the West," a stand-in for the universalistic norms and values of modernity? And what happens when the Asia abjected in revisionist discourse becomes an integral part of the America that is dearly held on to as "Japan's lifeline"? Increasingly, the memories of Japanese military and colonial violence have migrated across the Pacific to become part of the history and everyday scene of the U.S. empire at home. The next chapter explores this new phase of the transpacific order, one characterized by what I call the Asian Americanization of Japanese war crimes.

FOUR

Contagious Justice
Asian/America

The epistemological objectification of "comfort women" occurs because of the objectives underlying and constituting a given representation. Remembering this intimate and inseparable link among object, objectification, and objective is an important principle for Asian American studies. For, doing so can create a valuable sense of discomfort with respect to our critical practices—even and perhaps especially when they are mounted towards the ends of attempting to redress grievous injury.
Kandice Chuh, "Discomforting Knowledge: Or, Korean 'Comfort Women' and Asian Americanist Critical Practice"

These are strange times for thinking about what being "American" means.... Rather than enable a sympathetic identification with the "losers of History," a vengeful and newly emboldened yet selectively vigilant "American" militarized subject threatens to merge with and then to displace the mostly symbolic "American" judge and protector.
Laura Hyun Yi Kang, "Conjuring 'Comfort Women': Mediated Affiliations and Disciplined Subjects in Korean/American Transnationality"

Since around the turn into the new century, renewed calls for historical justice initiated in Asia and the Pacific Islands have begun to permeate American civic spheres. Numerous lawsuits and legislative measures have begun to utilize U.S. state apparatuses, demanding additional or new apologies and reparations from the Japanese government and corporations for their wartime violations. A highly illustrative example is the passing of House Resolution 121 (H. Res. 121) in 2007. In response to nationwide coalitional lobbying, Congress conducted hearings on "protecting the rights of 'comfort women,'" thus opening up an official public space of translation for testimonies of several women who were forced into sex labor. The resolution observed a series of events in Japan—including termination of the aforementioned Asian Women's Fund (1994–2007), the primarily government-run but officially private fund established to atone for the military comfort system, and the serious backlash against school textbooks' inclusions of the comfort women history—and concluded that the Japanese government should issue apologies and offer compensation more unequivocally and with greater sincerity than previously.

U.S. Cold War foreign policy concerns, as we have seen thus far, heavily influenced how war reparations settlements were choreographed throughout Asia and the Pacific, especially during the first two decades following Japan's surrender. Restoration of the juridico-political order under U.S. Cold War leadership paralleled the establishment of postwar economic arrangements under the Bretton Woods system, which through the dominance of U.S. currency sought to ensure stability for global finance and to maintain the industrialized countries' access to open markets, resources, and labor. The American administration of transitional justice was one of the key epistemic and material processes enabling the United States' midcentury ascendancy as the global power and authority. In other words, the Americanization of justice is by no means a new phenomenon. In contrast, the intra- and inter-Asia transnational redress culture has interrogated such Cold War institutional and epistemic arrangements, which took hold of the region in the war's aftermath. Elsewhere I used the term "counteramnes(t)ic" practices to name the struggles of citizens and activists in Korea and Japan who have pursued redress for losses brought on by Japanese imperial violence. In employing this phrasing I tried to capture a critical historical sensibility that not only warns against historical amnesia but also refuses to grant amnesty or forgiveness in exchange for state apology. More important for the purposes of this chapter, the significance of such practices lies in their affiliations with other networks of progressive activism. Attempting to radicalize democratic ideals and practices beyond formal procedures, such redress efforts sought a critical remembering in which past memories are recalled dialectically to become urgently relevant to present social and cultural transformations.[1]

The postnineties redress culture animated in the United States is not separate from this genealogy of intellectual critique and activism. It questions, at its most radical moments, oversight of the Cold War transitional justice which disavowed many instances of Japan's imperial violence and consequently left intact much of the prior colonial and other structures of violence, dispossession, and exploitation. Redress culture concerning Japanese war crimes offers, as I have suggested, a crucible indexing the deeply entangled, complex, and enduring structures of historical violence protracted into our late-colonial, late-capitalist world. Given such a longue durée of redress, what is distinctive about the relatively more recent involvement of the U.S. civic spheres and state apparatuses? What underlies the renewed American investment in the correct and just-war remembering of one of the many former Asian enemies? Focusing on developments in the U.S. juridical and legislative channels in the first decade of the new millennium, this chapter extends the preceding chapters' observations on the transpacific entanglements of memories of the Asia-Pacific War and its aftermath through an examination of the Americanization of justice—but in what appears to be a new phase.

Importantly, the redress activism reinvigorated in the United States since the turn of the new century has enlisted Asian/Americans as new subjects of historical justice.[2] Underpinning reemerging memories of Japanese imperial violence and the impetus to seek redress in the U.S. judicial system is the heightened presence of Asian immigrant-citizen-subjects and their growing importance in American representative politics. The demographic shift in the U.S. body politic is one crucial factor in the belated but increasing Asian/American presence in redress activism. The 1965 Immigration and Nationality Act abolished ethnonational and racial quotas, leading to a dramatic increase in immigration from Asia. Many new immigrants carried with them traumatic memories of suffering and loss wrought by Japanese colonialism as well as Japanese military invasions before and during the Asia-Pacific War. Much of the institutional drive for redress therefore comes from California and other North American locations where new and old Asian populations now pose a significant representational force. The Alliance for Preserving the Truth of Sino-Japanese War, the Global Alliance for Preserving the History of WWII in Asia (GA), and the Association for Learning and Preserving the History of WWII in Asia (ALPHA)—three overlapping North American network organizations demanding redress and apologies from the Japanese government and corporations not exclusively but largely for Chinese victims of Japan's aggressive war—are particularly noteworthy. Prompted by the publication of Iris Chang's *Rape of Nanking: Forgotten Holocaust of World War II* (1997), these organizations have also successfully mobilized the nineties discourse of international criminal justice and human rights to target Japanese war crimes.[3] With regard to "comfort women" redress, Korean/American and Asian/American transnational feminists have deployed American juridical venues, legislatures, communities, social media, and spaces of cultural production to disseminate memories of the Japanese military's sex trafficking and forced prostitution throughout the empire.

In ways that were not possible in the immediate aftermath of the war, Asian/Americans have emerged as new subjects of justice in the U.S. polity. The increasing visibility of Asian/Americans in U.S. redress culture at the same time reminds us of the ways in which the constitution of U.S. public institutions and discourses has been a racialized process.[4] More urgently, attention to the racial differences among subjects who pursue redress calls into question the history of the uneven distribution of power within America's nationalized liberal public sphere, forcing us to understand that reparation issues concern more than interstate normalization and reconciliation. Transborder redress culture affects colonial diasporic peoples as well as refugees and migrants who were violently uprooted by colonialism and war, and who became further displaced in many cases as a result of the political and economic disfranchisement they experienced in the process of decolonization. In analyzing the Americanization of Japanese war crimes, the redress practices of colonial diasporic and migrant peoples emerge as critical terrains of possibility and scrutiny for transnational practices seeking historical justice.

Americanization's new phase, at least in the above sense, thus registers the nationalization of Asian transnational migrants. Through subjectification to U.S. judicial, legislative, and other state apparatuses of knowledge, Asian immigrant-citizens are not only beckoned to speak as owners of and witnesses to memories of Japanese imperial violence in Asia. They also become speaking subjects by subjecting themselves to the institutional arrangements that enable their speech and visibility, but only to the extent to which they are recognized by the given parameters of historical knowledge and the idea of justice. The exploration of Japan's historical revisionists in the previous chapter demonstrated that National History performs a vital function as a normative epistemic apparatus that disciplines and interpellates nationalized citizen-subjects through mobilizing them toward the proper recitation of the nation's honorable and supposedly uniformly shared past. The normative remembering of the nation's past is intimately linked to the management of knowledge and subjectivities. Given such inseparable relationships among nationalism, normativity of citizenship, history, power, and knowledge, what are the ramifications of memories of Japanese imperial violence that travel from Asia and then become integrated with hegemonic American war memories and the persistent American discourse on historical justice? What type of political subject might we anticipate this process interpellates?

The special issue of the *Journal of Asian American Studies*, published in 2003, on "Korean Comfort Women" addressed precisely this question by focusing on the Asian American investment in Japan's wartime military "comfort women" issue. Guest-edited by the American literary critic Kandice Chuh, the special issue was based on an Association for American Studies (ASA) session, titled "Siting/Citing 'Comfort Women' Critically: Transnational Memories in Korea-Japan-U.S. Liaisons."[5] In her essay theorizing the Asian American investment in Japan's wartime military "comfort women" issue, Chuh raised a fundamental question regarding Asian Americanists' objectification of "comfort women."[6] Chuh examined the literary representation of comfort women by the works of two Korean American authors, *Comfort Woman* (1998), by Nora Okja Keller, and *A Gesture Life* (2000), by Chang-Rae Lee, calling into question the "highly troubling ideological and political ends" the Asian American knowledge of "comfort women" might accommodate (8). Laura H. Y. Kang's essay in the special issue likewise problematized the Americanization of Korean "comfort women" and its effect on knowledge and power.[7] Asking "who are and should be the 'we' who must remember and represent this subject," Kang argued for the urgent need to attend to the "multiple mediations and disciplinizations" (28) that are integral to the economy of Americanized "comfort women" knowledge, or the process she saw as "the various conjurings of 'comfort women'" (46). As an alternative to such an Americanization of "comfort women" discourse, Kang calls our attention to the issue of class, suggesting the need to consider "what U.S. citizenship might mean not only for differently racialized and gendered but also *differently capitalized subjects*" (47).

The investigations into the new phase of the Americanization of memories of Japanese imperial violence and the historical justice they call for can most productively yield critical politico-intellectual outcomes when situated in the perspectives put forward by the above Asian/American interventions. In keeping with Chuh's and Kang's theorizations, in what follows I explore the not-so-uniform effects of Asian/American mobilization into redress efforts within the U.S. public sphere. I will focus on juridico-historical discourse—a nexus of power and historical knowledge produced by juridical practices—and intend to closely examine the ways in which

Asian/Americans are erected as the law's agent-subject who enunciates, enacts, or at other times defers, not a single but multiple ideas of historical justice. American discourse on Japanese war crimes is profoundly shaped by U.S. nationalism and assumptions about modernity, liberalism, colonialism, and postcoloniality that are embedded in Cold War epistemologies. Asian/America, as a discursively constituted terrain, is deeply implicated in this knowledge production.[8] And yet Asian/Americans as new subjects of justice animated by the power invested in them as American citizen-subjects also necessarily illuminate contradictions of transnationality within the American civic sphere in such a way that they hold out the possibility of a radical politicization of justice and a critique of Americanization.[9] Asian/American involvement in redress unveils, often inadvertently, the long history of entanglements and the complicity of imperial violence, as well as the amnesia about these matters between Japan and the United States. In this process, juridico-historical discourse may produce new subjects and publicity that transnationally rally around antiracist, decolonial notions of history and justice. At the same time, however, this process is not automatic or easily decipherable. Asian/Americans, as the agent-subjects of U.S. state apparatuses, tend to secure their nationalized status by underwriting America's Cold War myth of liberation and rehabilitation vis-à-vis Asia. The North American liberal, multicultural nationalism, moreover, has effectively mobilized Asian ethnonationalisms as an enabling constituent element. Continuing the work of the previous chapters, in the following I seek out an analytic with which we might discern the risks, the possibilities, and the multiple and contested implications of this seemingly new phase in the Americanization of justice.

In considering the Americanization of Japanese war crimes as an emergent historical juncture, I wish to ask if and how this process of Americanization can productively repoliticize justice for the displaced and disenfranchised, both within and beyond the borders of nationalized public spheres. To what extent can we view such redress efforts that have taken shape in North American juridical and legislative venues as instances of critical remembering in which past memories are recalled dialectically to become urgently relevant to present social and cultural transformations? The Americanization of justice is neither entirely new nor singular. It needs to be situated in the longer Cold War trajectory of U.S. transpacific involvement. At the same time, it consists of multifold dimensions of transnational and national processes that involve actors and institutions at multiple levels both within and outside U.S. state interests and interpellations. By deploying the analytic of Asian/Americanization, this chapter hopes to capture the multivalent meanings of seeking truth and justice for Japanese war crimes in the United States. The contradictory effects the Asian/American critique may bring to that process raise a number of key issues regarding violence and historical justice. They call into question who represents injured parties, in what way and by whom are original losses reckoned to be grievous, how to ascertain proper reparations, and ultimately, where the sovereign power of redress resides.

Habits of War Remembering

In 1999 two important developments took place in the California state legislature. Together they gave significant symbolic and substantial support to those seeking reparations from Japan. One was an amendment to the previously established Code of Civil Procedure (§354.6). Originally the code had authorized those who were formerly victimized by Nazi persecution and forced labor, as well as their descendants, to bring lawsuits to demand compensation from companies and other organizations operating in California that had benefited from such forms of labor exploitation between 1929 and 1945. It eliminated the statute of limitations on the condition that legal actions commence by the end of 2010. Importantly for our context, it broadened the category of perpetrator that had previously been limited to the Nazi regime to include its allied Axis powers. The amendment thus expanded the category of the "Second World War slave labor victim" to "any person taken from a concentration camp or ghetto or diverted from transportation to a concentration camp or from a ghetto to perform labor without pay for any period of time between 1929 and 1945, by the Nazi regime, *its allies and sympathizers*, or enterprises transacting business in any of the areas occupied by or under control of the Nazi regime or *its allies and sympathizers*" (emphasis added).[10] Though ultimately ruled unconstitutional, §354.6 prompted the filing of a number of suits in California on behalf of not only former American prisoners of war but also people of Asia and the Pacific Islands who survived Japanese forced labor and who later immigrated to and became naturalized in the United States.

The amendment to the Code of Civil Procedure coincided with another crucial legislative development, Assembly Joint Resolution 27 (AJR 27). This legislation was originally initiated by Mike Honda, who was then a member of the California state assembly. Titled "Relative to the War Crimes Committed by the Japanese Military during World War II," AJR 27 "would urge the Government of Japan to finally bring closure to concerns relating to

World War II by formally issuing a clear and unambiguous apology for the atrocious war crimes committed by the Japanese military during World War II and immediately paying reparations to the victims of those crimes. This measure would also call upon the U.S. Congress to adopt a similar resolution and urge the President of the United States to take all appropriate action to bring about a formal apology and reparations by the Government of Japan."[11] Honda was later elected to the U.S. Congress and successfully lobbied for the earlier mentioned House Resolution 121.

The foremost obstacle to practically all legal battles that have sought new or additional compensation from the Japanese government and/or companies has been the consistent official position of the United States, Korea, China, Japan, and other signatory governments—namely that war reparations issues have been settled by the San Francisco Peace Treaty and other state-to-state normalization treaties (e.g., the 1965 Basic Treaty signed between the Republic of Korea and Japan and the 1972 Joint Communiqué of the Government of Japan and the Government of the People's Republic of China). The 1990s heightened aspirations for renewed justice notwithstanding—whether for Korean, Chinese, or Filipino civilians who were mobilized for hard labor at various strategic production sites during the war and who demand remittance of unpaid wages from companies such as Mitsubishi and Mitsui, or in lawsuits demanding official apologies and compensation for the survivors of the Japanese military comfort system, or for former American POWs who have filed lawsuits to obtain additional compensation—all their petitions have been consistently rejected on the grounds that the issue of war reparations have been concluded by the postwar settlement treaties. Whether in the case of the Asian Women's Fund or the former Chinese forced laborers' reparation settlements with Nishimatsu Construction Company, the resolutions for redress and compensation have been sought in extralegal venues. This is despite the counterargument made by a number of lawyers in Japan and elsewhere who have insisted for quite some time that, while these treaties relinquished the right of one government to demand further reparations from another, they do not necessarily preclude the right of individuals to seek compensation independently of their governments.

Given such juridical precedents, it is not surprising that California's new law was seen as a powerful alternative means by which to circumvent the international legal deadlock. Section 354.6 was meant to allow numerous litigation cases against Japanese corporations in the medical, shipbuilding, railroad, and other wartime industries that had not paid wages or had insufficiently compensated forced and other types of labor. During the brief period in which California's new legislation was in effect, plaintiffs and activists thus turned to the U.S. courtrooms as new transpacific venues for belated justice.

For redress efforts in Asia that called into question the shortcomings of Cold War transitional justice, those who would have benefited from California's new state law were unquestionably the peoples of and from Asia and the Pacific who had suffered from Japanese wartime violence. Yet a curious gap emerged in the ways the law's effects were represented and perceived in the U.S. national public sphere. The mainstream media in the United States, for instance, did not necessarily highlight the categories of people who took immediate advantage of the new legislation beyond the more or less familiar image of American war victims. The *Los Angeles Times* printed a full two-page article with a color photo of a couple living in Culver City, California. It reported that Frances and Louis Bachleder, who were interned in the concentration camp run by the Japanese army in Manila, were campaigning to obtain compensation for losses caused by the Japanese military invasion of the Philippines.[12] The NBC television show *Dateline* ran a segment on Frank Bigelow, a former POW who was imprisoned at Ōmuta and forced into hard labor by Mitsui.[13] Like the Bachleders, Bigelow was demanding compensation beyond the war-claims money he received through the U.S. government immediately after the war.[14] Both reports underscored the significance of California's new laws in enabling their pursuit of redressive justice.

While most U.S. legislators are unwilling to question the 1951 Peace Treaty, former American POWs received sympathetic support from such politicians as Senator Orrin Hatch, who appeared in a newspaper photo embracing the two former POWs. In 2000 Hatch successfully lobbied for a resolution (S. Cong. Res. 158) in which Congress urged the United States government to extend pressure on Japan to resolve the war reparation issues on behalf of the former American POWs who were forced into slave labor by Japanese companies.[15] Introducing the resolution, Hatch recounted the shortcomings of Cold War transitional justice as follows: "Fifty years have passed since the atrocities occurred, yet our veterans are still waiting for accountability and justice. Unfortunately, global political and security needs of the time often overshadowed their legitimate claims for justice—and these former POWs were once again asked to sacrifice for their country. Following the end of the war, for example, our government allegedly instructed many of the POWs held by Japan not to discuss their experiences and treatment. Some were even asked to sign nondisclosure agreements.

Consequently, many Americans remain unaware of the atrocities that took place and the suffering our POWs endured."[16] Faulting the U.S. government's foreign policy decisions sixty years earlier, Hatch insisted that the United States government is morally obliged to support the American veterans' renewed redress efforts as promoted through §354 and to "facilitate a dialogue" between them and the Japanese corporations that he found had benefited from American war settlement policies.[17]

The above instances illustrate that, at least in mainstream national public venues, §354.6 resulted in recentering once again former American POWs as the prime war victims and subjects of historical justice. Needless to say, acknowledging the hypervisibility of the Euroamerican Allied POWs in popularized America war memories is not meant in any way to discount or rank the sufferings experienced by individuals of different social backgrounds. Instead, only by doing so can we grasp what the iconic war images hide and the effects of the erasures in the broader politics of historical knowledge and justice. I will not reiterate the problems of Cold War transitional justice here, except to underscore the following. The anticolonial, antiracist critique has long faulted the Cold War architecture of transitional justice, not only because the IMTFE administered "victor's justice" and left the Allied powers' war crimes unprosecuted. More important, it has also questioned whether the IMTFE punished and executed Japanese political and military leaders for disturbing the peace and order preserved under European and U.S. domination and for violating their colonial entitlements, properties, and privileges in that region, rather than for the atrocities they committed against the people of Asia and the Pacific—who indeed constituted the majority of war victims.[18] The IMTFE's inability to fully perceive Japanese atrocities committed against tens of millions of people in the region's colonized condition as "crimes against humanity" has been criticized as indicative of the elisions and exclusions that have underwritten the genealogy of the West-centric notion of "humanity."[19]

Crucially, as I have discussed in the introduction, such critical interrogations dialectically connected the structure of unredressability generated by postwar transitional justice to the region's uneven structure of political and economic development—a Cold War contradiction that has remained intact since the war's ending. In contrast, the mainstream media's reporting on the effect of §354.6 yet again obscured the entangled history of colonialism, racism, and imperialism that had shaped the initial failure of historical justice, ironically a failure that the new amendment had set out to rectify. Against this tenacity of the habitual—and normative, in the sense that a historical discourse interpellates and disciplines subjects—way of knowing the U.S. wars in Asia and the Pacific Islands, what might be the implications of the new Americanization of Japanese war crimes in which Asian/American immigrant-citizens are emerging as subjects of redress?

Unredressable Injury and the Redressable Subject

Though ultimately ruled unconstitutional, §354.6 incited curious battles over legal interpretations concerning the federal government's exclusive right and authority to determine foreign affairs and the limits of the state's power. Some cases have explicitly addressed the constitutionality of California's new state law. One judge described a class action case filed by former American POWs as "a remarkable case, one in which the Attorney General of the United States and the Attorney General of the State of California are on opposite sides."[20] In contrast to the mainstream media's treatment, therefore, it is important to recognize that the Americanization of wartime Japanese crimes is not evenly distributed across the terrain of the U.S. public sphere. In the following discussion, I explore several cases of litigation brought under §354.6 with special attention to the language and memories appearing in these courts and the judicial opinions. I will attend especially to the following two issues: the perception that California's new law was a possible threat to national integrity; and the contradiction that the litigants' transnationality has introduced into U.S. courts.

In 2001 we witnessed two contradictory rulings on the constitutionality of §354.6. On September 17, U.S. district judge Vaughn Walker found §354.6 of the California Code of Civil Procedure unconstitutional unless ruled otherwise in the future by the Supreme Court because it "infringes on the federal government's exclusive power over foreign affairs" (*In re World War II Era Japanese Forced Labor Litigation*).[21] He thereby dismissed a class action case in which seven Korean and Chinese survivors of forced labor sued Mitsubishi, Nippon Steel, Kajima Corporation, and other companies. In contrast, the *Los Angeles Times* reported that Los Angeles Superior Court Judge Peter D. Lichtman, in his November ruling of a case brought by a Korean plaintiff named Jae Wong Jeong against the Onoda Cement Corporation and its successor, Taiheiyo Cement Corporation, had contradicted the federal court's opinion. According to the *LA Times*, Lichtman had rejected the defendants' argument that the case could not stand in California courts because the 1951 Peace Treaty precludes litigation of forced labor claims (*Taiheiyo Cement Corp. et al. v. Superior Court of California*).[22] The judge's

November decision, according to the report, took issue with the U.S. government's position by finding that unjust corporate enrichment through the exploitation of slave labor is a matter pertaining to the private sector, and that therefore adjudication of claims against private Japanese companies in U.S. courts would not cause "a diplomatic incident."[23] Lichtman furthermore noted the inconsistency and asymmetry between the U.S. government's position toward victims of slave labor in Europe, and in the war against Japan.

The rift between the federal and state courts' views with regard to §354.6 and its impact on interpretation of the 1951 Peace Treaty also continued in appellate courts. In January 2003 the Ninth Circuit U.S. Appellate Court Judge Stephen Reinhardt opined as follows: "Section 354.6 is impermissible because it intrudes on the federal government's exclusive power to make and resolve war, including the procedure for resolving war claims."[24] Reinhardt noted that according to the foreign affairs doctrine that grants power over external affairs exclusively to the national government, the court must regard §354.6 as unconstitutional: "The federal government, acting under its foreign affairs authority, provided its own resolution to the war; California has no power to modify that resolution" (1026). Thus in the absence of §354.6 the appellant's claims were time barred, and Reinhardt "reluctantly" (1015) vacated the appellate claims on behalf of the twenty-eight consolidated cases brought against Japanese corporations.[25] Contrastingly, in his ruling on an appeal brought by the Taiheiyo Cement Corporation concerning the *Jeong* case, made a few days before the ninth circuit court's decision, Judge Boland in the California Appellate Court had found that §354.6 was valid. Contrary to Reinhardt's view, Boland regarded §354.6 as essentially a procedural statute that applied only retroactively to assure the preexisting claims and rights of California denizens by simply extending the statute of limitation. "Not only is this a permissible state function," Boland opined, "but there is no reason to believe the adjudication of the claims will interfere with the federal government's ability to conduct foreign affairs. Any effect the adjudication of claims under section 354.6 may have on foreign nations is merely incidental and indirect" (420). He thus concluded that "the legislative enactment [of §354.6] was an appropriate exercise of the state's sovereign powers" (426) and allowed Jeong's case to proceed as mandated by Lichtman in the Los Angeles Superior Court.[26]

The California Appellate Court's view on the state's new law stood in sharp contrast to the February 2003 ruling of the Fourth District Court of Appeals of California in Orange County on the case filed by American POWs against multiple Japanese corporations (*Mitsubishi Materials Corp. et al. v. Su-*

perior Court of Orange Co.). The Orange County Appellate Court avoided the issue of the constitutionality of §354.6 but instead argued that once placed in the historical context in which it was signed, the 1951 Peace Treaty, which it acknowledged as the "supreme law of the land" (43), should be read as the "dispositive source of judicial decisionmaking [*sic*]" (51) with regard to the POWs' new claims against Japan.[27] In his historicist argument, Presiding Justice David G. Sills identified several key elements of the immediate postwar historical context in which the Allied forces waived war reparation claims. Most important, President Harry Truman understood that the Japanese economy needed to be restored "so that it could help serve as a bulwark against Communist aggression in Korea" (48).[28] Involvement in the Korean War required the United States to ensure that Japan's economy not be ruined by heavy war reparations claims. Furthermore, Truman emphasized that "the United States had not forgotten Bataan" but looked forward, according to Sills, to considering the idea that war reparations as punitive claims must be mitigated so that the treaty would not "contain the seeds of another war" (49). At the same time, citing the lesser known 1968 Shimoda case which had ruled that the U.S. atomic bombings violated international law, Sills observed that "the Japanese felt that they too had claims" (50) and concluded that "without a waiver of all war crime claims that could have been brought by either side, Japan and the United States might have wrangled endlessly about liabilities arising out of the war" (51). Suggesting agnostically that the cases against war crimes could have been made on both the Allied nations and Japan, Sills thus stressed the importance of accepting the officialized, statist account of the historical context in which the 1951 Peace Treaty had been signed and concluded that "the treaty, taken as a whole in historical context, precludes this lawsuit" (59).[29]

For our inquiry into the politicizing possibility of postnineties redress, especially intriguing is the way the above exchange of juridical opinions over the validity of §354.6 corroborated that the California legislation had been intended to address the unredressability resulting from colonial displacement and marginalization. A striking irony emerges when we juxtapose Jeong's case to the American POWs' litigation in Orange County. In colonial Korea Jeong had refused to serve in the Japanese imperial army. As a result he was forced to labor for Onoda Cement in Korea where he was subjected, according to the court document, to "physical and mental torture and forced to perform hard physical labor without compensation."[30] Jeong subsequently emigrated to the United States where he became a naturalized U.S. citizen. Yet Jeong's status as an expatriate from Korea, a non-Allied and nonsignatory nation to the 1951 Peace Treaty, had made the difference in court proceedings. Boland noted in his January 2003 California Appellate Court's ruling that the Taiheiyo Cement Corporation and its defendants failed to address whether the 1965 treaty had preempted Jeong's and other Korean nationals' claims for reparations. According to Boland, Taiheiyo and the United States instead placed emphasis solely on the 1951 San Francisco Peace Treaty and tried in vain to demonstrate how the U.S. Congress had preempted Jeong's war-related reparation claims. Consequently the court found that "the 1951 Treaty did not bar future claims by individuals [such as Jeong] of non-signatory nations and does not expressly preempt section 354.6" (410).[31] Likewise, even in deciding that §354.6 was unconstitutional, *In re World War II Era Japanese Forced Labor Litigation* distinguished the American POWs' cases from the claims of the Korean and Chinese plaintiffs by noting that the 1951 Peace Treaty did not intend to "control claims of individuals from non-signatory nations" and that §354.6 "provides a cause of action to such individuals."[32]

The court rulings that viewed §354.6 as infringing on federal jurisdiction over foreign affairs relied on the juridico-historical understanding, such as the one offered by Judge Sills, that the Japanese war crimes against American POWs and the enormity of the damages and losses they had suffered at the hands of the Japanese military were fully and keenly perceived by the state (Truman's "the United States had not forgotten Bataan") at the time. The U.S. government, as Sills recounted, waived the war reparation claims because it had already begun reparation payments through the War Claims Fund established with liquidated Japanese assets; and because the government acknowledged that the American POWs' suffering was beyond repair by any normal means. After citing a number of painful testimonies given by former Allied POWs, including Bigelow, and after noting that the brutality against them was a major reason for Truman's use of the atomic bombs, Sills noted: "The United States government knew that properly compensating them would be economically impossible."[33]

This juxtapositioning reveals the asymmetrical manner in which the two instances of historical loss were perceived as (un)redressable: while the gross violations against the propertied, rights-bearing American citizens were fully acknowledged over fifty years ago, the wartime claims by colonized and racialized victims like Jeong were only recently brought to light as part of American war memories. The full extent to which the U.S. government has acknowledged Japanese atrocities committed against American POWs stands in sharp contrast to the almost half-century absence of knowledge about Japanese war crimes against people in Asia and the Pacific Islands. While Jeong initially won his case, the U.S. Supreme Court's remand and denial of writ of certiorari to the California Appellate Court ultimately put an end to the lawsuit (January 18, 2005).[34] Yet, when we review Jeong's and other Korean and Chinese plaintiffs' cases in light of the not official and statist, but colonial and racialized historical context, it is evident that the Asian/Americanization of Japanese war crimes exemplified by redress suits like Jeong's has helped highlight the unevenness and voids in the American remembering of the Asia Pacific War(s) and its immediate aftermath. Jeong's case, in particular, illuminated the transwar, Cold War entanglement by clarifying how the Korean War had been crucial in determining the course of American orchestration of justice across the region. Asian/American transnationality in such a redress claim was indeed an "inconceivability a half a century ago," as Walker's decision put it.[35]

Finally, the juridical interpretative schisms did not only reflect the courts' different positions on the relation between the 1951 Peace Treaty and §354.6. To be sure, the state courts' opinions upholding the legality of suits filed under California's new law did not refer directly to the character of the 1951 Peace Treaty, nor did they deny its validity. They simply opined that §354.6 fits within the limits of state power assured by the constitution to protect the interests of California citizens. Yet the juridical inconsistency in understanding §354.6 and assessing the performative power it might exert over foreign relations eloquently spoke to the contradictions in the supposed sovereign integrity and supremacy of the federal government that Jeong's and the other plaintiffs' transnationality unveiled. The subnational divergence in California suggested by §354.6—a piece of state legislation considered to have violated a federal prerogative—revealed the predicaments inherent in any practical attempt to redress historical loss through existing juridical venues and other state apparatuses. By January 2005 all litigation prompted by §354.6 had ended in both U.S. and California courts.[36] Besides the two slave labor cases, *Hwang Geum Joo v. Japan*—the last of the series of litigations against Japan dismissed in the U.S. courts—was a "comfort women" case lodged by fifteen non-American female plaintiffs.[37] The U.S. Court of Appeals for the District of Columbia Circuit reaffirmed the U.S. District Court's 2001 decision and concluded that the case was nonjusticiable.[38] In sum, the law that could have benefited California residents seeking alternative channels for new or additional redress and reparations as war settlements was nullified by the legal argument that §354.6 would affect the standing international treaties and agreements. California legislators' attempts to rectify the shortcomings of earlier postwar settlements were thus yet again foreclosed by the very Cold War architecture it had set out to challenge.

In the brief period between its passage and nullification, §354.6 generated a prolific archive on Japanese war crimes and the failure of transitional justice in the early postwar years. For the most part, the juridico-historical discourse on the Asia-Pacific War incited by the introduction of §354.6 merely regurgitated the problems of earlier transitional justice. Some cases furthermore reinforced the pernicious racializing essentialism. In explaining the grounds on which the defendants refused to acknowledge the need for redress, some legal arguments relied not on geohistorical evidence on the production of unredressability, but on anthropological area studies knowledge of Japan rooted in wartime national character studies—for instance, following Ruth Benedict and others to describe Japanese culture and society in Orientalist and essentializing terms as dictated by "shame" culture, being "group-oriented and hierarchical."[39] In this way, some instances of the post-1990s redress culture sanctioned by the juridical and other state apparatuses reproduced the epistemic assumptions of Cold War knowledge formations.

Most important, however, by judging the cases against Japanese war crimes in the U.S. courts as constituting "a non-justiciable political question,"[40] the legal archives of §354.6 and the *Hwang Geum Joo v. Japan* case lay bare the problems of the Cold War arrangements that they themselves had inherited. The archives demonstrate the predicaments that have plagued the past efforts that had sought redress beyond the terms that had been agreed upon under Cold War geopolitics. Yet at the very moment of exposing justice's limits, the archives of the post-1990s redress culture simultaneously direct us to politicize questions of justice, historical knowledge, and the terms of reconciliation beyond their current judicialized states. The following section explores whether such an excess in the economy of juridico-historical discourse might potentially incite a newly politicized subject of justice precisely because of its very belatedness and unredressability.

Asian/American War Memories and Their Excess

Law's liberal premise formally disavows sociohistorically embedded differences among its subjects. For the purpose of grasping the cultural politics of juridico-historical discourse, however, it is crucial to acknowledge the ways in which the epistemological concerns and material conditions underpinning the Korean, Chinese, Filipino, and other Asian redress demands prompted by California's new law differ from those that circumscribe the simultaneous resurgence of American POW demands for additional compensation from Japanese corporations. At the same time that it was a symptom of the brief Cold War hiatus, the (re)emergence of reparation demands pertaining to Asian/Americans in the United States reflected the changing configuration of the U.S. citizenry since the 1965 Immigration Act. Insofar as Asian/American redress practices remain within the parameters of U.S. liberal multiculturalism and its politics of recognition, whose and which instances of victimization can be recognized and represented as a legitimate part of U.S. National History is a salient issue.

The two legislative measures in California reflected a critical shift in the racial and gendered configuration of the subject of remembering World War II. The amendment to the California Civil Code aimed to extend support to residents of California seeking reparations for damages caused by not only Germans and other Europeans but also Japanese and their collaborators. It shifted the anchoring point of the Californian, and by extension American, memory of World War II from the Atlantic to the Asia-Pacific. Assembly Joint Resolution 27 likewise gave voice to people of diverse geographical and national origins in Asia and the Pacific. In large part reflecting the new ethnonational configuration of the Asian-Pacific Islander (API) constituency in the state of California, the resolution supplemented the images of victims familiar in mainstream American memories of war with different racial, ethnic, and gendered faces. In other words, no longer only white Americans, but more crucially Asian Americans of various national and ethnic origins were becoming centered as subjects of remembering the U.S. war against Japan.

In considering the Asian/American formation through and within dominant U.S. war memories, it may be worthwhile recalling that the making of Asian America has been inseparably tied to the major U.S. wars since the mid-twentieth century. These were wars predominantly fought against and for Asian nations—whether the interimperial war against Japan; the two hot wars of the Cold War era in Korea, Vietnam, and Cambodia; or the more recent trade wars. Hence, one specific anti-Asian discursive formation continues to cast Asians as interchangeably perpetual aliens or ambivalent allies who can at any moment turn into enemies. Yet even as the state apparatus historically has subjected Asians to the suspect position of "unassimilable others," its liberal premise simultaneously has provided a means by which the ambiguously nationalized others can be mobilized as legitimately centered citizen-subjects.[41] For Japanese Americans in particular who were forced to choose their wartime allegiance, the disavowal of loyalties and cultural affinities with Japan at some point in their public lives, and demonstrations of assimilation to white, middle-class lifestyles and heteronormative domesticity, have arguably been prerequisites for acceptance as full, first-class cultural citizens. Similarly, to publicly disavow suspect Asian origins through the reiteration of the nation's orthodox Cold War American war memories—of not only the war against imperial Japan but the hot wars the United States has waged in and against different Asian countries—has been one intelligible gesture available to anyone in this precarious position to effectively prove Asian "assimilability" to America. In this regard, Mike Honda's initiatives for California's Joint Resolution and related bills in the Congress pertaining to Japanese war crimes can be read superficially as yet another rehearsal of a very familiar performance.

Indeed, Joint Resolution 27 inventoried Japanese war crimes as would any familiar American World War II narrative that is circulated and authorized by political speeches, commercial films, mainstream museum exhibits (chapter 5), and other cultural representations and images. The resolution notably lacks any reflection on the U.S. imperialist presence in the Pacific and Asia before and after the war.[42] Nor does it include any critical interrogation of the U.S. role in the IMTFE and how it made the past and ongoing colonial violence illegible—a reflection vital to the longue durée of redress in Asia. The resolution certainly does not reference the postwar, Cold War history in which U.S. foreign policies deliberately suppressed pro-democratic forces in Japan, Korea, the Philippines, Indonesia, and other parts of Asia where Japanese war crimes had only partially been scrutinized.[43] Neither does it question why the U.S. military continued to occupy regions that it had supposedly liberated. In highly archaic language, AJR 27 retains and reiterates the narrative of American justice and liberation. In these regards, California's two legislative actions arguably served as yet another set of state apparatuses for assimilating new immigrants from Asia. They order Asians to "stay put," so to speak, within the official account of the settler state's National History. It ensures that the discrepant memories of U.S. military involvement in Asia that immigrants have transported to the American public spheres are re-membered and re-enacted so as not to disrupt the imperialist myth of liberation and rehabilitation. The process of Asian/Americans becoming subjects of American National History is precisely where the contradictions that are inherent in any process of subjectification—in this case, national subjectification—also become apparent. It is worthwhile noting as well that, when juxtaposed to the intensification of anti–affirmative action and anti-immigration legislation in California (e.g.,

Propositions 209 and 187), the introduction of §354.6 reflected the uneven and selective enfranchisement of California's denizens.[44]

Still, the forces of nationalization cannot thoroughly contain transnational memories of U.S. wars in Asia. Certainly, to the extent that post–World War II U.S. Cold War policy in Asia has already shaped the political and ideological parameters of those choosing to emigrate to the United States, one might well expect a fit between some Asian immigrants' narratives and the official line on U.S. foreign policies.[45] Nevertheless, memories that travel are hardly consistent or containable. As geohistorically informed readings of Theresa Hak-Kyung Cha's *Dictée* by a number of Korean and other Asian/American critics have demonstrated, colonial and racialized memories of transnational Asian communities constantly disrupt the uniformly progressive narrative of the United States as the generous liberator and guardian of the free world.[46]

Nora Okja Keller's *Comfort Woman: A Novel* anticipates similar epistemic ruptures that traveling memories may potentially bring to dominant American World War II narratives. Written as the first in a trilogy on Korea-U.S. relations, the author's work took up the theme of transgenerational Asian immigrant-citizens' memories of the Japanese military comfort system.[47] *Comfort Woman* erects Asian immigrant-citizens as authentic subjects of U.S. National History. It presents the Asian/American historical experience in Asia as an integral part of mainstream American history. In this sense, the text produces the subject-ing effects that are analogous to the ones performed by AJR 27, or the litigation pursued under §354.6 and other forms of testimonial practices. At the same time, the novel lets its subjects recount Japanese militarism and colonialism in a manner that is inassimilable to the habitual American remembering of the U.S.-Japan War. *Comfort Woman* delineates a multifaceted history of the gender and class hierarchy in Korea, the Japanese colonial dispossession of Korea's sovereignty, the Korean people's and culture's subordination to the United States as well as to American missionaries, and the racial marginalization of Asian immigrants in the United States.

Comfort Woman opens up the incommensurable subjective worlds of two women, Beccah and her mother, Akiko. The two first-person narratives parallel each other as they move respectively between the two women's pasts and presents. Beccah's narrative shifts between the present in which Beccah works as a journalist for a local newspaper in Honolulu (for which she writes obituary columns), and the past in which she was raised in poverty and solitude by a single immigrant mother from Korea. *Comfort Woman* is a highly self-conscious attempt to critique the processes whereby colonial-ism, racism, and imperialism continue to subordinate "the feminine." In the novel the "United States," to which the narrator's mother immigrates, emerges as a site where individual emancipation and political realization are at least promised, while "Asia" remains an inert and undifferentiated realm of victimization and licit violence. In effect, the history of military sex slavery remains a supplementary text through which the second gen-eration daughter's/narrator's American political will is enabled. The novel's universalization of female victimization further risks subordinating "Asia" to what Chuh saw as the American "will to knowledge." The story, for in-stance, hints at an equation between sexual harassment in the contemporary First World workplace and the horrific abuse found in the wartime Japanese military comfort system. It even suggests that both are somehow resolved when the American narrator gains self-autonomy, not only as a professional Asian American woman but also as an enlightened subject of international humanitarianism through mention of the Red Cross. This assumed com-mensurability indicates the novel's problematic alignment with global femi-nism's universalist rendering of sexual violence against women, an issue that I have discussed earlier. Still, insofar as the geopolitical imaginary is concerned, through evoking the figure of a less than sincere American mis-sionary who rescues and marries Akiko, the narrator's mother who appar-ently survived the Japanese military comfort system, Keller's *Comfort Woman* offers an effective critique of the paternalistic relation between the United States and Asia. The novel suggests that historical justice concerning Japa-nese imperialist violence in Asia cannot be enunciated without intimating the volatile contradictions in the U.S. ideology of Asian assimilation, as well as the discourse of American innocence and justice.

While *Comfort Woman* can be read as a representation of an intraeth-nic, intergenerational transmission of historical memories among Korean Americans, I wish to read the text as a search for a collective subject of historical justice even in the absence of the stability of experiential truth and the apriority of identity. After the death of her mother, who earned a living as a spirit medium, Beccah prepares for the funeral and remembers a number of instances of discommunication between the two. Her mother's utterances, Korean songs, gods, the rituals her mother performed—none of these were meaningful to Beccah until her mother's death. Likewise Akiko's narratives shift between the past, in which she was forcibly taken to a Japanese military comfort system where she was dispossessed of her name and her body, and the present in which she gives birth to, names, and raises her biracial daughter. In both narrative worlds, the past is constantly called upon to make sense of the present. From the labor of giving birth to Beccah, Akiko cannot help but recall the pain she had to endure when the Japanese doctor forced her to have an abortion in the comfort station (22, 35). When Akiko remembers that the missionary husband's attempt to save his wife was no more than a tool with which to prove his own salvation, her memory of the American husband's narcissistic humanism is juxtaposed to the Japanese soldiers' brutal appropriation of comfort women for their selfish pleasure and imperialist pursuit (148). Beccah, too, remembers her mother's numerous enigmatic forewarnings about men as she decides to terminate her relationship with a married man who cannot leave his family. Beccah's relationship with her much older lover is nothing more than narcissistic dependence in which the aging man takes advantage of her to regain his youthfulness (138). Despite such formal symmetry, however, there is no point at which the two women's subjective worlds meet. Through this lack of identification, Keller's *Comfort Woman* suggests that the transmission of historical memories and the erection of a collective subject that can pursue justice do not necessarily presuppose a stable and positive connection between the victims of the original violence and those who stand in as agents of redress. Beccah cannot access her mother's past except as traces, through her remains and a disembodied voice left on a cassette tape. Even while readers know that Akiko was a survivor of the Japanese military comfort system, Beccah cannot confirm the final truth in her mother's absence. The novel thus suggests that in order to make it possible for Beccah to translate her mother's words into a "prayer for justice" (197), Beccah need not necessarily know if her mother actually lived through the past that now demands redress.

Throughout the text, Keller insinuates that her mother's shamanism was a ritual to nurture and mourn those women who died solitary deaths with no one to grieve for them or look after their spirits. Yet even when Beccah finally begins to make sense of her mother's rituals, the immediate relationship between her mother and the deceased women she has prayed for is not confirmed. Even when Beccah discovers that her mother's real name is Soon Hyo, she can do so only through official documents from such third-party authorities as the American embassy in Seoul and the Red Cross (173). In fact it was not even clear to Akiko whether the names she recalled of the women who were lost to the Japanese military violence—"Induk. Miyoko. Kimiko. Hanako. Akiko. Soon Hi. Soon Mi. Soon Ja. Soon Hyo"—were given at their birth, taken up by choice, or forced upon them (192). And yet, Beccah seems willing to inherit from her mother the task of offering prayers and rectifying past injustices. The task of carrying the pursuit of justice forward and mourning for the dead, then, requires not so much authentic restitution of the original, or uncritical identification with and empathy for the ultimate victims, as the contagious acknowledgment of and indignation toward the violence perpetrated by colonialism on the wholeness of life, language, body, and name.[48] Throughout, the text suggests the impossibility of re-presentation, the instability of language, and the irreparability of the original. At the same time, it probes the possibilities of action for historical justice that might be enabled precisely by such awareness of belatedness and incertitude.

The text's deferral of cognitive truth amid the pursuit of justice offers important implications for the politics of redress. That the text does not reveal, at least to Beccah, the final truth about the mother suggests that the legitimate subjects of remembrance and redress do not need to be the immediate survivors or their descendants but can be constituted by a collectivity that transcends the original time and place. Perhaps, then, the novel may be pointing to a radical reconstitution of subjectivity beyond the literal Korean-ness that ties Beccah to her mother and the community of the dead. It suggests that the collectivity to which the subjects of redress belong and their affective attachment need not necessarily exist prior to their engagement in the pursuit of justice. This community, moreover, consists not only of the living, here and now, but also of the dead out there—those unnameable and innumerable multitudes of beings and nonbeings. When approached from this critical transpacific perspective, Keller's *Comfort Woman* as well as Mike Honda's and other Asian/American redress efforts, may reveal much more than a familiar performance of Asian/American assimilation. Rather than gesturing toward a collectivity that rests on the given logic of ethnic or American nationalisms, the pursuit of historical justice for Asian/American victims of Japanese imperial violence may be grounded on a differently politicized sense of justice.

At the very least, by foregrounding race and colonialism, Keller's novel speaks to the productive ambivalence of the Asian immigrant-citizens' involvement in redressive practices. On the realpolitik front, even in the aftermath of the law's demise, Asian immigrant-citizens remain empowered in other venues of the U.S. public sphere and advance positive knowledge of the past by pressuring their government to disclose classified documents, archives, and other relevant evidence. In that process, Asian immigrant-citizens may indeed risk nationalization and disciplinization—that is,

"Americanization" of their excess ambivalence—to be consistent with their normative subject position in America's settler present. As the agent-subjects of redress, however, they can also disclose the extent to which knowledge about Japanese atrocities has been suppressed under the Cold War structure of impunity, even as certain losses have been selectively and strategically pronounced to sustain the "good war" narrative and the myth of liberation and rehabilitation. Asian/American subjectivity and agency rest on such multiple and often contradictory forces of history, knowledge, law, and the state. The Asian/Americanization of memories of Japanese colonialism and militarism can therefore both facilitate the formation of National History and simultaneously obstruct that same process.

During a conference on slave-labor and sex-slavery litigation organized in Los Angeles by the association which has since been renamed the Association for Preserving Historical Accuracy of Foreign Invasions in China (APHAFIC), one Korean American community participant somewhat abruptly mentioned the 1905 Katsura-Taft Secret Agreement and urged the audience to remember it in the discussion of slave-labor litigations.[49] The diplomatic agreement between representatives of the Japanese and American governments was a pact promising that neither side would interfere in the other's colonial projects—namely, the United States in the Philippines and Japan in Korea. But the agreement itself had no direct bearing on the wartime Japanese military forced labor. The odd dissonance generated by the participant's catachronic remembering illustrated how transborder redress culture constituting Asian/Americans as the new agent-subject cannot but conjure up the entangled histories of Japanese and U.S. colonialisms and their longue durée. Remembering the U.S. war against Japan critically linked one history of violence to other instances of loss and injustice. Thus the very process of pursuing redress may well incite knowledge that is much more complexly interconnected and unsettling than could be contained within the immediate juridical framing of individual cases. In this sense, and in ways that are unprecedented, Asian/American agency in the Americanization of Japanese war crimes and the inassimilable excess it brings to memories of Asia-Pacific War have the potential to proffer a radical reenvisioning of Cold War transpacific formations and their militarized-colonial legacies.

Indeed, whether and how seeking redress for war crimes committed seven decades ago can become meaningfully relevant to critical understandings of other past and present injustices has been a question repeatedly raised by younger generations of Asian/American participants in public gatherings. In a similar meeting in San Diego sponsored by the same group where American POWs, Chinese American Sino-Japanese War survivors, and international lawyers congregated to discuss boycotts, litigation, and other possible strategies against Japanese corporations, one Asian/American female college student asked why we are concerned exclusively about past Japanese atrocities and not ongoing injustices. As an exigent example she mentioned the then ongoing U.N. embargo against Iraq and the rise of infant mortality in the aftermath of the 1990 U.S.-led military attack.[50] The query was no doubt a provocation more than a question as such. It called out to conference participants to see conjunctions between past oversights of justice and the structures of violence in place today. I would respond to such an incitement by making a plea for vigilance, as I did in my earlier work on Hiroshima survivors' testimonial practices. That is, each and every instance of personal or collective injury ought to be dealt with as an absolute historical singularity dissociated from the arbitrary chains of signification and instrumentalization. At the same time, it is our responsibility as receivers of survivors' testimonies and witness accounts of egregious violations to critically discern justice's broader, more complex and radical politico-historical implications, whenever we are impelled, as the justice's subject, to ultimately determine requisite action.

Perils and Possibilities

Asian/American investments in knowledge production and representations of the Asia-Pacific War and Japanese imperial violence are not limited to juridical channels but have increasingly proliferated in other U.S. civic spheres. The decisions by state legislators in Maryland and Virginia to ensure that students will be taught in schools that the body of water between the Korean peninsula and Japan is named the East Sea in Korea and the Sea of Japan in Japan can likewise be seen as another attempt by Korean/Americans to rectify Japanese colonial injustice from their position as American citizen-subjects. The dispute over *So Far from the Bamboo Grove*, also known as *Yoko's Story*, a children's novel by an expatriate Japanese author, Yoko Kawashima Watkins, similarly involved public venues in Massachusetts and other states. Employing a plot reminiscent of Frances Hodgson Burnett's *A Little Princess*, this supposedly semiautobiographical story depicts a nine-year-old girl's turbulent and brave journey from Korea, where she grew up in a well-to-do Japanese colonists' family, to war-torn Japan, where she became orphaned and impoverished but learned to survive with honor.[51] The

FIGURE 4.1 The "Comfort Woman" statue in Glendale, California, erected in July 2013. A Korean sculptor couple, Kim Sŏkyŏng and Kim Unsŏng, has installed a series of "Peace Girl Statutes" in more than twenty locations. In this and other images the girl's youth highlights the many decades of silence that had lapsed before the sufferings of "comfort women" were brought to light as well as the belated justice which many still await. (AFP Photo / Frederic J. Brown/Getty Images.)

book sparked a nationwide and transpacific controversy when a local school board in Massachusetts found its depiction of "North Koreans" problematic and banned it from the district's school curriculum. The Korean American attempt to remove *Yoko's Story* from the school and libraries was viewed by some in Korea as a case of distant nationalism. In a different but related way, the city of Glendale, California, erected the "Comfort Woman" statute to commemorate and condemn the forced recruitment of Korean women into the wartime military comfort system (see figure 4.1).

At the time of this writing, a lawsuit has been filed by a group of Japanese/American citizens demanding that the city remove the statue, yet again judicializing the politics of memory and justice. This is an unfortunate development, for by shifting civic discord over popular justice into the juridical arena, the process has reestablished and reauthorized the State as the ultimate adjudicator. Such litigation, moreover, is likely to reduce the question of historical knowledge to a difference in ethnicized memories, as if the past could only be remembered through possessive investments in discrete, internally homogeneous and naturalized ethnonational identities. Instead, whatever grudges the litigants may have harbored, their discomfort could have been productively tied to interrogating why, despite its multiple attempts, the Japanese government's apologies have not been received as "sincere." At the same time, this incident could have provided an opportunity for critical thinking about the dialectics of (un)redressability. It could have generated questions about why now, why so belatedly, and how certain historical losses and violence have been privileged over others, not only in the representational politics of the U.S. public sphere but also in the transnational circuits of knowledge production. Indeed, the marked absence signified by the empty chair placed next to the statue of the girl unsettles viewers by reminding us of other injuries from state violence that remain equally unseen and unredressed. Finally, when read in conjunction with how the 1995 rape case of a twelve-year-old girl in Okinawa mobilized anti-base protests on an unprecedented scale, important questions remain regarding the seemingly universal affective power of condemnation that only an image of innocent girlhood can conjure up against sexual and other violence against women.

Considering the retrenchment of habitualized knowledge thus currently underway, how might we best reflect on the problematics put forward ten years ago in the special issue of the *Journal of Asian American Studies*? Chuh summarily opened the special issue with the following provocation: "Effectively masking U.S. imperialism and simultaneously reinstalling American exceptionalism, the 'comfort woman' as exemplary figure of subjugation under Japanese imperialism apparently argues for U.S. intervention in the peninsula's affairs."[52] Seen from this critical perspective, Korean/Americans' *American* condemnation of the history of Japanese imperial violence in the American public spheres seems to mean more than claiming a space for ethnonational representation in the multicultural politics of recognition. It may indeed serve as a conduit for facilitating precisely the sort of transpacific "U.S. intervention" Chuh warned about. Yet, despite the tendencies toward a seemingly purist and exclusionary identitarianism toward history, and indications that Asian/American ethnonationalism can supplement U.S. multicultural nationalism, the previous observation on the ambivalent effect of the American notion of Asian liberation I extrapolated in the above-mentioned journal may still remain viable.[53] Situated within and against the genealogy of America's relation to the idea of Asian liberation, the Asian/Americanization of justice may continue to be understood as a twofold process. On the one hand, the Asian/Americanization of justice can contribute to the obfuscation of past and present America's military and colonial violence. In the post–9/11 milieu in which the United States has yet again appointed itself to the position of the world's sole adjudicator, it is difficult to ignore how such legislative actions as H.S. 121 will further confirm the self-congratulatory faith in U.S. infallibility and justify its claim to possess the authority and power with which to define and punish every evil on behalf of the world. On the other hand, the transnationalization of juridico-historical discourse in U.S. courts, albeit for a brief period, may have inadvertently revealed how profoundly the United States has been implicated in facilitating twentieth-century culture of impunity and how it has subsequently suppressed and silenced the people and nations to whom it claims to have brought freedom and democracy. The dialectics of memory necessitated by transpacific demands for historical justice may thus effectuate an "un-American" consciousness of disidentification, even as it simultaneously disciplines and assimilates its new subjects into the cohesive National History of the settler colonial state.

Since 2013 we have witnessed several remarkable court rulings in Asia.[54] To name a few, courts in the Republic of Korea dispensed historic verdicts in litigation against the Nippon Steel and Sumitomo Metal Corp (NSSMC) (July 19, 2013) and Mitsubishi Heavy Industry (July 30, 2013) and ordered the companies to pay the survivors and their families unpaid wages and other compensation for wartime forced labor. This decision was rendered despite the executive office's announcement that the 1965 Basic Treaty had settled the forced labor violations, but not damages to Koreans victimized by the two atomic bombings and the military comfort system. In China, the Supreme People's Court temporarily impounded a carrier vessel owned by the Mitsui O.S.K. Line Ltd. for delinquent lease payments dating back to the 1930s (April 2014). To be sure, both Korean and Chinese government officials deny that these rulings infringe upon the previously signed normalization treaties. Still, these juridical developments—ensured by the separation of the three powers—have already created enough productive tensions between economic and political exigencies. Reportedly, the NSSMC announced that in the event that its appeal to the Korean Supreme Court is denied, it is prepared to comply with the court order in the interest of maintaining its global reputation and for the purpose of unobstructed commercial activities in Korea. Mitsui O.S.K. immediately submitted its payment, thus releasing its vessel from impoundment by the court and resuming its operations. The Japanese government, in contrast, has been pressuring these multinational corporations not to resolve reparations matters privately. These rulings in Asian courts have therefore begun to unsettle the relevant nations', if not their governments', official hardline views that postwar settlement issues have already been concluded by the standing peace and normalization treaties. Furthermore, the previously mentioned juridical interpretation that state-to-state treaties do not necessarily preclude individual rights to demand redress from private corporations appears to be empowering these new Asian cases.

The ongoing litigation and cases in Asia that generally appear to favor the victims and their surviving families seem to suggest that the long phase of the postwar Americanization of justice and the predicaments resulting from it have at last come to an end. It is certainly possible that the Japanese government might welcome American initiatives and mediation to establish a corporate reparations fund, as Germany did a decade ago following the dismissal of all litigations of the Nazis forced labor cases in U.S. courts. As we have seen in the previous chapters, the United States has consistently aided Japan's remilitarization throughout the postwar decades. In order to make palatable the long-deferred American design of deploying the officially legitimated robust Japanese army to serve the region's military-economic security, it also serves the U.S. interest if the Japanese government were to swiftly (re)settle the pasts and conjures away the war ghosts that loom over the region. The significance of such a possible accomplishment of reparative justice cannot be overemphasized. Yet it is equally necessary to be wary of the concurrent resurgence of Cold War language and realignments at this historical juncture. Indeed, anyone familiar with the history of U.S. trilateral relations with Korea and Japan will have noticed the irony of President Obama's Asia-centered diplomacy and his spring 2014 visits to these two countries, for Obama was welcomed in the respective nations by the offspring of the two powerful cold warrior leaders: Korea's Park Geun-hye, the daughter of Park Chung Hee and Japan's Abe Shinzō, the grandson of Kishi Nobusuke. On his visits, Obama underscored the American military commitment to defend Korea from North Korean's nuclear threat and Japan from China's maritime expansionism. The executive tour of America's old Cold War allies was primarily aimed to navigate successful free trade agreements through the proposed Trans-Pacific Partnership (TPP) and to demonstrate, vis-à-vis China, the trilateral military-political-economic alliance. On the same tour, Obama initiated the signing of a new military treaty between the United States and the Republic of the Philippines, which will resume U.S. use of military bases in the Philippines, including the former Subic naval base which has been closed since 1992. Likewise, Obama's visit reaffirmed the U.S.-Japan joint appropriation of Okinawa in the interests of making it possible to maintain the terms of the U.S.-Japan Security Treaty, thus further consolidating the controversial plan to use Henoko Beach as an alternative to the accident-plagued Futenma Naval Station.[55]

Given these indications of the obstinate persistence of the political, economic, and military architecture of the Cold War years, even as we can observe entirely different power dynamics currently under way due to the PRC's military and economic expansionism, the Americanization of Japanese war crimes and its (re)production of Cold War structures and epistemology may best be seen as a still evolving process. Despite the juridical closure in the United States, to draw any conclusions about the kinds of effects this new phase of Americanization will ultimately have on the politics of redress and historical memory would be premature. We need to carefully disentangle recalcitrant elements from emerging possibilities. We also need to vigilantly discern the contradictory process of the Americanization of justice, asking whether this in fact serves to reestablish the United States as the apparently innocent custodian of world peace and humanity while regimenting Asian/America and its "un-American" memories, or if that same process may foster, truly and critically, alliances of transnational publics that do not supplement the U.S. global multinational and multicultural management that has been familiar to us since the Cold War.

Insofar as the language and practice of redress and reparations inevitably holds out as its telos some form of closure, settlement, and sublation, the official acknowledgment of and accounting for past wrongs may be as perilous as it is enabling. In this process the state-corporate entity can disavow the oppression, grief, and marginalization that continue to exist for racialized and colonial minorities.[56] It moreover risks relegating justice, legitimacy, and even agency for redress and reconciliation to the very state-corporate entities that offer reparations and apologies (e.g., Japan), as well as to those that promote redress and authorize the rectification of injustice (e.g., the United States), rather than to the survivors of the original moment of violence.[57] Yet, transnational memories are never fully in sync with the nation's dominant collective memory or National History, even while they are constantly imperiled by nationalizing forces that, through domesticating and assimilating excess knowledge, threaten to produce a seamless narrative of national self-affirmation, victimology, and innocence. At a minimum, critical transnational memories can challenge such statist foreclosures and pose possibilities for interventions into the imagined inevitability and unilinear progress of universal history.

FIVE

Complicit Amnesia

For Transformative Knowledge

There is no document of civilization which is not at the same time a document of barbarism. And just as such a document is not free of barbarism, barbarism taints also the manner in which it was transmitted from one owner to another.
Walter Benjamin, "Theses on the Philosophy of History," *Illuminations*

Around the time the Japanese government initiated the Asian Women's Fund (1994–2007) in response to international condemnation of the wartime military sex enslavement and when such public admittance of the violence of the military comfort system prompted a powerful reaction and pushbacks from the Japanese conservative revisionists, the Smithsonian National Air and Space Museum (NASM) came to the forefront of another intense transnational public controversy. In 1994–1995, to commemorate the fiftieth anniversary of the ending of World War II, the museum prepared a display of *Enola Gay*, the bomber deployed in the Hiroshima mission of August 6, 1945, along with photo panels explaining the history that preceded and followed the world's first strategic use of a nuclear weapon. When the exhibit blueprint became known to the American publics, it was severely attacked and set off impassioned debates involving the U.S. news media, veterans' organizations, and their much younger supporters, the U.S. Congress, and professional historians. The controversy was finally "resolved" by the appointment of a new museum director and massive scaling down of the initial curatorial plan, leaving only a display of the fuselage and an enlarged crew photo. The Smithsonian dispute over how, with what, and where to commemorate the nation's past war was a multifaceted controversy that brought into focus many important issues regarding U.S. National History, militarized justice, narratives of victimization, and publicity. The mid-1990s history war in the United States was yet another symptom of the geopolitical and epistemic milieu at the end of the Cold War.

The atomic bombings of Hiroshima and Nagasaki obviously constituted an event that had grave and lasting material consequences for various parts of the world. Its signification has generated uneven and varied practices across and within the Pacific, including different nationalisms centered on the event's disparate meanings; anticolonial, antimilitarist objections to the American nuclear umbrella; anticapitalist dissent against the military-industrial-academic nuclear complex; and antinuclear environmentalism. The historical event of the Hiroshima and Nagasaki bombings has thus become a sign that rests at the intersections of multiple discourses. In U.S. National History, the narrative of the strategic use of nuclear weapons at the end of the Asia-Pacific War is as highly disciplined as well as disciplining of its subjects as the American myth of liberation and rescue. The dominant account of the truth—that the two atomic bombings "saved lives," not only of Americans but of multiple nationals including Japanese—empowers the ideology of militarized security that justifies the State violence for the sake of life. The embracing of such a nuclear discourse, however, is hardly unique to the United States. In this final chapter I will closely examine the controversy to argue that transpacific Cold War knowledge concerning the war, and the idea of American justice it enables, hinge on the selective forgetting and remembering of the Asia-Pacific War.

To recap the Smithsonian dispute, I begin with an inquiry into the fundamental predicaments underlying the production of a nation's public history and memory. What does it mean, and is it at all possible to produce a single and discrete public history and memory shared in common and objectively by a nation? The production of any overarching narrative about the past inevitably incites contestations and struggles over historical truths. This process furthermore raises the question of the limits of a mode of argumentation that uncritically assumes the force of factual authenticity and objectivity. Equally important, the controversy revealed that what appeared to be a conflict within the boundaries of one national public sphere was in fact composed of elements that went beyond national borders. The chapter's second half focuses on the tension common to any official memory making today. While various transnational and discordant factors inevitably participate in the production of a nation's hegemonic remembering, transnational movements in the production of collective memory are subjected to disavowal and censorship.[1] Even while reminding us of the tenacity of the nationalized imaginary and demonstrating that nationalisms and state apparatuses can still lay powerful claim to their possessive relations to a single, uniform collective historical consciousness for the nation, the Smithsonian dispute betrayed that the disparities in historical awareness concerning the Asia-Pacific War and the two atom bombings do not necessarily originate in national differences.

Yet transnationalization also risks depoliticization when critical remembering and alternative visions that are meant to be dissenting and oppositional in one context are transferred to another. This problem, which can be described as the transnational "warping" of politics, was evident in the Smithsonian controversy. Much like the conundrum of justice we observed in previous chapters, the anniversary dispute exposed the predicament of transnational ventriloquizing, a process through which progressive and anti-Statist, anticorporatist redress culture in Asia was cited and deployed in the U.S. national public sphere to discipline and domesticate diverse critical historical sensibilities. These latter were even incorporated into the orthodox National History narrative that shores up American exceptionalism. What fell out of this uncritical transnationalization of oppositional politics was awareness of redress's longue durée—that is, of the challenges to the enduring structure of illegibility of violence maintained by the Cold War U.S.-Japan complicity. By dissecting the problems of selective amnesia in a type of remembering that postulates an isomorphic relationship among a nation, the public sphere, and a single discrete historical consciousness, the chapter seeks alternative ways of remembering the Asia-Pacific War that might suggest a means of repoliticizing justice beyond relegitimation.

Facts, Commemoration, Critical Knowledge

The Smithsonian *Enola Gay* controversy concluded with a major departure from the comprehensive exhibit originally planned by the museum. Through negotiations that extended for more than a year between the public and the NASM curatorial staff, the scripts were rewritten a number of times, and in the end, all the following were eliminated: the details of debates among U.S. political leaders, scholars, and military commanders over the decision to use the atom bombs; an extensive number of photographs and descriptions concerning Japan's military invasions and colonial violence committed in East Asia, Southeast Asia, and the Pacific Islands; photographs showing physical and human damage in Hiroshima and Nagasaki; and general observations about the subsequent development of the atomic age and nuclear weapons proliferation.[2] The propriety and significance of commemorating *Enola Gay* in this national public space were never questioned, even though the media reports and academic writings referenced the controversy as the "*Enola Gay* controversy." In this sense, the Japanese-language news media might have captured what was really at the heart of the national dispute by naming it the "atom bomb exhibit controversy."

Let us begin by examining two strikingly similar, yet contrasting, statements in the U.S. news media. A *Los Angeles Times* editorial titled "Wrong Place for Anti-Nuclear Message: Smithsonian Scotches Enola Gay Exhibit amid a Controversy That Shouldn't Have Happened" (February 1, 1995), indicated that the *Enola Gay* dispute was "one of those historical arguments in which the factual context is often obscured by ideological presuppositions." While admitting the significance of warning against the destructive force of the atomic bombs and questioning the subsequent nuclear arms race, it concluded that "a Smithsonian exhibit that rightfully should have been primarily dedicated to commemorating the end of World War II and honoring those who fought to defeat Nazism and Japanese militarism clearly was not that place." Such a remark stands in sharp contrast to a *New York Times* editorial, "Hijacking History" (January 30, 1995). Cautioning against yielding to the political pressure of conservative Congress members and veterans, the editorial argued that "historians and museums of history need to be insulated from any attempt to make history conform to a narrow ideological or political interest." These two opposing statements remind us of the ways in which, as the sociologist John B. Thompson once put it, the term "ideological" always precludes references to the self and is summoned when used to condemn and discount others.[3] They also epitomize the way in which the notion of factual neutrality—despite the veterans' frequent claims of their experiential authority as witnesses—has served as the governing and most persuasive source of legitimacy across nearly the entire discursive terrain of disputes between those who supported and those who attacked the exhibit plans prepared by the NASM curators. In their heated exchanges, both the historians and the journalists who tried to save the much more comprehensive version of the exhibit and those who in the end succeeded in altering the exhibit so as to honor the plane's mission relied on the power of facticity to substantiate their credibility. Almost all who participated in the dispute emphasized that their positions were grounded in historical facts, thereby underscoring their objectivity and/or neutrality, while simultaneously denouncing their opponents as blinded by personal beliefs, political biases, and emotional investments.

The so-called revisionist historians who defended the curators' plans sought to refute their opponents by emphasizing the academic authenticity of the prepared texts. Kai Bird, perhaps one of the most vocal and active historians to denounce the politicians' violation of curatorial and academic freedom, argued that the controversy stemmed from the "inaccurate but understandable belief of the veterans that the atomic bomb saved their lives from being sacrificed."[4] Still others defended the exhibit plan by differentiating the concepts of "commemorative history" and "public history." The American studies scholar Edward T. Linenthal, who served on the advisory committee to plan the original exhibit, promoted such a distinction in his own efforts to counter the politicians' and veterans' interventions.[5] In his testimony of May 18, 1995, at one of the public hearings that were convened before the U.S. Senate Committee on Rules and Administration to investigate the controversy over the Smithsonian's proposed exhibition, Linenthal argued, "There is tension between the commemorative voice and the historical voice, which seeks to discern motives, understand actions, and discuss consequences that were impossible to analyze during the event itself. . . . It is a voice that to some can feel detached, even when those who speak out of this voice view their work as a way to deepen our understanding of an event."[6] When the newly appointed Smithsonian secretary Michael Heyman announced to the press cancellation of the display which would have shown the ground-level effects of the bombs as well as the radical scaling down of the exhibit as a whole, he, too, signaled that the controversy originated in "a basic error in attempting to couple a *historical treatment* of the use of atomic weapons with the 50th anniversary *commemoration* of the end of the war" (emphasis added).[7] The Smithsonian staff's defenders, though of course in various ways, argued that the controversy stemmed from the clash between the academic attempt to produce a comprehensive and objective public history and the desire of those who witnessed the event to celebrate their—and, by imaginary extension, the nation's—honorable past.

Such characterizations, however, provoked vehement rebuttals from many veterans and conservative journalists and historians. Earlier, Martin Harwit, the director of the NASM who was eventually forced to resign as a result of the controversy, had portrayed the dispute as a conflict between a historical view that "appeals to our national self-image" and another historical perspective that is "more analytical, critical in its acceptance of facts and concerned with historical context."[8] A *Washington Post* editorial titled "Context and the *Enola Gay*" (August 14, 1994) reacted sharply to this depiction of the debate. The editorial criticized Harwit in no uncertain terms, charging that although he and others were quick to dismiss their critics' take on the *Enola Gay* exhibit as lacking in "intellectual sophistication," the problem in fact lay in the "curatorial inability to perceive that political opinions are embedded in the exhibit or to identify them as such—opinions—rather than as universal, 'objective' assumptions all thinking people must necessarily share." The editorial also attributed the source of the problem to what the editors perceived as a growing "postmodern" relativism in the academy, an issue to which I will return. To counter the charges that they were simply being subjective and not academic, those who attacked the NASM curators tried to demonstrate the objective and analytical nature of their criticisms with a long list of publications they relied on to construct their arguments.[9]

With respect to this endless exchange of facts, during the Senate committee hearing on May 18, 1995, Linenthal expressed the distress and frustration shared by many of the museum's academic staff. He pointed out that despite the immediate and substantial changes made to the exhibit plans in response to criticisms of veterans and the historian of the Office of the Secretary of Defense (who at one point reportedly approved of the revised comprehensive version of the prepared text), the media's and the Air Force Association's attacks continued to intensify. At the same time, the museum staff was forced to negotiate with those who criticized the omission of photographs of the human devastation caused by nuclear weapons. Linenthal summarized the process as follows:

> As script after script deleted material about historical controversies regarding the decision to drop the bomb, added photographs of mushroom clouds and structural damage, and removed most photographs of dead Japanese, historians and peace activists met with museum officials to argue for what they believe should be restored or newly incorporated. The scripts were a kind of Rorschach test. People were concerned with different questions, paid attention to different "facts," and interpreted the same facts differently. In the end, everyone believed their history had been "stolen," resulting either in a "revisionist" exhibit or in one showing a disregard for the complexity and irony of history.[10]

Linenthal's observation that the two opposing camps were talking past each other even as each side equally grounded its legitimacy on selective use of historical facts and events unwittingly puts into relief a number of issues inherent in the politics of knowledge in general. Most important, his remark suggests that there are limits to a mode of argumentation that relies solely on the epistemic certainty of facts to gain access to the power to represent in a public sphere. This limitation also extends to the idea that habitually presupposes—as in Secretary Heyman's inaugural remark "Let the object speak for itself"[11]—that positive historical knowledge can automatically deliver an unproblematically shared, authentic history.

It is not my intention to undermine the importance of factual knowledge produced by archival work that has revealed multiple sets of competing, contingent, and often indeterminate factors ultimately resulting in a single historical event—in this case, President Truman's executive order to use the two atomic bombs. Challenges to the master historical narrative through the archival investigations have increasingly made evident not only the significance of excavating and examining documents and records, but also the instrumental power that resides in the presentation of "facts." The archival findings of the so-called liberal revisionist historians in the United States have played a pivotal role in putting the naturalized image of the past into critical perspective, however gradually.[12] In relativizing the hegemonic historical narrative by calling attention to particular "facts," historians have unmistakably disturbed our common sense, offering vital ground for suspicion about received knowledge. Moreover, as the historian Barton Bernstein has emphasized, new fact finding can raise awareness that knowledge has been deliberately suppressed or withheld from the public, thus further generating healthy skepticism of the government's censorship and the general ways in which the world is made known to us.[13] The revelation of the fact of suppression can itself prompt further demystification of officialized historical accounts.

What needs to be interrogated, then, is not so much the use of historical facts as such, but rather the simplistic distinction between "history" and "memory," or "public history" and "commemorative desire." These binaries frequently figured in the discourses of both those who defended and those who attempted to sabotage the exhibit. Despite their instrumental value for rhetorical purposes, such oppositions cannot be posited a priori. History, like commemorative rituals, can always be mediated by the desire to speak in voices of and for the dead, to honor victims and martyrs, and to memorialize past events. Furthermore, the clear distinction between, on the one hand, a "commemorative exhibit" that is created out of empathy and the subjective judgment of those who hold shared communal ties to the remembered event, and on the other, a "public history" fashioned out of the analytical and detached examination of a historical incident assumes the possibility of attaining a transcendent and universal position from which a subject can observe and present the past. This understanding may also lead to the categorical dismissal of testimonial voices on the grounds that they are personal, conjectural, and mystified, thus subordinating them too hastily to the knowledge produced by institutionalized authorities. In a given situation of amnesic hegemony, a singular witness account, as a reconstructed memory of a firsthand experience, can illuminate a heretofore suppressed past even if not in its originary form. Such a dismissal is likely to lead to a condition Dominick LaCapra observed in the German *Historikerstreit* over European memory and the history of Nazism. In his commentary on historians' texts on everyday life under the Nazi regime, LaCapra argued that the "overly simple oppositions between history and 'mythical memory' or between dry reconstruction of facts and ritualization" may not only serve as a psychological defense mechanism to disavow traumatic experiences, but may also encourage the repressed to return as a supplement in a reified, uncritically valorized state.[14] In the Smithsonian debates, attempts to divert attacks by charging that opponents of the original exhibit plan were infatuated with their personal memories and that they lacked the intellectual authenticity that scientific history required inadvertently prompted the return of what had been repressed by the counterfeit distinction between history and memory. The prepared text was comprehensive and analytical, and thus objective at the level of cognitive knowledge in its explication, for instance, of the processes that led to the decision to use the bombs. It was, however, no less perspectival, engaged, and committed than the opponents' narrative. Aesthetic and moral factors came into play in the construction of knowledge on all sides.[15]

To be sure, there were a number of instances in which conservative politicians and activists deliberately refused to acknowledge the existence of certain information and records, thus precluding a more comprehensive view of the event. Distortions in this sense indeed shaped some of the most vocal oppositions to the planned exhibit. At the same time, if we direct our attention to only interrogating such misrepresentations we would miss the constitutive antagonism that structured the controversy. The crux of the Smithsonian debate centered around questions of for whom, for what objectives, and for whose community the event needed to be remembered. Many veterans, members of the Air Force Association, conservative politicians, and far-right intellectuals desired to commemorate the important mission that led America to victory. They strove to memorialize the martyrs of their sacred war and to remember the atomic bombings through the mediation of the Cold War paradigm, which justified the use of military power to achieve and maintain Pax Americana. In contrast, those who planned the canceled exhibit aspired to remember the millions of war victims, including those who were killed before and by *Enola Gay*'s mission, those who were suffering from the effects of radiation, and those who might in the future become victimized by yet another nuclear catastrophe. It is imperative, then, that we reconsider in this particular light the significance of Harwit's choice of words when he described the curators' perspective as being "more analytical, critical in its acceptance of facts." To put it differently, the originally planned narrative was framed by a specifically situated "critical" perspective on our naturalized view of history, while it also warned of the present global condition in which we find ourselves thoroughly contaminated by the nuclear.

To put it differently, the *Enola Gay* debate brought to light the predicament of representation within the liberal understanding of the public sphere and its history.[16] Contrary to the ideal of a national public sphere that operates as an open forum in which plural voices freely enter into dialogues and negotiate with each other, certain voices that insist on representation are in reality capable of drawing disproportionate authority and power from the structural positions they occupy within existing social, economic, and political arrangements, and not only from experiential truths or factual authenticity. Likewise, it urges us to attend perhaps even more urgently to some of the controversy's unintended consequences. Simply by virtue of its venue, that which is represented in a nation's official public sphere in such places as the Smithsonian is less susceptible to questions about partiality. This was indeed the case with knowledge about the military comfort system, which was produced and disseminated by NHK through its censored program discussed in chapter 3. Given the reality that their representation of history was in the end disallowed at the museum, there is risk in even acknowledging that the position taken by Harwit and the other curators was grounded in "critical" perspectives.

This uneven ascription of constructiveness and partiality to different historical representations was fully in evidence when conservative politicians and veterans repeatedly criticized the "presentism" and "historical relativism" of the prepared text. They argued that one cannot apply the Vietnam War generation's 1990s sensitivity to reconstruct the history of the 1940s.[17] Similarly, in a testimony that I discuss below in more detail, retired U.S. Air

Force Major General Charles W. Sweeney, a member of the *Enola Gay* crew and the commander of the Nagasaki mission, alleged that the revisionists' intrusion into even this very patriotic site was caused by "the advancing erosion of our history, of our collective memory."[18] What is remarkable in this statement is that while it betrays the intimate association between a nation's history and the memory possessed by a specific collectivity, at the same time it authorizes the historicist position by grounding the speaker's perspective on experiential truths, thereby castigating the "presentist" view of history as an inauthentic construction. In their study on the production and consumption of Colonial Williamsburg, Eric Gable, Richard Handler, and Anna Lawson succinctly summarize the danger I am describing here: "A relativizing rhetoric—in this case, an explicit recognition of historical 'presentism'—seems easier to apply to the cultures and histories of minorities than to those of the mainstream."[19] Peter Novick's historical account of the way the question of objectivity has been transfigured primarily in the U.S. academic sphere is equally helpful in understanding the hegemonic tendency of misappropriating those arguments that take into account the aesthetic dimensions, positionality, and constructedness of knowledge. Given the post–World War II condition Novick described, in which the empiricism of the social sciences came to stand in for objectivism to offer a vital source of ideological and intellectual legitimation, it is not surprising that attacks against "anti-American" ideals and ways of life are articulated as positivist critiques against constructionist arguments.[20]

The Smithsonian controversy thus eloquently demonstrated that one cannot effectively seek proper representation in the national public sphere solely by claiming to possess knowledge that is grounded on factual authenticity. To subscribe to the distinction between factual history and imaginary commemoration—an opposition enabled by simple trust in the power of facticity—is problematic precisely because it can prove debilitating when trying to prevail over those who adhere to diametrically opposed understandings of history. Moreover, as observed in the Smithsonian dispute, to rationalize the demand for representation in the public sphere by grounding one's legitimacy on factual authenticity alone may unwittingly help perpetuate the myth that the subaltern history is more partial, conjectural, and constructed than mainstream history. The recovery and accumulation of knowledge about the past—what Walter Benjamin called the "additive" method of universal history—do not themselves automatically produce new knowledge and sensibilities. As much as the question of how much we know about the past, what matters is inquiring into the historically conditioned discourses that set the parameter of knowledge and through which we come to an awareness of that past.

Warped Politics

The dissension over whether it was necessary and justifiable for the United States to use atom bombs against the two Japanese cities is often explained reductively as a clash of national differences in historical outlook. In the Smithsonian dispute it was common to portray the disagreement as reflecting a "U.S.-Japan gap."[21] At times scholarly arguments were also perceived through the national affiliations of their proponents, as if individual scholars represented the views upheld by an entire nation. The tendency to regard the disparities in perceptions and memories of Hiroshima and Nagasaki as corresponding isomorphically to national differences has governed the popular discourse on the Smithsonian controversy. For the offended veterans and their supporters in the United States, compassion for those who suffered at ground level as a result of the *Enola Gay*'s mission was often considered as under the influence of the "Japanese" viewpoint. Likewise, in Japanese-language news reports—as the expression "[the differing] atom-bomb perceptions between the Japanese and American nations" (*Nichibei ryōkokukan no genbakukan*) illustrates—the clash of opinions continued to be represented and understood within national frames.[22]

Yet it is also true that reporting on the Smithsonian debates simultaneously revealed that the national boundaries of collective memories have constantly been infiltrated. In the Japanese-language media the controversy has offered opportunities for people in Japan to rethink a simple nationalized perspective on history. Practically every major newspaper reported on the intense negotiations between the museum staff and their advisers on the one hand, and representatives of the American Legion, the Air Force Association, and conservative historians and journalists on the other. The newspapers and journals published their own interviews with individuals who protested publicly against Congress's intervention in curatorial research and intellectual engagements. Detailed reports on the controversy's background moreover explained that censures against sympathetic portrayals of Japanese casualties in the prepared texts were not generated solely by World War II veterans, but had been fostered by a series of recent neoconservative turns in U.S. society, including the patriotic reemphasis in history education, anti-immigrant sentiments exemplified by the passing of Proposition 187 in California, intensifying anti-abortion terrorism, and attacks on affirmative action. Later in the year, when a Japanese student initiated a public symposium with its own exhibits on Hiroshima and Nagasaki at American University in Washington, the news media in both countries very quickly introduced the alternative exhibits' contents along with accounts of yet another counterexhibit on the Rape of Nanjing that was organized by protesting Chinese Americans. Unlike conventional stories, therefore, the disputes over the Smithsonian's planned exhibit were reported as reflecting dissension within American society and helped debunk the prevailing perception that the United States upholds a single unified view about Hiroshima, Nagasaki, and other related nuclear matters.[23]

Evidence of this transnational penetration and the national censoring of memory processes can be found in the language and activities of those who supported as well as those who opposed the initial Smithsonian plans. Several NASM staff members visited Hiroshima and Nagasaki at an early planning stage. By borrowing artifacts from the two cities, the curators sought to add a ground-level perspective to the pilot's-eye view of the atomic explosions. The latter's aerial images had thus far dominated American memory of Hiroshima and Nagasaki.[24] The curators also hoped to complicate that historical moment so as to remember it not solely as the war's last act, but as simultaneously the inaugural event in the subsequent nuclear age. However, for conservative politicians, journalists, academics, veterans, and others who opposed the display of photographs depicting what they saw as "Japanese" victimization, the Smithsonian curators' contact with the former enemy was nothing less than an "un-American" move. Herman G. Harrington, the chairman of the American Legion's National Internal Affairs Commission, for instance, angrily denounced what he saw as the museum curators' willingness to "conform to the Japanese perspective" when they attempted to borrow artifacts from Hiroshima and Nagasaki.[25]

At the same time, while some tried to limit the Smithsonian debate to the U.S. national context,[26] those who opposed the exhibit frequently made transnational citations, so to speak, for their arguments. They attempted to justify their demands to eliminate artifacts and photographs that showed the effects of the atom bombs on humans by calling attention to present Japanese amnesia about the nation's past conduct, both before and during the war. Unless one elaborated on the "historical contexts" leading to the bombs' use, they argued, displays of the Hiroshima and Nagasaki destructions would only contribute to the historical understanding they saw as prevalent in Japan, namely, that the Japanese were solely victims and not perpetrators of war atrocities. The opponents of the ground-level exhibits thus linked their resistance to the American remembering of the atomic bombing as a civilian atrocity to what they saw as Japan's inability to apologize for past wrongs.

Major General Sweeney's testimony before the U.S. Senate Committee on Rules and Administration illustrates the case well. He identified what he found problematic about the text prepared by the museum by referring to the situation in Japan. Replicating the orthodoxy of the global World War II historical memory, Sweeney argued that knowing the "facts" and understanding the historical context leading up to the destruction would make one appreciate why it was necessary for President Truman to decide to use the bombs. He recounted Japan's invasion of China and other parts of Asia for the purpose of building the Greater East Asia Co-Prosperity Sphere and the numerous instances of plunder, torture, and massacres that took place throughout the area, beginning with Nanjing. The testimony mentioned the "sneak" attack on Pearl Harbor, together with the loss of American servicemen in Saipan, Iwo Jima, and Okinawa. Furthermore, it emphasized that Japan had not surrendered despite the commencement of air raids on Japan's major cities. It should be underscored that at one point such details of the longer trajectory of war prior to the bombing were included in the museum's script. The purpose of Sweeney's recounting, then, was to remind the Japanese of what he believed they had forgotten.

Sweeney asked why conflicts continued to occur about the necessity of dropping the atomic bombs despite the American consensus that doing so had ended the war. He answered this question in the following way:

> Fifty years after their defeat, Japanese officials have the temerity to claim they were the victims. That Hiroshima and Nagasaki were the equivalent of the Holocaust.
>
> And believe it or not, there are actually some American academics who support this analogy, thus aiding and giving comfort to a 50-year attempt by the Japanese to rewrite their own history, and *ours* in the process.
>
> There is an entire generation of Japanese who do not know the full extent of their country's conduct during World war [sic] II.
>
> This explains why they do not comprehend why they must apologize.[27]

He then cited such matters as the "comfort women" issue and the biological experiments on Allied POWs as cases for which the Japanese have failed to apologize properly. He concluded: "In a perverse inversion, by forgetting our own history, we contribute to the Japanese amnesia, to the detriment of both our nations."[28]

In his transnational citation of Japan's historical amnesia, Sweeney maintained that remembering only Japanese victimization in Hiroshima and Nagasaki occludes Japanese aggression in war, including the almost fifteen-year duration of military and colonial expansion, which began at the turn of the century. Sweeney's reasoning is remarkable in that it employs the same arguments that, as we have seen throughout the book, Japan's multiple publics have routinely used to counter the cluster of deeply entangled issues that have contributed to the Japanese government officials' and political elites' repeated disavowal of the loss and destruction wrought by Japanese colonialism and the atrocities committed by the Japanese imperial army during the war. Some progressive citizens of Japan, including some survivors of the Hiroshima and Nagasaki bombings, have reflected that remembering a historical event exclusively in terms of victimization may lead to the mystification of other dimensions of the nation's history and its present condition. Their conviction that securing memories of Japan's imperial violence in school textbooks and other public apparatuses that produce National History is inseparably linked to the radicalization of ideas and practices associated with antimilitarism, antiracism, and radical democracy. For those who are engaged in counteramnes(t)ic practices in Japan, the act of remembering Japan's military and colonial violence constitutes an integral part of critical reflection on the legacy of Japanese imperialism as well as Japan's postwar neocolonial economic exploitations in Asia and the Pacific.

The irony, then, is that in the Japanese context the politics advanced by those who have pushed for redress and who have long questioned their country's inability to fathom the suffering it inflicted on the people of Asia and the Pacific Islands are primarily aligned with the oppositional politics of the progressives and the liberal to radical left who have long antagonized the pro–United States Cold War regime. They have long challenged the Japanese orthodoxy of the conservative just-war narrative that regards the Asia-Pacific War as not a war of invasion, but as a war of self-defense and for the emancipation of Asia from Western imperialism (see chapter 3). Thus in the Smithsonian dispute it was as if U.S. conservatives who attacked the Smithsonian staff had taken up the claims of progressives in Japan, "warping" the latter's politics to aid different or sometimes even opposing political ends. The contradiction I am trying to identify here can be summarized as follows: as a result of its transference into a different national public sphere, the critical discursive practice in one national context became appropriated in support of a political position that was unintended, often resulting in contradictory political effects. In other words, the transnational movement of ideas created a warping in politics.

This warping has a number of troubling effects. To transnationally transfer a critique situated in one context and to ventriloquize it in another obscures the way in which the problem that the critique originally set out to question may very well be found, albeit in different forms, in the context into which it has been transferred. As a result, the uncritical transnational citation comes to the aid of self-mystifying nationalism—an effect which participates in the occlusion of many issues that can and need to be addressed across national and other borders. Such warps, in other words, obscure the fact that the problems of knowledge associated with histories of violence and historical amnesia plague not only other nations, but ours as well; and that they need to be addressed in a critical transnational fashion, as questions not only common across different nationalisms but as conditions sustained by mutual collusions. Warps render invisible the ways in which seemingly opposed nationalisms, as well as many other elements in the nation-state-centered global order, are in fact interconnected and mutually constitutive.

Despite their antipodal appearance, the selective amnesia Sweeney identified in Japan in many respects intersects with the forgetfulness found in the United States. Those in the United States who opposed displays of atomic bomb victims tended to share an arbitrary and selective amnesia about the American history of colonial and military aggression. This is evident in some of the basic assumptions concerning the U.S. role in Asia and the Pacific that underpinned not only this particular testimony, but also other similar arguments deployed by many others to attack the planned exhibit. Although it interrogated Japan's colonial invasions, Sweeney's narrative omitted any mention of the United States' self-interest and imperial expansion into the Asia-Pacific region, including its capitalist drive to secure markets in China and how it often aided and relied on the Japanese subimperial presence. It condemned the Japanese military's attack on Pearl Harbor but ignored the questions of how the United States had secured colonial possessions in the Pacific Islands, including Hawai'i, and why a U.S. naval base existed there. Nowhere in his testimony, or by extension in other accounts objecting to the ground-level exhibit, can we find any reference to the history of U.S. Cold War interventions in postwar transitional justice and how the U.S. dominance short-circuited the redress people in Asia and the Pacific were entitled to claim. In other words, the binational warping hides the complicity with which American and Japanese nationalisms and imperial investments in fact mutually coproduce amnesia about their histories of colonialism and military expansion in the Asia-Pacific. The binational warping of political positions, in short, is an effect that results from the ways in which national and transnational framings of historical narratives deflect our analyses away from histories of global capitalism, military expansion, colonialism, and xenophobic nationalism that do not only run parallel but actually collude across national borders. The narrating of history premised on the self-contained national unit also allows the victimization of one segment of a society to stand for the victimization of the entire national collectivity. What is at stake, ultimately, is this: insofar as the assumptions of National History remain unquestioned, it will not be possible to recognize that during most of the twentieth century, the conservatives in the United States (which has sought, for instance, to obstruct "nonpatriotic" activities) and the conservatives in Japan (which continue to suppress dissenting practices, including opposition to the monarchy) are in many respects complicit with each other in their capitalist and nationalist endeavors.

Sweeney's Senate hearing testimony summarily expresses the widely shared conviction that, if Americans are to properly discipline the Japanese to possess a correct view of history, we as Americans, too, ought to seize unadulterated knowledge about our National History. Sweeney maintained that it was precisely because his country used the atomic weapons when it did that the Japanese people were able to receive various benefits in the postwar years. The lengthy testimony stated that the atomic bombings saved Japanese lives and rescued the Japanese people from fanatic militarist rule. It also alluded to the view that the American supremacy achieved by use of the atom bombs deterred a Soviet occupation and prevented Japan from becoming Communist, while establishing the conditions for Japan's subsequent democratic reforms and incredibly swift economic recovery. According to this narrative—one shared by a considerable portion of pro–United States conservatives and centrist liberals in Japan—Japanese people are expected to be as grateful to the United States for its "benevolent" and timely use of the atom bombs as other liberated Asians and the Pacific Islanders.[29] In short, the Smithsonian controversy produced yet another rehearsal of the Cold War epistemology that has long framed the historical sensibilities and geopolitical knowledge about the war and its afterlives. It reiterated the midcentury idea of American justice by insisting that the U.S. nuclear umbrella and its military supremacy shielded the region against the Soviet and Chinese threats while facilitating the economic development of Japan and other U.S. Cold War allies.

It may be worthwhile observing what happened at the other end of the binational warping. In the first draft of the plan for the Smithsonian exhibit, one phrase indicated that the United States fought the war in the Pacific in ways that were fundamentally different from the war waged against Germany and Italy. The draft stated that Americans had fought the war against the Japanese as a "war of vengeance. For most Japanese, it was a war to defend their unique culture against Western imperialism."[30] This phrase appeared in the script as an ironic summary of the way Japanese self-lauding nationalists' view of the Asia-Pacific War as a war of defense in effect serves as gross justification for the atrocities Japan committed during the war.[31] The historian Martin Sherwin, among others, advocated contextualizing this phrase, particularly for a Japanese audience.[32] Sherwin's intervention was an especially important one, for even while placing Japanese aggression within the broader historical context of the Western imperialist expansion into Asia and other parts of the world that preceded it, he also precluded appropriation of this historicization by the Japanese revisionists. In other words, Sherwin's cautionary remarks to the Japanese audience sought to deter yet another warping of politics by obstructing the dovetailing of the U.S. revisionist historians' progressive position, which was skeptical of the promises of the nuclear age, with that of the Japanese far-right militarists and conservatives.

The assaults on the NASM staff continued despite the fact that the curators, from a very early stage in the negotiations, agreed to incorporate what were often called the absent "historical contexts" into their exhibit narratives. The infuriated members of the American Legion, the Air Force Association, Congress, and a number of journalists and academics challenged what they saw as the NASM curators' "un-American" and insulting attitude toward the glorious accomplishments of former political leaders and soldiers. The conservative offensive did not subside until all displays of Japanese casualties were removed and Director Harwit was forced to resign. According to the *Washington Post* editorial of August 14, 1994, cited earlier, the museum's critics charged that the planned exhibit would "build sympathy for the Japanese" by portraying the *Enola Gay* mission as the cause of "death, radiation sickness, despair and the beginning of nuclear terror."[33] Tom Crouch, chairman of the NASM Aeronautics Department, who had played a central role in designing the prepared exhibit, astutely observed that the critics continued to be offended not so much by how the story about the ground-level destruction was presented, as that the "whole story" was told.[34]

The Smithsonian controversy was primarily an American disagreement over the parameters of U.S. National History and what a nation should remember and not remember in order to properly commemorate the past war. Ultimately, the way the dispute came to a close reaffirmed the tenacity of the Cold War legacy and the way it reproduces, through the maintenance of America's "good war" narrative, consensus over historical knowledge about use of the atomic bombs and its aftermath. Resistance to the heterodoxy of National History, however, was part of the broader backlash against interdisciplinary critical thinking in U.S. academia. What was perceived to be seriously alarming about the cancelled exhibit was in fact intimately linked to the type of emerging critical scholarship, largely categorized as cultural studies, which was gaining increasing intellectual attention and even some institutional ground in the human and social sciences at the time. Nothing better illustrates this point than the flamboyant "linguistic turn" in Sweeney's Senate testimony. He censured his foes, arguing that to remember the Japanese not just as villains but also as victims of the U.S. atom bombings was an "assault on our language and history by the elimination of accurate and descriptive words." It was, he maintained, equivalent to saying "Up is Down, Slavery is Freedom, Aggression is Peace"; in contrast, fifty years ago, "the threat was clear, the enemy well defined."[35] This striking problematization signals that the discomfit generated by the atom bombs' "whole story" in fact concerned the broader condition of U.S. academia. Though perhaps entirely unwittingly, it extended much further beyond the commemorative exhibit's time and location.

Cast broadly and rather vaguely as cultural studies, the critical intellectual inquiries that characterized cutting-edge scholarship of the 1990s pushed for the further radical rethinking and complicating of our familiar knowledge, analytical categories, and disciplinary boundaries. These inquiries questioned the transparency of taken-for-granted knowledge in the study of history, modernity, and social identities. Cultural studies' discomfort, however, did not stem merely from the shock of the destabilization of signs or the denaturalization and defamiliarization of accepted knowledge. The cultural critic Rey Chow has observed that ever since works by the Centre for Contemporary Cultural Studies at Birmingham traveled to North America in the eighties, four "prominent types of analyses" developed. They include the critique of Orientalism initiated by Edward Said; inquiries into subaltern identities complicated by Gayatri Spivak; the investigation of "minority discourses" by Gilles Deleuze, Félix Guattari, David Lloyd, Abdul Jan-Mohamed, and others; and the rendering of colonial cultures and empires as hybrid and hence inherently unstable by Homi Bhabha and others. In Chow's view, despite their enormous diversity the four prominent cultural studies rubrics share a proximity to poststructural "theory," which is rooted in the continental philosophy.[36] And yet, Chow provocatively asked, why it is that such scholars as Harold Bloom, "who, during the 1960s and 1970s, were staunch promoters and defenders of what is called 'theory' when theory itself was derogated and attacked by reactionary humanists as some metaphysical garbage that found its way from continental Europe to higher education sectors of North American society," today brandish such negative sentiments toward cultural studies?[37]

Chow identified two reasons. One, cultural studies is seen as "a kind of dangerous supplement to poststructuralist theory" (4). In other words, cultural studies is considered to be dangerous and disturbing, according to Chow, because it exposes the tacit Eurocentrism of postmodern theories even in its radical "epistemological subversiveness" (5). Secondly, cultural studies obliges the postmodernists to see the material violence embedded in the history of colonialism and racialized modernity which precedes the violence of signs and the system of meanings problematized by postmodern theories. In other words, cultural studies prompts particularly negative responses because it brings to the fore the longue durée of geohistorical violence disavowed by many who sought security and comfort in the political unconscious of intellectual Eurocentricity, which underpinned the universalistic claim to "theory." Closely engaging with the historical material dimension of culture and signs, cultural studies' poststructuralism thus asks, to take Sweeney's example: whether what we have assumed to be the progress of civilization (read "up") might instead connote a regression toward barbarism (read "down"), as Walter Benjamin and other critical theorists would argue; whether what has been uncritically acclaimed as liberation from the old regime might in fact entail our enslavement to an oppressive society of self-surveillance and control (read "slavery is freedom"), as Michel Foucault would have it; or whether what has been unproblematically promoted as the means to achieve peace might be inseparable from tools of aggression (read "aggression is peace"), as the Smithsonian curators tried to call into question.

Without making any substantive or explicit reference to the intellectual dynamics of cultural studies, when Newt Gingrich declared "victory" in the Smithsonian controversy, his defense of the stable American National History therefore needs to be situated in the above 1990s academic milieu. In his anti-intellectual debasement of American populism and the (mis) appropriation of what he believed to be the subaltern voice, Gingrich insisted that "the *Enola Gay* fight was a fight, in effect, over the reassertion by most Americans that they're sick and tired of being told by some cultural elite that they ought to be ashamed of their history."[38] More than a mere celebration of the victory of patriotism, this paternalistic gesture of speaking on behalf of the people should be understood as exultation over the successful defense of the epistemic stability of the language of National History against the infiltration of critical and self-reflective inquiries. Perhaps this best explains why the conservative elites concluded that the controversy had ended in a victory over academic "political correctness."[39] In short, the Smithsonian dispute ended in the defeat of those who sought critical rethinking, those who questioned the self-evident, the naturalized social identities, and history's inevitability. The victorious, then, were those who successfully defended habitual thinking against the heterogeneous and alien elements that threatened to obfuscate the contours of conventional knowledge. It is in this sense that the controversy centering on the Smithsonian ought to be understood as but one symptom of America's still waging culture wars.

Toward a Conjunctive Critique of the Transpacific

The normative grammar of American National History interpellates subjects who understand that the use of nuclear weapons against Hiroshima, and to a lesser extent Nagasaki, saved lives and was necessary to bring Japan to surrender. Historical studies have shown for quite some time that the Truman administration was aware that Japan had already indicated its terms of surrender through different intermediaries, including the Soviet government, which did not officially revoke its neutrality with Japan until April 1945, and that the official narrative of the bomb's inevitability was crafted ex post facto to avert postwar international criticism. The notion that only the U.S. atomic bombing could have ended the war, a belief which carried enormous poignancy among many who were subjected to the immediate violence of the occupying Japanese army, came to form an official consensus in the aftermath of the Asia-Pacific War. Subsequently, in spite of deep-seated grass-roots antinuclearism across the region, the suppression of the details of the bomb's immediate and long-term destructive effects helped promote the Cold War "Atoms for Peace" campaign, in which the Eisenhower administration aggressively promoted the export of nuclear-power technology to Asia. To put it differently, in American National History as well as in some prominent renditions of the transpacific memory of the Asia-Pacific War, the inauguration of the nuclear age marked by the atomic bombings of Hiroshima and Nagasaki is remembered as an act of American justice in war and peace. The Smithsonian controversy was one of many instances in which challenges to revise, negate, or question this knowledge formation have met formidable resistance. What the Senate hearing demonstrated above all is that insofar as it colludes with America's "good war" narrative, the redress culture on Japanese war crimes is inextricably intertwined with justification of the use of the atom bombs—resulting in the unredressability of the nuclear-related suffering and losses in the world after Hiroshima and Nagasaki. The "warping" of politics, in which the transborder redress culture in Asia that originated with the anticolonial and antiracist Cold War critique travels to the U.S. public spheres to endorse American exceptionalism, is a constitutive part of this entanglement.

In the Name of the Emperor (1997), a documentary on the Nanjing Massacre made by two Asian American directors, Christine Choy and Nancy Tong, offers an important alternative approach to violence and justice that responds to the urgency for effective transnational engagement and critique.[40] While often described as a film focusing on Chinese victimization at the hands of the Japanese, the documentary is also an important example of how a critical transnational remembering of the Nanjing Massacre can be made acutely relevant to challenging the world under the Anglo-American leadership that came into effect in the war's aftermath. The work also suggests how these memories might even play a part in forging new alliances of popular justice and critical thinking across nationality, ethnicity, and class.

The documentary is composed primarily of historical film footage and interviews concerning the Japanese army's atrocities in Nanjing in 1937. The film not only reconstructs conditions at the time of the massacre visually and through testimonies. It also effectively intervenes in the question of knowledge production by interrogating the processes through which forgetfulness about the event has been manufactured in Japan and elsewhere. It centers on contemporary film footage of the mass civilian killing shot by the American missionary priest John Magee to ask why the film was not fully consulted at the time of the Japanese invasion, or in the Tokyo War Crimes Trial (IMTFE), despite its adoption as evidence of atrocities, and why it had been secreted away from public knowledge ever since. The documentary uses this case to signal the overall inadequacy of postwar transitional justice for failing to consider the war responsibility of the Japanese monarch Hirohito, who was head of state and commander in chief of the imperial army during the war. This oversight, as the film demonstrates, was part of what I have been problematizing as the transwar Cold War formation. Historical records unequivocally indicate that as early as 1942 the United States already perceived instrumental value in retaining Japan's monarchy after the war's conclusion.[41] It regarded the monarchical system as a pro-capitalist, anticommunist institution that would facilitate U.S. geopolitical advancement in the war's aftermath. What is tragic then is that the Allied powers had insisted on making *unconditionality* the *condition* under which Japan would surrender, thereby making the postwar disposition of the emperor and his sovereign status uncertain. This prolonged the war and added even further catastrophic losses, especially during the war's final months. The film's title, *In the Name of the Emperor*, points to such deadly ironies. To be sure, the mass civilian killing in Nanjing was among the Japanese war crimes that were examined and prosecuted during the IMTFE. *In the Name of the Emperor* therefore does not understand marginalization of the film footage as the sole cause of the forgetting of Japanese war crimes. More important, the film suggests that the disappearance of Magee's images of Chinese victimization from global World War II memories is symptomatic of the Cold War management of knowledge about the war and its aftermath.

Echoing in many ways with the critique of the Cold War elaborated throughout this study and the historical sensibility underpinning much of the post-1990s redress culture, Choy and Tong's documentary suggests that the IMTFE was premised on a West-centric historical worldview and that it interrogated primarily Japan's crimes against the Western colonial powers. The film touches on the way the "comfort women" redress activism necessarily reveals multiply overlapping Cold War/cold war histories that resulted in the long marginalization and failure to understand the Japanese military comfort system *as* an egregious violation. By showing how the United States has been implicated in the process, the documentary convincingly demonstrates how Cold War geopolitics suppressed in Asian countries over many years progressive leftist movements—including those active in immediate postwar Japan—that had tried to expose Japan's military and colonial violence.

The documentary furthermore raises a series of "what if" questions regarding memory and history. By interrogating the peripheral status of Magee's film in the postwar decades, and by extension, the marginalization of knowledge concerning the Nanjing Massacre, it asks, what if Magee's film footage was fully consulted both during the war itself and in the postwar trial? Had it not been for the Cold War, could the immense suffering of the Chinese people resulting from the Japanese military invasion have been more thoroughly imbedded in memory and law? Or, in turn, if evidence of the Nanjing Massacre and other instances of Chinese victimization had been more properly disseminated, might the Cold War management of the war's aftermath, decolonization, and the post–World War II international order taken a different and more just course? In conjunction with the Smithsonian controversy, such an epistemic challenge, and the way the film unleashes the unthought of hegemonic knowledge, can moreover be extended to the way we understand the war's conclusion. The orthodox World War II narrative has customarily asked, "what if Americans did not use the atom bombs?" to reach the consensus that without the two bombs the Japanese would not have surrendered in a timely fashion. In contrast, the documentary's focus on the status of sovereignty reminds us that we have not asked often enough the other possible "what if" question: if the United States and the Allies had not made unconditionality the absolute condition, how soon might Japan have surrendered and how many more lives might have been saved in the war's myriad locations? Such an epistemic exercise brings to light that historiographies have not eschewed the "what if" questions but posed them unevenly and one-dimensionally, especially when it comes to the triumphalist narrative of the use of the atom bombs.

Finally, while holding Japan's political elites and governmental bodies absolutely accountable for their misconduct, Choy and Tong furthermore refuse to represent nations as uniform and undivided subjects. Concerning the crimes committed by the Japanese military, the documentary reminds its viewers that the state-corporate political and economic elites' interests in Japan and the United States were in fact accomplices in promoting forgetfulness. And even as the film makes it unequivocally clear that the Japanese army committed racialized atrocities against those identified as enemy Chinese, it highlights one woman survivor's witness account to emphasize that the experience of the atrocity was at the same time inflected by class, to the extent that the wealthy and resourceful were able to flee the city before its fall to the invading Japanese. At the same time, while condemning the Japanese government's decades-long refusal to acknowledge the mass civilian killing as a "massacre," the two directors do not fail to describe the activism by which Japanese progressive historians have for many years interrogated the statist occlusion of Japan's wartime atrocities. The two directors point out that there is a long intra-Asia and transpacific transnational genealogy of activism on the issue of historical justice that involves feminists, labor activists, and other progressives in Korea, Japan, and Asian/American communities. In this way, Choy and Tong effectively prevent memories of the Nanjing Massacre from becoming instrumentalized by an internally homogeneous ethnonational collectivity and its victimology. Filled with abundant catachronic moments, their film may be viewed as an instance of what the late historian Miriam Silverberg once termed an "associative history," a method of history that transgresses national and other borders of identitarian categories and is attentive to the deep entanglement of cotemporaneous processes, interlocking relations, and interconnected genealogies.[42]

Perhaps one of the most valuable outcomes of the mid-1990s Smithsonian dispute is that the incident generated a sense of urgency for envisaging transpacific and transnational—or more precisely post-Statist—public spheres in which diverse memories of historical violence might intersect and be shared coalitionally. The crafting of such spaces will help us discern the critical ways of remembering that have been banned in order for the orthodoxy of National History to be maintained. To forge a position suspicious of epistemologies that confine our memory work to the boundaries of the state, nationhood, and other sources of social identification and interpellation will also keep us from resorting to patriotic appeals when seeking legitimation, as some historians involved in the Smithsonian debates inadvertently did when countering accusations that their activities were "un-American."[43] Crucially, the Smithsonian controversy demonstrated the need to distinguish critical transnationalism from transnational ventriloquism.

This final question pertains to many of this book's discussions. What kind of warping of politics, for instance, might the critique of the Americanization of the "comfort women" redress discourse instigate when it travels to Japan? It is one thing to be wary of the Asian/Americanization of Japanese war crimes and its effect on the discourse of Asian assimilation and American exceptionalism (chapter 4). But to ventriloquize the same critique without critically situating it in Japan where conservative revisionists hold representative power is another matter (chapter 3). And yet, if we refrain from challenging U.S. nationalism, racism, and paternalism out of fear that such a critique might inadvertently come to the aid of an unintended politics, we compromise the ability to interrogate the complicity of conservative nationalists in the United States and Japan, who continue to sustain institutionalized and epistemic Cold War formations. Historical sensibilities found in Okinawa under U.S. occupation illuminate the urgency of addressing precisely such transpacific complicities by revealing how violence and justice intersect. They simultaneously highlight the predicament that, given Okinawa's liminality, such an address cannot but risk being marshalled into neat alliances with already established politics, languages, and other institutionalized categories (chapter 1). Similarly, if we were to simply reiterate the language of American gender justice and the women's human rights regime against their antifeminist detractors without coming to grips with the history of violence and the dialectics of (un)redressability that are constitutive of the universalist ideals of rights, freedom, and liberation, we would remain powerless to confront the new faces of imperialism in other contexts that might assert sovereign power in the form of protecting other humans and other women (chapter 2).

What the above investigations have suggested, therefore, are the vexing risks of transnational critique. They remind us of the need to be vigilant about the ways in which a situated critique proven transformative in one context might participate in an entirely different configuration of knowledge and power in another. Such a critical imagination and acuity to the situatedness of knowledge, however, cannot be gained without attention to the connectivities and specificities that make up each geohistorical context. Accountability to history, then, must also entail the commitment to such an unwieldy but vitally important task of multilayered critical historical thinking. To coalesce the denationalized and discrepant yet entwined historical memories into an intelligible and effectively politicizing narrative, as Choy and Tong managed to do in their documentary, requires labor. It also asks us for patience and humility toward the unseen. But it is a task well worthwhile undertaking.

Epilogue

Many Americans are now aware...that the dropping of the atomic bombs on Japan was not necessary....How better to make a contribution to amends than by offering Japan the means for the peaceful utilization of atomic energy. How better, indeed, to dispel the impression in Asia that the United States regards Orientals merely as nuclear cannon fodder!
Peter Kuznick, Washington Post, 1954

It is therefore quite significant, a structural element in the realm of human affairs, that men are unable to forgive what they cannot punish and that they are unable to punish what has turned out to be unforgivable.
Hannah Arendt, The Human Condition

No other image more fabulously captures post-Cold War redress culture than the late Kang Duk-Gyeong's (Kang Tŏk-kyŏng) painting, "Punish the Responsible—For Peace."[1] Kang publicly identified herself as a former "comfort woman" in 1992. She then moved into the House of Sharing (Nanum Jip), a residential collective which a Buddhist association initiated for the support of aging survivors.[2] Until she succumbed to terminal lung cancer in 1997 at the age of sixty-nine, Kang spent her final years leading weekly rallies in front of the Japanese embassy in Seoul, calling for an unequivocal state apology and reparations from the Japanese government.[3] Kang also produced a series of paintings dedicated to the lives and afterlives of those who perished under the

Japanese military comfort system. "Punish the Responsible," which appears on the book's cover, portrays an imaginary scene of execution. Hannah Arendt famously aligned forgiveness and punishment as opposed to vengeance. While vengeance is an automatic and passive reaction to wrongdoing, for Arendt forgiving and punishing, though far from equivalent, are both creative interventions that are neither conditioned nor prescribed by the original context to which one is responding. It is an act, in her words, "to put an end to something that without interference could go on endlessly."[4] In Kang's piece, too, punishment is not tantamount to vengeance. Indeed, as an alternative to forgiveness, punishment must be available to those against whom the violence has been perpetrated. This is especially so as a matter of practice, given that the Japanese government has never asked its victims for forgiveness, thus long precluding the latter from becoming the sovereign of justice (chapter 3). Making the wartime Japanese military comfort system punishable, furthermore, has the potential to put an end to otherwise habitualized practices and what has been unthought, in this case, the impunity automatically afforded to violences committed against those in a carceral state of exception. Kang's painting has thus offered an affective ground zero, so to speak, in the aftermath of the Asian Women's Fund and inspired many into renewed redress activism, including those who established the 2000 Women's International War Crimes Tribunal on Japan's Military Sexual Slavery.[5]

Despite its surreal style, the embodied images in "Punish the Responsible" are often deemed to have a straightforward and monovalent referent. The blindfolded man in khaki military uniform is said to represent the Japanese military leaders, including the Japanese monarch and commander in chief.[6] White doves, the icon of peace, congregate around the tree with their piercing gaze, as if to ascertain the execution. Witness to the unspeakability of organized sexual violence, Kang's work at once mourns the loss and condemns the Japanese government's obdurate refusal to commit to full-fledged redress. In this sense, "Punish the Responsible" reflects the normative call for State-led justice, which the author collectively shared with many former "comfort women." It is thus not difficult to read the artwork's message as suggesting that justice and peace will be restored with proper prosecution and punishment.

Yet, why does an ominous air rather than triumphant jubilation prevail? The tree to which the military man is tied is dark and lifeless yet uncannily robust. His legs are melded into the tree's roots, which grow tenaciously in the soil as if to foretell the man's persistence even after execution. At the gloomy treetop is a nest where the doves have laid their eggs. White doves, according to the artist, are the reincarnated souls of the former "comfort women." But their redemption may be overshadowed by the perniciousness which engulfs the tree's roots. Viewed in this way, the scene of execution is where the historical amnesia of violence commences. Also, the curious question of who is doing the punishing remains. It is suggestive that the executioners are faceless in Kang's painting. It is not obvious to the viewers whether the hands aiming pistols at the prosecuted represent states, the peace keeping forces, the police, or other familiar agents of the international criminal justice system. Insofar as the prosecutors remain faceless and thus unnamable, this fable-like image of the tree of execution may indeed be alluding to the possibility of popular justice beyond obviously available means and conventions. Kang's work, then, opens up a number of difficult questions concerning the illegibility of violence, the limits of criminalization, the cycle of impunity, and above all the meaning of justice beyond judicialization. Resisting interpretive certitudes and the foreclosure of meanings, the painting invites us to ask what is being punished, on whose behalf, by what means, and with what far-reaching intended and unintended consequences.

Compelled in part by the profound tension Kang's artwork suggests between redress's multivalence and singularity, *Cold War Ruins* has examined the multiple ideas, agents, and practices of justice concerning the history of Japanese military and colonial violence in order to consider their complex effects on the politics of culture and knowledge. If, as historical records have clearly indicated, the Cold War impaired postwar transitional justice, to what extent can we understand renewed calls for historical justice since the 1990s as facilitating or disrupting the transpacific entanglements that are rooted in post–World War II institutional and epistemic formations? The longer trajectory of redress activism has illuminated that postwar transitional justice ushered in a regime of il/legibility which has rendered some cases of violence against specific bodies invisible while spectacularizing others. What does it mean, then, to rectify the divides between the legibilities and illegibilities of violence, loss, and injustice through the available terms of law, the State, and ethnonations? What are some of the transnational and extrajuridical practices and imaginaries that challenge the ways in which certain historical injuries have been rendered unredressable, that is, both beyond redress and not requiring redress? How can redress, apologies, and reparations be achieved without relegitimating the institutions and other arrangements that were responsible for the original injustices that now demand rectification? In what ways might we make redress efforts for past wrongs urgently relevant to questioning presently unfolding injustices? These have been some of the overarching questions guiding my inquiry.

Instead of limiting the question of unredressability to the metaphysical level, *Cold War Ruins* has attended to concrete geohistorical contexts and directed universalistic concerns for justice, trauma, and irreparability toward situated questions of power and knowledge production. Throughout the pages of the book, I have deployed conjunctive cultural critique to capture the not-so-obvious linkages and connections among the incommensurable losses, injuries, grievings, and pursuits for redress. My investigations have transgressed conventional periodizations, ethnonational boundaries, and statist geopolitical orderings of the world. Such an approach has required a particular kind of vigilance. It asks readers to eschew humanist or other universalized versions of history, as well as to resist the path whereby different collectivities might mutually cancel out accountabilities for their past wrongdoings. It is my hope that, at the very least, the preceding pages have demonstrated the possibilities of a historical inquiry through which we can address past instances of violence in their distinct singularities and local specificities, while remaining critically perceptive of the way their genealogies complexly intersect with other violences and apparent nonviolences.

Cold War Ruins developed over many years of engagement, both inside and outside formal academia, with issues broadly related to memories of war and colonialism. Dissensus over war and colonial memories has often manifested as culture wars in different nationalized public spheres. Following the inauguration of the Japan Society for History Textbook Reform, Japanese legislators passed a law in 1999 that recognized Hinomaru and "Kimigayo" as Japan's official national flag and national anthem. The international campaign to halt classroom adoption of the Society's new textbook, which was closely tied to protests against the national flag–national anthem legislation, drew me into the prolific world of Internet activism. The campaign regarded the legislation as part of Japan's neonationalist developments which, it was felt, would deeply though differently affect both nonnational and national denizens of Japan as well as overseas expatriates and their closest associates. I subsequently became centrally albeit unintendedly involved in the dispute over NHK's censorship of a program on the 2000 Women's

International War Crimes Tribunal on Japan's Military Sexual Slavery, the details of which I have discussed in chapter 3. At the same time, Japan's history war shared the same space and time as the American debate on the National Standards for United States History, which was initiated in 1994 by the former chair of the National Endowment for the Humanities, Lynne V. Cheney. This debate paralleled the controversy observed in chapter 5 over the commemorative exhibit at the Smithsonian Air and Space Museum. Moreover, these processes were simultaneous with the 1990s galvanization of the Korean and other diasporic Asian American communities through transnational memories of the Japanese military comfort system. If the history war waged by Japan's far right was underpinned by the disavowed violence toward racial, national, sexual, and other differences, the series of legislations and the introduction of state ballots throughout the 1990s that negatively and immanently affected migration, public health, criminal justice, and affirmative action policies in California further demonstrated for me yet again how the struggles over history and memory are closely associated with the dissensus over the boundaries of national citizenry. My concerns about the Americanization of transnational memories and efforts to redress Japanese imperial violence, in particular, the histories of wartime forced labor and so-called comfort women, initially grew out of these transpacific observations and involvements.

But I began outlining what later became the book's central argument on justice and its Americanization in the midst of America's new wars of the new century, which drew upon many previous U.S. military involvements to all too successfully mobilize the familiar tropes of justness, liberation, the ultra-enemy, and the world order. In 2001 the United States led a retaliatory military attack on the Taliban regime in Afghanistan in response to the events of September 11. The USA Patriot Act passed in the same year (extended in 2011) capitalized on the prolonged national emergency to legally expand state and police power. This enabled further surveillance measures and the curtailment of civil liberties, but especially with regard to migrants' rights and border controls even as it fueled anti-Muslim and anti-Arab sentiments. The military invasion and occupation of Iraq followed shortly after, led by the same administration whose failed disaster relief effort after Hurricane Katrina (2005) left New Orleans's already aggrieved black community and other communities of color in devastation as the city headed toward further privatization and consumerism.[7] America's new wars furthermore immediately affected military-security arrangements in and across the Pacific. Even as Japanese conservatives were rapidly garnering the informal and formal power to further militarize Japan and to defeat grassroots efforts to redress the failed justice concerning Japan's past wrongs, in 2002 the U.S. and Japanese governments reached an agreement to relocate facilities at Marine Corps Air Station Futenma, partly to Guam and partly to Henoko beach in Okinawa. These are only a few instances among many that pushed me, sometimes inadvertently, into thinking transnationally and conjunctively as I transited between the English and Japanese linguistic realms and across other translations. What became increasingly evident was that after a brief hiatus in the 1990s we were witnessing, at least in the transpacific arena, the retrenchment of Cold War structures and epistemologies, albeit with significant "amendments" to some of the ways that certain injuries have been rendered illegible and unredressable.[8] The heightened incitement into transborder redress culture, it appeared to me, needed to be scrutinized within and against this turn-of-the-new-century milieu.

America's new global war on terror led some anthropologists in the United States to interrogate the discipline's close ties to military intelligence and U.S. national security concerns on an unprecedented scale. The U.S. Army established the Human Terrain System (2007–2014) as a program to embed anthropologists in the military so as to facilitate the effective use of their expert cultural knowledge for U.S. military operations. According to a U.S. Army review, the Human Terrain System is expected to "address cultural awareness shortcomings at the operational and tactical levels by giving brigade commanders an organic capability to help understand and deal with 'human terrain'—social, ethnographic, cultural, economic, and political elements of the people among whom a force is operating."[9] A significant number of American anthropologists responded to the call to patriotic duty by enlisting, while others expressed moral faith in the discipline by recalling cultural anthropology's founding forefather, Franz Boas, who is known to have objected publicly to the mobilization of anthropologists during World War I. Still, those who organized a collective voice objecting to the military's deployment of anthropology argued that the problem of anthropological knowledge goes beyond its *application*.[10] Anthropologists, they suggested, must reckon with the intrinsic assimilability of certain kinds of anthropological knowledge to military intelligence and governance over the local populations under siege. The transwar continuity in the utility of anthropological knowledge that we explored in chapter 1 illustrated just such an assimilability. The ethnological information Alfred Tozzer, George Peter Murdock, and others produced transitioned from knowledge that had earlier served the purpose of knowing the enemy's hearts and minds in order to win the war to on-the-ground information about places and people that were to be occupied, rehabilitated, and governed. American anthropological knowledge deployed in this way helped facilitate the biopolitical selection and management of the target population, and not necessarily its extermination. And it is in these former uses that the military has found the efficacy of field-based anthropological knowledge for current programs such as the Human Terrain System.

Recent self-reflective discussions on the mobilization of anthropologists into America's current wars, however, do not easily extend to their mid-century deployment during and after the War in the Pacific. American anthropology's political unconscious, even while condemning the Cold War's manifestly illiberal aspects, remains tethered to orthodoxies of World War II as a just and "good war." Yet, as we have seen in the cases of Tozzer, Murdock, and others whose work inaugurated anthropological area studies during the transwar decade, there are connections and linkages among the different wars that America has fought since the midcentury. The geopolitical discourse of the new century, which Mahmood Mamdani has called "Culture Talk," likewise had its precedent in World War II's Pacific theater. Mamdani observed that the concept of "culture" has regained increasing primacy in problematic representations of "Islamic terrorism" in the wake of September 11, 2001.[11] Culture Talk "assumes that every culture has a tangible essence that defines it, and it then explains politics as a consequence of that essence" (17). It originates largely in two academic traditions in the United States: Orientalist studies led by Bernard Lewis, who has long served as a U.S. policy adviser on the Middle East; and the branch of political science represented by such scholars as Samuel Huntington, who famously argued that all political and territorial conflicts after the Cold War constitute what Lewis had earlier called the "clash of civilizations." Important differences notwithstanding, Mamdani succinctly sums up the way in which "Culture Talk" selectively conjoined the two schools to aid realpolitik by offering "intellectual support for the notion that there are 'good' as opposed to 'bad' Muslims, an idea that has become the driving force of American foreign policy" (23). What was ironic about the American anthropology of the midcentury war, then, is that while Tozzer and others may have advocated the "Ryukyuans" as "good Japs," a population selected within the enemy empire for its "operative usefulness," the Cold War ultimately left postwar Okinawa under the carceral regime of military occupation. By attending to such transwar connections and contradictions within anthropological and other knowledge formations we can begin to see the shared genealogies of militarization of knowledges in America's old and new wars, both "good" and not so good. More fundamentally, the critical remembering of America's midcentury involvement in Asia and the Pacific in association with the current war on terror further begs the question as to what has been at stake beyond saving lives when a just war is waged against a named collectivity the State perceives as its absolute enemy.

Although I cannot pinpoint the book's definitive origin, the title, *Cold War Ruins*, has been in place for some time. By "ruins" I not only hoped to highlight the sheer belatedness of justice and unredressability, but what that deferment might have allowed. Throughout, I have tried to point to the enabling impossibility of justice beyond the confines of the Cold War—that is, beyond the nomos of the post–World War II world we currently inhabit. A spatial and temporal concept, ruins are in fact traces of geohistorical violence. There one comes to "know" the loss but only when it is too late, after this knowledge has already been compromised and impaired. Yet when critically illuminated, ruins are repositories of debris that in the present offer wisdom associated with failed strategies, unrealized possibilities, and paths that could have but were never taken. They remind us, too, of the excisions and exclusions in what appears complete and victorious, as in the Cold War's triumphant, forward-looking ideologies—of liberation, the new international order, postcolonial nation-building, economic take-off, and so forth. The Cold War's ruins and their remainders, as I have tried to demonstrate, comprise at once the seemingly immutable institutional and intellectual premises *and* the historical skepticisms of the present they necessarily beget. Ruins are vestiges bequeathed to us that are at once liabilities endured from the past and assets for the future, both repressive and emancipatory. It is then left to each one of us to fathom the debris, but without instrumentalizing them.

If Kang's artwork, "Punish the Responsible," epitomizes the intensifying articulation of redress culture since the nineties, among the images circulating throughout the world that capture the material poignancy of the Cold War's ruins, the rubble from the Fukushima nuclear meltdown in the aftermath of the 2011 mega-earthquake and tsunami is perhaps one of the most literal and recent. Fukushima's nuclear crisis swiftly prompted a critical remembering of the transpacific history of nuclearization. It conjured up memories of the Cold War collusion between the U.S. and Japanese nuclear industrial-military-academic establishments as they promoted the use of nuclear energy across the Pacific. Earlier during the Cold War hiatus of the 1990s, the NHK television documentary *Contemporary History Scoop, Documented: Scenario for the Introduction of Nuclear Power—Nuclear Policy under the Cold War* (1994) offered a stunningly candid and detailed account of how the "Atoms for Peace" campaign successfully introduced U.S. nuclear power technology to postwar Japan. The documentary exposed the clandestine collaboration between U.S. foreign intelligence and conservative Japanese media-corporate oligarchs and politicians as they jointly worked to transform the image of nuclear technology away from the death and destruction resulting from U.S.-Japan hostilities to peace and prosperity as secured by the two states' cross-Pacific alliance. Following reports on the Fukushima meltdown, the documentary was uploaded onto blogosphere for a brief period and disseminated this important piece of Cold War history.[12] Alternative discursive networks furthermore offered narratives that recalled the asymmetrical capitalist development of modern Japan and how Fukushima and other places previously known for similar histories of underdevelopment—including Minamata, a seaside community devastated by mercury poisoning from a local chemical factory's release of contaminated wastewater during the 1950s and '60s—have had to negotiate with metropolitan desires and demands for suppliers of disposable labor, raw materials, and land.[13]

Likewise in the United States, the historian Peter Kuznick brought to light the American Cold War media opinions that had helped promote the Eisenhower administration's "Atoms for Peace" campaign. Kuznick released his timely online essay to show how the Eisenhower administration understood the strategic importance of Japan for the worldwide success of the American nuclear-power industry.[14] The 1954 *Washington Post* article, which I quoted as the epigraph for this epilogue, reveals the remarkable transvaluation the "Atoms for Peace" campaign initiated on two fronts. One concerns, of course, the biopolitical shift in the meaning of the new technology from that associated with death and annihilation to that which promotes life, civilizational comfort, and well-being. Less obvious yet central to this book's overarching discussion are the implications of the editorial's timing, that is, its publication in the immediate aftermath of the Korean War. In this new military conflict the use of nuclear weapons existed as an imminently viable strategic option for President Truman. According to the editorial, the targeted audience of the "Atoms for Peace" campaign consisted of the "Orientals" who might hold suspicions and implacable grudges against an excessive U.S. military presence. Equating exports by the U.S. nuclear industry to gestures of national atonement—a gift to "make amends"—to the nuclear-devastated Japan, the same discourse turned the "Atoms for Peace" campaign into a new technology of transpacific management.

The Cold War ruins, which were and are in the making at Fukushima and beyond, thus illuminated albeit briefly the discursive lacunae and disconnects in knowledge concerning the meaning of the nuclear in times of war and peace. They simultaneously signal the repressed transwar continuity I have been discussing between the Asia-Pacific War and the Cold War. The genealogy of the transpacific entanglement we observed in Okinawa, especially concerning the U.S. military-base issue, is inseparably linked to that of Fukushima's ongoing nuclear predicament. The two sites, moreover, are not disconnected from other Pacific locations. The reduction of U.S. troops in Okinawa has an immediate bearing on the further militarization of Guam. We have also begun to receive reports about radioactive debris reaching the U.S. northwest coastlines. Yet there are further asymmetries and divides even in the way we perceive such connectivities. The silence Teresia K. Teaiwa observed two decades ago in her analysis of the construction of the notion "B/bikini" in the aftermath of the U.S. nuclear testing in the Marshall Islands remains to prevent our metropolitan geography from imagining how irradiated currents might be affecting people throughout the Pacific Islands.[15]As I write this epilogue in winter 2014, the massive leakage of radioactive waste water generated by the Tokyo Electric Power Company (TEPCO)'s decommissioning of the Fukushima Daiichi Power Station belies Prime Minister Abe's earlier claim that the condition was "under control."[16]

Eisenhower's "Atoms for Peace" campaign, by disavowing death, displacement, and destruction, may have succeeded in helping to bring otherwise inimical Asian populations into the militarized and nuclearized space of Cold War biopolitics. And yet, as the cultural studies scholar Josen Masangkay Diaz's discussion of Bataan as a remarkable palimpsest site of deeply entwined transpacific histories cautions us, we need not accept such a process as a fait accompli. The construction of a nuclear power plant in Bataan began under the Ferdinand Marcos regime with American support. Yet, as Diaz demonstrates, the operation came to a halt with the Philippines' antidictatorial People Power Revolution, but especially through the local efforts of a group of Filipinas. They protested the construction through their bodily intimacy, by the vital "human chain" their bodies formed around the nuclear power plant.[17] Bataan is not only the iconic site of the Japanese wartime atrocity that is known as the Bataan death march. From 1980 to 1994, according to Yen Le Espiritu, the Bataan Peninsula also accommodated the Philippines Refugee Processing Center, "the most prominent transit center for almost all of the U.S.-bound refugees" from Southeast Asia.[18] The Taiwanese nuclear scientist Wen Ho Lee's case similarly evinced not only the structuring forces but also the contradictions and inherent unpredictability of transpacific nuclear connections. Lee was born in Taiwan under Japanese colonial rule, left for the United States during Chiang Kai-shek's regime, and was charged with espionage in 1999 while he was working at the University of California's Los Alamos National Laboratory. Lee's case mobilized the protests of Asian American and other communities, which understood the incident as part of the long history of anti-Asian racism.[19] The transpacific nuclear military-industry-academic complex has a shared material genealogy that can be traced back to the World War II/Cold War ruins of the Manhattan Project, which was secretly advanced in the American Northwest and aided by uranium mined from indigenous land. Localized manifestations across Asia and the Pacific are far from uniform or preordained; each demands an analysis and understanding that is attentive to intertwined geohistorical contingencies, contradictions, and serendipitous turns.

Wittingly or not, postnineties redress culture ultimately calls attention to its own negative trajectories and failures. As redress debates concerning Japan's war crimes continue to occur within the demands of Cold War international protocols, juridical standings, institutions, and habitualized knowledge, they tend to reiterate and buttress the conventional language of justice, to reproduce cultural assumptions, and to facilitate the management of redressability and its Americanization. Those elements of redress culture that tenaciously resist the Cold War regime—including, the persistent antibase discourse in Okinawa, the recalcitrant demands to clarify State accountability for the wartime military comfort system, the tenacious efforts to preserve memories of the Japanese war of invasion, the deep-seated grass-roots antinuclear activism in Asia and the Pacific Islands, and the ongoing local redress negotiations to amend the shortcomings of the previous state-sponsored redress—these will continue to be imperiled by the familiar forces of containment, foreclosure, nationalization, and assimilation. But such processes can simultaneously mobilize new and older critical engagements with earlier arrangements, thereby unsettling and potentially rendering problematic the legacy of the Cold War order of knowledge along with the global colonial constellations that extend much further into the past. As I have tried to demonstrate throughout this book, the transborder culture of redress and some of its most contentious demands have proferred a myriad of fabulous imaginaries for history, future justice, and alliances. It is then incumbent upon each of us to discern and unleash the transformative meanings they embrace if we are to counter past and present injustices, both seen and unseen.

ACKNOWLEDGMENTS

While there have been many unexpected turns, key events, and new encounters that have shaped this book's main orientation, in many ways *Cold War Ruins* inherits the theoretical concern for the politics of forgetting and remembering I explored in *Hiroshima Traces: Time, Space and the Dialectics of Memories* (Berkeley: University of California Press, 1999). It also remains loyal to many of the problematics shared in the collaborative project *Perilous Memories: The Asia-Pacific War(s)* (Durham, NC: Duke University Press, 2001). In part responding to the end of the Cold War milieu, *Perilous Memories* questioned many dominant assumptions and conventions concerning World War II memories in the Pacific theater. It challenged the prevailing binary with which the war has been remembered—in other words, as a war primarily fought between the United States and Japan—through the observations of events, subjectivities, and experiences that had been suppressed for nearly half a century since the war's end. I want to thank the contributors to *Perilous Memories* and especially the two coeditors, Geoffrey M. White and T. Fujitani, for one of the first opportunities to think collectively through, against, and beyond the Cold War/post–Cold War dialectics.

After completing *Hiroshima Traces*, I continued to publish on the politics of war memories, colonial amnesia, history wars, racism and neonationalism in Japan and the United States. Some of these writings appeared in a Japanese language volume entitled *Violence, War, Redress: Politics of Multiculturalism* (*Bōryoku, sensō, ridoresu: Tabunkashugi no poritikusu*, Tokyo: Iwanami Shoten, 2003). I was able to complete the second book relatively quickly because I had the fortune of receiving a University of California Humanities Research Institute (UCHRI) Resident Fellowship. But the UCHRI fellowship and the two quarter-length resident fellows' seminars in which I participated also opened up an entirely new horizon of inquiries such that the completion of one book project only became the beginning of another. The UCHRI seminar Redress in Literature and Social Thought was organized by Saidiya Hartman and Stephen Best, who ran the sessions concurrently with their Mellon Foundation Sawyer Seminar on a shared theme. It was through weekly exposure to stimulating conversations on the risks and possibilities of redress, specifically focusing on African American reparations, the history of transatlantic slavery, the globality of race, and antiblack violence as constitutive of American modernity that I began to appreciate transpacific redress discourse on Japanese war crimes in relationship to the long trajectories of persistent colonial, racial, and other asymmetrical arrangements. *Cold War Ruins'* overarching concern with the problem of redressability was initially formulated out of this thought process. I cannot thank Stephen and Saidiya enough. They generously took me in despite my distance from the discipline of African American studies. Thanks also to David Theo Goldberg and Lisa Lowe, who made it possible for me to participate.

Different chapters of *Cold War Ruins* benefited from the invaluable feedback I received on my visits to various institutions. These opportunities were made possible by the following friends and colleagues: Leo Ching and Aimee Kwon at Duke University, Shu-mei Shih and Françoise Lionnet at UCLA, Christina Schwenkel at UC Riverside, Lisa Rofel at UC Santa Cruz, Moon-ho Jung and Chandan Reddy at the University of Washington, Hiromi Mizuno and Roderick A. Ferguson at the University of Minnesota, Nam-lin Hur at the University of British Columbia, Igarashi Yoshikuni at Vanderbilt University, Jeff Hanes at the University of Oregon, Ken Ruoff at Portland State University, Brett Walker at Montana State University, John Davis at Michigan State University, Tomomi Yamaguchi and Hitomi Tonomura at the University of Michigan, Andre Schmid at the University of Toronto, Shih-szu Hsu and Pin-chia Feng at National Chiao Tung University, Andy Wang at Academia Sinica, Brigitte Steger and Barak Kushner at the University of Cambridge, Glenn Hook and Mika Ko at the University of Sheffield, and Chris Gerteis and Angus Lockyer at the School of Oriental and African Studies (SOAS), University of London. The SOAS session was a precious opportunity to consider Japanese women's enfranchisement under occupation in light of the then ongoing occupation of Iraq. The 2009 Korean Studies Regional Seminar in New York, Truth and Reconciliation: Remembering War Crimes on the Korean Peninsula, 1948–1953, allowed me to rearticulate my thoughts on historical justice and the question of unredressability through the complex transwar histories that led to the

Korean War. Although ill health prevented me from physically attending, I am thankful to Henry Em and Ted Hughes for having me as a discussant and to Jae-Jung Suh who invited me to submit my workshop comments for publication in a special issue of *Critical Asian Studies* 42, no. 4 (November 2010): 653–71. Some of these comments have been further developed and incorporated into this book's introduction.

The 1999 American Studies Association session, "War, Memory, and Post-Nationalist American Studies," organized by Shelley Streeby and Curtis Marez, gave me the initial insights into considering Okinawa's recent history as part of transnational American studies inquiries. Although the focus has shifted, Chapter 1 initially evolved out of this earlier conversation. The 2001 American Studies Association session, "Siting/Citing 'Comfort Women' Critically: Transnational Memories in Korea-Japan-U.S. Liaisons," was one of the first opportunities to explicitly center Asian America in my consideration of post–Cold War redress and the Americanized claim to world justice. I owe special thanks to Kandice Chuh, Laura Hyun Yi Kang, and Leti Volpp for joining me and making it happen. The session papers appeared in the *Journal of Asian American Studies'* special issue guest-edited by Kandice. Chapter 4 is an extensively revised and updated version of the article I contributed to this special issue (vol. 6, no. 1 [February 2003]: 57–93). I also wish to extend my appreciations to Keith Camacho, Christine Hong, Jodi Kim, Rika Nakamura, and Cathy Schlund-Vial, among others, for seriously engaging my rather idiosyncratic Asian American critique in their respective investigations of various transpacific connections. *Cold War Ruins* is also indebted to the new and old conversations and memorable exchanges I have had with scholars in anthropology, history, and a number of other disciplines, whose names I have not yet mentioned: Nancy Abelmann, Harumi Befu, Daniel Botsman, Oscar V. Campomanes, Kuan-Hsing Chen, Chungmoo Choi, Rey Chow, James Clifford, Bruce Cumings, Brett de Barry, Vicente M. Diaz, Arif Dirlik, James Ferguson, Norma Field, James A. Fujii, Andrew Gordon, Akhil Gupta, Hugh Gusterson, Gail Hershatter, Miyako Inouye, Marilyn Ivy, Elaine Kim, Dorinne K. Kondo, J. Victor Koschmann, John Lie, David Lloyd, Liisa Malkki, Martin F. Manalansan IV, David Palumbo-Liu, Renato Rosaldo, Sonia Ryang, Setsu Shigematsu, Marita Sturken, Tessa Morris-Suzuki, Neferti X. M. Tadiar, Yuki Tanaka, John W. Treat, Samuel Yamashita, Sylvia J. Yanagisako, and Mari Yoshihara. If transnational American and Asian American studies scholars have opened up a space for the kind of transpacific critique I develop in this study, it is equally true that such a critique could not have been articulated without the production of a critical yet welcoming discursive space within North American Japanese studies that pioneering scholars such as Naoki Sakai, Harry Harootunian, Carol Gluck, Mark Selden, the late Mariam Silverberg, and others have long cultivated. I thank them all.

One of the serious concerns for a book like *Cold War Ruins* has been that it does not have a disciplinary home or an established readership community. While the risks of not fully belonging are real, the current study has been inspired and guided by works which have brought together problematics that do not conventionally belong to given disciplines or academic fields and which have successfully generated new questions for new readerships. Many of my former colleagues and students at the University of California, San Diego—especially in the Department of Literature, the Ethnic Studies Department, and the Critical Gender Studies Program—did exactly that. If not for the presence of this amazing scholarly community, I could not have explored as fully the interdisciplinary potential of this book or its transregional conceptualization, although I dare not claim that my work lives up to the high standards they have set. For nearly two decades, I had the tremendous fortune of participating in and learning from members of this rare collectivity. The founding philosophy and the institutional ethos of the UCSD Literature Department, and especially the visionary leadership of Lisa Lowe who served as department chair from 1998 to 2001, encouraged historically situated, multilingual, cross-hemispheric and transdisciplinary scholarship. Affiliations with Ethnic Studies and Critical Gender Studies, both of which likewise emphasized the merit of a transnational approach, were equally vital to my thinking in that these constantly pushed me to reflect on the relevance of academic inquiries to urgent predicaments in the here and now. If there's any value in the kind of transnational and interdisciplinary work I put forward in *Cold War Ruins*, it is entirely owing to the precious insights and input of my former colleagues and students in these three critical UCSD locations. An informal off-campus writing group merits special mention here, as it was instrumental to the book's production. The group read my first book outline in 2006 and a 2009 version of the introduction. They will see that I have learned so much from their input. I wish to express my sincerest gratitude to the following former colleagues, some of whom were in that writing group. Although several of them eventually departed from San Diego, they made my life in San Diego so enriching, fun, and meaningful: Patrick Anderson, John D. Blanco, Lisa Bloom, Dennis Childs, Page duBois, Ann DuCille, Fatima El-Tayeb, Yen L. Espiritu, T. Fujitani, the late Rosemary Marangoly George, Judith Halberstam, Marcel Henaff, Todd Henry, Tara

Javidi, Sara Johnson, Nicole King, Dorothy Ko, Martha Lampland, Jin-kyung Lee, Ping-hui Liao, George Lipsitz, Lisa Lowe, Curtis Marez, Luis Martin-Cabrera, the late Masao Miyoshi, Vincente Rafael, Roddey Reid, Rosaura Sanchez, Nayan Shah, Denise Ferreira da Silva, Stephanie Small-wood, Brett St Louis, Shelley Streeby, Stefan Tanaka, Christena Turner, Daniel Widener, Yingjin Zhang, and Oumelbanine Nina Zhiri. San Diego brings back not only fond memories but also feelings of immense loss. I want to thank Chandan, Gayatri, Jack, Maca, Ken, Nayan, Lisa, and Tak, who once were affiliated with UCSD in one way or other, for coming together to grieve the untimely departure of our dearest friend Rosie. Badri and Jayshree, we will miss her, forever.

The institutional setup of UCSD graduate programs allowed me to work with students in multiple disciplines and with a wide range of intellectual concerns. Graduate teaching has always been inspiring and I would like to thank the following former students, many of whom are now accomplished scholars in their respective areas of expertise, for so many stimulating conversations over the years: Maile Arvin, Neda Atanasoski, Benjamin Balthaser, Michael Bevacqua, Alex Chang, Emily Cheng, Yu-Fang Cho, Juliana Choi, Kimberly Chung, Thuy Vo Dang, Greg dePies, Josen Diaz, Kyung Hee Ha, Grace Kyungwon Hong, Shih-szu Hsu, Julietta Hua, Junghyun Hwang, Jessica Jordan, Ji Hee Jung, Satoko Kakihara, Jinah Kim, Su Yun Kim, Ashvin Kini, Cathi Kozen, Chien-ting Lin, Stefanie Moore, Ryan Moran, Kit Myers, Amie Parry, Cindy Pinhal, Ayako Sahara, Tomo Sasaki, Ramie Tateishi, Tomoko Tsuchiya, Ma Vang, Chuong-Dai Vo, Yin Wang, and Randall Williams. I learned and continue to learn so much from your work.

Activist-intellectual networks in Japan have constantly provided me with grounding and inspiration to further the investigations of *Cold War Ruins*, especially in regards to intra-Asia relations, Japan's far-right politics, nationalism, militarization, and racism. I am indebted to the support and encouragement of a number of progressive Japanese scholars and critics who have invited me to participate in their various collaborative projects. I wish to reiterate my special gratitude to Itagaki Ryūta, Iwasaki Minoru, Jung Yeonghae, Kitahara Megumi, Kim Puja, Komagome Takeshi, Lee Hyo-duk, Matsuda Motoji, Mitsui Hideko, Nakano Toshio, Narita Ryūichi, Nishino Rumiko, Ōba Eri, Ōhashi Yukako, Tomiyama Ichirō, and Yoshida Toshimi, for many years of intellectual and spiritual support. Had it not been for the mentorship I received as an undergraduate student from Tsurumi Kazuko and Murai Yoshinori I could not have written this book. They passed in 2006 and 2013 respectively and I miss them dearly. Through Murai-sensei

I met Utsumi Aiko whose lifelong academic and activist engagement with the legacy of Japanese colonialism has played a major part in laying the foundation for critical studies of the postwar "settlement," a body of work to which this book is hugely indebted. Hirota Masaki and Yasumaru Yoshio approached my nonhistorian's writings on history on a number of occasions with robust curiosity, incisive critique, and heartening support. I also wish to extend special gratitude to Nishikawa Yūko who invited me to contribute to her "Post/State, Post/Family" special issue in the journal *Shisō* (November 2003), where I first presented the core argument of chapter 2. An earlier version of this chapter in a different form appeared in *American Quarterly* 57, no. 3 (September 2005): 885–910.

Bereavements, political affairs, household and health emergencies, and more recently the challenging move to a new workplace in a new country— all contributed in one way or another to considerably delaying the book's completion. Yet the challenges have also brought new opportunities and inspirations. My heartfelt thanks to the new colleagues and friends I have gained in Toronto, both in and outside the university, for their friendship, guidance, and support: Ritu Birla, Elspeth Brown, Eric Cazdyn, Hae Yeon Choo, Jennifer Jihye Chung, Denise Cruz, Robert Diaz, Linda Feng, Richard Fung, Yi Gu, Ju Hui Judy Han, Franca Iacovetta, Kajri Jain, Eric Jennings, Ken Kawashima, Tom Keirstead, Janice Kim, Tong Lam, June Larkin, Tania Li, Victor Li, Marieme Lo, Deidre Lynch, Tim McCaskell, Bonnie McElhinny, Thy Phu, Janet Poole, Marian Reed, Allison Ringer, Atsuko Sakaki, Shiho Satsuka, Meghan Sbrocchi, Andre Schmidt, Rachel Silvey, Jesook Song, Alissa Trotz, Natasja Vanderberg, Rinaldo Walcott, Joseph Wong, Yiching Wu, Meng Yue, and Yurou Zhong. The new environment presented me with a few surprises and unanticipated turns. But I feel very blessed to be welcomed by a community of Asian studies scholars who are deeply cosmopolitan and multilingual, and who have for some time far surpassed the discipline's Cold War tenets. I owe special thanks to Joshua Pilzer, who despite the busy schedule offered to help facilitate the communication with the House of Sharing. M. Jacqui Alexander, Roland Coloma, and Jin-kyung Park, all three of whom unfortunately left Toronto not long after my arrival, gave me precious initial introductions to the university and the city even though our associations were relatively brief. I will cherish the legacies they left with us. Working with University of Toronto graduate students has been equally rewarding and inspiring. For many engaging and insightful conversations during and outside our seminars, I extend my thanks to Jenny Choi, Sonny Dhoot, Nicholas Feinig, Na Sil Heo, Jeremy Hurdis, Sinhyeok Jung,

Yoo Kyung Jung, Banu Kaygusuz, Derek Kramer, Elena Kusaka, Laura Kwak, Lynn Ly, Zenee Maceda, Sara Osenton, Tomoe Otsuki, Alexandre Paquet, Michael Roellinghoff, and Grace Yoo. Asako Masubuchi not only helped me with the bibliography but also shared many important observations on Okinawa based on her own research.

The book could not have been completed without the institutional support of the University of Toronto, Faculty of Arts and Science. I am thankful to Duke University Press and its staff, Jade Brooks, Christine Riggio, Heather Hensley, and Christopher Robinson, for their generosity and professionalism, but especially Ken Wissoker for his patience and faith in my work over many years. The project editor Sara Leone's meticulous editorial support tremendously enhanced the book's quality and readability. The final stage of writing also benefited from the profoundly insightful feedback from David Eng, whose suggestions on chapter organization and the subtitle were definitive, and another anonymous reviewer. Finally, my special thanks to Mr. HoCheol Jeong at the House of Sharing for responding positively to my request to use one of the late Kang Duk-Kyoung halmoni's paintings for the book's cover art.

During the course of writing this book, I lost many important people—mentors, friends, families—who gave me nothing but love and kindness. My late father wouldn't be offended if I placed most of the blame on him for my slowness. When he passed in 2006 he left me with the colossal postmortem task of cleaning up his study, where he had squirreled away every new and old thing he had collected. What I pulled out of his study over several summers amounted to some 1.8 tons of waste and dust mites. The first fifteen years of my father's life were saturated by Japanese militarism. From scattered pieces of his autobiographical writings I could gather that during the war years he felt so embarrassed about his maternal family's literati class background and the nonnormative household his professional mother formed with his anarchist-vagabond father in a remote rural village that he volunteered for the youth fighter pilot program to prove his patriotism—but only to fail due to his poor health and to become a radical cultural relativist after the war. As a graduate student of agricultural economy in the 1950s, he was by happenstance recruited as the anthropologist Julian Steward's native assistant. I later learned that the Eisenhower administration encouraged comparative peasant and village studies as part of the promotion of global Cold War knowledge. My father continued to work as a research assistant at the University of Illinois. The Champaign County Bank account book, which I found among all that he had kept, showed he was receiving a monthly paycheck worth ten times more than a new fulltime public employee would be making in Japan at that time. He returned to Japan to teach, indeed to become a public employee, at a national university, where he pursued field-based research on agricultural societies in several African countries. There were several stories my father would recall from time to time about my birth. He wanted to name me Tomoko but his teacher and colleagues dissuaded him, arguing that the nickname for Tomoko would then be "Tommy," a story suggestive of the Cold War normativity in which such gender bending would be considered inappropriate. My anglicized birth name must also have had to do with the postinternment assimilationist milieu. Then I also heard repeatedly about the day I arrived in Japan. When we flew back to Japan in June 1960, our landing at Haneda Airport was interrupted due to a mass protest against press secretary James Hagerty's deplaning. He had flown in to prepare for President Eisenhower's upcoming visit to Japan to mark the signing of the renewed U.S.-Japan security treaty. Due to the protest Hagerty could not leave the airport that day and had to be rescued out of Japan by Marine airlift. A product of transwar, Cold War contradictions, my father also unwaveringly supported the Liberal Democratic Party's centrist and Cold War U.S.-Japan alliance. His radical cultural relativism might have been a product of the *après-guerre*, shattering encounter with the unexpectedly amicable former "enemy," combined with the ethos of 1950s American cultural anthropology. But I think it also had to do with the fact that he was a kind of hoarder. In his universe everything existed in equal (non)value and demanded equal (non)attachment: he would let go of many things as freely as he kept others. Among the 1.8 tons of debris and so many other things, my father left me with these Cold War memories. He left it to me to fathom just how much could be hidden in such seemingly only personal—and binary—U.S.-Japan stories.

When I wrote my acknowledgments for the book that appeared in 2003, I selfishly and foolishly thought I would write another one soon and have another opportunity to thank the many people I continue to owe many unrepayable debts. It's been more than ten years since I last had such a luxury. Losses and farewells, for sure, but some things have remained constant. So, I repeat. Lisa, Yen, Fatima, Nicole, and Rosie, then and in memory, I could not and will not survive any of it without you. Harumi and Kei Befu, Guillermo Delgado and Norma Klahn, Jeff Hanes, Linda Angst, Andrew Barshay and Kimiko Nishimura, Rev. Masami and late Kyoko Fujitani, Mari, Kenji, Yuri, Takuya and friends in the San Francisco Bay Area—CI, Verna, AY, Patti, Mark, the Momono sisters, Kenny, Karen, Steve, Lynn, but this time especially to Darrel and Lisa K.—thank you for watching over us. My mother, who exemplifies for me a nonacademic reader who appreciates complex and challenging new ideas, continues to amaze me with her admirable self-discipline and the ability to stay honorably solitary. En witnessed my writerly struggles more closely than anyone else. At age nineteen he valiantly flew across the continent with failing kidneys, but did not live to see how the book ended. It is beyond comprehension how I finished any writing let alone a book manuscript without his company. But the biggest, still accumulating, unrepayable debt I owe is to Tak. I am utterly at a loss how I could even begin to thank him, my trusted ally, soulmate, partner for over thirty years, who took meticulous care in reading over, commenting on, and edited a literally endless number of different drafts and parts of this book, while patiently allowing me to test the limits of what is known as the English language. His integrity, humor, erudition, and resoluteness have saved me at every old and new phase of my thinking, writing, and embattlement. And he has never failed to offer me laughter, solace, and perfect food—the gifts of a good life. No qualms about the paths taken together, even sometimes snowy ones.

NOTES

Preface

1. Priscilla B. Hayner, *Unspeakable Truths: Confronting State Terror and Atrocity* (New York: Routledge, 2001). Out of twenty-five truth commissions Hayner noted since 1970, nineteen of them took place after 1990.

2. The Cold War "empire for liberty" can be regarded as another phase of what Oscar V. Campomanes called the "anticolonial empire." Campomanes built on the idea of "imperial anticolonialism," coined by William Appleman Williams, who famously characterized the Open Door Policy consistently sought in twentieth-century U.S. diplomacy as "America's version of the liberal policy of informal empire or free-trade imperialism" (67), which was at the same time driven by "the benevolent American desire to reform the world in its own image" (47). William Appleman Williams, *The Tragedy of American Diplomacy* (New York: World Publishing Company, 1959). See Oscar V. Campomanes, "1898 and the Nature of the New Empire," *Radical History Review* 73 (winter 1999): 139. For a genealogy of the link between liberalism and the development of the United States as a national empire, see Richard H. Immerman, *Empire for Liberty: A History of American Imperialism from Benjamin Franklin to Paul Wolfowitz* (Princeton, NJ: Princeton University Press, 2010). From the opposite end of the political spectrum, in *America's Inadvertent Empire* (New Haven, CT: Yale University Press, 2004), William E. Odom and Robert Dujarric present the idea of the United States as a "liberal empire." They offer a post–Cold War reaffirmation of the American imperium as a militarized defender of free market fundamentalism.

3. See especially Gavan McCormack, *Client State: Japan in the American Embrace* (London: Verso, 2007); and Chalmers Johnson, *The Sorrows of Empire: Militarism, Secrecy, and the End of the Republic* (New York: Metropolitan Books, 2004).

4. Elaine Kim and Chungmoo Choi's *Dangerous Women: Gender and Korean Nationalism* (New York: Routledge, 1998) was the pioneering collaborative work by Korean and Korean American feminist scholars who, for the first time in North America, brought light to the transwar, transpacific continuities among Japanese colonialism, U.S. Cold War military-security imperialism, and Korean nationalism. For my own early attempt to theorize the transpacific, U.S.-Japan Cold War

complicity in forgetting the history of colonialism, see "Complicit Amnesia: The Smithsonian 'Atom Bomb Exhibit' Controversy in Japan and the U.S.," Honolulu, Hawaii: East-West Center, 1995. Most fundamentally, Naoki Sakai's concept of "co-figuration" has offered an important analytic for understanding the supplementary relation between the universalism of the West and the provincialism of the non-West; what we regard as universalistic is simply the particular masquerading as the universal. See his groundbreaking essay, "Kindai no hihan: Chūzetsu shita tōki: posutomodan no shomondai," *Gendai shisō* 15, no. 15 (1987): 184–207. More recently, Sakai discussed the coconstitutiveness of American modernity and Japanese nationalism as a "trans-Pacific arrangement." See his "On Romantic Love and Military Violence: Transpacific Imperialism and U.S.-Japan Complicity," in Setsu Shigematsu and Keith L. Camacho, eds., *Militarized Currents: Toward a Decolonized Future in Asia and the Pacific* (Minneapolis: University of Minnesota Press, 2010), 205–21. Sakai's choice of the term "arrangement" in describing the transpacific complicity is especially effective in capturing its gendered and sexualized dimension and performativity (as in "marriage arrangement" and "legal arrangement"). For the purpose of *Cold War Ruins*, I have adopted "formations" and "order" to highlight the militarized dimension and tenacity of that transpacific historical product. For important observations on the midcentury transpacific configuration of racism, see Yukiko Koshiro, *Trans-Pacific Racisms and the U.S. Occupation of Japan* (New York: Columbia University Press, 1999).

5. See, among others, Candace Fujikane and Jonathan Y. Okamura, eds., *Asian Settler Colonialism: From Local Governance to the Habits of Everyday Life in Hawai'i* (Honolulu: University of Hawai'i Press, 2008) on this point. Likewise pointing to the predicament of Asian Americans' use of the "transpacific" as an analytic, Denise Cruz nonetheless underscores, following Aihwa Ong, the "capacity of *trans-* to describe not only movement across borders, but also states of transition and change" (8). Denise Cruz, *Transpacific Femininities: The Making of the Modern Filipina* (Durham, NC: Duke University Press, 2012).

6. By centering the Pacific region in their analyses, Setsu Shigematsu and Keith L. Camacho challenged the ways in which both Asian and American studies, even when critical of their geopolitical contexts, treated the Pacific Land/Ocean "as an open frontier to be crossed, domesticated, occupied, and settled" according to the militarized logics of security. Setsu Shigematsu and Keith L. Camacho, "Introduction: Militarized Currents, Decolonizing Futures," in Shigematsu and Camacho, *Militarized Currents*, xv–xlviii. Camacho further extended the notion of "transoceanic flow" to mark the emerging interisland indigenous epistemologies and practices in the Pacific Islands and diaspora. Keith Camacho, "Transoceanic Flows: Pacific Islander Interventions across the American Empire," *Amerasia Journal* 37, no. 3 (2011): ix–xxxiv.

7. See *Hiroshima Traces* (1999) on the politics of how to name and remember the war.

8. For example, historian Ustumi Aiko, who was among the scholars who advocated renaming the war, coauthored *Sekidōka no Chōsenjin hanran* (Tokyo: Keisō Shobō, 1980) with late economist Murai Yoshinori. They offered an account of Korean

soldiers who fought as Japanese imperial soldiers and remained in Indonesia to participate in the anticolonial armed struggles that continued after 1945. Utsumi and Murai moved on to publish several related works, including *Chōsenjin BC kyū senpan no kiroku* (Tokyo: Keisō Shobō, 1982), the first sustained investigation on the Korean men who fought as Japanese soldiers in Indonesia during the war and who were subsequently prosecuted in local B and C class war crimes trials. Korean soldiers were often deployed as prison guards for the Allied POWs. Because of their daily contact with the prisoners, they tended to be identifiable as individuals and were in many cases held accountable for abuses against POWs. An excerpt of the latter work is available in English: "Korean 'Imperial Soldiers': Remembering Colonialism and Crimes against Allied POWs," in *Perilous Memories* (2001). Utsumi summarized, "There were twenty-three Koreans and twenty-one Taiwanese among the 984 individuals who were executed for war crimes. And of the 3,419 people sentenced to life or limited imprisonment, 125 were Korean and 147 were Taiwanese" (211). These pioneering works have pointed to the urgent need for non-Statist, transborder, subnational redress efforts in Asia.

9. For the standard distinction between "Cold War" and "cold war": "A. In the sixteenth edition of *CMS*, we make a distinction between the Cold War (i.e., between the United States and the former Soviet Union) and any old cold war (e.g., between feuding families). See 8.74." *Chicago Manual of Style Q and A*, 16th ed. http://www.chicagomanualofstyle.org/qanda/data/faq/topics /CapitalizationTitles/faqoo10.htm.

Introduction

1. Writings on transitional justice are numerous. See for some of the most useful overviews and discussions on the practicality of transitional justice, Ruti G. Teitel, *Transitional Justice* (Oxford: Oxford University Press, 2000); and Elazar Barkan, *The Guilt of Nations: Restitution and Negotiating Historical Injustices* (Baltimore: Johns Hopkins University Press, 2000). For a recent development in intra- and inter-Asia discussion of historical justice in English, see Gi-Wook Shin, Soon-Won Park, and Daqing Yang, eds., *Rethinking Historical Injustice and Reconciliation in Northeast Asia: The Korean Experience* (New York: Routledge, 2007).

2. While the two surrendered states experienced war crimes trials unprecedented in the history of international law, their paths to postwar settlements diverged in critical ways immediately following the cease-fire. Before unification, Germany's post–World War II redress measures had been directed with far more intensity toward the prosecution and compensation of Nazi crimes than state indemnities for losses and damages suffered by neighboring countries.

3. The Treaty of Peace between the Union of Burma and Japan (effective 1955), the Reparations Agreement between the Republic of the Philippines and Japan (1956), the Treaty of Peace and Agreement on Reparations and Economic Cooperation (1958), and the Japan-South Vietnam Agreement on Reparations (1959) are the four treaties in which Japan agreed to indemnity payments. Cambodia, which insisted on reparations in the form of an indemnity payment but reluctantly

signed the San Francisco Treaty, later won agreement from Japan to compensate its people for wartime damages in 1950 through the Japan-Cambodia Agreement on Economic and Technical Cooperation. Singapore, Thailand, and Malaysia also signed follow-up treaties. See Utsumi Aiko's *Sengo hoshō kara kangaeru Nihon to Ajia* (Tokyo: Yamakawa Shuppansha, 2002) for the details as well as on the troubling implications of such state-to-state reparations agreements.

4. On the issue of the Philippines, see Ricardo Jose, "Nihon no sengo kokusai shakai e no fukki to Firipin," trans. Nakano Satoshi, *Kōwa mondai to Ajia*, a special issue of *Nenpō Nihon gendaishi* 5 (1999): 78–84; Takushi Ohno, *War Reparations and Peace Settlement* (Manila: Solidaridad, 1986); and Utsumi Aiko, *Sengo hoshō kara kangaeru Nihon to Ajia*.

5. The treaty with Taiwan, officially called the Sino-Japanese Peace Treaty between the Republic of China and Japan, relinquished the republic's rights to demand reparations from Japan. The treaty was signed in 1952 but was nullified after the 1972 Joint Communiqué of the Government of Japan and the Government of the People's Republic of China, whereby the latter formally relinquished its rights to demand reparations from Japan. As discussed later, while the war indemnity issues between Japan and the two governments of Taiwan and PRC respectively are said to have been concluded, the question remains as to whether the two interstate agreements also relinquished individual rights to demand compensations from Japan.

6. See John Dower, *Empire and Aftermath: Yoshida Shigeru and the Japanese Experience, 1878–1954* (Cambridge, MA: Harvard East Asian Monographs, 1979), 371. Kimie Hara underscores the constitutive force of the 1951 San Francisco Peace Treaty as shaping the foundation for the postwar Asia-Pacific region under U.S. Cold War hegemony, and especially by leaving what she identifies as "blind-spots" in the treaty that led to ambiguities regarding territorial boundaries and sovereignty. Kimie Hara, *Cold War Frontiers in the Asia Pacific: Divided Territories in the San Francisco System* (New York: Routledge, 2007). Likewise, Alexis Dudden situates the current territorial disputes regarding Dokdo/Takeshima Island and other issues related to postwar settlements in a triangulated relationship among the United States, South Korea, and Japan. Alexis Dudden, *Troubled Apologies among Japan, Korea, and the United States* (New York: Columbia University Press, 2008).

7. See especially Kurasawa Aiko, "Indonesia no kokka kensetsu to Nihon no baishō," *Kōwa mondai to Ajia*, a special issue of *Nenpō Nihon gendaishi* 5 (1999): 35–77.

8. Fatima El-Tayeb, *European Others: Queering Ethnicity in Postnational Europe* (Minneapolis: University of Minnesota Press, 2011), 38. El-Tayeb succinctly notes, Papon "was never disciplined for his role as police prefect in Algeria or police chief in Paris" (38). See also Kikuchi Keisuke, "Shokumichi shihai no rekishi no saishin: Furansu no 'kako no kokufuku' no genzai," in Kim Puja and Nakano Toshio, eds., *Rekishi to sekinin: "Ianfu" mondai to 1990 nendai* (Tokyo: Seikyūsha, 2008), 216–34, for a critical examination of the Papon trial in relation to the French inability to come to terms with its history of colonialism.

9. And yet, the U.S. military's maneuvering has been guided by the "Project for a New American Century" (PNAC), a conservative think tank named after the 1950s U.S. Cold War enterprise, "The American Century."

10. While they have increasingly become a central part of South Korea's authentic National History, the testimonies of women who survived the Japanese military comfort system had been silenced for more than four decades due to their non-heteronormative femininity and sexuality. See, among others, Chungmoo Choi, ed., *The Comfort Women: Colonialism, War, and Sex*, a special issue of *positions: east asia cultures critique* 5, no. 1 (1997); and C. Sarah Soh's *The Comfort Women: Sexual Violence and Postcolonial Memory in Korea and Japan* (Chicago: University of Chicago Press, 2008). Pyong Gap Min underscores the feminist understanding of the wartime Japanese military sex slavery through the intersections of colonial power and gender hierarchy in "Korean 'Comfort Women': The Intersection of Colonial Power, Gender, and Class." *Gender & Society* 17, no. 6 (December 2003): 938–57. In Japan, the 1988 proposal for the Law Pertaining to Postwar Reparations and the Guarantee of Human Rights for Resident Aliens from Former Colonies (Zainchi kyū-shokuminchi shusshinsha ni kansuru sengo hoshō oyobi jinken hoshō hō) was drafted by several members of the Coalition to Combat Ethnic Discrimination (Minzoku Sabetsu to Tatakau Renraku Kyōgikai, or Mintōren, for short), who have since then organized themselves into a group, the Association to Demand Postwar Reparations for Resident Aliens (Zainichi no Sengo Hoshō o Motomeru Kai). The legislation's objective was to enable reparations and ensure human rights for those who had originally been displaced from Japan's former colonies (i.e., Taiwan and Korea) to the Japanese mainland any time before 1952, and for their descendants. Similarly, the lawsuits by Korean survivors of the atomic bombing of Hiroshima and Nagasaki, in demanding redress for wartime injury caused by the Japanese imperial policy, reveal the litigants' diasporic and precarious position deriving from colonial intimacy and violence.

11. See *Hiroshima Traces: Time, Space and the Dialectics of Memory* (Berkeley: University of California Press, 1999) and introduction to T. Fujitani, Geoffrey M. White, and Lisa Yoneyama, eds., *Perilous Memories: The Asia-Pacific War(s)* (Durham, NC: Duke University Press, 2001).

12. Although this would preclude the American POWs who received reparations in the form of individual payments through the U.S. government, which used Japanese liquidated assets, the same argument has great exigencies, for example, for averting the Joint Communiqué of the Government of Japan and the Government of the People's Republic of China (1972), which waived the latter's entitlement to reparations.

13. As in the German situation prior to the U.S.-initiated establishment of the Remembrance, Responsibilities and Future Foundation (2000)—which summarily put an end to litigations for corporate compensation of Nazi forced labor while setting aside the question of the state's legal accountability—the Asian redress cases, too, are increasingly seeking reparations from private corporations. Michael Bazyler, "Japan Should Follow the International Trend and Face Its

History of World War II Forced Labor," *The Asia-Pacific Journal* 5–3–09 (January 29, 2009). At least one such instance has led to a reparative settlement after the law had denied claimants' rights in Japan (former Chinese forced laborers' reparation settlements with Nishimatsu Construction Company, 2009). The Asian Women's Fund (Josei No Tame No Ajia Heiwa Kokumin Kikin, 1994–2007), the government-sponsored private atonement fund that aimed to morally redress the violations of women's humanity by the Japanese military comfort system (*jūgun ianjo seido*), was another such privatized redress attempt, albeit a problematic one.

14. The anthropologists John D. Kelly and Martha Kaplan observe that the word "nation-state" did not gain currency in English until the mid-twentieth century, suggesting that the promotion of nation-states was an American post-World War II project. John D. Kelly and Martha Kaplan, "Nation and Decolonization: Toward a New Anthropology of Nationalism," *Anthropological Theory* 1, no. 4 (2001): 419–37.

15. Roderick A. Ferguson, *Aberrations in Black: Toward a Queer of Color Critique* (Minneapolis: University of Minnesota Press, 2004), 17.

16. Allen Feldman, "Memory Theaters, Virtual Witnessing, and the Trauma-Aesthetic," *Biography* 27, no. 1 (winter 2004): 163–202.

17. Randall Williams, *The Divided World: Human Rights and Its Violence* (Minneapolis: University of Minnesota Press, 2010).

18. Lisa Lowe, "The Intimacies of Four Continents," in Ann L. Stoler, ed., *Haunted by Empire: Geographies of Intimacy In North American History* (Durham, NC: Duke University Press, 2006), 206.

19. See Dipesh Chakrabarty, *Provincializing Europe: Postcolonial Thought and Historical Difference* (Princeton, NJ: Princeton University Press, 2000), for the contradictions that post-Enlightenment universal humanism and historicism have posed on the West's rest.

20. Leti Volpp, "Feminism versus Multiculturalism," *Columbia Law Review* 101 (June 2001): 1181–218, esp. 1201. On women's human rights, see also Inderpal Grewal, " 'Women's Rights as Human Rights': Feminist Practices, Global Feminism, and Human Rights Regimes in Transnationality," *Citizenship Studies* 3, no. 3 (1999): 337–54; and Julietta Hua, *Trafficking Women's Human Rights* (Minneapolis: University of Minnesota Press, 2011). Wendy S. Hesford and Wendy Kozol have further developed Grewal's insights to discuss the predicaments of universalistic feminism after U.S. military action in Afghanistan. See their introduction to *Just Advocacy? Women's Human Rights, Transnational Feminisms, and the Politics of Representation* (New Brunswick, NJ: Rutgers University Press, 2005), 1–29. In general, critical transnational feminists have questioned the uneven ways in which the global feminists' women's rights regime functions as a new form of colonial governmentality through its uneven deployment of the concept of human rights to women in the "developing" non-West, once again portraying them as objects of rescue and protection.

21. For those works that try to mediate the risks and possibilities of achieving postviolence justice as described here, see especially Martha Minow, *Between Vengeance*

and *Forgiveness: Facing History after Genocide and Mass Violence* (Boston: Beacon Press, 1998); and Robert Rotberg and Dennis Thompson, eds., *Truth v. Justice: The Morality of Truth Commissions* (Princeton, NJ: Princeton University Press, 2000).

22. Jacques Derrida, *On Cosmopolitanism and Forgiveness*, trans. Mark Dooley and Michael Hughes (London: Routledge, 2001).

23. This observation parallels Wendy Brown's discussion on the pitfalls of justice sought within the liberal state and its institutionalized public spheres. *States of Injury: Power and Freedom in Late Modernity* (Princeton, NJ: Princeton University Press, 1995).

24. Ann Russo, "The Intersections of Feminism and Imperialism in the United States," *International Feminist Journal of Politics* 8, no. 4 (December 2006): 557–80.

25. Jacques Derrida, "Force of Law: The 'Mystical Foundation of Authority,'" in Drucilla Cornell, Michel Rosenfeld, David Gray Carlson, eds., *Deconstruction and the Possibility of Justice* (New York: Routledge, 1992), 24. It may be worthwhile noting as well that even though he warned of the perils of the post-1990s quest for international justice, shortly before his death Derrida explicitly endorsed the *BRussells* Tribunal, a transnational people's court that adjudicated the American war of aggression against Iraq. Lieven De Cauter, "For a Justice to Come: An Interview with Jacques Derrida," The *BRussells* Tribunal: People vs Total War Incorporated, April 2004, last accessed February 7, 2010, http://www.hydra.umn .edu/derrida/brussels.html.

Like the TRCs, the *BRussells* court is yet another form of new cosmopolitanism, but one that operates in a juridical manner with imaginary prosecution and sentencing. The 2000 Women's International War Crimes Tribunal on Japan's Military Sexual Slavery, which passed judgment on violations against women's lives under Japan's wartime military comfort system (see chapter 3), took a similar people's court form.

26. This was the essential Buddhist characteristic of the Moon Light Masked Man, a pan-Asianist postwar Japanese popular hero. His motto was: "do not hate, do not kill, let's forgive."

27. Derrida, "Force of Law," 27.

28. Feldman, "Memory Theaters, Virtual Witnessing, and the Trauma-Aesthetic," 168, 185.

29. Slavoj Žižek, "Carl Schmitt in the Age of Post-Politics," in Chantal Mouff, *Challenge of Carl Schmitt* (New York: Verso, 1999), 28.

30. Žižek, "Carl Schmitt in the Age of Post-Politics," 28.

31. Jacques Rancière, "Overlegitimation," trans. Kristin Ross, *Social Text* 10, no. 2 (1992): 252–57.

32. Jacques Rancière, "Who Is the Subject of the Rights of Man?" *South Atlantic Quarterly* 103:2/3 (spring/summer 2004): 297–310.

33. Rancière, of course, is reluctant to offer historical instances of such politicizations and what he calls dissensus beyond the historical instance of the demand for universal suffrage by European women, many of whom were already included in the biopolitical sphere due to their class and sexuality. In order to engage in

a thoroughgoing critique of the coextensiveness of carceral violence on a mass scale and the Rights of Man, the supplementary relationship—that is, between the enabling of liberal political subjects and such illiberal formations as slavery, colonialism, incarceration, foreign occupation, and so forth—needs to be examined through the analytics of racialized modernity and its local manifestations. For recent work that makes a compelling American case on this point, see Lisa Marie Cacho's *Social Death: Racialized Rightlessness and the Criminalization of the Unprotected* (New York: New York University Press, 2012).

34. Žižek, "Carl Schmitt in the Age of Post-Politics," 28.

35. Feldman, "Memory Theaters, Virtual Witnessing, and the Trauma-Aesthetic," 198.

36. Robert S. McNamara, for instance, confessed that during the war against Japan he was aware that the bombing of civilians constituted a war crime. McNamara recalled: "[Curtis] LeMay said, 'If we'd lost the war, we'd all have been prosecuted as war criminals.' And I think he's right. He, and I'd say I, were behaving as war criminals." *The Fog of War: Eleven Lessons from the Life of Robert S. McNamara*, directed by Errol Morris (New York, NY: Sony Pictures Classics, 2003), DVD.

37. The historian Richard H. Minear was the first to observe that the IMTFE served "victor's justice" because it failed to prosecute the Allied Forces' war crimes. Richard H. Minear, *Victor's Justice* (Princeton, NJ: Princeton University Press, 1971).

38. See Yoneyama, "Traveling Memories, Contagious Justice: Americanization of Japanese War Crimes at the End of the Post–Cold War," *Journal of Asian American Studies* 6, no. 1 (February 2003): 80–81. In tracing the discursive transition and emergence of new relations of power and subjugation around the idea of freedom in the U.S. post-Reconstruction era, Saidiya Hartman incisively points out how the trope of debt was deployed to bind the newly emancipated to a new system of bondage and indentureship. Hartman writes: "Emancipation instituted indebtedness. . . . The emancipated were introduced to the circuits of exchange through *the figurative deployment of debt*. . . . The transition from slavery to freedom introduced the free agent to the circuits of exchange through this construction of *already accrued debt*, an abstinent present, and a mortgaged future. In short, *to be free was to be a debtor—that is, obliged and duty-bound to others*" (emphasis added). See Saidiya V. Hartman, *Scenes of Subjection: Terror, Slavery, and Self-Making in Nineteenth-Century America* (New York: Oxford University Press, 1997), 131. Hartman's analysis succinctly captures the constitutive contradiction of the post-Enlightenment world. While firmly situated in the specific geohistorical context of the failure of American Reconstruction, Hartman's observation of the "figurative deployment of debt" helps us understand how the notions of freedom, emancipation, equality, and self-determination have been stabilized relationally to the modernity's other.

This radical contradiction of modernity is also what undergirds what I have referred to as "the imperialist myth of liberation and rehabilitation," a discursive economy of geopolitics that consolidated the logic of subjugation and bondage in the U.S. relationship to many Asian nations from World War II through the Cold War. The American myth of rescue and rehabilitation leaves indelible markers on the liberated of not only inferiority, subordination, and belatedness (to freedom and democracy), but also indebtedness (see also chapters 2 and 4). It prescribes "the already accrued debt" for the liberated. Once marked as "the liberated" and therefore "the indebted," one can hardly ever enter into an evenly reciprocal relationship with the liberators. Related, Kennan Ferguson discusses the anthropological studies on the concept of gift in the context of U.S. liberation of Iraq. Kennan Ferguson, "The Gift of Freedom," *Social Text* 25, no. 2 (2007): 39–52. More recently, Mimi T. Nyugen took up the notion of "debt" and "gift" to discuss the discourse of rescue and liberation of the Vietnam War refugee in the United States. *The Gift of Freedom: War, Debt, and Other Refugee Passages* (Durham, NC: Duke University Press, 2013).

39. An important case indicative of the unredressability of U.S. war crimes in Asia can be found in the work of the South Korean Truth and Reconciliation Commission (TRCK). The commission's findings presented unassailable evidence of the moral and legal criminality of U.S. military operations during the Korean War. And yet, while the TRCK "acknowledged" the overwhelming losses resulting from U.S. counterinsurgency operations, it fell short of seriously ascertaining them. See Suh Hee-Kyung, "TRCK's Verification Process for Mass Civilian Killings during the Korean War," *Critical Asian Studies* 42, no. 4 (November 2010): 553–88; and Kim Dong-Choon, "The Long Road toward Truth and Reconciliation: Unwavering Attempts to Achieve Justice in South Korea": 525–52, in the same issue.

　One of TRCK's legal claims is that the South Korean government should be held accountable for Korean War damages because the state cannot justifiably exercise its rights to self-defense unless it can ensure the protection of the rights, sovereignty, and well-being of its people. Such a theoretical stance cannot be unproblematically applied to those contexts in which less powerful states must defend themselves against overwhelmingly superior political, military, and economic external forces. According to this perspective, for instance, it is equally possible to condemn the democratically elected Hamas regime because it has failed to safeguard its people, while leaving unquestioned the Israeli occupation that produces Gaza's unlivable conditions. To pursue historical justice within a single national sphere without implicating such extraneous hegemonic forces as the United States and the United Nations also leaves the uneven structure of global power relations unchallenged. I discussed this point in "Politicizing Justice: Post–Cold War Redress and the Truth and Reconciliation Commission" in the same issue of *Critical Asian Studies*. See also Kim Dong Choon, "Beneath the Tip of the Iceberg: Problems in Historical Clarification of the Korean War," *Korea Journal* (autumn 2002): 60–86.

40. The critical methodology I am advocating here with which to perceive the idea and practice of justice as incommensurable yet interlinked within the history of geopolitical entanglement resonates with ones deployed in the following critical comparative studies: Yen L. Espiritu, *Body Counts: The Vietnam War and Militarized Refuge(es)* (Berkeley: University of California Press, 2014); and Lisa Lowe, *The Intimacies of Four Continents* (Durham, NC: Duke University Press, 2015).

41. For the discursive turn and internationalization of Cold War American studies, see especially Mary L. Dudziak, *Cold War Civil Rights: Race and Image of American Democracy* (Princeton, NJ: Princeton University Press, 2000); Penny M. Von Eschen, *Race against Empire: Black Americans and Anticolonialism, 1937–1957* (Ithaca, NY: Cornell University Press, 1997); Christina Klein, *Cold War Orientalism: Asia in the Middlebrow Imagination, 1945–1961* (Berkeley: University of California Press, 2003); Thomas Borstelmann, *The Cold War and the Color Line: American Race Relations in the Global Arena* (Cambridge, MA: Harvard University Press, 2001); and Melani McAlister, *Epic Encounters: Culture, Media, and U.S. Interests in the Middle East, 1945–2000* (Berkeley: University of California Press, 2001). For the pioneering work on the postnationalist turn in the study of Americas, John Carlos Rowe, ed., *Post-nationalist American Studies* (Berkeley: University of California Press, 2000).

42. Christian G. Appy, "Introduction: Struggling for the World," in Christian G. Appy, ed., *Cold War Constructions: The Political Culture of United States Imperialism, 1945–1966* (Amherst: University of Massachusetts Press, 2000), 3.

43. Jonathan Nashel, "The Road to Vietnam: Modernization Theory in Fact and Fiction," in Appy, *Cold War Constructions: The Political Culture of United States Imperialism*, 134.

44. McAlister, *Epic Encounters.*

45. T. Fujitani, "The Reischauer Memo: Mr. Moto, Hirohito, and Japanese American Soldiers," *Critical Asian Studies* 33, no. 3 (2001): 379–402.

46. See especially Colleen Lye, *America's Asia: Racial Form and American Literature, 1893–1945* (Princeton, NJ: Princeton University Press, 2005), 232–43.

47. Gerald Horne, *Race War! White Supremacy and the Japanese Attack on the British Empire* (New York: New York University Press, 2004). See also Marc Gallicchio, *The African American Encounter with Japan and China: Black Internationalism in Asia, 1895–1945* (Chapel Hill: University of North Carolina Press, 2000).

48. See Lye, *America's Asia*, 239, on the notion of racial rehabilitation and how this process in fact started during the wartime. T. Fujitani has also observed a wartime shift from exclusion to assimilation and the use of liberal governmentality in the Japanese American war relocation camps, as well as the homology between the strategy for ruling Japanese Americans and Japan. See Fujitani, *Race for Empire: Koreans as Japanese and Japanese as Americans during World War II* (Berkeley: University of California, 2011). On an earlier observation of how the anthropological knowledge, deployed both for the management of the wartime Japanese American internment camps and for the postwar blueprints for the U.S. occupation of Japan, helped enable such transwar homology of American governmentality, see Yoneyama, "Habits of Knowing Cultural Differences: *Chrysanthemum and the Sword* in U.S. Liberal Multiculturalism," *Topoi* 18 (1999): 71–80.

49. "Japan's Women Could Be Model in Postwar Iraq," *Rocky Mountain News*, April 16, 2003. A few months later, Gordon wrote a letter to the editor of the *New York Times* and reiterated her point. See the *New York Times*, October 1, 2003, as well as her autobiography, *Only Woman in the Room: A Memoir* (Tokyo: Kodansha, 1997).

50. Judith Butler, *Frames of War: When Is Life Grievable?* (London: Verso, 2009).

51. Heonik Kwon, *The Other Cold War* (New York: Columbia University Press, 2010), 6.

52. On the ways in which the continuity of structures of violence from the colonial to the postcolonial era has been suppressed in the mainstream memories and historiographies of the Korean War in both South Korea and the United States, see among others Jae-Jung Suh, "Truth and Reconciliation in South Korea: Confronting War, Colonialism, and Intervention in the Asia Pacific," *Critical Asian Studies* 42, no. 4 (November 2010): 503–24.

53. For an insightful discussion on the American forgetfulness about the Korean War and its implications on the Cold War dialectics of history, see Junghyun Hwang, "Specters of the Cold War in America's Century: The Korean War and Transnational Politics of National Imaginaries in the 1950s" (PhD dissertation, University of California, San Diego, 2008).

54. Nancy Scheper-Hughes and Philippe I. Bourgois, eds., *Violence in War and Peace* (Malden, MA: Wiley-Blackwell, 2004).

55. Klein, *Cold War Orientalism*.

56. Aimé Césaire, *Discourse on Colonialism*, trans. Joan Pinkham (New York: Monthly Review Press, [1955] 2000), 77.

57. For a renewed discussion of American discourse on Japanese war crimes based on recently declassified archives, see Edward Drea et al., *Researching Japanese War Crimes Records: Introductory Essays* (Washington, DC: Nazi War Crimes and Japanese Imperial Government Records Interagency Working Group, 2006); and Toshiyuki Tanaka, Timothy L. H. McCormack, and Gerry J. Simpson, eds., *Beyond Victor's Justice? The Tokyo War Crimes Trial Revisited* (Leiden: Martinus Nijhoff Publishers, 2011).

58. Setsu Shigematsu and Keith L. Camacho, eds., *Militarized Currents: Toward a Decolonized Future in Asia and the Pacific* (Minneapolis: University of Minnesota Press, 2010), xxv–xxvi.

59. Utsumi Aiko was among the pioneer activist historians who offered a comprehensive critique of how the San Francisco Treaty and the subsequent individual postwar reparations settlement treaties were compromised by U.S. Cold War policies, which resulted in the formation of a neocolonial political economy organized under the regional hegemonies of the United States and Japan, as well as the IMF, the World Bank, and other nongovernmental organizations. *Sengo hoshō kara kangaeru Nihon to Ajia* (note 3 above) summarizes her argument. For a more recent intervention that brought inter- and intra-Asia scholarship and activisms to the North American readership, see Kuan-Hsing Chen, *Trajectories: Inter-Asia Cultural Studies* (London: Routledge, 1998); and Kuan-Hsing Chen and Beng H. Chua, eds., *The Inter-Asia Cultural Studies Reader* (London: Routledge, 2007).

60. See in English, Keith Howard, ed., *True Stories of the Korean Comfort Women: Testimonies Compiled by the Korean Council for Women Drafted for Military Sexual Slavery by Japan and the Research Association on the Women Drafted for Military Sexual Slavery by Japan*, trans. Young Joo Lee (London: Cassell, 1995).

61. Earlier English publications on "comfort women" redress can be found in Choi, *The Comfort Women*. Of late, C. Sarah Soh's *The Comfort Women* (see note 10

above) is perhaps the most comprehensive account available in English on the complex and diverse ways in which the Japanese military comfort system operated historically and how it has been remembered and represented in the "history wars" between Korean and Japanese nationalists. While I agree with her argument that the issue of Japan's wartime military comfort system is a product of "long-standing structural violence (intersecting with class, ethnicity, and nationality factors) embedded in the still-prevalent masculinist sexual cultures of the two countries (240)," and while I appreciate her nuanced critique of the problematic appropriation of "comfort women" issues by domestic and overseas nationalisms, I take issue with her representation of Korean redress activism, especially her binary presentation of Korean feminists and activists as nationalistically holding on to the "one-dimensional" truth, in contradistinction to her own cosmopolitan "middle-ground" and multifaceted scholarly understanding. Korean as well as Japanese feminist redress activists, though far from uniform, are critically aware of the complex, multifaceted, and collaborative nature of Japan's military comfort system. Moreover, Soh's distinction between activist and nonactivist feminist scholars is arbitrary. Needless to say, scholarly neutrality is not the same as objectivity; one can present an objective analysis from a position of commitment, as Soh in fact does. Nonetheless, Soh's work is invaluable for clearing the paths for further, better informed debates on this matter.

62. Yuki Tanaka, *Japan's Comfort Women: Sexual Slavery and Prostitution during World War II and the US Occupation* (London: Routledge, 2002).

63. For the pioneering collaborative project that put forward such a transpacific and transwar critique of militarized sexual violence, see Elaine Kim and Chungmoo Choi's *Dangerous Women: Gender and Korean Nationalism* (New York: Routledge, 1998). See also Katharine H. S. Moon, *Sex among Allies: Military Prostitution in U.S.-Korea Relations* (New York: Columbia University Press, 1997); Seungsook Moon, "Regulating Desire, Managing the Empire: U.S. Military Prostitution in South Korea, 1945–1970," in Maria Höhn and Seungsook Moon, eds., *Over There: Living with the U.S. Military Empire from World War Two to the Present* (Durham: Duke University Press, 2010), 39–77; and Grace M. Cho, *Haunting the Korean Diaspora: Shame, Secrecy, and the Forgotten War* (Minneapolis: University of Minnesota Press, 2008).

64. On this point see especially Neferti Xina M. Tadiar, *Fantasy-Production: Sexual Economies and Other Philippine Consequences for the New World Order* (Hong Kong: Hong Kong University Press, 2004/5).

65. One of the conveners, the late journalist Matsui Yayori, reminisced that stories of wartime Japan's military comfort system had been a haunting presence as early as the seventies when she investigated the commercial sex-tour industry. Matsui Yayori, "Naze sabaku ka, dō sabaku ka: 'Josei Kokusai Senpan Hōtei' ga mezasu mono," *Sekai* 682 (December 2000): 108–15.

66. Nihon Chōsen Kenkyūsho, *Nichi-Chō-Chū sangoku jinmin rentai no rekishi to riron* (Tokyo: Nihon Chōsen Kenkyūsho, 1964). I thank Itagaki Ryūta for calling my attention to this pamphlet.

67. Itagaki Ryūta, "Shokuminchi sekinin o teiritsu suru tame ni," in Iwasaki Minoru et al., eds., *Keizoku suru shokuminchishugi: Jendā, minzoku, jinshu, kaikyū* (Tokyo: Seikyūsha, 2005), 310. The second part of the essay is: "Datsureisen to shokuminchi shihai sekinin no tsuikyū: Zoku/shokuminchi shihai sekinin o teiritsu suru tame ni," in Kim and Nakano, *Rekishi to sekinin*, 260–84. Discussion on the Japanese colonial restitutions for Korea can be found in English in Catherine Lu, "Colonialism as Structural Injustice: Historical Responsibility and Contemporary Redress," *The Journal of Political Philosophy* 19, no. 3 (2011): 261–81.

68. Nakano Toshio, "Higashiajia de 'sengo' o tou koto: Shokuminchishugi no keizoku o hasoku suru mondai kōsei towa," in Iwasaki Minoru et al., eds., *Keizoku suru shokuminchishugi*. The collaborative project produced three milestone publications: *Keizoku suru shokuminchishugi: Jendā, minzoku, jinshu, kaikyū* (2005); *Okinawa no senryō to Nihon no fukkō: Shokuminchishugi wa ikani keizoku shitaka* (2006); and most important to the current project, Kim and Nakano, *Rekishi to sekinin* (2008), which was translated into Korean almost simultaneously.

69. That Americans singlehandedly drafted the charter for the Tokyo War Crimes Trial, unlike the joint authorship of the London Charter before the Nuremberg International Military Tribunal (formally the Agreement and Charter for the Prosecution and Punishment of Major War Criminals of the European Axis, 1945–1946), also contributed to greater U.S. maneuvering regarding the prosecution. See Richard Minear's comparison: "Long negotiations among the Big Four at the London Conference had produced the Nuremberg Charter. No similar conference preceded the promulgation of the Tokyo Charter. Instead, the Tokyo Charter was an executive decree of General Douglas MacArthur, Supreme Commander for the Allied Powers in Japan, acting under orders from the United States Joint Chiefs of Staff. The charter itself had been drawn up by Americans, primarily by Chief Prosecutor Joseph B. Keenan. America's allies were consulted only after the charter had been issued." Minear, *Victor's Justice*, 20.

70. Tōkyō Saiban Handobukku Henshū Iinnkai, ed., *Tōkyō saiban handobukku* (Tokyo: Aoki Shoten, 1999), 5, 17.

71. The television media dealt with the Unit 731 in the early seventies, but it was not until Morimura Seiichi's nonfiction novel, *Akuma no hōshoku*, published in 1981–1982, that the history became widely known. The negotiations over medical information during the IMTFE were documented by Nippon Hōsō Kyōkai (NHK), or Japan Broadcasting Corporation. Sheldon H. Harris's *Factories of Death: Japanese Biological Warfare 1932–45 and the American Cover-up* (New York: Routledge, 1994) was one of the first to introduce this piece of history in English.

72. For scrupulous studies of the massacre at Nanking, see especially Daqing Yang, "The Malleable and the Contested: The Nanjing Massacre in Postwar China and Japan," in Fujitani, White, and Yoneyama, *Perilous Memories*, 50–86; and Takashi Yoshida, *The Making of the "Rape of Nanking": History and Memory in Japan, China, and the United States* (New York: Oxford University Press, 2006).

73. Ajia Minshū Hōtei Junbi Kai, ed., *Toinaosu Tōkyō saiban* (Tokyo: Ryokufū Shuppan, 1995). The "Asian People's Tribunal" also sought to redeem Japanese

sovereignty by administering its own justice in the prosecution of war crimes. Such a plan was indeed in place in the war's immediate aftermath; but the terms of surrender rendered it moot.

74. More recently, the historian Chŏng Yŏng-hwang reintroduced the earlier *zainichi* Korean critique of the IMTFE. According to Chŏng, at the time of the trial zainichi Korean intellectuals used the press to publicly express an anticolonial critique of the IMTFE. Chŏng Yŏng-hwang, "Shiryō to kaisetsu: Tōkyō saiban o meguru zainichi Chōsenjin hakkō zasshi shinbun/kikanshi no ronchō," *Nikkan sōgo ninshiki* 1 (2008): 19–67.

75. For example, Gary Jonathan Bass, *Stay the Hand of Vengeance: The Politics of War Crimes Tribunals* (Princeton, NJ: Princeton University Press, 2000); Yuma Totani, *The Tokyo War Crimes Trial: The Pursuit of Justice in the Wake of World War II* (Cambridge, MA: Harvard University Asia Center, 2008); and Nicola Henry, "Memory of an Injustice: The 'Comfort Women' and the Legacy of the Tokyo Trial," *Asian Studies Review* 37, no. 3 (September 2013): 362–80. A different approach to the two military tribunals that historicizes their societal impact in the Japanese national contexts can be found in Madoka Futamura's *War Crimes Tribunals and Transitional Justice: The Tokyo Trial and the Nuremburg Legacy* (London: Routledge, 2008).

76. Danilo Zolo, *Victors' Justice: From Nuremberg to Baghdad* (London: Verso, 2009). Rory Rowman, among others, criticizes Zolo's and others' appropriations of Carl Schmitt's argument and argues that the advocacy of multipolar international orders replicates the Schmittian pitfalls of a pluralistic approach to geopolitics through "a set of large-scale spatial units [*Großraum*]": "A New Nomos of Post-Nomos? Multipolarity, Space, and Constituent Power," in Stephen Legg, ed., *Spatiality, Sovereignty and Carl Schmitt: Geographies of the Nomos* (London: Routledge, 2011), 143–62. While I agree with Rowman on this point, exposing the predicaments of international law's criminalization of war does not necessarily or exclusively lead to such geopolitical pluralism as its alternative.

77. See Carl Schmitt, *The Nomos of the Earth in the International Law of the Jus Publicum Europaeum*, trans. G. L. Ulmen (New York: Telos Press, [1950] 2003), 259–80.

78. This radically opened the path to a potential "global civil war" (93). Schmitt's two famous examples were Lenin and Mao against whose "revolutionary class enmity" a "global civil war" would be waged. Carl Schmitt, *Theory of the Partisan: Intermediate Commentary on the Concept of the Political*, trans. G. L. Ulmen (New York: Telos Press, [1975] 2007), 93–95.

79. Achille Mbembe, "Necropolitics," trans. Libby Meintjes, *Public Culture* 15, no. 1 (2003): 11–40.

80. Sun Ge, "Shikō no shūkan: Tōkyō saiban to sengo Higashi Ajia," trans. Satō Ken, *Posuto Higashi Ajia* (Tokyo: Sakuhinsha, 2006), 197. My translation.

81. Takeuchi Yoshimi, "Kindai no chōkoku" (1959), in, eds., Kawakami Tetustarō et al., ed. (Tokyo: Toyamabō, [1979] 2010), 306. My translation.

82. Michael Hardt and Antonio Negri, *Empire* (Cambridge, MA: Harvard University Press, 2000). The problem of their totalizing narrative notwithstanding, they

offer useful observations of new imperialist formations since the 1990s. See especially the chapter, "Network Power: U.S. Sovereignty and the New Empire," 160–82.

83. Elizabeth Kiss, "Moral Ambition within and beyond Political Constraints: Reflections on Restorative Justice," in Robert I. Rotberg and Dennis Thompson, eds., *Truth v. Justice: The Morality of Truth Commissions* (Princeton, NJ: Princeton University Press, 2000), 92.

84. I refer to the term, "Pacific Century," as it appeared in Hillary Clinton, "America's Pacific Century," *Foreign Policy* 189 (2011). In it Clinton laid out the Obama administration's refocalization on Asia in U.S. foreign policies. Obviously, "Pacific Century" is a misnomer—the focus of the article is northeast Asia, especially China. The Pacific is relegated to an empty space to be crossed over by U.S. capital to effectively reach the other side of the rim. See also Arif Dirlik, ed., *What Is in a Rim? Critical Perspectives on the Pacific Region Idea* (Lanham, MD: Rowman and Littlefield, 1998).

85. Eleanor Lattimore, "Pacific Ocean or American Lake?" *Far Eastern Survey* (November 7, 1945): 313–16.

Chapter 1. Liminal Justice

1. For further details on the Futenma issue see, Yoshio Shimoji, "The Futenma Base and the U.S.-Japan Controversy: An Okinawan Perspective," *The Asia-Pacific Journal*, 18–5–10, May 1, 2010.

2. These areas stretch from the Far East, to which the U.S.-Japan Security Treaty formally delimits U.S. military operations involving Japan, to Southeast Asia and the Middle East. For Okinawa's relation to the U.S. war in Afghanistan, see *Ryūkyū Shimpō*, March 11, 2010.

3. Information obtained through *Wikileaks* was reported in local and national newspapers. See *Ryūkyū shimpō*, May 5, 2011 and *Asahi Shimbun*, May 4, 2011. They disclosed that high-ranking Japanese bureaucrats had contacted Washington officials and advised the U.S. government not to make any concessions when negotiating Futenma base issues with the Hatoyama regime or the Democratic Party.

4. Annmaria Shimabuku broadly terms this overall arrangement a "transpacific colonialism." See her "Transpacific Colonialism: An Intimate View of Transnational Activism in Okinawa," *CR: The New Centennial Review* 12, no. 1 (2012): 131–58.

5. Due to the widespread antibase protest in the aftermath of the 1995 rape case, an amendment was made to the existing agreement regarding the status of U.S. armed forces in Japan. Article 17.5(c) reads: "The custody of an accused member of the United States armed forces or the civilian component over whom Japan is to exercise jurisdiction shall, if he is in the hands of the United States, remain with the United States until he is charged by Japan." The revised agreement reads: "The United States will give sympathetic consideration to any request for the transfer of custody prior to indictment of the accused which may be made by Japan in specific cases of heinous crimes of murder or rape." "Nichibei chii kyōtei dai 17jō 5(c) oyobi, keiji saiban tetsuzuki ni kakawaru Nichibei Gōdō Iinkai gōi,"

Gaimushō, accessed March 1, 2014, http://www.mofa.go.jp/mofaj/area/usa/sfa /rem_keiji_o1.html#contents.

6. The brief "end of the Cold War" hiatus did indeed bring in a momentary rupture. In 1995 the socialist prime minister Murayama Tomiichi led a cabinet that diverged dramatically from the previous LDP historical outlook by reckoning that Japan's actions in the Asia-Pacific War did not constitute self-defense, but invasion. And yet, his coalition cabinet did not differ from the former cabinet position on the U.S.-Japan military alliance and the official position regarding the San Francisco Treaty and other postwar settlements. Two decades later, the Obama regime's return to the American foreign affairs policy that stresses the strategic importance of Asia appears to have given license to Japan's LDP-led cabinet, which has recaptured power, to further entrench Okinawa into the militarized state.

7. Ōshiro Tatsuhiro, "*Kakuteru pātī*," in *Kakuteru pātī* (Tokyo: Iwanami Shoten, 181–258. For an English translation, see Ōshiro Tatsuhiro, "*The Cocktail Party*," trans. Steve Rabson, in Steve Rabson, ed., *Two Postwar Novellas* (Berkeley: Center for Japanese Studies, 1989), 35–80. I find Rabson's colloquial readability helpful. But I adopted my own translation of *Kakuteru pātī* in order to capture the text's logocentrism, which permeates even conversational exchanges among the characters. Much of the conversation appearing in the story is supposedly conducted in Chinese, and the Japanese renderings reflect the bookishness characteristic of literary translations.

8. Ōshiro Tatsuhiro, " 'Ryūkyū shobun' sawagi," *Ryūkyū Shimpō*, January 20, 2011. Ōshiro observes the rhetorical use of the term "Ryukyu Disposition" in Okinawa. Unlike on the mainland it has often been used to characterize the Japanese government's autocratic policies on base-related issues. The Futenma issue, for example, came to be known as "the second Ryukyu Disposition."

9. The novel had once been republished in 1972. Following Kan's sensationalized remark, it almost immediately appeared in a popular paperback edition in August 2010.

10. Tomiyama Ichirō has most insightfully articulated this process of imperial subjectification: *Kindai Nihon shakai to Okinawajin: Nihonjin ni naru to iu koto* (Tokyo: Nihon Keizai Hyōronsha, 2006). See Leo Ching's *Becoming "Japanese": Colonial Taiwan and the Politics of Identity Formation* (Berkeley: University of California Press, 2001) for a comparable process in colonial Taiwan under Japanese imperialization (*kōminka*).

11. Earlier I observed a similar discursive habit in the absenting of colonial memories of ethnic Koreans in the representation of Hiroshima's atom bombing. See *Hiroshima Traces: Time, Space and the Dialectics of Memory* (Berkeley: University of California Press, 1999).

12. In his critique of Marx's critical ontology and arguing that his theory of commodity fetishism and the relationship between the base and superstructure were enabled by the "conjuring away" or "exorcising" of various societal and spiritual elements, Jacques Derrida offered hauntology as a key method for deconstructing

Western metaphysics. *Specters of Marx: The State of the Debt, the Work of Mourning, and the New International* (New York: Routledge, 1994).

13. Avery F. Gordon, *Ghostly Matters: Haunting and the Sociological Imagination* (Minneapolis: University of Minnesota Press, 2008), 202. Underscoring the concerns for transformation and change in the works of Luisa Valenzuela and Toni Morrison, Gordon concludes: "The ghostly phantom objects and subjects of modernity have a determining agency on the ones they are haunting" (201). See, in contrast, Fredric Jameson, "Marx's Purloined Letter," in Michael Sprinker, ed., *Ghostly Demarcations: A Symposium on Jacques Derrida's* Specters of Marx (London: Verso, [1999] 2008), 26–67.

14. See among others, Chungmoo Choi, "The Discourse of Decolonization and Popular Memory: South Korea," *positions: east asia cultures critique* 1, no. 1 (spring 1993): 77–102; and Bruce Cumings's pioneering work, *The Origins of the Korean War: Liberation and the Emergence of Separate Regimes 1945–1947* (Princeton, NJ: Princeton University Press, 1981). See also his "Colonial Formations and Deformations: Korea, Taiwan, and Vietnam," in *Parallax Visions: Making Sense of American–East Asian Relations at the End of the Century* (Durham, NC: Duke University Press, 1999).

15. Heonik Kwon, *The Other Cold War* (New York: Columbia University Press, 2010), 137.

16. The incident on February 28, 1947, in which an estimated total of more than twenty thousand Taiwanese were killed by the Republic of China's military force led by the Nationalist government, is another example of postliberation violence.

17. On the colonial nature of international law, see Antony Anghie, *Imperialism, Sovereignty, and the Making of International Law* (Cambridge: Cambridge University Press, 2005).

18. Toriyama Atsushi, "Okinawa's 'Postwar': Some Observations on the Formation of American Military Bases in the Aftermath of Terrestrial Warfare," trans. David Buist, in Kuan-Hsing Chen and Beng H. Chua, eds., *The Inter-Asia Cultural Studies Reader* (London: Routledge, 2007), 273.

19. U.S. policy makers regarded the Ryukyu and other Pacific islands as spoils of war, so to speak. In his studies of the United States' military involvement in the post–World War II Pacific, the historian Hal M. Friedman describes this American perception as follows: "High casualties, in particular, helped form a strong postwar strategic mindset about annexing island groups and creating an American lake in the Pacific basin. For example, American casualties sustained in the Marshall, Mariana, Caroline, Volcano, and Ryukyu Islands campaigns had a telling effect on American officials who specifically and repeatedly discussed the islands in the context of the 'blood and treasure' expanded from them. In fact, in July 1945, Secretary of the Navy James Forrestal *used American casualty figures in these campaigns to justify American postwar rights in the Pacific* by eagerly providing this information to Senator Harry Byrd in order to reinforce in congressional circles the idea of annexing the islands after the war" (italics added). Hal M. Friedman, *Creating an American Lake: United States Imperialism and Strategic Security in the Pacific Basin, 1945–1947* (Westport, CT: Greenwood Press, 2001), 4.

20. For the most comprehensive assessment of Ōshiro's writings on Okinawa that is attentive to their multivalent quality when read against the backdrop of East Asia's postcoloniality, see Namihira Tsuneo, "Ōshiro Tatsuhiro no bungaku ni miru Okinawajin no sengo," *Gendai shisō* 29, no. 9 (July 2001): 124–53.

21. Chalmers A. Johnson, *The Sorrows of Empire: Militarism, Secrecy, and the End of the Republic* (London: Verso, 2004).

22. See, for instance, Michael S. Molasky, *The American Occupation of Japan and Okinawa: Literature and Memory* (London: Routledge, 1999). In his exploration of the literary construction of Okinawan identity and difference, Molasky relied on Fredric Jameson's reading of Third World literatures as national allegory and concluded, "Like many men's narratives of the occupation, *The Cocktail Party* revolves around rape yet relegates the act and its victim to the margins of the text. The rape appears as a lacunae, as an absence that primarily serves to establish the victimhood of the male protagonist. . . . In *The Cocktail Party* the bodily act of rape thus becomes disembodied, reduced to a symbolic and structural role that conveys none of the violence and violation inherent in the act itself" (52).

23. Miyagi Kimiko, "Gunji senryō to seibōryoku: mondai no shozai," in Nakano Toshio et al., eds., *Okinawa no senryō to Nihon no fukkō: Shokuminchishugi wa ikani keizoku shitaka* (Tokyo: Seikyūsha, 2006), 31–41. For an important critique of Molasky's binarism in his gender and sexuality analysis of Okinawan literatures, see especially Shinjō Ikuo, "Okinawa senryō to gei shintai seijisei: Shokuminchi no dansei sekushuariti," in Nakano et al., *Okinawa no senryō to Nihon no fukkō*, 85–107. Shinjō argues that such a gender and sexual binary reproduces what he calls the "heterosexual matrix." Focusing on the representation of Okinawan gay male figures, Shinjō notes: "Molasky's commentaries completely lack thoughts about the complex power relations of male sexuality pertaining to both the occupier and the occupied because it grasps the sex/politicity [*sei=seijisei*] of the American occupation through the gender contradistinction between masculinity (i.e., the occupying American soldiers) and femininity (i.e., the native Okinawans including 'men')" (89).

24. *Kakuteru pātī* (Tokyo: Iwanami Shoten, [1967] 2011), 150.

25. For critical historical assessment of the prewar Japanese empire's multiracial, multiethnic soldiering, see Utsumi Aiko, "Korean 'Imperial Soldiers': Remembering Colonialism and Crimes against Allied POWs," in *Perilous Memories: Asia-Pacific War(s)*, edited by Takashi Fujitani, Geoffrey M. White, and Lisa Yoneyama (Durham, NC: Duke University Press, 2001), 199–217; and T. Fujitani, *Race for Empire: Koreans as Japanese and Japanese as Americans during World War II* (Berkeley: University of California Press, 2011).

26. See, for example, Ishihara Masaie, *Okinawasen ni okeru Nihongun to jūmin gisei: Kyōkasho saiban (daisanji soshō kōsoshin) no shōgen "ikensho"* (Tokyo: Kyōkasho Kentei Soshō o Shien suru Zenkoku Renrakukai, 1991).

27. In the aforementioned work Ishihara Masaie has collected testimonials of so-called collective suicide (shūdan jiketsu), in which survivors describe circumstances under which many residents were forced into mass suicide or were driven to murdering their own family and community members, primarily due to the Japanese military

doctrine of refusing capture. The excavation of these memories led to the high-profile incident in which a local grocer named Chibana Shōichi destroyed the rising-sun flag in protest against Japanese policy over Okinawa. The latter case is detailed in Norma Field, *In the Realm of a Dying Emperor* (New York: Pantheon Books, 1991).

28. See especially Edward Friedman and Mark Selden, eds., *America's Asia: Dissenting Essays on Asian-American Relations* (New York: Pantheon Books, 1971). See also the introduction to E. H. Norman and John W. Dower, *Origins of the Modern Japanese State: Selected Writings of E.H. Norman* (New York: Pantheon Books, 1975). Indeed, this group of scholars and their close associates continue to raise critical voices on U.S. transpacific affairs. Equally important for the critique of area studies, there is a generalizable difference between the interventions of the late sixties and the early nineties. If the earlier instance left intact many assumptions about North American liberal values and historiography, the nineties disciplinary self-examination extended beyond the ontological to include reflections on some of the most foundational premises of modernity.

29. Bruce Cumings, "Boundary Displacement: Area Studies and International Studies during and after the Cold War," *Bulletin of Concerned Asian Scholars* 29, no. 1 (1997): 8.

The international dissemination of American-style area studies resulted, for example, in financial aid from such foundations as Ford and Rockefeller, which helped establish two major research centers in Japan, each devoted to the study of languages and cultures of the so-called developing countries of Southeast Asia and Africa. In 1963 the Center for Southeast Asian Studies was founded at Kyoto University, and the Research Institute for Languages and Cultures of Asia and Africa at the Tokyo University of Foreign Studies.

30. A. B. Shamsul also links what he calls "methodological nationalism" to deploy knowledge "based mainly on the 'territoriality' of the nation-state" to Cold War area studies. See "Producing Knowledge of Southeast Asia: A Malaysian View," in Kuan-Hsing Chen and Beng H. Chua, eds., *The Inter-Asia Cultural Studies Reader* (London: Routledge, 2007), 140–60.

31. The anthropologists Akhil Gupta and James Ferguson explained in detail the problems of this type of anthropological knowledge production. See "Beyond 'Culture': Space, Identity, and the Politics of Difference," in Akhil Gupta and James Ferguson, eds., *Culture, Power, Place: Explorations in Critical Anthropology* (Durham, NC: Duke University Press, 1997), 33–51. In part responding to the 1990s post–Cold War moment and in part urged by the heightened awareness of accelerating globalization, transnationalization, and other border crossing phenomena, Gupta and Ferguson, among others, led a cohort of anthropologists who challenged the epistemic categories that have been foundational to the discipline of anthropology. Arguing that "the geographical territories that cultures and societies are believed to map onto do not have to be nations," Gupta and Ferguson pointed out that even cutting-edge anthropological studies tend to rely on what they regarded as the "assumed isomorphism of space, place, and culture" (34). The "assumed isomorphism of space, place, and culture," moreover, puts border-crossers

such as "immigrants, refugees, exiles, and expatriates" (34) outside the purview of anthropological observation.

32. To illustrate, in cross-cultural kinship study the anthropologist George Peter Murdock and others observed a vast array of gender and family relations through the "nuclear family" unit that was to be found universally. Likewise, the sociologist Robert Bellah's study famously identified parallels between Protestantism and early modern Japanese religion and argued that the latter had facilitated Japan's capitalist development and modernization in a way that was different from, and yet equivalent to, the process the advanced Euro-American nations were understood to have undergone. Robert N. Bellah, *Tokugawa Religion: The Values of Pre-Industrial Japan* (New York: Free Press, [1957] 1969). I became exposed to the critique of modernization theory through my undergraduate supervisor, Tsurumi Kazuko. Tsurumi was among the first generation of scholars in Japan during the mid-seventies who systematically pointed out the problems of modernization theory propagated by the American sociologists Marion J. Levy and others. See for the seminal work, Tsurumi Kazuko and Ichii Saburō, eds., *Shisō no bōken: Shakai to henka no atarashii paradaimu* (Tokyo: Chikuma Shobō, 1974).

33. In observing the U.S.-Japan context, T. Fujitani likewise underscores the importance of examining the transwar connectivity. He observed that as early as September 1942 policy advisers such as Edwin O. Reischauer were already making plans to remake Japan into a postwar friend and ally and to utilize Japanese-Americans as cultural and racial brokers. This "triggered a fundamental transformation of popular images about Japan and the Japanese people that clearly accelerated in the postwar and Cold War years" (230). According to Fujitani the recent critique of Cold War area studies has not fully appreciated the wartime origins of Cold War knowledge: "Though critical scholarship on Cold War modernization theory has already unveiled its ties to U.S. imperialism, much less has been made of the transwar linkages between this theory and U.S. plans for hegemony in Asia that were already being hatched during the hot war" (*Race for Empire*, 231). Bruce Cumings may be a notable exception. Cumings traced a genealogy between the fact observed previously by historian Akira Iriye "that as early as 1942 a small cadre of internationalists in the American State Department and in Japan began moving on remarkably parallel lines to reintegrate Japan into the postwar American hegemonic regime" and "that by 1947 George Kennan had elaborated plans for Japan's industrial revival; and that these plans called for a modified restoration of Japan's former colonial position in northeast Asia." "Archaeology, Descent, Emergence: American Mythology and East Asian Reality," in *Parallax Visions*, 31.

34. Rexmond C. Cochrane, *The National Academy of Sciences: The First Hundred Years, 1863–1963* (Washington, DC: The Academy, 1978).

35. "The Okinawas: A Japanese Minority Group, Summary Statement (Second Edition)," *Okinawan Studies* 1, Office of Strategic Services, Honolulu, Hawaii, March 16, 1944. I am indebted to Ishihara Shun's MA thesis for alerting me to Tozzer's report: "Gunji senryō o meguru chi no jūsōteki hensei: Okinawa ni okeru <rekishi no shūdatsu>" *Soshioroji* 44, no. 1 (May 1995): 3–19.

36. This passage is taken from Alfred M. Tozzer's full report, *The Okinawas of the Loo Choo Islands: A Japanese Minority Group* (Honolulu: Office of Strategic Services, Research and Analysis Branch, 1944), republished in Okinawa Kenritsu Toshokan Shiryō Henshūshitsu, ed., *Okinawa kenshi, shiryōhen 2: Okinawasen 2 (genbunhen)* (Okinawa: Okinawaken Kyōiku Iinkai, 1996), 123. *The Okinawas of the Loo Choo Islands* is slightly different from the "Summary Statement" I cited earlier and offers a more extensive recommendation of the operative usefulness of Okinawans through the utilization of the historical rift between Okinawa and the mainland. For example, the former includes the following strategic recommendation: "If in South America the cleft between Loo Chooans and Naichijin can be utilized, why not in their own archipelago, in the Mandates and in the Philippines where in each area the Okinawas [*sic*] form the larger part of a Japanese population?" *Okinawa kenshi, shiryōhen 2*, 123.

37. Ruth Benedict's canonical work of anthropology, *The Chrysanthemum and the Sword*, likewise illustrates this transference between wartime knowledge and the postwar management of the former enemy-turned-ally. See Yoneyama, "Habits of Knowing Cultural Differences: *Chrysanthemum and the Sword* in U.S. Liberal Multiculturalism," *Topoi* 18 (1999): 71–80. In Benedict's analysis, the same features of Japanese national culture—for example, excessive situationalism, shame culture, the authoritarian, hierarchical personality, and so forth—that had negatively defined the Japanese as a despicable, ferocious enemy during the war turned out to offer favorable characteristics that would facilitate the U.S. occupation of postwar Japan. Benedict thought that the U.S. occupation policy of rebuilding Japan as an American ally was not only accepted but even facilitated, "precisely because of the culturally conditioned character of the Japanese." Ruth Benedict, *The Chrysanthemum and the Sword: Patterns of Japanese Culture* (Boston: Houghton Mifflin Company, [1946] 1989), 299. Wartime national character studies of the enemy Japan soon evolved into a psychological "culture and personality" school that flourished in postwar American anthropology.

38. Murdock also founded the Scientific Investigation of the Ryukyu Islands (SIRI, 1951–1954). He reported from Okinawa and is frequently cited in declassified documents on psychological warfare compiled in *Okinawa kenshi, shiryōhen 2* mentioned above, 145–243. Writings on Murdock are many. See, for example, Ward H. Goodenough, "George P. Murdock, 1897–1985," National Academy of Sciences, Washington DC, 1994; and David H. Price, *Threatening Anthropology: McCarthyism and the FBI's Surveillance of Activist Anthropologists* (Duke University Press, 2004).

39. Tomiyama, "'Chiiki kenkyū' to iu arīna: Sengo Okinawa kenkyū o megutte," in Kokuritsu Minzokugaku Hakubutsukan Chiiki Kenkyū Kikaku Kōryū Sentā, ed., *Chiiki kenkyū ronshū 2*, no. 1 (1999): 7–17; see 11.

40. According to the anthropologist Mahmood Mamdani, despite the anthropologists' theoretical intervention over the past decade, the notion of culture as static, impenetrable, and commanding is deployed to explain and give meaning to the conflict and violence associated with Muslim nations. Mamdani called such a speech act "Culture Talk." Mahmood Mamdani, *Good Muslim,*

Bad Muslim: America, the Cold War, and the Roots of Terror (New York: Pantheon Books, 2004).

41. See Masamichi S. Inoue, *Okinawa and the U.S. Military: Identity Making in the Age of Globalization* (New York: Columbia University Press, 2007). Borrowing from historian Kano Masanao, Inoue showed that the U.S. Civil Administration of the Ryukyu Islands (USCAR) attempted to restore the pride and identity of Ryukyu and undertook measures toward "Ryukyuanizing (i.e., 'un-Japanizing') Okinawa" (49).

42. Gayatri Chakravorty Spivak, "Can the Subaltern Speak?" (1988), in Patrick Williams and Laura Chrisman, eds., *Colonial Discourse and Post-Colonial Theory: A Reader* (New York: Columbia University Press, 1994), 102.

43. Namihira Tsuneo, "Ōshiro Tatsuhiro no bungaku ni miru Okinawajin no sengo," 133.

44. "Chosha no oboegaki 9: Ugoku jikan to ugokanai jikan," in *Ōshiro Tatsuhiro Zenshū*, vol. 9 (Tokyo: Bensei Shuppan, 2002), 467. In this short reflection, Ōshiro noted, for example, that while there is an unmistakable lightheartedness (*akarusa*) in Okinawa's otherwise troubled relationship with the American forces, such an understanding is lost when the Japanese on the mainland observe Okinawa. Similarly, with regard to his short story "Kamishima," in which he depicted the return of a former Japanese lieutenant to the island where he had been rumored to have ordered residents to commit mass suicide or domicide during the war, Ōshiro suspected that local sentiments and memories toward the former colonizer could not be reduced to hatred alone.

45. The historian Toriyama Atsushi examined the political documents in the immediate postwar Okinawa to observe the transitions in the idea of Okinawa's self-determination, or more precisely, self-governance. While the idea of "Okinawa *minzoku* (ethnos)" and "*Okinawajin*" became possible under the American occupation that signified Okinawa's "liberation" from Japanese rule, as disillusionment with U.S. military governance deepened, hopes for Okinawa's self-determination became increasingly pronounced through equating liberation of Okinawa with regaining sovereign independence as part of Japan. Toriyama noted that many people in Okinawa felt they had earned the political status as Japanese through their wartime sacrifices. Toriyama Atsushi, "'Okinawa no jichi' e no katsubō: Sengo shoki seitō kankei shiryō o chūshin ni miru seiji ishiki," *Okinawa kenshi kenkyū kiyō* 4 (March 1997): 61–80.

46. On this point, see especially Hiyane Teruo's "Kindaishi ni okeru Okinawa zō" (1970), republished in *Kindai Okinawa no seishinshi* (Tokyo: Shakai Hyōronsha, 1996). With great exigency for the historical moment, Hiyane argued that within the call for "Homeland Reversion" it was necessary to distinguish between the image of the homeland imposed "from the top," as outlined in the U.S.-Japan Security Treaty, and an alternative idea of homeland envisioned "from the bottom" (108). The latter aspired to a radically transformed nationhood that would resonate with anticolonial nationalisms in other parts of Asia and Africa.

47. Rabson, "Introduction," in *Two Postwar Novellas*, 1–31; Namihira, "Ōshiro Tatsuhiro no bungaku ni miru Okinawajin no sengo," see esp. 141; also Moto-

hama Hidehiko, "Kaisetsu," in *Kakuteru pātī* (Tokyo: Iwanami Shoten, 2011), 305–17.

48. For critiques of the conventional periodization of wars, see *Perilous Memories: Asia-Pacific War(s)*, esp. Arif Dirlik, " 'Trapped in History' on the Way to Utopia: East Asia's 'Great War' Fifty Years Later," 299–322.

49. Chiang's leniency policy resulted in war trials for Japanese POWs between 1946 and 1949 in ten locations, and the prosecution of over a hundred individuals for conventional war crimes. Some recent studies on the leniency policies are Arai Toshio, "Chūka Jinmin Kyōwakoku no senpan saiban," in VAWW-NET Japan, ed. *Senpan saiban to seibōryoku, Nihongun seidoreisei o sabaku: 2002nen Josei Kokusai Senpan Hōtei no kiroku, vol. 1* (Ryokufu Shuppan, 2000), 123–53; Toyoda Masayuki, "Chūgoku no tainichi senpan shori seisaku: Genbatsushugi kara 'kandai seisaku' e," *Shien* 69 (2009): 15–45; Wada Hideo, "Kokumin seifu no tainichi sengo shori hōshin no jissai: Senpan mondai to baishō mondai," *ICCS Research Report of Youth Researchers* 1 (2006): 123–33; Adam Cathcart and Patricia Nash, "War Criminals and the Road to Sino-Japanese Normalization," *Sino-Japanese Relations: History, Politics, Economy* 2 (2011): 49–70; and " 'To Serve Revenge for the Dead': Chinese Communist Responses to Japanese War Crimes in the PRC Foreign Ministry Archive, 1949–1956," *China Quarterly* 200 (2009): 1053–69. See also Barak Kushner, "Pawns of Empire: Postwar Taiwan, Japan and the Dilemma of War Crimes," *Japanese Studies* 30, no. 1 (2010): 111–33. I will discuss the politics of memory and forgiveness concerning the Japanese POWs from the PRC's Fushun Management Center in chapter 3.

50. Many of the Japanese POWs detained by the PRC were captured initially by the Soviet Union in northern China and who were later transferred to PRC jurisdiction with the signing of the 1950 Sino-Soviet Treaty of Friendship, Alliance and Mutual Assistance. The PRC delivered final judgment on these and other Japanese POWs in 1956.

51. Toyoda Masayuki, "Chūgoku no tainichi senpan shori seisaku," 15–45.

52. Charles Villa-Vicencio and Erik Doxtader, eds., *The Provocations of Amnesty: Memory, Justice, and Impunity* (Trenton, NJ: Africa World Press, 2003).

53. Janice Radway, "What's in a Name? Presidential Address to the American Studies Association, 20 November, 1998," *American Quarterly* 51, no. 1 (1999): 2.

54. I originally presented what later became this chapter's core argument as a paper at the American Studies Association session "War, Memory, and Post-Nationalist American Studies" (Montreal, October 28, 1999), organized by Shelley Streeby and Curtis Marez.

55. Giorgio Agamben, "Beyond Human Rights," in *Means without End: Notes on Politics* (Minneapolis: University of Minnesota Press, 2000), 19.

56. Agamben, Giorgio. *Homo Sacer: Sovereign Power and Bare Life* (Stanford, CA: Stanford University Press, 1998), 128.

57. Ōshiro Tatsuhiro, "Bangai Nihonjin e no michi," *Nami* (May 1989), 2; quoted in Namihira, "Ōshiro Tatsuhiro no bungaku ni miru Okinawajin no sengo," 133.

Chapter 2. Liberation under Siege

1. David E. Sanger and Eric Schmitt, "U.S. Has a Plan to Occupy Iraq, Officials Report," *New York Times*, October 11, 2002.
2. Amy Kaplan, "Confusing Occupation with Liberation," *Los Angeles Times*, October 24, 2003.
3. Yen Espiritu likewise locates this discursive dynamic and its grave material consequences regarding the Vietnam War. Yen L. Espiritu, *Body Counts: The Vietnam War and Militarized Refuge(es)* (Berkeley: University of California Press, 2014).
4. "Bush Says War on Terror Led to Women's Freedom," *Los Angeles Times*, March 13, 2004; "Bush Likens War on Terror to WWII," *Los Angeles Times*, June 3, 2004.
5. "Another Pose of Rectitude," *Newsweek*, September 2, 2002, 70.
6. On the concept of American exceptionalism, see Amy Kaplan, *The Anarchy of Empire in the Making of U.S. Culture* (Cambridge, MA: Harvard University Press, 2002).
7. *Hiroshima Traces: Time, Space and the Dialectics of Memory* (Berkeley: University of California Press, 1999), chapter 6, "Postwar Peace and Feminization of Memory," 190–91.
8. Susan J. Pharr, *Political Women in Japan: The Search for a Place in Political Life* (Berkeley: University of California Press, 1981), 30–31.
9. Melani McAlister, *Epic Encounters: Culture, Media, and U.S. Interests in the Middle East since 1945* (Berkeley: University of California Press, 2001), 82–83.
10. Naoko Shibusawa's *America's Geisha Ally: Reimagining the Japanese Enemy* (Cambridge, MA: Harvard University Press, 2006) is a notable exception. Scholarship on the effects of U.S. occupation policy in Japan continues to be prolific, ranging from the seminal work by Robert E. Ward and Yoshikazu Sakamoto, eds., *Democratizing Japan: The Allied Occupation* (Honolulu: University of Hawaii Press, 1987) to John W. Dower, *Embracing Defeat: Japan in the Wake of World War II* (New York: W. W. Norton/The New Press, 1999); and Eiji Takemae, *The Allied Occupation of Japan* (New York: Continuum, 2002). See also Maho Toyoda, *Senryōka no josei rōdō Kaikaku: Hogo to byōdō o megutte* (Tōkyō: Keisō Shobō, 2007); Mark Caprio and Yoneyuki Sugita, *Democracy in Occupied Japan: The U.S. Occupation and Japanese Politics and Society* (London: Routledge, 2007); and Mire Koikari, *Pedagogy of Democracy: Feminism and the Cold War in the U.S. Occupation of Japan* (Philadelphia, PA: Temple University Press, 2010). Earlier studies that focused specifically on the occupation policies' effects on Japanese women's status, as well as Japanese women's active involvement in SCAP programs are: Yasuko Ichibangase, *Kyōdō tōgi sengo fujin mondaishi* (Tokyo: Domesu Shuppan, 1971); Kiyoko Nishi, *Senryōka no Nihon fujin seisaku: Sono rekishi to shōgen* (Tokyo: Domesu Shuppan, 1985); and Susan Pharr, "Politics of Women's Rights," in Ward and Sakamoto, *Democratizing Japan*, mentioned above.
11. Critical transnational feminism is linked to the genealogy of women of color feminism. See M. Jacqui Alexander's *Pedagogies of Crossing: Meditations on Feminism, Sexual Politics, Memory, and the Sacred* (Durham, NC: Duke University Press, 2005) for an important articulation of women of color feminist epistemology.

For important works of critical feminisms, see among others: Angela Y. Davis, *Women, Race and Class* (New York: Random House, 1981); Cherríe Moraga and Gloria Anzaldúa, eds., *This Bridge Called My Back: Writings by Radical Women of Color* (New York: Kitchen Table, 1981, 1983); Teresa de Lauretis, ed., *Feminist Studies/Critical Studies* (Bloomington: Indiana University Press, 1986); Patricia Hill Collins, *Black Feminist Thought: Knowledge, Consciousness, and the Politics of Empowerment* (London: HarperCollins Academic, 1991); Judith Butler and Joan W. Scott, eds., *Feminists Theorize the Political* (New York: Routledge, 1992); Inderpal Grewal and Caren Kaplan, eds., *Scattered Hegemonies: Postmodernity and Transnational Feminist Practices* (Minneapolis: University of Minnesota Press, 1994); M. Jacqui Alexander and Chandra Talpade Mohanty, eds., *Feminist Genealogies, Colonial Legacies, Democratic Futures* (New York: Routledge, 1997); and Gabriela F. Arrendondo et al., eds., *Chicana Feminisms: A Critical Reader* (Durham, NC: Duke University Press, 2003).

12. Helen Moscicki, "The Unhappiest Women in the World," *Saturday Evening Post* 27 (July 8, 1944): 19, 37.

13. The image of subservient and oppressed Japanese women has been dominant not only within the United States but also among Japan's modernist elites. However, the feminine ideal of chastity, subservience, and subordination to men had been shared only among a limited elite segment of society until the late nineteenth-century period of modernization and Westernization. For an ethnographic counterimage see, for instance, Robert J. Smith and Ella Lury Wiswell, *Women of Suye Mura* (Chicago: University of Chicago Press, 1989).

14. "A Japanese Women's Changing World," *New York Times*, December 7, 1941.

15. "Japan's Kimono Eclipsed by 'Uniform' for Women," *New York Times*, February 21, 1942. For similar reports in popular magazines, see, for instance, Bataviaasch Nieuwsblad, "An End to the Flippant Kimono," *Living Age* 360 (April 1941): 112; "Japanese 'Girls in Uniform,'" *Asia* 41 (May 1941). Later, "Japan Mobilizes Women" reported that Japanese premier Tōjō Hideki spoke to the public of the "necessity for mobilization of women." *New York Times*, November 12, 1943.

16. *New York Times*, September 23, 1942.

17. "2 Japanese Women Die in Action," *New York Times*, May 18, 1944. For similar emphasis on the fear of the armed Japanese women warriors, see also "Japanese Women get War Duty in Burma," May 19, 1942; "Japanese Women Snipers Reported at Guadalcanal," December 1, 1942; and "Japanese Women are Told to Fight," June 17, 1945.

18. See Sasaki Yōko on the official stipulation of Japanese women as "combatants" in 1945. *Sōryokusen to josei heishi* (Tokyo: Seikyūsha, 2001), 124.

19. I thank Shelley Streeby for calling my attention to this aspect of Japanese women warrior representation.

20. Robert Bellaire, "Slave Women of Japan," *Woman's Home Companion* 70 (February 1943): 64.

21. John Dower, *War without Mercy: Race and Power in the Pacific War* (New York: Pantheon Books, 1986).

22. "U.S. in Japan," *Life*, February 18, 1946, 32.

23. *New York Times*, October 12, 1945.

24. *New York Times*, October 14, 1945.

25. *Newsweek*, March 25, 1946, 51.

26. *New York Times*, April 11, 1946; June 2, 1946; August 23, 1946.

27. *New York Times*, August 23, 1946.

28. "The Rising Sun of Democracy," *Senior Scholastic* 48 (May 13, 1946): 12–13.

29. "Now a Japanese Woman Can Be a Cop," *New York Times Magazine*, June 2, 1946, 18, 56.

30. Marion May Dilts, "New World for Japanese Women: Elevation to Eminence Offers Opportunities and Makes Problems," *Christian Science Monitor*, August 23, 1947, 1–2.

31. *Newsweek*, October 22, 1945, 64.

32. See, for instance, "Chaplain's Aid Asked to End Fraternizing," *New York Times*, April 3, 1946. The article appeared shortly after SCAP's order to abolish the Recreation and Amusement Association (RAA), the licensed prostitution system which the Japanese government had introduced immediately following the war's end in order to accommodate the occupying troops. Yuki Tanaka considers the RAA an extension of the wartime Japanese military comfort system. In both systems the state sought to regulate militarized sexualities and gender along the lines of class and race. *Japan's Comfort Women: Sexual Slavery and Prostitution during World War II and the US Occupation* (London: Routledge, 2002), see especially 133–66. See also Keisen Jogakuen Heiwa Bunka Kenkyūjo, ed., *Senryō to sei: Seisaku, jittai, hyōshō* (Kyoto: Inpakuto Shuppankai, 2007) for a recent collaborative investigation into the complex management of sexuality in occupied mainland Japan.

33. Lindesay Parrott, "Out of Feudalism: Japan's Women," *New York Times Magazine*, October 28, 1945, 10.

34. Lindesay Parrott, "Now a Japanese Woman Can Be a Cop," *New York Times Magazine*, June 2, 1946, 18, 56. Ichikawa's name is misspelled as "Ishikawa." Similar remonstrations concerning U.S. women's sense of superiority toward Japanese women were communicated personally from Mary R. Beard to Ethel B. Weed in 1946. Chikako Uemura, "Nihon ni okeru senryō seisaku to josei kaihō: Rōdōshō fujin shōnenkyoku no seiritsu katei o chūshin toshite," *Joseigaku kenkyū* 2 (1992): 5–28.

35. See, for instance, John Dower, *Empire and Aftermath: Yoshida Shigeru and the Japanese Experience, 1878–1954* (Cambridge, MA: Council on East Asian Studies, Harvard University, 1988) and his "Occupied Japan and the American Lake, 1945–1950," in Edward Friedman and Mark Selden, eds., *America's Asia: Dissenting Essays on Asia-American Relations* (New York: Pantheon Books , 1971).

36. "Japan: Fumbling Toward Democracy," *Newsweek*, May 12, 1947, 40.

37. Lafe Franklin Allen, "Democracy in Japan," *Commonweal* 46 (September 1947): 542–46. For the enduring implications of the Congress of Industrial Organizations' suppression of workers' direct actions and wildcat strikes in the Cold War, see George Lipsitz, *Rainbow at Midnight: Labor and Culture in the 1940s* (Urbana: University of Illinois Press, 1994).

38. Works dating from this period in this genre are many, but a list of some of the more commonly read books might begin with Mikiso Hane, *Peasants, Rebels, and Outcastes: The Underside of Modern Japan* (New York: Pantheon, 1982) and *Reflections on the Way to the Gallows: Rebel Women in Prewar Japan* (Berkeley: University of California Press, 1988).

39. In her analysis of official U.S. policy over Japanese women's issues under occupation, Mire Koikari notes that the occupation authorities promoted "a white, middle-class progressive motherhood" from the beginning. "Rethinking Gender and Power in the US Occupation of Japan, 1945–1952," *Gender and History* 11, no. 2 (July 1999): 319. To a great extent, U.S. media representations loyally reflected this official policy, but not without contradiction or significant shift in emphasis.

40. See Yoneyama, "Hihanteki feminizumu no keifu kara miru Nihon senryō," *Shisō* 955 (November 2003): 60–84.

41. The two quotes are from the title of her two respective autobiographies: Beate Sirota Gordon, *The Only Woman in the Room: A Memoir* (Tokyo: Kodansha, 1997); and Beate Sirota Gordon, *1945nen no Kurisumasu: Nihonkoku kenpō ni "danjo byōdō" o kaita josei no jiden* (Tokyo: Kashiwa Shobō, 1995). Biographical accounts about Gordon in Japanese are numerous.

42. "The Constitution of Japan," Prime Minister of Japan and His Cabinet, accessed March 15, 2014, http://japan.kantei.go.jp/constitution_and_government_of _japan/constitution_e.html.

43. Statement by Gordon made in 1999 and quoted in "Feminist Secretly Wrote Part of Japan's Constitution," *New York Times*, January 24, 2013.

44. Gertrude Penrose, "Reporting on Japan's Women," *Independent Woman* 27 (November 1948): 322–24.

45. *New York Times*, April 9, 1949.

46. Miriam Frank et al., *The Life and Times of Rosie the Riveter: The Story of Three Million Working Women During World War II* (Emeryville, CA: Clarity Educational Publication, 1982).

47. Elaine Tyler May, *Homeward Bound: American Families in the Cold War Era* (New York: Basic Books, 1988). For further analyses of gender, sexual, and others forms of Cold War domestic containment, see, for instance, Caroline Chung Simpson, *An Absent Presence: Japanese Americans in Postwar American Culture, 1945–1960* (Durham, NC: Duke University Press, 2001); Joanne Meyerowitz, "Sex, Gender, and the Cold War Language of Reform" and Jane Sherron De Hart, "Containment at Home: Gender, Sexuality, and National Identity in Cold War America," in Peter J. Kuznick and James Gilbert, eds., *Rethinking Cold War Culture* (Washington, DC: Smithsonian Institution, 2001); and John D'Emilio, "The Homosexual Menace: The Politics of Sexuality in Cold War America," in John D'Emilio, ed., *Making Trouble: Essays on Gay History, Politics, and the University* (New York: Routledge, 1993).

48. Mary L. Dudziak, *Cold War Civil Rights: Race and Image of American Democracy* (Princeton, NJ: Princeton University Press, 2000); Penny M. Von Eschen, *Race against Empire: Black Americans and Anticolonialism, 1937–1957* (Ithaca, NY:

Cornell University Press, 1997); Christina Klein, *Cold War Orientalism: Asia in the Middlebrow Imagination, 1945–1961* (Berkeley: University of California Press, 2003); Thomas Borstelmann, *The Cold War and The Color Line: American Race Relations in the Global Arena* (Cambridge, MA: Harvard University Press, 2001); Eric Foner, *The Story of American Freedom* (New York: W. W. Norton, 1998).

49. McAlister, *Epic Encounters*, 76.

50. Vicente L. Rafael, "Colonial Domesticity: White Women and United States Rule in the Philippines," *American Literature* 67 (December 1995): 639–66; Amy Kaplan, "Manifest Domesticity," *American Literature* 70, no. 3 (September 1998): 581–606; Shelley Streeby, *American Sensations: Class, Empire, and the Production of Popular Culture* (Berkeley: University of California, 2002); Laura J. Briggs, *Reproducing Empire: Race, Sex, Science and U.S. Imperialism in Puerto Rico* (Berkeley: University of California Press, 2002); Mari Yoshihara, *Embracing the East: White Women and American Orientalism* (New York: Oxford University Press, 2003); Yu-Fang Cho, *Uncoupling American Empire: Cultural Politics of Deviance and Unequal Difference, 1890–1910* (Albany: State University of New York Press, 2013).

51. Christian G. Appy, "Introduction: Struggling for the World," in Christian G. Appy, ed., *Cold War Constructions: The Political Culture of United States Imperialism, 1945–1966* (Amherst: University of Massachusetts Press, 2000), 3.

52. *New York Times*, April 15, 1951.

53. See, for instance, "Japan's 'Second-Class Citizens,'" *New York Times*, August 22, 1954; "Japan: The Women," *Time* 63 (April 26, 1954): 37–38; and Beryl Kent, "Is Democracy Making Japanese Women Neurotic?" *American Mercury* 78 (June 1954): 139–40.

54. "Japan: The Women," 38.

55. "Women of Japan Sensing New Era," *New York Times*, November 7, 1954.

56. Leti Volpp, "Feminism versus Multiculturalism," *Columbia Law Review* 101 (June 2001): 1181–218; 1190. The pitfalls of Cold War feminism become sorely evident when we turn to critical feminist analyses that have interrogated the unitary concept of women's liberation, which obfuscates the interlocking power relations that make up the very category of "women." Though far from uniform, critical feminisms have observed the "simultaneity of oppressions" rooted in the entangled histories of racialized modernity, global capitalism, colonialism, and foreign military domination through which they must seek transformation. Norma Alarcón has succinctly stated the problem as follows: "The pursuit of a 'politics of unity' solely based on gender forecloses the 'pursuit of solidarity' through different political formations and the exploration of alternative theories of the subject of consciousness." "The Theoretical Subject(s) of This Bridge Called My Back and Anglo-American Feminism," in Gloria Anzaldúa, ed., *Making Face, Making Soul/ Haciendo Caras: Creative and Critical Perspectives by Feminists of Color* (San Francisco: Aunt Lute Books, 1990), 364. See also Cherríe Moraga and Gloria Anzaldúa, eds. *This Bridge Called My Back: Writings by Radical Women of Color* (New York: Kitchen Table, 1981, 1983). Alarcón's insight that identifies a nonunitary, multiple-voiced subjectivity and process of disidentification in

women of color feminism further resonates with the poststructuralist rearticulation of gender categories offered by Judith Butler and many others. See *Bodies That
Matter: On the Discursive Limits of "Sex"* (New York: Routledge, 1993). Chandra
Talpade Mohanty, among others, theorized that the homogeneous category of
"women," abstracted out of the web of social relations and represented as the
universal victim of patriarchy and male dominance, projects a uniform, progressive course of women's liberation. "Under Western Eyes: Feminist Scholarship
and Colonial Discourses," *boundary 2* 12, no. 3/13, no. 1 (spring/fall 1984): 338–58.
Republished in *Feminist Review* 30 (1988): 65–88. Once feminist emancipation is
envisioned in such a single, linear trajectory, it creates a hierarchy among the more
and less advanced women according to the unitary ladder of feminist progress.

57. Gayatri Spivak, "Three Women's Texts and a Critique of Imperialism," in Henry
Louis Gates Jr., ed., *"Race," Writing and Difference* (Chicago: University of Chicago
Press, 1985, 1986), 262–80. Of course, in practice, racialized American women's
participation in this discursive process complicates such a simple dichotomy.

58. Eyal Benvenisti, *The International Law of Occupation* (Princeton, NJ: Princeton
University Press, 1993), 91–98.

59. The full quote reads: "Unlike Germany . . . the Japanese government still
functioned when it signed the Instrument of Surrender. That was hardly a situation of debellatio. Japanese sovereignty was probably retained, and therefore
the legal source of Allied authority was the Instrument of Surrender, which
was based upon the Potsdam Declaration and the Japanese responses to it.
Nevertheless, that instrument's terms were sufficiently broad to enable the oc-
cupant to implement—mainly through the Japanese government, serving as an
intermediary—fundamental changes of Japan's laws and institutions, similar in
scope to those effected in vanquished Germany." Benvenisti, *The International Law
of Occupation*, 92–93.

60. Thus such scholars as Danilo Zolo who are critical of the criminalization of aggressive war—the post-Nuremberg protocol with which, according to Zolo and
others, supranational bodies such as the United Nations have consistently given
immunity to those powerful countries that emerged victorious in World War
II—argue that what is considered lawful occupation may have paradoxically
given justification to the aggressive use of the military force which had initially
generated the situation requiring occupation. Zolo characterizes the relationship
between the crime of aggression and territorial occupation as follows: "a legal
process in which, through a sort of magical normative transubstantiation, the
fact that the armed aggression was successful, leading to the military occupation of another people's territory, produces an automatic act of indemnity for
the 'supreme crime' committed by the aggressors, and makes the effects of their
aggression legitimate." Danilo Zolo, *Victors' Justice: From Nuremberg to Baghdad*
(London: Verso, 2009), 41. Histories of conquest, colonialism, and occupation
have shown us that the post-Enlightenment cultural discourse on civilizational
and racial uplift has consistently provided the condition of possibility for what
Zolo observes as "a sort of magical normative transubstantiation" in the recent

international law. See, for instance, Antony Anghie, *Imperialism, Sovereignty, and the Making of International Law* (Cambridge: Cambridge University Press, 2005).

61. Jenny Edkins, *Trauma and the Memory Politics* (Cambridge: Cambridge University Press, 2003), 179. On the intersection of biopolitics and thanatopolitics, see Giorgio Agamben. *Remnants of Auschwitz: The Witness and the Archive* (New York: Zone Books, 1999), 83. Also see chapter 1 of this book for a discussion of Agamben's critique of the liberal democratic state's biopolitics and sovereign power.

62. Morris-Suzuki noted further that "in December 1945, for example, the occupation authorities had acquiesced to the introduction of a new Japanese voting law which, as part of Allied policies to democratize Japan, extended the franchise to women, but also removed the franchise from Koreans and Taiwanese in Japan (who had been eligible to vote under the old imperial system). The change apparently came about because of pressure from Japanese politicians, who feared the radical tendencies of newly liberated former colonial subjects. Four months later, in March 1946, SCAP informed the Japanese government that 'non-Japanese' who were repatriated to their homelands would not be allowed back in Japan without the express permission of the SCAP. Most of the 'non-Japanese' in question were Koreans." See Tessa Morris-Suzuki, "Guarding the Borders of Japan: Occupation, Korean War and Frontier Controls," *Asia-Pacific Journal* 9, Issue 8, no. 3 (February 21, 2011). Earlier in his path-breaking archival study, the historian Mizuno Naoki explained that behind the Japanese cabinet's decision in 1945 to disenfranchise Korean and Taiwanese men above age twenty-five who were living in the imperial metropole was the fear that the Communists and socialists among these colonial subjects might call for the abolition of the monarchical system. At least ten of them were expected to be elected to the Diet immediately after the war. See Mizuno Naoki, "Zainichi Chōsenjin/Taiwanjin sanseiken 'teishi' jōkō no seiritsu: Zainichi Chōsenjin sanseiken mondai no rekishiteki kentō (1)," *Sekai Jinken Mondai Kenkyū Sentā kenkyū kiyō* 1 (March 1996): 43–65. Mizuno's and Morris-Suzuki's studies reveal that the occupation created a situation in which the nationality of Koreans (and Taiwanese despite the agreement between the Nationalist Party and Japan) remained suspended in an ambiguous status as a result of the perfect collusion between the Japanese nationalists' racism and the occupation authority's desire to secure the Far Eastern border against Communist insurgencies.

63. Kurt Steiner, "The Occupation and the Reform of the Japanese Civil Code," in Ward and Sakamoto, *Democratizing Japan*, 188–220.

64. See Yoshie Kobayashi, "A Path toward Gender Equality: State Feminism in Japan" (PhD dissertation, University of Hawaii, 2002), 52–82.

65. "Japan's Women Could Be Model in Postwar Iraq," *Rocky Mountain News*, April 16, 2003.

66. Roger Pulvers, "Beate Sirota Gordon, An American to Whom Japan Remains Indebted," *Japan Times*, January 13, 2013. See also the documentary on Gordon's biography, Tomoko Fujiwara, dir., *The Gift from Beate* (Committee of *The Gift from Beate*, Tokyo: Nippon Eiga Shinsha, 2004). In March 2010 I was invited together

with the gender studies scholar Nadje Al-Ali and the modern Japanese historian Chris Gerteis to participate in a session in honor of Gordon and the screening of this documentary at the School of Oriental and African Studies, University of London. A remarkably inspiring, dignified, and charming woman, Gordon concluded the session with her authoritative eyewitness account and emphasized that "Japanese women had nothing" that counted as rights or power prior to the American occupation. On the "figurative deployment of debt," see Saidiya V. Hartman, *Scenes of Subjection: Terror, Slavery, and Self-Making in Nineteenth-Century America* (New York: Oxford University Press, 1997), 131.

67. I discussed, for instance, the historian Kano Mikiyo's grassroots activism in which she problematized the link between the forgetting of women's complicity in imperialist war and the popular discourse on Japanese women as "innocent and passive victims" (209) in *Hiroshima Traces*; see chapter 6.

68. See *Hiroshima Traces*, 191.

Chapter 3. Sovereignty, Apology, Forgiveness

Epigraph. On the final day of the Women's International War Crimes Tribunal, which is analyzed below, the judges read the verdict summary aloud. They prefaced their statements with quotes from several witnesses who had testified during the trial. The judgment, which does not include this court performance, can be found in International Organising [sic] Committee for the Women's International War Crimes Tribunal, "The Women's International War Crimes Tribunal: Judgement [sic]" (Hague: December 4, 2001), last accessed February 2014, http://vawwrac .org/war_crimes_tribunal. Yuen testified on the Tribunal's second day. Born in 1922, she was brought into a comfort station through deception and coercion. The facility was operated by a couple, a Japanese man and Chinese woman, inside the Japanese military occupied zone. When she was impregnated by a soldier who had refused to use a condom she was forced to have an abortion. After having survived fifteen months of forced prostitution and physical abuse, she escaped with the help of a former Japanese soldier. During her confinement at the comfort station Yuen was separated from her child, who died of starvation in her absence. The Chinese prosecutor team presented her case as a violation of her rights to freedom, choice, life and rearing one's own child. Yuen's and other survivor-witnesses' testimonies as well as the details of the Tribunal in their entirety can be found in VAWW-NET Japan, ed. *Josei Kokusai Senpan Hōtei no zenkiroku I, Nihongun seidoreisei o sabaku: 2002nen Josei Kokusai Senpan Hōtei no kiroku, vol. 5* (Ryokufū Shuppan, 2002), 38–247. See also the video documentary containing the essential testimonies of former "comfort women": Video Juku, dir., *"Josei Kokusai Senpan Hōtei" no kiroku: Chinmoku no rekishi o yabutte* (Tokyo: Video Juku; VAWW-NET Japan, 2001).

1. In its official English name the group translated the neologism *jiyūshugi shikan* as "unbiased view of history." I have chosen to retain the more literal translation I used in earlier works, "liberal historical view," because it bears the contradictions of positivist liberal historiography, which generally does not problematize the epistemic certainty of facts. We have seen similar liberal historiographical

attitudes in the U.S. controversy over the Smithsonian's *Enola Gay* exhibit. See chapter 5.

In part reflecting the end of Cold War milieu, the Study Group was founded upon the idea that history should not side with either the historical materialist view of Japan's modernity, or the romantic view that glorifies "The Greater East Asia War," the term introduced by the conservative critic Hayashi Fusao to affirm the just cause of Japan's war in Asia. In this sense, the initial impetus and the grass-roots popularity of the Study Group can be attributed to its attempt to move beyond the confines of conventional post–World War II historical narratives. The initial members were less ideologically opposed to telling the history of the military comfort system, but treated it as yet another "untold story" kept hidden under the Cold War binary. It was only after 1996, when Fujioka publicly censured the mention of the comfort system in school textbooks, that the Study Group became explicitly aligned with the Textbook Reform Society and other conservative and far-right nationalist groups.

2. When it was first established in 1997, the Group of Concerned Diet Members was headed by Abe Shinzō, twice prime minister who inherited the pro-U.S. hawkish political stance from his grandfather Kishi Nobusuke. To recall, Kishi was acquitted of the A-class war crime charge during the occupation and later led the controversial signing of the 1960 U.S.-Japan Security Treaty as a prime minister. The group was formerly known as Nihon no Zento to Rekishi Kyōkasho o Kangaeru Wakate Giin no Kai. See Nihon no Zento to Rekishi Kyōkasho o Kangaeru Wakate Giin no Kai, ed., *Rekishi kyōkasho e no gimon: Wakate kokkai giin ni yoru rekishi kyōkasho mondai no sōkatsu* (Tokyo: Tentensha, 1997). The Concerned Diet Members and the Textbook Reform Society are closely affiliated with the Nihon (Nippon) Kaigi, or the Japan Conference. The latter is widely regarded as the largest conservative organization in Japan and consists of legislators, far-right religious leaders, the Japan War-Bereaved Association (Nihon Izoku Kai) affiliates, corporate executives, schoolteachers and academics. In cabinets appointed by Abe more than ten seats have consistently been assigned to the affiliates of the Japan Conference.

3. See, for instance, Oguma Eiji and Ueno Yōko, <*Iyashi*> *no nashonarizumu: Kusano ne hoshuundō no jisshō kenkyū* (Tokyo: Keiō Gijyuku Daigaku Shuppankai, 2003. Kobayashi Yoshinori and Nishibe Susumu, *Hanbei to iu shuhō* (Tokyo: Shōgakkan, 2002) exposes the feuds and deep-seated antagonism that existed in the Reform Society from the outset. Kobayashi and Nishio left the Society after the 9/11 attacks. Fujioka Nobukatsu acknowledged that the Japanese colonization of Korea was wrong and differs on this point from centrists of the Concerned Diet Members. Fujioka Nobukatsu and Izawa Motohiko, *Nō to ieru kyōkasho: Shinjitsu no Nikkan kankeishi* (Tokyo: Shōdensha, 1998).

4. See, among others, Amano Keiichi, *Jiyūshugi shikan o kaidoku suru* (Tokyo: Shakai Hyōronsha, 1997); Komori Yōichi and Takahashi Tetsuya, et al., eds., *Nashonaru/ hisutorī o koete* (Tokyo: Tokyo Daigaku Shuppankai, 1998); Nagahara Keiji, *"Jiyūshugi shikan" hihan: Jikokushi ninshiki ni tsuite kangaeru*, Iwanami Booklet

505 (2000); and Komori Yōichi et al., *Rekishi kyōkasho nani ga mondai ka: Tettei kenshō Q&A* (Tokyo: Iwanami Shoten, 2001).

5. The sociologist Itō Kimio offers a useful summary of the backlash against Gender Equality and "gender free" education in *"Danjo kyōdō sankaku" ga toikakeru mono: Gendai Nihon shakai to jendā/poritikusu* (Inpakuto Shuppankai, 2003).

6. Takahashi Shirō, "Feminisuto ni yugamerareru kaisei kyōiku kihonhō: Sore hodo aikokushin ga okirai ka," *Seiron* 366 (January 2003): 320–29.

7. "Rekishi to minzoku e no sekinin (1): Danjo kyōdō sankaku to 'jūgun ianfu' ni tsūtei suru yamai," *Seiron* 394 (March 2005): 134.

8. Fujioka Nobukatsu and Izawa Motohiko, *Nō to ieru kyōkasho*, 16.

9. *Asahi Shimbun*, April 4, 2001.

10. The case of the home economics teacher Nezu Kimiko eloquently reveals how the three fields I am articulating here are inseparably interlinked in revisionist discourse. Nezu was a prime target for the revisionists' attack on public education because she integrated the three issues—namely, critical thinking about heteronormative gender distinctions, the history of wartime military "comfort women," and compulsory salutation to the national flag and anthem—as subjects of her home economics classroom pedagogy.

11. Article 9 reads: "Aspiring sincerely to an international peace based on justice and order, the Japanese people forever renounce war as a sovereign right of the nation and the threat or use of force as means of settling international disputes. In order to accomplish the aim of the preceding paragraph, land, sea, and air forces, as well as other war potential, will never be maintained. The right of belligerency of the state will not be recognized." "The Constitution of Japan," Prime Minister of Japan and His Cabinet, last accessed, February 12, 2014, http://www.kantei.go.jp /foreign/constitution_and_government_of_japan/constitution_e.html.

12. The Edwin O. Reischauer Institute of Japanese Studies, Harvard University, highlights the revision to the Constitution as the Society's primary concern. "Atarashii Kyōkasho o Tsukuru Kai," Reischauer Institute of Japanese Studies Constitutional Revision in Japan Research Project, last accessed March 12, 2014, http://nrs .harvard.edu/urn-3:FCOR.REISCH:2254350.

13. Satō Manabu, Komori Yōichi, Kang Sang-jung, et al. "Taiwa no kairo o tozashita rekishikan o dō kokufuku suru ka? Hikarete iku 'kokumin'/'hikokumin' no kyōkaisen," *Sekai* 645 (May 1997): 187.

14. Fujioka Nobukatsu, "Watashi ga hannichi rekishi kyōiku ni idonda ketteiteki na dōki," *Seiron* 293 (January 1997): 195.

15. Fujioka Nobukatsu, "Watashi ga hannichi rekishi kyōiku ni idonda ketteiteki na dōki," 202.

16. Nishio Kanji and Kobayashi Yoshinori, " 'Nihon no rekishi' no hokori takaki jigazō ni mezameyō," *Sapio* 12, no. 1 (January 2000): 19.

17. For the details of the political pressure the Society and the Concerned Diet Members exerted on local schools to adopt the Fusōsha textbook, see "Rekishi kyōkasho kentei 'ianfu' sakujo ni migi ni narae, chiratsuku seiji atsuryoku," *Chūgoku shimbun*, April 4, 2001; and "Tsugi no nerai 'saitaku 10%,' " "Tsukuru

Kai kyōkasho tanjō made," *Asahi shimbun*, April 4, 2001. The Reform Society announced a change in publishing venue from Fusōsha to Jiyūsha in 2007.

18. Komori Yōichi et al., *Rekishi kyōkasho nani ga mondai ka*, vii.

19. Komori Yōichi et al., *Rekishi kyōkasho nani ga mondai ka*, 91–92.

20. Nosaka Akiyuki, in *Amerika hijiki, Hotaru no haka* (Bungei Shunjū, [1968] 1988). Quoted passages are my translations. See also "American Hijiki," trans. Jay Rubin, in Howard Hibbett, ed., *Contemporary Japanese Literature: An Anthology of Fiction, Film, and Other Writing Since 1945* (New York: Knopf, 1977), 436–62.

21. In her scathing criticism of the conservative literary critic Nishibe Susumu, the feminist sociologist Ueno Chizuko described him as someone suffering from the trauma of the American encounter. Although once an active member of the Textbook Reform Society, Nishibe along with Kobayashi left the organization because their staunch anti-Americanism became increasingly incompatible with the revisionists' centrist position, especially after a rift formed over the U.S. invasion of Iraq and Afghanistan. These men, according to Ueno, shared the traumatic experience of the generation that had experienced national defeat. They projected their sense of loss as the defeated nation onto the image of postwar Japanese women. In their eyes these women were "whimsically seduced by the victors." Ueno Chizuko, *Kindai kazoku no seiritsu to shūen* (Iwanami Shoten, 1994), see especially 213–17.

22. Asian American studies scholars have long problematized the image of emasculated and effeminate Asian men in popular culture and historical narrative as well as in established institutional venues such as the public news media, politics, and law. Particularly pertinent to our discussion is that the sexually deviant Asian male image critiqued so powerfully by Asian American studies concerns more than the U.S. history of race and immigration. The image of Asian men as effeminate, infantile, and insufficiently masculine, or perversely sexualized as hyper- or asexual deviants from normative virility, was integral to not only U.S. but global racial discourse throughout the age of imperialism. The representation of deviant Asian masculinity was no less a product of modern Western colonialism and the globalized ideology of white supremacy (both necessitated by the demands of the universal humanism which was a corollary of colonialism) than the histories of military defeat, displacement, and dispossession. Whether in identification or counteridentification, "Asian men" produced *as* the difference from normative white masculinity was subjected to interpellation by historically hegemonic gendered racial ideologies and heteronorms. See especially Gary Y. Okihiro, *Margins and Mainstreams: Asians in American History and Culture* (Seattle: University of Washington Press, 1994); Robert G. Lee, *Orientals: Asian Americans in Popular Culture* (Philadelphia: Temple University Press, 1999); Nayan Shah, *Contagious Divides: Epidemics and Race in San Francisco's Chinatown* (Berkeley: University of California Press, 2001); and David Eng, *Racial Castration: Managing Masculinity in Asian America* (Durham, NC: Duke University Press, 2001).

23. For instance, the literary critic Elaine Kim famously identified in the 1970s civil rights struggles how many Asian American male writers who struggled to represent themselves in the U.S. national public sphere also sought counteridentifica-

tion in patriarchal ethnic nationalism. Elaine Kim, *Asian American Literature: An Introduction to the Writers and Their Social Context* (Philadelphia: Temple University Press, 1982). In a more recent account, the sociologist Hyun Suk Kim pointed to the ways in which Korean and Korean American nationalism tends to represent the wartime Japanese military comfort system as the failure of colonized men who failed to "protect" their own women. Hyun Sook Kim, "History and Memory: The 'Comfort Women' Controversy," *positions* 5, no. 1 (spring 1997): 73–106. Reflecting on the earlier works of the cartoonist Kobayashi mentioned above, the historian Tessa Morris-Suzuki has similarly noted "a rather obsessive association of the nation with imperiled male sexual potency." Tessa Morris-Suzuki, *The Past within Us: Media, Memory, History* (London: Verso, 2005), 186.

24. "Algeria Unveiled," in *A Dying Colonialism*, trans. Haakon Chevalier, introduction by Adolfo Gilly (New York: Grove Press, [1959] 1965). Fanon wrote, "In the colonialist program, it was the woman who was given the historic mission of shaking up the Algerian man. Converting the woman, winning her over to the foreign values, wrenching her free from her status, was at the same time achieving a real power over the man and attaining a practical, effective means of destructuring Algerian culture" (39). Fanon insisted in this piece that, despite the powerful colonial fantasy, "unveiling" did not derive only from colonial policy but also from Algerian women's revolutionary agency, which had emerged out of their participation in anticolonial struggles.

25. On the supplementary relationship between universal humanism and racism, see, among other works, Etienne Balibar, "Is There a 'Neo-Racism'?" trans. Chris Turner, in Etienne Balibar and Immanuel Wallerstein, *Race, Nation, Class: Ambiguous Identities* (New York: Verso, 1991), 17–28.

26. Yamatani Eriko and Yagi Hidetsugu, "<Han feminizumu taidan> kokka, shakai kihan, kazoku no kaitai ni zeikin o tsukauna!" *Seiron* 366 (January 2003): 299.

27. It should be underscored, however, that the Women's Tribunal's transnational feminist position critically diverged from the UN-based global feminists' universalistic position as well as the latter's "gender standpoint epistemology." For the exemplary argument of global feminism, see Charlotte Bunch, "Women's Human Rights: The Challenges of Global Feminism and Diversity," in Marianne DeKoven, ed., *Feminist Locations: Global and Local, Theory and Practice* (New Brunswick, NJ: Rutgers University Press, 2001), 129–45. Bunch was centrally involved in the UN Public Hearing held in conjunction with the Tribunal, where victims of more recent sexual violence in military conflicts came to testify. For the critique of "gender-standpoint epistemology," see Norma Alarcón, "The Theoretical Subject(s) of *This Bridge Called My Back* and Anglo-American Feminism," in Gloria Anzaldúa, ed., *Making Face, Making Soul: Haciendo Caras: Creative and Critical Perspectives by Women of Color* (San Francisco: Aunt Lute Foundation Books, 1990), 356–69. Inderpal Grewal and others differentiate transnational feminist critique from the universalistic feminism of the sort advocated by Bunch. Grewal succinctly observed that the global feminists' position of treating women's subordination as a universal human rights issue has formed a geo- and biopolitical

regime akin to imperial-colonial governmentality in "'Women's Rights as Human Rights': Feminist Practices, Global Feminism, and Human Rights Regimes in Transnationality," *Citizenship Studies* 3, no. 3 (1999): 337–54; and *Transnational America: Feminisms, Diasporas, Neoliberalisms* (Durham, NC: Duke University Press, 2005), see especially 129.

The Tribunal was rooted in the decades-long, local genealogy of anti-imperialist, critical transnational feminist activism (see the introduction), but it was not without internal differences. The difference between the universalist, gender standpoint feminism and the (post)colonial, anti-imperialist feminism also had to be negotiated among the Tribunal's organizers. Yun Chung-Ok wrote that her longtime activist partner late Matsui Yayori had understood that "the Japanese military sexual slavery as the outcome of the patriarchal system only" and had difficulty in grasping "the Japanese military sexual slavery was not only gender discrimination but also segregation of Asian peoples" (191). Yun Chung-Ok, "In Memory of Yayori Matsui," *Inter-Asia Cultural Studies* 4, no. 2 (2003): 190–92. See also Yoneyama, "Hihanteki feminizumu to Nihongun seidoreisei: Ajia/Amerika kara miru josei no jinken rejīmu no kansei," in *Rekishi to sekinin: "Ianfu" mondai to 1990 nendai*, Kim Puja and Nakano Toshio, et al., eds. (Tokyo: Seikyūsha, 2008), 235–49.

28. VAWW-NET Japan, *Josei Kokusai Senpan Hōtei no zenkiroku I, Nihongun seidoreisei o sabaku: 2002nen Josei Kokusai Senpan Hōtei no kiroku*; see 51–55 for Ustinia Dolgopol's opening remark in translation.

29. C. Sarah Soh, *The Comfort Women: Sexual Violence and Postcolonial Memory in Korea and Japan* (Chicago: University of Chicago Press, 2008), 44.

30. "Statement by the Chief Cabinet Secretary Yohei Kono on the Result of the Study on the Issue of 'Comfort Women'" (August 4, 1993), Ministry of Foreign Affairs of Japan, last accessed, February 28, 2014, http://www.mofa.go.jp/policy/women /fund/state9308.html.

31. Taking up the question of healing, Hyunah Yang raises the issue of positionality in representing the subaltern voice. "Finding the 'Map of Memory': Testimony of the Japanese Military Sexual Slavery Survivors," *positions: east asia cultures critique* 16, no. 1 (2008): 79–107. Cautioning against too hasty dismissal in academia of the possibility of speaking, intelligibility and reparability, Soyang Park offers a nuanced account on how the intersubjective dialectics between the survivors of the Japanese military comfort system as "the traumatized subalterns" and their intellectual listeners can generate transformative effects not only on historical knowledge but also lead to the former's healing, redress, and redemption. Soyang Park, "Silence, Subaltern Speech and the Intellectual in South Korea: The Politics of Emergent Speech in the Case of Former Sexual Slaves," *Journal for Cultural Research* 9, no. 2 (April 2005): 169–206.

32. For instance, Barak Kushner, "Pawns of Empire: Postwar Taiwan, Japan and the Dilemma of War Crimes," *Japanese Studies* 30, no. 1 (2010): 111–33.

33. Through examining the narrative of Tomasa Dioso Salinog, the late Filipina survivor who rejected the "sympathy money," the anthropologist Hideko Mitsui

likewise challenges the Asian Women's Fund's inability to respond to the survivors' call for justice and compensation. "The Politics of National Atonement and Narrations of War," *Inter-Asia Cultural Studies* 9, no. 1 (2008): 47–61. For an insightful critique of the masculinist nature of apology with which "the party that perpetrated the wrongs frequently assumes the position of the powerful, and 'reminds' everyone involved of the hierarchical differences between the perpetrator and the victim," see You-me Park, "Comforting the Nation: 'Comfort Women,' the Politics of Apology and the Workings of Gender," *Interventions* 2, no. 2 (2000): 203.

34. Chungmoo Choi, "The Politics of War Memories toward Healing," in Fujitani, White, and Yoneyama, eds., *Perilous Memories: Asia-Pacific War(s)* (Durham, NC: Duke University Press, 2001), 395–409.

35. See my initial reporting on this incident in "NHK's Censorship of Japanese Crimes against Humanity," *Harvard Asia Quarterly* 6, no. 1 (winter 2002): 15–19.

36. See Yoneyama, "Media no kōkyōsei to hyōshō no bōryoku," *Sekai* 690 (July 2001): 209–19.

37. The subcontracting company had already "completed" the production process and delivered the program to NHK for final review on January 24. The studio recording took place a month prior.

38. The normal viewership of the ETV series was no more than 0.5 percent. Low as it may seem, this still amounts to 500,000 viewers. Yoshida Toshimi, "Sanpunkan no sakeme: Hōmurareta mou hitotsu no koe o megutte," in Media no Kiki o Uttaeru Shimin Nettowāku, ed., *Bangumi wa naze kaizan sareta ka: "NHK/ETV jiken" no shinsō* (Ichiyōsha, 2006), 335–45. See 337 for the figure. Many who objected to the NHK censorship felt that had the edifice of knowledge gathered at the tribunal been properly disseminated over the Japanese airwaves, especially through the public broadcasting venue that carries a type of credibility distinct from other media, public opinion in Japan might be different today.

39. Throughout the course of my arbitration case (see below) and the court battle between VAWW-NET and NHK, we produced an archive on the NHK-ETV censorship issue. For information on how and why the unprecedented alteration occurred, see the following list of the media coverage, exposés, testimonies, and expert analyses: Media no Kiki o Uttaeru Shimin Nettowāku (Mekiki-net), ed., *Bangumi wa naze kaizan sareta ka: "NHK/ETV jiken" no shinsō* (Ichiyōsha, 2006); VAWW-NET Japan, ed., *Kesareta sabaki: NHK bangumi kaihen to seiji kainyū jiken* (Gaifūsha, 2005); and VAWW-NET Japan, eds., *Abakareta shinjitsu: NHK bangumi kaizan jiken, Josei Kokusai Senpan Hōtei to seijikainyū* (Gendaishokan, 2010). A full exposé of the entire censorship process can be found in Nagata Kōzō, *NHK, tetsu no chinmoku wa dare no tame ni* (Kashiwa Shobō, 2010). In it Nagata names the people involved and details the conversations that took place. The book reveals the repeated pressure that the producers received from NHK's high administrators as well as Nagata's subsequent struggles. Nagata, who was the chief producer of the ETV series at the time, also repents that he did not come forward sooner.

40. Shortly before the broadcast, Sakagami had widely circulated an e-mail to her network of friends and media workers, alerting them to the possibility that NHK

might buckle under political intimidation. Sakagami Kaori, "Seisaku genba de mita NHK bangumi kaihen no genjitsu," *Tsukuru* 32, no. 1/2 (January/February 2002): 98–107. Many publications by those who were not directly involved in the production process but nonetheless called immediate attention to the problem of the NHK-ETV program also appeared. See, among others, Nishino Rumiko's "NHK ni nani ga okita no ka: Josei Kokusai Senpan Hōtei o meguru bangumi kaihen sōdō," *Tsukuru* 31, no. 4 (May 2001): 110–17. Kitahara Megumi was first to point out the "fabricated" nature of the program in "Chinmoku saserareta no wa dare ka: NHK bangumi kaihen mondai/terebi eizo ni okeru netsuzō," *Inpakushon* 124 (April 2001): 126–31.

41. Because my role in the studio had been to discuss the tribunal's historical significance, as the main subject was drastically cut from the program, many of my original remarks were also deleted. The severe mangling of my remarks, to the point where the tribunal itself became unintelligible, was one of the few unassailable pieces of evidence available at the time that demonstrated the extraordinariness of what had happened. To be sure, filing a personal case did not seem apposite when the tribunal, the central subject under erasure, problematized collective and structural violations. I also felt wary that the issue of the media's accountability might overshadow the question of historical accountability. Still, because I kept my studio comments in writing, I was in a rare position to show how the program had been dramatically diverted away from what it had originally intended to convey. The media lawyer Yamashita Yukio worked pro bono, while concerned citizens and my closest colleagues in Japan pulled together a massive amount of evidence concerning the violations. In 2003 the BRC concluded that NHK had committed an ethical violation and recommended that it offer me a formal apology as well as announce the judgment to its viewers. See Yoneyama, "Ken'etsu, kaizan, netsuzō: Towarenakatta senji seibōryoku," in VAWW-NET Japan, ed., *Kesareta sabaki: NHK bangumi kaihen to seiji kainyū jiken* (Gaifūsha, 2005), 250–72; and "Kesareta sabaki to feminizumu," in VAWW-NET Japan, eds., *Abakareta shinjitsu: NHK bangumi kaizan jiken, Josei Kokusai Senpan Hōtei to seijikainyū* (Gendaishokan, 2010): 106–34.

42. Because of the involvement of high-profile LDP members, Abe Shinzō and the late Nakagawa Shōichi, the investigation evolved into a question of the public media's autonomy. To frame the censorship incident in this way proved to be a double-edged sword: while it marshaled a broad spectrum of civic sectors to interrogate the infringement of the public media's independence by political partisanship, it also gave ammunition to the NHK to remain unaccountable. The lawsuit was primarily fought not to prove the political pressures but to pursue the question of the media's "editorial rights [*henshūken*]." Historically, the idea of "editorial rights" came about out of the need to stave off the encroachment of the Allied occupation authority on the Japanese media. Six decades later, ironically, the NHK succeeded in appropriating the idea, which originally aimed to protect the media's autonomy from the sovereignty of the foreign occupiers and to allow itself to be shielded from the public inquisitions. Detailed accounts and analysis can

be found in the above-mentioned edited volume *Bangumi wa naze kaizan sareta ka* (Why was the program censored?). Edited by the Mekiki-net, an international group of concerned scholars and citizens including myself, the volume has more than a dozen contributors and is divided into three parts: the witness accounts of what actually happened to the program, analysis of the broader structural condition that invites such censorship, and commentaries on what this specific incident means and what can be learned from it. Media no Kiki o Uttaeru Shimin Nettowāku, *Bangumi wa naze kaizan sareta ka*.

43. Saitō Takao, "Futatabi 'teikoku' o shikō suru shakai to senji kenryokusha e no masumedia no kutsujū: 21seiki no 'Hakkō Jiken' dewa nai no ka," in Mekiki-net, ed, *Bangumi wa naze kaizan sareta ka*, 296–320. In the 1918 Hakkō Jiken, the Asahi newspaper reported on the famous "Rice Riots" (the mass protests that swept the country over the inflated price of rice), other related corruptions, and cases in which "Rice Riot" protesters were charged for sedition and attempting to overthrow the government.

44. Nihon no Zento to Rekishi Kyōkasho o Kangaeru Wakate Giin no Kai, *Rekishi kyōkasho e no gimon*, 35–36.

45. Nihon no Zento to Rekishi Kyōkasho o Kangaeru Wakate Giin no Kai, *Rekishi kyōkasho e no gimon*, 36–37.

46. The feminist literary critic Susan Jeffords's analysis of militarization and masculinity helps clarify the ideological work behind the male revisionists' response to redress efforts led by other Japanese men. In her now-classic study of the post–Vietnam War militarization of American masculinity, Jeffords makes a suggestive observation concerning representations of militarized rape. In her reading of gang rape which, according to Jeffords, "combines collectivity and display as the masculine bond performs as a group, with itself as audience," she reveals that the collectivity (the military, the nation-state) and its identity as male are produced and maintained not only through their distinction from women, but by the enforcement of the collective homosocial bond. Jeffords's insights can be extended to explore the broader implications of the revisionists' discontent beyond their immediate displays of repudiation. Susan Jeffords, *The Remasculinization of America: Gender and the Vietnam War* (Bloomington: Indiana University Press, 1989), 69.

47. Nishino Rumiko, *Jūgun ianfu: Moto heishitachi no shōgen* (Akashi Shoten, 1992).

48. The psychiatrist Noda Masaaki's work, *War and Accountability*, investigates the psychosocial trajectory that has come to structure the feelings of guilt, remorse, and their disavowal in postwar Japan. Noda points out that the "martial spirit" of the Japanese military, which was idealized and demanded from its soldiers, not only profoundly impaired the wartime individual male psyche but lived on into the postwar decades. The Japanese military ideology, according to Noda, exalted "a spiritual non-death even in the face of physical injury, in another word, desensitization" (353). It instituted various micromechanisms to produce a "desensitized self" that ontologized death. Such military indoctrination not only governed wartime soldierly subjectivity but, according to Noda, remained after the war in the form of a collective disavowal of the devastating impact of the Japanese war

on the enemy Other. The disavowal of accountability—the inability, that is, to respond to the ethical demands of the Other—is intimately tied to the inability to mourn and grieve for the others' death. Noda Masaaki, *Sensō to zaiseki* (Tokyo: Iwanami Shoten, 1998).

49. See Arai Toshio, "Chūka Jinmin Kyōwakoku no senpan saiban," in VAWW-NET Japan, ed. *Senpan saiban to seibōryoku, Nihongun seidoreisei o sabaku: 2002nen Josei Kokusai Senpan Hōtei no kiroku, vol. 1* (Tokyo: Ryokufū Shuppan, 2000), 123–53. Details on how Zhou Enlai negotiated with Chiang Kai-shek's legal adviser and formulated the leniency policy after the establishment of the PRC and acceptance of the POWs transferred from the Soviet Union can be found in Toyoda Masayuki, "Chūgoku no tainichi senpan shori seisaku: Genbatsushugi kara 'kandai seisaku' e," *Shien* 69 (2009): 15–45. Adam Cathcart and Patricia Nash have referenced the newly opened archives on the PRC's leniency policy in "War Criminals and the Road to Sino-Japanese Normalization," *Sino-Japanese Relations: History, Politics, Economy* 2 (2011): 49–70; and " 'To Serve Revenge for the Dead': Chinese Communist Responses to Japanese War Crimes in the PRC Foreign Ministry Archive, 1949–1956," *China Quarterly* 200 (2009): 1053–69.

50. These memoirs were published previously in Chūkiren's periodical and reappeared in Kumagai Shin'ichirō, *Naze kagai o katarunoka: Chūgoku Kikansha Renrakukai no sengoshi* (Tokyo: Iwanami Shoten, 2005).

51. Jacques Derrida, *On Cosmopolitanism and Forgiveness* (London: Routledge, 2001).

52. In addition to the periodical published by Chūkiren, see also Chūgoku Kikansha Renrakukai and Yomiuri Shosha, eds., *Shinryaku: Chūgoku ni okeru Nihon senpan no kokuhaku* (Shin Dokushosha, 1958); Chūgoku Kikansha Renrakukai, eds., *Kanzenban sankō: Yakitsukushi, ubaitsukushi, koroshitsukusu, kore o "sankō" to iu* (Tokyo: Kōbunsha, [1957] 1984); Chūgoku Kikansha Renrakukai, eds., *Watashitachi wa Chūgoku de nani o shitaka: Moto Nihonjin senpan no kiroku* (Tokyo: San'ichi Shobō, 1987); Tōru Hoshi, *Watashitachi ga Chūgoku de shita koto: Chūgoku Kikansha Renrakukai no hitobito* (Tokyo: Ryokufū Shuppan, 2002). I am thankful to UCSD librarian Dr. Eiji Yutani for collecting the out-of-print Chūkiren publications. Most recently, Okabe Makio et al., eds., *Chūgoku shinryaku no shōgensha tachi: "Ninzai" no kiroku o yomu* (Tokyo: Iwanami Shoten, 2010).

53. Kumagai Shin'ichirō, *Naze kagai o katarunoka*.

54. Although NHK-ETV failed to air the image, it is included in the aforementioned video documentary, "Chinmoku no rekishi o yabutte."

55. Sakagami in Media no Kiki o Uttaeru Shimin Nettowāku, ed., *Bangumi wa naze kaizan sareta ka: "NHK/ETV jiken" no shinsō*, 58; also Nagata, *NHK, tetsu no chinmoku wa dare no tame ni.*

56. Kumagai Shin'ichirō, *Naze kagai o katarunoka*, 25–27.

57. On the leniency policy and other cultural policies interpreted as an instrumental part of the PRC's well-calculated Cold War/cold war diplomatic strategies, see Justin Jacobs, "Preparing the People for Mass Clemency: The 1956 Japanese War Crimes Trials in Shenyang and Taiyuan," *China Quarterly* 205 (2011): 152–72.

58. David Eng, *Racial Castration*.

59. Slavoj Žižek's phrase is from *The Sublime Object of Ideology* (New York: Verso, 1989), 113; quoted in David Eng, *Racial Castration*, 170, 176.

60. According to Eng, the "racial hysteria" manifests differently for Asian American men. The narrator of Maxine Hong Kingston's *Woman Warrior: A Memoir of Girlhood* exhibits what he describes as "total withdrawal from the public realm" (168). Plagued by a mysterious illness, the narrator refuses to attend school. She locks herself up in her house in Chinatown without coming into contact with people beyond her immediate family. The story portrays this adolescent time as the most blissful period in the narrator's life. For the narrator this time was necessary to restore her psychic equanimity, a period during which she was able to remove herself from the public space of assimilation where she was expected to become a normative American subject. In Eng's reading, there is no negative connotation associated here with the symptoms of "withdrawal." In contrast, America's racialized heteropatriarchal laws produce different effects for the Asian American male characters. Closely analyzing the male protagonists in Louis Chu's and David Wong Louie's stories, Eng describes them as manifesting "mysterious symptoms all relating to sexual impotence and resulting in complicated withdrawals from the social realms" (168), which would include "a type of emotional segregation from whiteness" (196) and "internal exile" (197).

61. Also, David Palumbo-Liu, *Asian/American: Historical Crossings of Racial Frontier* (Stanford, CA: Stanford University Press, 2000).

62. On the supplementary relations between color-blind ideology and white supremacy, see Neil Gotanda, "A Critique of 'Our Constitution Is Colorblind': Racial Categories and White Supremacy," *Stanford Law Review* 44 (1991): 1–68. On the concept of "liberal racism" and how multiculturalism is not only coextensive with but facilitates capitalist social structures without decentering normative whiteness, see Avery F. Gordon, "The Work of Corporate Culture: Diversity Management," *Social Text* 13, no. 3 (1995): 3–30; and Avery F. Gordon and Christopher Newfield, "Introduction," in Avery F. Gordon and Christopher Newfield, eds., *Mapping Multiculturalism* (Minneapolis: University of Minnesota Press, 1996).

63. Here I am borrowing the concept of "model minority nation" from the historian T. Fujitani's study of Nisei soldiers. Fujitani drew a parallel between the making of the Nisei soldiers into a "model minority" in the American racial discourse toward the end of the war and the way defeated Japan became America's loyal anticommunist "model minority nation" in the U.S.-Soviet Cold War confrontation. T. Fujitani, "*Go for Broke*, the Movie: Japanese American Soldiers in U.S. National, Military, and Racial Discourse," in Fujitani, White, and Yoneyama, eds., *Perilous Memories: Asia-Pacific War(s)*, 239–66; see 253.

64. In November 2013 the United Nations General Assembly First Committee adopted the resolution for nuclear disarmament, "United action toward the total elimination of nuclear weapons," the draft of which was submitted by the Japanese government. "Statement by the Minister of Foreign Affairs on the Adoption of Japan's Draft Resolution on Nuclear Disarmament at the First Committee of the United Nations General Assembly" (November 5, 2013), Ministry of Foreign

Affairs of Japan, last accessed March 2, 2014, http://www.mofa.go.jp/press/release /press4e_000060.html. Even in this historic case in which the Japanese government officially participated in such a resolution for the first time in UN history, the wording carefully avoided reference to the illegality of nuclear weapons.

65. Historical studies attentive to the early twentieth century's global race discourse have demonstrated over the past decade that Japan's official rhetoric of antiwhite supremacy as the "champion of the darker races" had garnered far broader popular support among the nations of color across the colonized world than had been commonly acknowledged. George Lipsitz, " 'Frantic to Join . . . the Japanese Army': Black Soldiers and Civilians Confront the Asia-Pacific War," in Fujitani, White, and Yoneyama, eds., *Perilous Memories*, 347–77; Gerald Horne, *Race War: White Supremacy and the Japanese Attack on the British Empire* (New York: New York University Press, 2004); Marc Gallicchio, *The African American Encounter with Japan and China: Black Internationalism in Asia, 1895–1945* (Chapel Hill: University of North Carolina Press, 2000); Reginald Kearney, *African American Views of the Japanese: Solidarity or Sedition* (Albany: State University of New York Press, 1998); T. Fujitani, "The Reischauer Memo: Mr. Moto, Hirohito, and Japanese American Soldiers," *Critical Asian Studies* 33, no. 3 (September 2001): 379–402; and *Race for Empire: Koreans as Japanese and Japanese as Americans during World War II* (Berkeley: University of California Press, 2011). See especially Colleen Lye on the necessity of gaining knowledge about the global racial alliances and counteralliances at the time of World War II. *America's Asia: Racial Form and American Literature, 1893–1945* (Princeton, NJ: Princeton University Press, 2005), 232–43.

66. See Kang Sang-jung's remark in Satō Manabu et al., "Taiwa no kairo o tozashita rekishikan o dō kokufuku suru ka," 198.

67. Takubo Tadae, "Hitsuyō na 'haueba' no shikō," *Seiron* 316 (December 1998): 236–40, 239.

68. Gavan McCormack, *Client State: Japan in the American Embrace* (London: Verso, 2007).

69. That such national self-victimology can be seen as an outcome of the long disavowal of Japan's imperial violence is discussed in Yoneyama, *Hiroshima Traces: Time, Space and the Dialectics of Memory* (Berkeley: University of California Press, 1999).

70. See Yoneyama, "Kokki kokka ni hantai suru koto ni tsujite," in Ishida et al., *"Hinomaru, Kimigayo" o koete* (Tokyo: Iwanami Shoten, 1999), 53–59.

71. Nishio Kanji, "Hachigatsu jūgonichi izen no Nihonjin, igo no Nihonjin," *Seiron* 298 (June 1997): 57.

72. "Sensō no katari to posuto-reisen no masukyuriniti," in Tessa Morris-Suzuki et al., eds., *Iwanami kōza: Ajia/Taiheiyō sensō*, vol. 1, *"Naze, ima, Ajia/Taiheiyō sensō ka"* (Iwanami Shoten, 2005), 317–56.

73. Foucault famously demonstrated that the positive power through which modern states govern by managing and promoting the life of the population (i.e., the biopower) has been coterminous with the power to let die (i.e., necropower). See Michel Foucault, *Society Must Be Defended: Lectures at the Collège De France, 1975–76* (New York: Picador, 2003). Giorgio Agamben further abstracted

Foucault's argument and painstakingly demonstrated that the politicization of life and its intimacy to death, the exception to life, has always been at the heart of Western metaphysics. Giorgio Agamben, *Homo Sacer* (Stanford, CA: Stanford University Press, 1998). Explicitly referencing Carl Schmitt's definition of sovereignty as that which decides on the exception, Agamben points to the way the State's decisions on extrajudicial measures (martial law, capital punishment, war, the final solution) are exceptions written within the law. He provocatively states that the Nazi state was "the first radically biopolitical state" (Agamben, *Homo Sacer*, 143). There is a continuity, he argues, among modern polities in the way the State passes on the decision to kill or let die—from camps, prison complexes, gas chambers, and euthanasia to humanitarian wars—in the name of defending and preserving what is believed to be the politically qualified, valued life, except that ours is sanctioned democratically by the sovereignty of the people.

74. Mbembe, "Necropolitics," trans. Libby Meintjes, *Public Culture* 15, no. 1 (2003): 73.

75. Mbembe's argument appears to reiterate some of Carl Schmitt's observations of the post-1945 transformation that supposedly marked the demise of the European system of war presented in his *The Nomos of the Earth in the International Law of the Jus Publicum Europaeum* (New York: Telos Press, 2003). The European protocol and the idea of *justus hostis*, according to Schmitt, had long mitigated the war's escalation into a bellum justus, the ultimate aim of which is to annihilate the absolute evil. Mbembe, however, differs critically from Schmitt in that he does not see the war of annihilation as a new post–World War II development but as constitutive of Jus publicum Europaeum. It is revealing that Schmitt only began to perceive the annihilating character of wars waged by Europeans in the post–World War II milieu when the armed anticolonial struggles and the (post) colonial realities of the metropole came to fundamentally unsettle *Jus Publicum Europaeum*.

76. Naoki Sakai, *Kibō to kenpō: Nihonkoku kenpō no hatsuwa shutai to ōtō* (Tokyo: Ibunsha, 2008).

77. Sakai has written numerous essays on this topic. For example, Sakai writes of this complicity: "The preservation of national history and of the putative unity of national culture was thus an exceedingly effective means of keeping the occupied population, first, under direct American rule and then indirectly complicit with U.S. hegemony. The most ironic and interesting aspect of the postwar relationship between the United States and Japan can perhaps be found in the fact that the United States effectively continued to dominate Japan by endowing the Japanese with the sense of Japanese tradition and the grounds for their nationalism. It is through the apparent sense of national uniqueness and cultural distinctiveness that people in Japan were subordinated to U.S. hegemony in East Asia." Naoki Sakai, "You Asians, On the Historical Role of the West and Asia Binary," *South Atlantic Quarterly* 99, no. 4 (2000): 809–10.

78. Sakai, *Kibō to kenpō*, 47–48.

79. The historian John W. Dower's classic study demonstrates that, with the onset of the Cold War confrontation, the U.S. government had misgivings about its earlier

disarmament policy and began rearming Japan during the occupation. It continued to do so after Japan's independence, thus virtually nullifying Article 9. Dower,
Empire and Aftermath: Yoshida Shigeru and the Japanese Experience, 1878–1954
(Cambridge, MA: Harvard East Asian Monographs, 1979). Dower argued how
postwar Japan's "subordinate independence" was born out of the calculated diplomatic decision by statesmen like Yoshida Shigeru who sought Japan's national
survival under the absolute and lasting U.S. military presence. See especially
415–70.

80. Chalmers A. Johnson, "Japan in Search of a 'Normal' Role,'" *Daedalus* 121, no. 4
(Fall 1992): 26

81. *Nihonkoku Kenpō: Japan's Peace Constitution*, directed by John Junkerman and
Tetsujiro Yamagami (Brooklyn, NY: First Run/Icarus Films, 2005), DVD.

82. Lafe Franklin Allen, "Democracy in Japan," *Commonweal* 46 (September 1947):
546. See chapter 2.

Chapter 4. Contagious Justice

1. In *Hiroshima Traces: Time, Space, and the Dialectics of Memory* (Berkeley: University of California Press, 1999), I have discussed the counteramnes(t)ic—namely,
unforgetting and unforgiving practices in postwar Hiroshima, as well as the
intimate ties present in Japan that link the politics of representing the country's
war of aggression, memories of colonialism, minoritization of Korean colonial
diasporic populations, and the testimonial practices of the atomic bomb survivors. The link between memories, historical redress and efforts to extend and secure minority rights is best expressed in the 1988 proposal for the Law Pertaining
to Postwar Reparations and the Guarantee of Human Rights for Resident Aliens
from Former Colonies (Zainichi kyū-shokuminchi shusshinsha ni kansuru sengo
hoshō oyobi jinken hoshō hō). Minzoku Sabetsu to Tatakau Renraku Kyōgikai,
ed., *Zainichi Kankoku Chōsenjin no hoshō/jinken hō: Zainchi kyū-shokuminchi
shusshinsha ni kansuru sengo hoshō oyobi jinken hoshō hō seitei o mezashite* (Osaka:
Akashi Shoten, 1991).

2. I use the term, "Asian/America" to extend David Palumbo-Liu's observation of the
mutually constitutive formation of Asia, the United States, and Asian America
with or without hyphenation.

3. For information regarding the Global Alliance for Preserving the History of WW II
in Asia, http://www.global-alliance.net/home.htmlwww.GAinfo.org. The network
among regional organizations can be found at http://www.alpha-canada.org/about
/global-alliance-sister-organizations (last accessed November 1, 2014).

4. For seminal historical and cultural studies on this point, see Ronald Takaki,
Strangers from a Different Shore: A History of Asian Americans (New York: Penguin,
1989); Gary Okihiro, *Margins and Mainstreams: Asians in American History and Culture*
(Seattle: University of Washington Press, 1994); and Robert G. Lee, *Orientals:
Asian Americans in Popular Culture* (Philadelphia: Temple University Press, 1999).

5. In the article I submitted to the special issue I shared a few preliminary observations of the then emergent Asian/Americanization of transpacific justice. The

earlier analysis was extensively developed, updated, and incorporated into this chapter. See "Traveling Memories, Contagious Justice: Americanization of Japanese War Crimes at the End of the Post–Cold War," *Journal of Asian American Studies* 6, no. 1 (February 2003): 57–93.

6. Kandice Chuh, "Discomforting Knowledge: Or, Korean 'Comfort Women' and Asian Americanist Critical Practice," *Journal of Asian American Studies* 6, no. 1 (February 2003): 8. Especially with regard to Keller's work, which I will later explore from another viewpoint, Chuh observed: "According to this novel, the importance of recovering the history of 'comfort woman' locates not to those who were so conscripted, but to us, to satisfy *our will to knowledge*" (19; emphasis added). Chuh thus suggested the importance of asking to what end is the "comfort women" history remembered, and what is being empowered by such representations.

7. Laura Hyun Yi Kang, " 'Conjuring 'Comfort Women': Mediated Affiliations and Disciplined Subjects in Korean/American Transnationality," *Journal of Asian American Studies* 6, no. 1 (February 2003): 25–55. Kang focused on three sites of knowledge mobilization in the United States: Korean American politicization as American citizen-subjects; institutionalization and academic objectification; and expansion of U.S.-based transnational feminism which, according to Kang, "risks forgetting that there is a distinct 'Americanization' of the subject" (43). On the question of the latest Americanization of justice, Kang took special note of the following curious development. In December 1996 the U.S. Department of Justice announced the new inclusion into the government "watch list" of sixteen Japanese nationals suspected of involvement in wartime biological experimentation and the operation of the military comfort system. In asking whether the state's retroaction might signify yet another Americanization of "comfort woman" discourse, Kang described the new legislative development as a "self-congratulatory appointment of the 'U.S. government' as the inclusive repository of 'the victims and their sufferings' in the past and as the guarantor of a just future for all" (41–42). Kang's critical gaze on the academic institutionalization of "comfort women" knowledge is worth reiterating. Referring to the women's studies scholar Margaret Stetz, who observed that "the body of material . . . around 'comfort women' issues has grown so rapidly, over just the last decade, that we can now speak of there being a ' "comfort women's" literature,' in the same way that we refer to a 'Holocaust literature,' " Kang asked whether "this prognosis presumes that formalization [of comfort women knowledge] as 'an academic subject' is both a desired goal and a neutral process" (43).

8. Jodi Kim thoroughly investigates this point in her study of Asian American cultural production as an index to American Cold War geopolitics and epistemologies. *Ends of Empire: Asian American Critique and the Cold War* (Minneapolis: University of Minnesota Press, 2010).

9. When I refer to Asian/American transnationality, I am thinking of the predicament and ambivalence Kandice Chuh observed when a racialized collectivity is perceived as transnational. Citing the violation and exclusion of Japanese Americans, whose

presence during World War II was deemed to be in excess of the boundaries of the United States and Japan, Chuh astutely pointed out that "the transnation suggests the possibilities for affiliations other than as determined by the nation-state, and at the same time identifies nationalism's coercive practices." Chuh advocated attending to such an ambivalence of the "transnation" as a necessary element in resistance politics, while at the same time cautioning us against the disciplinization and violence such transnational excess and ambivalence necessarily invites. "Transnationalism and Its Pasts," *Public Culture* 9, no. 1 (1996): 109.

10. California Senate Bill 1245, Chapter 216, §4, February 26, 1999. The Congressional Research Service reported as of May 2000 that some twenty-eight cases had been filed since introduction of the law. Gary K. Reynold, "U.S. Prisoners of War and Civilian American Citizens Captured and Interned by Japan in World War II: The Issue of Compensation by Japan," Congressional Research Service, Library of Congress, 27.

11. Assembly Joint Resolution 27, Chapter 90, Legislative Counsel's digest by Mike Honda, June 22, 1999.

12. *Los Angeles Times*, May 14, 2000.

13. *Dateline*, NBC, June 5, 2000.

14. Under the War Claims Act of 1948, the United States government seized and liquidated Japanese assets in the amount of $228,750,000 and created a War Claims Fund which paid $60 for each month of internment. See Reynold, "U.S. Prisoners of War and Civilian American Citizens Captured and Interned by Japan in World War II."

15. Senate Concurring Resolution 158 (October 31, 2000). It concludes, "*Resolved by the Senate (the House of Representatives concurring),* That it is the sense of Congress that it is in the interest of justice and fairness that the United States, through the Secretary of State or other appropriate officials, put forth its best efforts to facilitate discussions designed to resolve all issues between former members of the Armed Forces of the United States who were prisoners of war forced into slave labor for the benefit of Japanese companies during World War II and the private Japanese companies who profited from their slave labor." 146 Cong. Rec. S11,433 (daily ed. Oct. 31, 2000).

16. 146 Cong. Rec. S11,432 (daily ed. Oct. 31, 2000) (statement of Sen. Hatch).

17. 146 Cong. Rec. S11,432 (daily ed. Oct. 31, 2000) (statement of Sen. Hatch).

18. The anticolonial, antiracist, and anticapitalist critique of the IMTFE I summarize here and in the introduction is drawn from such Japanese historians as Awaya Kentarō and Utsumi Aiko who have problematized the fact that the West-centricism of the Tokyo Tribunal left the injustices of Japanese colonialism unquestioned, and thus virtually exonerated the subsequent continuation of colonization and neocolonization of much of Asia and the Pacific by the United States and others. They have proposed for many decades to hold an international people's court to reopen cases of crimes against colonized people that were not addressed adequately in the IMTFE. The Japanese plan to administer their own war crimes court and prosecute Japanese officials was precluded by the terms of

Japan's surrender to the Allied powers. Ustumi Aiko, for one, has been a pioneer in linking the failure of justice at the war's end with postwar Japan's institutional racism against former colonial subjects as well as the neocolonial political economic development that came to restructure the prewar unevenness in Asia and the Pacific.

19. For example, Chungmoo Choi was the first to point out how differently the international community handled the cases of the Dutch "comfort women" from those of the Asian and Pacific Islanders. Introduction to *"The Comfort Women": Colonialism, War, and Sex*, ed. Chungmoo Choi, a special issue of *positions: east asia cultures critique* 5, no. 1 (spring 1997): v–xiv.

20. Mitsubishi Materials Corp. et al. v. Superior Court of Orange Co., 106 Cal. App. 4th 39 at 41 (2003).

21. *In re World War II Era Japanese Forced Labor Litigation*, 164 F. Supp. 2d 1160, 1168 (N.D. Cal. 2001). In his opinion Walker cited Zschernig v. Miller, 389 U.S. 429 (1968), which deemed unconstitutional those state activities that may influence foreign affairs and concluded that "California and all states enacting legislation touching upon foreign affairs are thus bound by the doctrines of *Zschernig* until the Supreme Court instructs otherwise" (1171).

22. *Jae Won Jeong v. Taiheiyo Cement Corp.* was mandated to proceed by Judge Peter D. Lichtman as 105 Cal. App. 4th 398 (January 15, 2003).

23. "Slave-Labor Suit against Japanese Firms to Continue," *Los Angeles Times*, December 1, 2001.

24. *Deutsch v. Turner Corp.*, 317 F.3d 1005, 1023. On the foreign affairs powers, the opinion noted: "The Supreme Court has long viewed the foreign affairs powers specified in the text of the Constitution as reflections of a generally applicable constitutional principle that power over foreign affairs is reserved to the federal government" (317 F.3d 1005 at 1020).

25. *Deutsch*, at 1026, 1015. Reinhardt's ruling argued that §354.6 creates a cause of action; hence it must be viewed not as procedural but substantive. The amendment's power to create or alter the rights and obligations beyond what the federal government has defined is thus deemed to infringe upon the foreign affairs power doctrine.

26. Taiheiyo Cement Corp. et al. v. Superior Court of California, 105 Cal. App. 4th 398, 426 (January 15, 2003). The opinion also tries to decouple the state assembly joint resolution from the statute and argued, "§354.6 does not provide a forum to criticize Japan's current policies or practices" (105 Cal. App. 4th at 418).

27. *Mitsubishi Materials Corp. et al.*, at 43 and 51.

28. The opinion cites Public Papers of the Presidents of the United States Harry S. Truman, 1951, U.S. Government Printing Office 1965, 505, 506.

29. Incidentally, this court's opinion also cited the long-term memory of U.S. adjudication of Japanese war crimes in their relation to U.S. nationals. Citing past litigation known as the *Kawakita* treason case (Kawakita v. United States 343 U.S. 717 [1952]), in which an American national of Japanese descent who worked for a Japanese corporation during the war and mishandled American POWs was found

guilty of treason, Sills dissented from Boland's opinion that adjudication of claims brought against Japanese companies under §354.6 would not implicate a foreign government or affect foreign policy. In the *Kawakita* treason case, even though the defendants argued that he worked not for the Japanese military but for a private company, Kawakita was found guilty of treason on the grounds that all Japanese corporations operated through the Japanese Army during the war. Sills therefore concluded that the issue of a private corporation's unjust enrichment through slave labor does pertain to the "prosecution of the war" and therefore falls within the jurisdiction of the 1951 treaty (and is preempted by it). See *Mitsubishi Materials Corp. et al.*, at 53–56.

30. See *Taiheiyo Cement Corp.*, at 404–5.

31. Boland later vacated the court's opinion upon review and ruled that §354.6 was unconstitutional because it conflicted with the 1951 San Francisco Peace Treaty. With respect to the non-signatory status of Korea, the revised opinion noted its view on the treaty as follows: "While neither Japan nor Korea was required to implement any specific resolution, and Korea was under no obligation to even negotiate with Japan concerning the settlement of war claims, the treaty nonetheless expressed the foreign policy determination of the Allied Powers, including the United States, that such claims should be resolved diplomatically between the Japanese and Korean governments." Taiheiyo Cement Corp. et al. v. Superior Court of California, 117 Cal. App. 4th 380, 392–93 (March 2004). Furthermore, it cited the court opinion of *Hwang Geum Joo v. Japan* and resolved the transnational contradictions of American justice as follows: "As a matter of foreign policy it would be odd indeed for the United States, on the one hand, to waive all claims of its nationals against Japan and, on the other hand, to allow non-nationals to proceed against Japan in its courts." See 117 Cal. App. 4th at 394; Hwang Geum Joo v. Japan, 332 F.3d 679, 685 (D.C. Cir. 2003).

32. *In re World War II Era Japanese Forced Labor Litigation*, at 1168.

33. *Mitsubishi Materials Corp. et al.*, at 57.

34. 543 U.S. 1089.

35. *In re World War II Era Japanese Forced Labor Litigation*, at 1167.

36. *Deutsch*, at 1005; U.S. App. Ninth Circuit (January 21, 2003), amended 324 F.3d 692 (March 6, 2003), certiorari denied by the U.S. Supreme Court, 540 U.S. 820 (October 6, 2003). Taiheiyo Cement Corp. v. Superior Court, 117 Cal. App. 4th 380 (July 2004), certiorari denied, 543 U.S. 1089 (January 18, 2005).

37. This would have been a problematic case because in order to enable the alien plaintiffs' claims to proceed in the U.S. courts the American juridical team argued that Japan's military comfort system was commercially run businesses, a view promoted by Japan's conservative revisionists, but consistently rejected by the majority of former "comfort women" as well as the transnational feminists in Asia who organized the 2000 Women's Tribunal (see chapter 3).

38. Hwang Geum Joo v. Japan, 172 F. Supp.2d 45, 52 (October 4, 2001), vacated and remanded, 542 U.S. 901 (June 4, 2004), reaffirmed (June 28, 2005), certiorari denied, 546 U.S. 1208 (February 21, 2006).

39. The lawyer Barry A. Fisher, for instance, relied on Ruth Benedict and Ian Buruma: "According to some scholars, Japanese society is fundamentally group-oriented, hierarchical, and focused on what others in society think, and European culture is more concerned with individuals, their consciences, and their moral and religious rules. tinder [*sic*] the 'shame' principle, maintaining face or appearance is essential to Japanese society, and admitting failures or crimes brings shame to the entire group. Japan also values its dependence on stronger entities: in this case, the United States. When expectations fall short, Japanese feelings of group victimization become strong." "Notes from the World War II Redress Trenches: The Disparate Treatment of Victims East and West," *Loyola of Los Angeles International and Comparative Law Review* 95 (winter 2010): 8, 20. In contrast, in analyzing the case of a "cultural defense" made on behalf of a Chinese man who murdered his wife, Leti Volpp painstakingly demonstrated the problematic use of the "culture and personality" school's anthropological notion of culture in courtrooms. "(Mis)identifying Culture: Asian Women and the 'Cultural Defense,'" *Harvard Women's Law Journal* 17 (1994): 57–101.

40. *Taiheiyo Cement Corp.*, at 245. See also Hwang Geum Joo, et al. v. Japan 413 F.3d 45 at 52 for a similar argument.

41. On theorization of the fundamental contradictions the liberal state poses on racialized citizenship in the capitalist formation, see Lisa Lowe, *Immigrant Acts: On Asian American Cultural Politics* (Durham, NC: Duke University Press, 1996). Yen Espiritu has pointed to the historical process whereby Asians and other groups of color have been made integral to the American nation but only through their "designated subordinated standing." See, for instance, Yen Le Espiritu, *Home Bound: Filipino American Lives across Cultures, Communities, and Countries* (Los Angeles: University of California Press, 2003), 42. For the historical importance of law and the state of emergencies in regulating the lines between aliens and citizens in the United States, see especially Mae M. Ngai, *Impossible Subjects: Illegal Aliens and the Making of Modern America* (Princeton, NJ: Princeton University Press, 2004).

42. *Pacific Citizen*, the semimonthly newspaper published by the Japanese American Citizens League, reported in detail on the debates among Japanese and other Asian/American communities over the Joint Resolution 27 initiative. Concrete debates ranged from whether such a legislative move would further anti-Japanese and anti-Asian racism by reinforcing popular stereotypes that tend to portray Asians as potential U.S. enemies, to whether the United States should also apologize and offer compensation for the atomic attacks on Hiroshima and Nagasaki and its violation of international laws. But overall, Resolution 27 was collectively welcomed as fostering a new coalition among the increasingly diverse community of Asian and Pacific Islander Americans, uniting different North and Southeast Asians and Pacific Islanders. See *Pacific Citizen* 129, no. 8 (August 20–26, 1999). See also Teresa Watanabe's article, "Measure Urges Japan to Apologize for Atrocities" in the *Los Angeles Times*, August 24, 1999.

43. Chalmers Johnson's *Blowback: The Costs and Consequences of American Empire* (New York: Metropolitan Books, 2000) best summarizes how U.S. Cold War

policies have achieved their imperialist goals through propping up pro–United States, antidemocratic, dictatorial regimes throughout Asia and the Pacific. I wish to add to his list the Liberal Democratic Party's antidemocratic Cold War regimes in Japan which were led by Kishi, later his brother Sato Eisaku, and others, and which was funded and guarded by such far-right wingers as Kodama Yoshio and Sasagawa Ryōichi (both of whom, like Kishi, were arrested as A-class war criminal suspects soon after the war).

44. §354.6 was introduced to reflect the California legislature's collective moral interest in "assuring that its residents and citizens are given a reasonable opportunity to claim their entitlement to compensation for forced or slave labor performed prior to and during the Second World War." Senate Bill 1245, §1, (c).

45. For the most insightful and compelling discussion of the links between the formation of knowledge about the United States in South Korea and the production of Korean gendered subjectivities, see Elaine Kim and Chungmoo Choi, eds., *Dangerous Women*. In critiquing the heteronormative implications of the concept, "diaspora," JeeYeun Lee also alludes to this point, following the Korean studies scholars Nancy Ablemann and John Lie's argument that the image of the United States popularized by the South Korean government is that of the United States as the "colonial liberator and Korean War savior." JeeYeun Lee, "Toward a Queer Korean American Diasporic History," in David L. Eng and Alice Y. Hom, eds., *Queer in Asian America* (Philadelphia: Temple University Press, 1998), 189–90.

46. Elaine H. Kim and Norma Alarcón, eds., *Writing Self, Writing Nation: Essays on Theresa Hak Kyung Cha's* Dictée (Berkeley: Third Woman Press, 1994). See especially, Lisa Lowe, "Unfaithful to the Original: The Subject of *Dictée*" and Laura Hyun Yi Kang, "The 'Liberatory Voice' of Theresa Hak Kyung Cha's *Dictée.*"

47. Nora Okja Keller, *Comfort Woman: A Novel* (New York: Penguin Books, 1997).

48. It is certainly possible to read Keller's novel as endorsing a conservative position that retrenches existing categories and identitarian relationalities. From her text it is difficult to discern why Beccah must urgently restore justice to her mother's past, except for the radical feminist impetus to reject all male violence against women. Nationalism also urges Beccah to explore her mother's past. The process whereby Beccah gains knowledge of her mother's past parallels that in which she becomes increasingly aware of her Korean-ness through the acknowledgment of shared blood, body, and biologically inherited spirituality. Nationalism in *Comfort Woman* thus emerges not so much as a political collectivity as an essentialized embodiment of the biological. To the extent that Japanese colonialism often attempted to legitimate its administration of Korea by insisting on the primordial oneness of blood and biological ties between Koreans and Japanese, to assert Korean biological distinctiveness might serve as a viable anticolonial strategy. Nationalism as a form of identification also has the potential to critically interrogate existing hierarchical arrangements of power, for it can highlight the inequity among supposedly equal members of the national community. However, in most cases, the version of nationalism that assumes identification based upon blood, culture, or other prediscursive elements cannot effectively counter the colonial-

ist thinking that has sustained its technology of management through the same system of categorizing bodies according to biological and cultural racism.

49. "Japanese Crimes against Humanity: Sexual Slavery and Forced Labor," international conference, Radisson Wilshire Plaza Hotel, November 29–30, 2001.

50. Global Alliance for Preserving the History of WWII in Asia, the Fifth Biennial Conference, the Clarion Hotel Bay View Hotel, San Diego, November 15–17, 2002.

51. For a detailed analysis, see Yoneyama, "Nihon shokuminchishugi no rekishi kioku to Amerika: *Yōko monogatari* o megutte," in Komori Yōichi et al., eds., *Higashi Ajia rekishi ninshiki ronsō no metahisutorī: Kannichi, rentai 21 no kokoromi* (Tokyo: Seikyūsha, 2008), 267–84.

52. Chuh, "Discomforting Knowledge," 7.

53. See Yoneyama, "Traveling Memories, Contagious Justice."

54. Mizuho Aoki, "War Redress Reversal in South Korea," *Japan Times*, January 27, 2014; Lucy Hornby, "Mitsui OSK Settles to Free Ship Impounded in China," *Financial Times*, April 24, 2014, last accessed April 27, 2014, http://www.ft.com/intl /cms/s/0/0ddc073a-cb60–11e3-ba95–00144feabdc0.html#axzz308WtLm2w; and Carlos Barria, "Japan's Mitsui pays China to Release Seized Ship-Court," *Reuters*, April 24, 2014, last accessed April 27, 2014, http://www.reuters.com/article/2014 /04/24/us-japan-china-lawsuit-idUSBREA3N0A920140424.

55. Hillary Clinton, "America's Pacific Century," *Foreign Policy* 189 (2011).

56. See Roy Miki, *Redress: Inside the Japanese Canadian Call for Justice* (Vancouver: Raincoast Books, 2004), who observed that the Japanese Canadian redress case needs to be viewed from a more critical perspective when considering that Canada's state-sanctioned official multiculturalism celebrates this instance of historical justice as a national success.

57. Following Frantz Fanon, the cultural critic Randall Williams described such a process an "appellative mode of recognition." Randall Williams, *The Divided World: Human Rights and Its Violence* (Minneapolis: University of Minnesota Press, 2010), 100.

Chapter 5. Complicit Amnesia

1. Geoffrey White observed that the Smithsonian controversy was rooted in the inability to negotiate national and extranational ways of remembering what was in essence an international event: the war. He writes, "The particular difficulties for this exhibit in navigating between opposed calls for critical history and patriotic history stem from the fact that it was dealing with an intensely international subject in an intensely national site." See White, "Memory Wars: The Politics of Remembering the Asia/Pacific War," *AsiaPacific Issues*, no. 21 (July 1995): 1–8. See also White's earlier analysis of Guadalcanal's fiftieth-anniversary commemorative on the transnational memory-making processes, "Remembering Guadalcanal: National Identity and Transnational Memory Making," *Public Culture* 7 (spring 1995): 529–55.

2. Two important collaborative projects were produced in response to the legislators' censorship of National History. See "Remembering the Bomb: The Fiftieth

Anniversary in the United States and Japan," special issue of *Bulletin of Concerned Asian Scholars* 27, no. 2 (April–June 1995), and the articles collected in "Hiroshima in History and Memory: A Symposium," special issue of *Diplomatic History* 19, no. 2 (spring 1995). For readers of Japanese, the historian Yui Daizaburō has succinctly summarized the entire course of events and the problems with the dominant historical understanding in the United States about the use of atom bombs. Yui's book also examines the U.S.-Japan gap in perceptions of the Pacific War, the Korean War, and the Vietnam War. See Yui Daizaburō, *Nichibei sensōkan no sōkoku: Masatsu no shinsō shinri* (Tokyo: Iwanami Shoten, 1995).

3. See John B. Thompson, *Studies in the Theory of Ideology* (Berkeley: University of California Press, 1984), 1.

4. Kai Bird, "A Humiliating Smithsonian Retreat from the Facts of Hiroshima," *International Herald Tribune*, October 12, 1994.

5. See Michael King, "Revisiting the *Enola Gay*," *Post-Crescent* (Appleton, WI), November 20, 1994.

6. U.S. Senate Committee on Rules and Administration, *Hearing: The Smithsonian Institution Management Guidelines for the Future*, 104th Cong., 1st sess., May 11 and 18, 1995, 48.

7. Eugene L. Meyer and Jacqueline Trescott, "Smithsonian Scuttles Exhibit," *Washington Post*, January 31, 1995.

8. Martin Harwit, "The *Enola Gay*: A Nation's, and a Museum's, Dilemma," *Washington Post*, August 7, 1994.

9. See the statement of Herman G. Harrington in U.S. Senate, *Hearing: The Smithsonian Institution Management Guidelines*, 20–27.

10. U.S. Senate, *Hearing: The Smithsonian Institution Management Guidelines*, 49. The Rorschach test image also appears in Gaddis Smith, "Hiroshima: The Rorschach Test of the American Psyche," *Los Angeles Times*, July 30, 1995.

11. "Enola Gay Exhibit Remains Unsettled," *San Diego Union Tribune*, March 12, 1995.

12. The most important of earlier seminal works by revisionist historians include Gar Alperovitz, *Atomic Diplomacy: Hiroshima and Potsdam* (New York: Simon and Schuster, 1965); Martin J. Sherwin, *A World Destroyed: The Atomic Bomb and the Grand Alliance* (New York: Knopf, 1975); and Barton Bernstein, "Atomic Diplomacy and the Cold War," in Barton Bernstein, ed., *The Atomic Bomb: The Critical Issues* (Boston: Little, Brown, 1976), 129–35. The argument that Truman was aware in early July of Japan's likely surrender appeared in Gar Alperovitz, "Enola Gay: A New Consensus . . . ," *Washington Post*, February 4, 1995. In his more recent *Decision to Use the Atomic Bomb and the Architecture of an American Myth* (New York: Knopf, 1995), Alperovitz rearticulates the revisionist view and juxtaposes it in great detail to the ways in which the mainstream U.S. understanding about the bomb's use was manufactured. For the official manipulation of the estimated American casualties and deaths, see Barton Bernstein, "Understanding the Atomic Bomb and the Japanese Surrender: Missed Opportunities, Little-Known Near Disasters, and Modern Memory," *Diplomatic History* 19, no. 2 (spring 1995): 227–73. For a summary of the historians' new consensus, see J. Samuel Walker,

"History, Collective Memory, and the Decision to Use the Bomb," *Diplomatic History* 19, no. 2 (spring 1995): 319–28.

13. This point was made by Bernstein in his remarks at the conference "Hoping for the Worst: The Planning, Experience, and Consequences of Mass Warfare, 1930–1950," University of California, Berkeley, November 1995.

14. Dominick LaCapra, "Representing the Holocaust: Reflections on the Historians' Debate," in Saul Friedlander, ed., *Probing the Limits of Representation: Nazism and the "Final Solution"* (Cambridge, MA: Harvard University Press, 1992), 122. LaCapra proposed instead that, in addition to the scientific inquiry of historical accuracy, we recognize the significance of identifying the ritualized aspects of psychological transference that shape any historical representation. For the ways in which the subject positions of scholars/rememberers are cathected to their objects of inquiry/remembering will determine the degree to which the processes of working through (*Durcharbeitung*) historical trauma will be effective or evaded. For an earlier discussion of the difficulties and possibilities in the act of confronting the past, see Theodor W. Adorno, "What Does Coming to Terms with the Past Mean?" in Geoffrey H. Hartman, ed., *Bitburg in Moral and Political Perspective*, (Bloomington: Indiana University Press, 1986), 114–29. See also Eric L. Santner, "History beyond the Pleasure Principle: Some Thoughts on the Representation of Trauma," in Saul Friedlander, ed., *Probing the Limits of Representation: Nazism and the "Final Solution"* (Cambridge, MA: Harvard University Press, 1992), 143–54. Santner links LaCapra's discussion on "working through" to his conceptualization of the possibility of redemption through the proper form of "mourning" loss. Santner points out that the German inability to mourn emerges as what he calls "narrative fetish," which serves as yet another repression of the repressed, in a manner similar to the "acting out" of historians that LaCapra observes.

15. See Hayden White, "The Value of Narrativity in the Representation of Reality," and "Narrativization of Real Events," in W. J. T. Mitchell, ed., *On Narrative* (Chicago: University of Chicago Press, 1981), 1–23, 249–54.

16. Ping-hui Liao urges us to extend our rethinking of the Habermasian utopian presumption of a single, unitary public sphere to historical consciousness and memories. Following the critiques of Nancy Fraser and others, Liao underscores the significance of modifying the liberal public sphere notion with respect to the postcolonial condition in Taiwan, where multiple layers of modern experiences and historical identities coexist. See Liao, "Rewriting Taiwanese National History: The February 28 Incident as Spectacle," *Public Culture* 5 (winter 1993): 281–96.

17. Among numerous examples of this reasoning, see especially Edwin M. Yoder Jr., ". . . Or Hiroshima Cult?" *Washington Post*, February 4, 1995.

18. U.S. Senate Committee, *Hearing: The Smithsonian Institution Management Guidelines*, 11.

19. Eric Gable, Richard Handler, and Anna Lawson, "On the Uses of Relativism: Fact, Conjecture, and Black and White Histories at Colonial Williamsburg," *American Ethnologist* 19, no. 4 (1992): 792. I am especially thankful to Richard Handler for

pushing me to think through the conflation of history and memory in Sweeney's Senate hearing.

20. See Peter Novick, *That Noble Dream: The "Objectivity Question" and the American Historical Profession* (New York: Cambridge University Press, 1988).

21. When a Harvard professor stated at the United Nations Hiroshima Disarmament Conference that he believed use of the atom bombs helped hasten the war's end and saved both American and Japanese lives—which indeed is the dominant view shared by most people in the United States—*Asahi Shimbun* reported on the contention his statement elicited with the headline, " 'Nuclear Consciousness,' Japan-U.S. Gap," December 11, 1992.

22. *Chūgoku Shimbun*, September 30, 1994.

23. See *Asahi Shimbun*, June 14, 1995, for one of the most detailed articles dealing with the overall social and political environment in the United States.

24. The pilot's view simultaneously structured the dominant memoryscape of postnuclear Hiroshima and Nagasaki. The gaze from above came to shape the subsequent development of medico-legal discourse on the damages caused by the bombs as well as the survivors' testimonial practices. See *Hiroshima Traces: Time, Space, and the Dialectics of Memory* (Berkeley: University of California Press, 1999), 113–14.

25. U.S. Senate Committee, *Hearing: The Smithsonian Institution Management Guidelines*, 24.

26. For instance, the spokesperson for the Air Force Association, Jack Giese, described the Smithsonian controversy as "an internal American debate with an American institution that wasn't doing their job." See Nigel Holloway, "Museum Peace: U.S. Curators Seek Truce over the Plane That Atom-Bombed Hiroshima," *Far Eastern Economic Review*, February 2, 1995, 32.

27. U.S. Senate Committee, *Hearing: The Smithsonian Institution Management Guidelines*, 11.

28. U.S. Senate Committee, *Hearing: The Smithsonian Institution Management Guidelines*, 11.

29. For a statement that most succinctly reveals the understandings of history and U.S.–East Asia relations described here, see James R. Van de Velde, "Enola Gay Saved Lives, Period," *Washington Post*, February 10, 1995. The Smithsonian controversy also demonstrated that some of the Cold War perceptions that justified the use of the atomic bombs and the subsequent nuclear buildup are still strongly upheld by many in the United States. See, for example, Thomas Sowell, "The Right to Infiltrate," *Forbes*, March 13, 1995, 74. It should further be noted that the view held by Sweeney, Van de Velde, and others need not necessarily be identified as national (i.e., American), for such a historical awareness is also widely found among citizens of Japan and other Asian nations. The irony, of course, is that such justifications for the bombs' use are premised on an argument that the prepared text's opponents have themselves been refuting. This Cold War historical narrative in fact unwittingly appropriates the factual grounds used by the U.S. revisionist historians to argue that the atomic bombs were unnecessary

from a strictly military point of view, that is, the argument that the decision to drop the bombs was necessary not primarily for the purpose of bringing the war to a rapid close, but rather to contain the Soviets in the postwar settlement.

30. Holloway, "Museum Peace," 32.

31. National Air and Space Museum, "The Crossroads: The End of World War II, the Atomic Bomb, and the Origins of the Cold War, First Script," National Air and Space Museum, Washington, DC, 1994, mimeograph, 5.

32. Martin Sherwin, "Hiroshima gojūnen, rekishi to kioku no seijigaku" (Hiroshima fifty years, politics of history and memory), *Kokusai bunka kaikan kaihō* 6, no. 4 (October 1995): 8.

33. "Context and the Enola Gay," *Washington Post*, August 14, 1994. See also Richard Serrano, "Smithsonian Says It Erred, Scraps Exhibit on A-Bomb," *Los Angeles Times*, January 31, 1995, for William M. Detweiler's comment in which he noted "the museum curators' attempt to depict the Japanese as victims and Americans as coldhearted avengers."

34. Hugh Sidney and Jerry Hannifin, "War and Remembrance," *Time* (May 23, 1994), 64. Crouch had been explaining to the public that survivors' testimonies and displays of articles demonstrating the ground-level effects of the bombs would make up the planned exhibit's "emotional center." It would have included photographs of mutilated women and children and audiovisual tapes of survivors' testimonies. Throughout the controversy, the museum curators' critics problematized the proposed exhibit for placing the emotional center on the destruction caused by the atomic bombing. See also James Risen, "War of Words," *Los Angeles Times*, December 19, 1994; and "War of Words: What Museum Couldn't Say," *New York Times*, February 5, 1995. Journalists such as *Air Force Magazine* editor John Correll expressed their disgust at the fact that the museum curators' script would have included more photographs of Japanese casualties than of American soldiers. See "The Mission That Ended the War," *Washington Post*, August 14, 1994. That the number of Chinese killed by the Japanese military far exceeded either American or Japanese casualties was the least of their concerns.

35. U.S. Senate Committee, *Hearing: The Smithsonian Institution Management Guidelines*, 12.

36. "Theory, Area Studies, Cultural Studies: Issues of Pedagogy in Multiculturalism," in Joyce E. Canaan and Debbie Epstein, eds., *A Question of Discipline: Pedagogy, Power, and the Teaching of Cultural Studies* (Boulder, CO: Westview Press, 1997), 11–26; also republished in Rey Chow, *Ethics after Idealism: Theory, Culture, Ethnicity, Reading* (Bloomington: Indiana University Press, 1998).

37. Chow, *Ethics after Idealism*, 1.

38. Gingrich's speech is quoted in Stephen Budiansky et al., "A Museum in Crisis: The Smithsonian Heads into Rough Times after the Enola Gay Debacle," *U.S. News and World Report*, February 13, 1995, 73–74.

39. For characterizations of the NASM curators' effort to include multiple dimensions of the two atom bombs' use as stemming from the sensitivities of "political correctness" and of the 1960s Vietnam War generation, see above all, Sowell,

"Right to Infiltrate," 74; the testimony of Evan S. Baker, president of the Navy League of the United States, in U.S. Senate Committee, *Hearing: The Smithsonian Institution Management Guidelines*, May 11, 1995; and Risen, "War of Words." William M. Detweiler, who was one of the first to openly attack the NASM staff, drew a connection between the Smithsonian controversy and the National History Standards for U.S. and world history, through which "students will learn more about the politically correct people, places and events." See "Assault on American Values," *Washington Post*, February 11, 1995.

40. Christine Choy and Nancy Tong, dir., *In the Name of the Emperor* (New York: Film News Now Foundation, AMVNM, 1995), VHS.

41. T. Fujitani, "The Reischauer Memo: Mr. Moto, Hirohito, and Japanese American Soldiers," *Critical Asian Studies* 33, no. 3 (2001): 379–402. Also for an alternative view, Tsuyoshi Hasegawa, *Racing the Enemy: Stalin, Truman, and the Surrender of Japan* (Cambridge, MA: Harvard University Press, 2005).

42. Miriam Silverberg, "Remembering Pearl Harbor, Forgetting Charlie Chaplin, and the Case of the Disappearing Western Woman: A Picture Story," *positions: east asia culture critique* 1, no. 1 (spring 1993): 24–76.

43. Kai Bird, for instance, argued that the Smithsonian script did not assault "the patriotism of World War II veterans. But neither should one question the patriotism of scholars who labor in the archives at the difficult task of peeling away layers of historical truth." See his "Humiliating Smithsonian Retreat." Martin Sherwin also responded to the press: "I'm appalled that Congress has come into this with an official history over the debate, leaving no room for informed debate. In my view, this cancellation undermines the democratic process for which these veterans fought in World War II." See Karen De Witt, "U.S. Exhibit on Bomber Is in Jeopardy," *New York Times*, January 28, 1995. It is unclear from this quote whether Sherwin himself is equating the democratic process with the particular U.S. constitutional process. But when read against the larger context of Detweiler's and others' accusation that the NASM staff and their supporters lack American patriotism, it produces precisely such an effect.

Epilogue

Washington Post Epigraph. Quoted in Peter Kuznick, "Japan's Nuclear History in Perspective: Eisenhower and Atoms for War and Peace," *Bulletin of the Atomic Scientists*, April 30, 2011, last accessed January 28, 2012, http://thebulletin.org/print/web-edition /features/japans-nuclear-history-perspective-eisenhower-and-atoms-war-and-peace.

1. Michel de Certeau suggested that "fables" and "fabulous stories" can offer spaces for alternative histories akin to those proffered by Walter Benjamin. According to de Certeau the space of "fabulous stories" suspends dominant categories and institutionalized power so that the existing social order is not inevitably reproduced and the past does not necessarily dictate the future. See *Hiroshima Traces: Time, Space, and the Dialectics of Memory* (Berkeley: University of California Press, 1999), 112–35; and Michel de Certeau, *The Practice of Everyday Life*, trans. Steven F. Rendall (Berkeley: University of California Press, 1984).

2. The House of Sharing was initially located in Seoul and later moved to the countryside in Kyŏngi-Do. In addition to housing, the building accommodates a historical museum where visitors can learn the history of Japan's wartime military comfort system and experience the testimonials and artwork produced by and for the survivors.

3. Pyŏn Yŏng-ju's documentary film on the lives at the House of Sharing, "Habitual Sadness" (1997), which was a sequel to "The Murmuring" (1995), evokes a profound sense of the belatedness of justice in presenting Kang's untimely passing. See *The Murmuring/Najŭn moksori 1*, directed by Pyŏn Yŏng-ju (Seoul: Korean Film Council, [1995] 2005), DVD; and *Habitual Sadness/Najŭn moksori 2*, directed by Pyŏn Yŏng-ju (Seoul: Korean Film Council, [1997] 2005), DVD.

4. "Forgiving," wrote Arendt, "is the only reaction which does not merely re-act but acts anew and unexpectedly, unconditioned by the act which provoked it and therefore freeing from its consequences both the one who forgives and the one who is forgiven." Vengeance, in contrast, locks in "both doer and sufferer [of the evil deed] in the relentless automatism of the action process, which by itself need never come to an end." Hannah Arendt, *The Human Condition* (Chicago: University of Chicago Press, [1958] 1965), 241.

5. The late journalist Matsui Yayori, one of the primary organizers of the tribunal, explained how Kang's artwork stimulated feminists in Japan to become involved in the tribunal "from the position of women belonging to the perpetrating country" as a response to Kang's and other survivors' calls for unequivocal justice. Matsui Yayori, "Naze sabaku ka, dō sabaku ka: 'Josei Kokusai Senpan Hōtei' ga mezasu mono," *Sekai* 682 (December 2000): 109.

6. Nanumu no Ie Rekishikan Kōenkai, ed., *Nanumu no Ie Rekishikan: Handobukku* (Tokyo: Kashiwa Shobō, 2002), 93.

7. See George Lipsitz, "Learning from New Orleans: The Social Warrant of Hostile Privatism and Competitive Consumer Citizenship," *Cultural Anthropology* 21, no. 3 (August 2006): 451–68.

8. See Chandan Reddy on how the liberal states can sustain the status quo through instituting "amendments" in the form of counterviolence. *Freedom with Violence: Race, Sexuality, and the US State* (Durham, NC: Duke University Press, 2011).

9. Jacob Kipp, PhD, Lester Grau, Karl Prinslow, and Captain Don Smith, "The Human Terrain System: A CORDS for the 21st Century," *Military Review* (September/October 2006). The U.S. Army Professional Writing Collection. Last accessed July 22, 2011. http://www.army.mil/professionalWriting/volumes/volume4/december_2006/12_06_2.html. See also *The U.S. Army/Marine Corps Counterinsurgency Field Manual: U.S. Army Field Manual No. 3–24, Marine Corps Warfighting Publication No. 3–33.5* (Chicago: University of Chicago Press, 2007).

10. Hugh Gusterson, for instance, extended his critique to the Cold War origin of the militarization of anthropological knowledge, while Catherine Lutz incisively understood the commercial market publication of the *US Army/Marine Corps Counterinsurgency Field Manual* as part of larger problems inherent in the history of U.S. empire and what she called "the military normal," or "the overall

militarization of the American everyday life through the entangled system of the military-industrial-Congressional-media-entertainment-university complex" (29). Andrew Bickford, furthermore, reflected on the affinity between ethnographic field research and the work of the intelligence collection and saw it as "anthropology's potentially dangerous side" (138). Similarly, Greg Feldman censured that the *Counter-Insurgency Field Manual* "reads like an introduction to cultural anthropology" (85) and called for critical examination of the discipline's "epistemic framework" (90). Hugh Gusterson, "Militarizing Knowledge"; Catherine Lutz, "The Military Normal"; Greg Feldman, "Radical or Reactionary?"; Andrew Bickford, "Anthropology and HUMINT", in The Network of Concerned Anthropologists, *The Counter-Counterinsurgency Manual: Or, Notes on Demilitarizing American Society* (Chicago: Prickly Paradigm Press, 2009).

11. Mahmood Mamdani, *Good Muslim, Bad Muslim: America, the Cold War, and the Roots of Terror* (New York: Pantheon Books, 2004).

12. The original title is *Gendaishi skūpu dokumento: Genpatsu dōnyū no shinario~reisenka no genshiryoku senryaku~*. See also Arima Tetsuo, *Genpatsu, Shōriki, CIA: Kimitsu bunsho de yomu Shōwa uramen shi* (Tokyo: Shinchō Bunko, 2008).

13. See, for example, Kainuma Hiroshi, *"Fukushima"ron: Genshiryoku mura wa naze umareta no ka* (Tokyo: Seidosha, 2011).

14. Kuznick, "Japan's Nuclear History in Perspective: Eisenhower and Atoms," *Bulletin of the Atomic Scientists*, April 30, 2011, last accessed January 28, 2012, http://thebulletin.org/print/web-edition/features/japans-nuclear-history -perspective-eisenhower-and-atoms-war-and-peace. For a transpacific critique of the collusion of the American and Japanese nuclear industrial-military-academic establishments in promoting the use of nuclear energy across the Pacific, see also Kuznick's collaborative work with Toshiyuki (Yuki) Tanaka, *Genpatsu to Hiroshima:"Genshiryoku heiwa riyō" no shinsō, Iwanami bukkuretto* 819 (2011).

15. Teresia K. Teaiwa, "bikinis and other s/pacific n/oceans," *Contemporary Pacific* 6, no. 1 (1994): 87–109.

16. In August 2013 TEPCO reported that some 79,000 gallons of contaminated water leaked into the ocean as a result of overflow above the subterranean ice wall, which had been designed to prevent the spread of radioactive water. Phred Dvorak, "Japan Studies Plan to Contain Radioactive Water; Japan to Stem Spread of Radioactive Water at Fukushima with Subterranean Ring of Ice," *Wall Street Journal*, August 29, 2013, last accessed December 14, 2014, http://www.wsj.com /articles/SB10001424127887324324404579040520540137690. Another report from the same period warned that "some 400 metric tons of water a day is still being used to cool the melted fuel cores—though much of that water is now recycled. More troubling is another 400 tons a day of groundwater that flows down from hills and mountains into the compound, and toward the sea." Mari Iwata and Phred Dvorak, "At Fukushima, Fear of a Losing Battle: Tepco Builds Sunken Barrier to Ring-Fence Site, but Water May Have Already Overtopped Wall," *Wall*

Street Journal, August 6, 2013, last accessed December 14, 2014, http://www.wsj
.com/articles/SB10001424127887323420604578651713545887032.

17. Josen Masangkay Diaz, "The Subject Case: The Filipino Body and the Politics of Making Filipino America" (PhD dissertation, University of California, San Diego, 2014).

18. Yen Le Espiritu, *Body Counts: The Vietnam War and Militarized Refuge(es)* (Berkeley: University of California Press, 2014), 58.

19. Wen Ho Lee and Helen Zia, *My Country versus Me: The First-Hand Account by the Los Alamos Scientist Who Was Falsely Accused of Being a Spy* (New York: Hyperion, 2001).

BIBLIOGRAPHY

Adorno, Theodor W. "What Does Coming to Terms with the Past Mean?" In *Bitburg in Moral and Political Perspective*, edited by Geoffrey H. Hartman, 114–29. Bloomington: Indiana University Press, 1986.

Agamben, Giorgio. "Beyond Human Rights." In *Means Without End: Notes on Politics*, 15–26. Minneapolis: University of Minnesota Press, 2000.

———. *Homo Sacer: Sovereign Power and Bare Life*. Translated by Daniel Heller Roazan. Stanford, CA: Stanford University Press, 1998.

———. *Remnants of Auschwitz: The Witness and the Archive*. New York: Zone Books, 1999.

Ajia Minshū Hōtei Junbi Kai, ed. *Toinaosu Tōkyō saiban*. Tokyo: Ryokufū Shuppan, 1995.

Alarcón, Norma. "The Theoretical Subject(s) of This Bridge Called My Back and Anglo-American Feminism." In *Making Face, Making Soul/ Haciendo Caras: Creative and Critical Perspectives by Feminists of Color*, edited by Gloria Anzaldúa, 356–69. San Francisco, CA: Aunt Lute Books, 1990.

Alexander, M. Jacqui. *Pedagogies of Crossing: Meditations on Feminism, Sexual Politics, Memory, and the Sacred*. Durham, NC: Duke University Press, 2005.

Alexander, M. Jacqui, and Chandra Talpade Mohanty, eds. *Feminist Genealogies, Colonial Legacies, Democratic Futures*. New York: Routledge, 1997.

Alperovitz, Gar. *Atomic Diplomacy: Hiroshima and Potsdam*. New York: Simon and Schuster, 1965.

———. *Decision to Use the Atomic Bomb and the Architecture of an American Myth*. New York: Knopf, 1995.

Amano Keiichi. *Jiyūshugi shikan o kaidoku suru*. Tokyo: Shakai Hyōronsha, 1997.

Anghie, Antony. *Imperialism, Sovereignty, and the Making of International Law*. Cambridge: Cambridge University Press, 2005.

Appy, Christian G. "Introduction: Struggling for the World." In *Cold War Constructions: The Political Culture of United States Imperialism, 1945–1966*, edited by Christian G. Appy, 1–8. Amherst: University of Massachusetts Press, 2000.

Arai Toshio. "Chūka Jinmin Kyōwakoku no senpan saiban." In *Senpan saiban to seibōryoku, Nihongun seidoreisei o sabaku: 2002nen Josei Kokusai Senpan Hōtei no kiroku*, vol. 1, edited by VAWW-NET Japan 123–53. Tokyo: Ryokufū Shuppan, 2000.

Arendt, Hannah. *The Human Condition.* Chicago: University of Chicago Press, (1958) 1965.

Arima Tetsuo. *Genpatsu, Shōriki,* CIA: *Kimitsu bunsho de yomu Shōwa uramen shi.* Tokyo: Shinchō Bunko, 2008.

Arrendondo, Gabriela F., et al., eds. *Chicana Feminisms: A Critical Reader.* Durham, NC: Duke University Press, 2003.

Balibar, Etienne. "Europe: Vanishing Mediator." *Constellations* 10, no. 3 (2003): 312–38.

———. "Is There a 'Neo-Racism'?" Translated by Chris Turner. In Etienne Balibar and Immanuel Wallerstein, *Race, Nation, Class: Ambiguous Identities,* 17–28. New York: Verso, 1991.

Barkan, Elazar. *The Guilt of Nations: Restitution and Negotiating Historical Injustices.* Baltimore, MD: Johns Hopkins University Press, 2000.

Bass, Gary Jonathan. *Stay the Hand of Vengeance: The Politics of War Crimes Tribunals.* Princeton, NJ: Princeton University Press, 2000.

Bazyler, Michael. "Japan Should Follow the International Trend and Face Its History of World War II Forced Labor." *The Asia-Pacific Journal* 5-3-09, January 29, 2009.

Bellah, Robert N. *Tokugawa Religion: The Values of Pre-Industrial Japan.* New York: Free Press, (1957) 1969.

Benedict, Ruth. *The Chrysanthemum and the Sword: Patterns of Japanese Culture.* Boston: Houghton Mifflin, (1946) 1989.

Benjamin, Walter. "Theses on the Philosophy of History." In *Illuminations,* edited by Hannah Arendt, translated by Harry Zohn, 253–64. New York: Schocken Books, 1969.

Benvenisti, Eyal. *The International Law of Occupation.* Princeton, NJ: Princeton University Press, 1993.

Bernstein, Barton. "Atomic Diplomacy and the Cold War." In *The Atomic Bomb: The Critical Issues,* edited by Barton Bernstein, 129–35. Boston: Little, Brown, 1976.

———. "Understanding the Atomic Bomb and the Japanese Surrender: Missed Opportunities, Little-Known Near Disasters, and Modern Memory." *Diplomatic History* 19, no. 2 (spring 1995): 227–73.

Borstelmann, Thomas. *The Cold War and the Color Line: American Race Relations in the Global Arena.* Cambridge, MA: Harvard University Press, 2001.

Briggs, Laura J. *Reproducing Empire: Race, Sex, Science and U.S. Imperialism in Puerto Rico.* Berkeley: University of California Press, 2002.

Brown, Wendy. *States of Injury: Power and Freedom in Late Modernity.* Princeton, NJ: Princeton University Press, 1995.

Bunch, Charlotte. "Women's Human Rights: The Challenges of Global Feminism and Diversity." In *Feminist Locations: Global and Local, Theory and Practice,* edited by Marianne DeKoven, 129–45. New Brunswick, NJ: Rutgers University Press, 2001.

Butler, Judith. *Bodies That Matter: On the Discursive Limits of "Sex."* New York: Routledge, 1993.

———. *Frames of War: When Is Life Grievable?* London: Verso, 2009.

Butler, Judith, and Joan W. Scott, eds. *Feminists Theorize the Political.* New York: Routledge, 1992.

Cacho, Lisa Marie. *Social Death: Racialized Rightlessness and the Criminalization of the Unprotected*. New York: New York University Press, 2012.

Camacho, Keith L. *Cultures of Commemoration: The Politics of War, Memory, and History in the Mariana Islands*. Honolulu: University of Hawaii Press, 2011.

———. "Transoceanic Flows: Pacific Islander Interventions across the American Empire," *Amerasia Journal* 37, no. 3 (2011): ix–xxxiv.

Campomanes, Oscar V. "1898 and the Nature of the New Empire." *Radical History Review* 73 (winter 1999): 130–46.

Caprio, Mark, and Yoneyuki Sugita. *Democracy in Occupied Japan: The U.S. Occupation and Japanese Politics and Society*. London: Routledge, 2007.

Cathcart, Adam, and Patricia Nash. "'To Serve Revenge for the Dead': Chinese Communist Responses to Japanese War Crimes in the PRC Foreign Ministry Archive, 1949–1956." *China Quarterly* 200 (2009): 1053–69.

———. "War Criminals and the Road to Sino-Japanese Normalization." *Sino-Japanese Relations: History, Politics, Economy* 2 (2011): 49–70.

Certeau, Michel de. *The Practice of Everyday Life*. Translated by Steven F. Rendall. Berkeley: University of California Press, 1984.

Césaire, Aimé. *Discourse on Colonialism*. Translated by Joan Pinkham. New York: Monthly Review Press, (1955) 2000.

Chakrabarty, Dipesh. *Provincializing Europe: Postcolonial Thought and Historical Difference*. Princeton, NJ: Princeton University Press, 2000.

Chen, Kuan-Hsing. *Trajectories: Inter-Asia Cultural Studies*. New York: Routledge, 1998.

Chen, Kuan-Hsing, and Beng H. Chua, eds. *The Inter-Asia Cultural Studies Reader*. New York: Routledge, 2007.

Ching, Leo. *Becoming "Japanese": Colonial Taiwan and the Politics of Identity Formation*. Berkeley: University of California Press, 2001.

Chinkin, Christine M. "Women's International Tribunal of Japanese Military Sexual Slavery." *American Journal of International Law* 95, no. 2 (2001): 335–41.

Cho, Grace M. *Haunting the Korean Diaspora: Shame, Secrecy, and the Forgotten War*. Minneapolis: University of Minnesota Press, 2008.

Cho, Yu-Fang. *Uncoupling American Empire: Cultural Politics of Deviance and Unequal Difference, 1890–1910*. Albany: State University of New York Press, 2013.

Choi, Chungmoo, ed. *The Comfort Women: Colonialism, War, and Sex*. A special issue of *positions: east asia cultures critique* 5, no. 1 (1997).

———. "The Discourse of Decolonization and Popular Memory: South Korea." *positions: east asia cultures critique* 1, no. 1 (spring 1993): 77–102.

———. "The Politics of War Memories toward Healing." In *Perilous Memories: Asia-Pacific War(s)*, edited by Takashi Fujitani, Geoffrey M. White, and Lisa Yoneyama, 395–409. Durham, NC: Duke University Press, 2001.

Chŏng Yŏng-hwang. "Shiryō to kaisetsu: Tōkyō saiban o meguru zainichi Chōsenjin hakkō zasshi shinbun/kikanshi no ronchō." *Nikkan sōgo ninshiki* 1 (2008): 19–67.

Chow, Rey. "Theory, Area Studies, Cultural Studies: Issues of Pedagogy in Multiculturalism." In *A Question of Discipline: Pedagogy, Power, and the Teaching of Cultural*

Studies, edited by Joyce E. Canaan and Debbie Epstein, 11–26. Boulder, CO: Westview Press, 1997.

———. *Ethics after Idealism: Theory, Culture, Ethnicity, Reading.* Bloomington: Indiana University Press, 1998.

Choy, Christine and Nancy Tong, dirs. *In the Name of the Emperor.* New York: Film News Now Foundation, AMVNM, 1995.

Chuh, Kandice. "Discomforting Knowledge: Or, Korean 'Comfort Women' and Asian Americanist Critical Practice." *Journal of Asian American Studies* 6, no. 1 (February 2003): 5–23.

———. "Transnationalism and Its Pasts." *Public Culture* 9, no. 1 (1996): 93–112.

Chūgoku Kikansha Renrakukai, ed. *Kanzenban sankō: Yakitsukushi, ubaitsukushi, koroshitsukusu, kore o "sankō" to iu.* Tokyo: Kōbunsha, (1957) 1984.

———. *Watashitachi wa Chūgoku de nani o shitaka: Moto Nihonjin senpan no kiroku.* Tokyo: San'ichi Shobō, 1987.

Chūgoku Kikansha Renrakukai/Yomiuri Shosha, eds. *Shinryaku: Chūgoku ni okeru Nihon senpan no kokuhaku.* Tokyo: Shin Dokushosha, 1958.

Cochrane, Rexmond C. *The National Academy of Sciences: The First Hundred Years, 1863–1963.* Washington, DC: Academy, 1978.

Crenshaw, Kimberlé. "Demarginalizing the Intersection of Race and Sex: A Black Feminist Critique of Antidiscrimination Doctrine." *University of Chicago Legal Forum* (1989): 139–67.

Cruz, Denise. *Transpacific Femininities: The Making of the Modern Filipina.* Durham, NC: Duke University Press, 2012.

Cumings, Bruce. "Boundary Displacement: Area Studies and International Studies during and after the Cold War." *Bulletin of Concerned Asian Scholars* 29, no. 1 (1997): 6–27.

———. *The Origins of the Korean War: Liberation and the Emergence of Separate Regimes 1945–1947.* Princeton, NJ: Princeton University Press, 1981.

———. *Parallax Visions: Making Sense of American-East Asian Relations at the End of the Century.* Durham, NC: Duke University Press, 1999.

Davis, Angela Y. "Interview with Lisa Lowe, Angela Davis: Reflections on Race, Class, and Gender in the USA." In *The Politics of Culture in the Shadow of Capital*, edited by Lisa Lowe and David Lloyd, 303–23. Durham, NC: Duke University Press, 1997.

———. *Women, Race and Class.* New York: Random House, 1981.

De Hart, Jane Sherron. "Containment at Home: Gender, Sexuality, and National Identity in Cold War America." In *Rethinking Cold War Culture*, edited by Peter J. Kuznick and James Gilbert, 124–55. Washington, DC: Smithsonian Institution, 2001.

de Lauretis, Teresa, ed. *Feminist Studies/Critical Studies.* Bloomington: Indiana University Press, 1986.

D'Emilio, John. "The Homosexual Menace: The Politics of Sexuality in Cold War America." In *Making Trouble: Essays on Gay History, Politics, and the University*, edited by John D'Emilio, 57–73. New York: Routledge, 1993.

Derrida, Jacques. "Force of Law: The 'Mystical Foundation of Authority.' " In *Deconstruction and the Possibility of Justice*, edited by Drucilla Cornell, Michel Rosenfeld, and David Gray Carlson, 3–67. New York: Routledge, 1992.

———. *On Cosmopolitanism and Forgiveness*. Translated by Mark Dooley and Michael Hughes. London: Routledge, 2001.

———. *Specters of Marx: The State of the Debt, the Work of Mourning, and the New International*. New York: Routledge, 1994.

Diaz, Josen Masangkay. "The Subject Case: The Filipino Body and the Politics of Making Filipino America." PhD diss., University of California, San Diego, 2014.

Dirlik, Arif. " 'Trapped in History' on the Way to Utopia: East Asia's 'Great War' Fifty Years Later." In *Perilous Memories: The Asia-Pacific War(s)*, edited by T. Fujitani, Geoffrey M. White, and Lisa Yoneyama, 299–322. Durham, NC: Duke University Press, 2001.

———. *What Is in a Rim? Critical Perspectives on the Pacific Region Idea*. Lanham, MD: Rowman and Littlefield, 1998.

Dower, John. *Embracing Defeat: Japan in the Wake of World War II*. New York: W. W. Norton, 1999.

———. *Empire and Aftermath: Yoshida Shigeru and the Japanese Experience, 1878–1954*. Cambridge, MA: Harvard East Asian Monographs, 1979.

———. "Occupied Japan and the American Lake, 1945–1950." In *America's Asia: Dissenting Essays on Asia-American Relations*, edited by Edward Friedman and Mark Selden, 146–206. New York: Pantheon Books, 1971.

———. *War without Mercy: Race and Power in the Pacific War*. New York: Pantheon Books, 1986.

Drea, Edward, et al. *Researching Japanese War Crimes Records: Introductory Essays*. Washington, DC: Nazi War Crimes and Japanese Imperial Government Records Interagency Working Group, 2006.

Dudden, Alexis. *Troubled Apologies among Japan, Korea, and the United States*. New York: Columbia University Press, 2008.

Dudziak, Mary L. *Cold War Civil Rights: Race and Image of American Democracy*. Princeton, NJ: Princeton University Press, 2000.

Edkins, Jenny. *Trauma and the Memory Politics*. Cambridge: Cambridge University Press, 2003.

El-Tayeb, Fatima. *European Others: Queering Ethnicity in Postnational Europe*. Minneapolis: University of Minnesota Press, 2011.

Eng, David. *Racial Castration: Managing Masculinity in Asian America*. Durham, NC: Duke University Press, 2001.

Espiritu, Yen Le. *Body Counts: The Vietnam War and Militarized Refuge(es)*. Berkeley: University of California Press, 2014.

———. *Home Bound: Filipino American Lives across Cultures, Communities, and Countries*. Los Angeles: University of California Press, 2003.

Fanon, Frantz. "Algeria Unveiled." In *A Dying Colonialism*. Translated by Haakon Chevalier. Introduction by Adolfo Gilly, 35–67. New York: Grove Press, (1959) 1965.

Feldman, Allen. "Memory Theaters, Virtual Witnessing, and the Trauma-Aesthetic."
  Biography 27, no. 1 (winter 2004): 163–202.
Ferguson, Kennan. "The Gift of Freedom." *Social Text* 25, no. 2 (2007): 39–52.
Ferguson, Roderick A. *Aberrations in Black: Toward a Queer of Color Critique*. Minne-
  apolis: University of Minnesota Press, 2004.
Field, Norma. *In the Realm of a Dying Emperor*. New York: Pantheon Books, 1991.
Fisher, Barry A. "Notes from the World War II Redress Trenches: The Disparate Treat-
  ment of Victims East and West." *Loyola of Los Angeles International and Comparative
  Law Review* 95 (winter 2010): 1–22.
Foner, Eric. *The Story of American Freedom*. New York: W. W. Norton, 1998.
Foucault, Michel. *Society Must Be Defended: Lectures at the Collège De France, 1975–76*.
  Edited by Mauro Bertani, Alessandro Fontana, François Ewald, and David Macey.
  New York: Picador, 2003.
Frank, Miriam, et al. *The Life and Times of Rosie the Riveter: The Story of Three Million
  Working Women during World War II*. Emeryville, CA: Clarity Educational Publica-
  tion, 1982.
Friedman, Edward, and Mark Selden, eds. *America's Asia: Dissenting Essays on Asian-
  American Relations*. New York: Pantheon Books, 1971.
Friedman, Hal M. *Creating an American Lake: United States Imperialism and Strategic
  Security in the Pacific Basin, 1945–1947*. Westport, CT: Greenwood Press, 2001.
Fujikane, Candace, and Jonathan Y. Okamura, eds. *Asian Settler Colonialism: From
  Local Governance to the Habits of Everyday Life in Hawai'i*. Honolulu: University of
  Hawai'i Press, 2008.
Fujioka Nobukatsu. "Watashi ga hannichi rekishi kyōiku ni idonda ketteiteki na dōki."
  Seiron 293 (January 1997): 192–203.
Fujioka Nobukatsu and Izawa Motohiko. *Nō to ieru kyōkasho: Shinjitsu no Nikkan
  kankeishi*. Tokyo: Shōdensha, 1998.
Fujitani, T. "*Go For Broke*, the Movie: Japanese American Soldiers in U.S. National,
  Military, and Racial Discourse." In *Perilous Memories: Asia-Pacific War(s)*, edited by
  Takashi Fujitani, Geoffrey M. White, and Lisa Yoneyama, 239–66. Durham, NC:
  Duke University Press, 2001.
———. *Race for Empire: Koreans as Japanese and Japanese as Americans during World
  War II*. Berkeley: University of California Press, 2011.
———. "The Reischauer Memo: Mr. Moto, Hirohito, and Japanese American Sol-
  diers." *Critical Asian Studies* 33, no. 3 (2001): 379–402.
Fujitani, T., Geoffrey M. White, and Lisa Yoneyama, eds. *Perilous Memories: The Asia-
  Pacific War(s)*. Durham, NC: Duke University Press, 2001.
Fujiwara, Tomoko, dir. *The Gift from Beate*. Committee of "The Gift from Beate."
  Tokyo: Nippon Eiga Shinsha, 2004.
Futamura, Madoka. *War Crimes Tribunals and Transitional Justice: The Tokyo Trial and
  the Nuremburg Legacy*. London: Routledge, 2008.
Gable, Eric, Richard Handler, and Anna Lawson. "On the Uses of Relativism: Fact,
  Conjecture, and Black and White Histories at Colonial Williamsburg." *American
  Ethnologist* 19, no. 4 (1992): 791–805.

Gallicchio, Marc. *The African American Encounter with Japan and China: Black Internationalism in Asia, 1895–1945.* Chapel Hill: University of North Carolina Press, 2000.

Gilman, Nils. *Mandarins of the Future: Modernization Theory in Cold War America.* Baltimore, MD: Johns Hopkins University Press, 2003.

Goodenough, Ward H. "George P. Murdock, 1897–1985." Washington, DC: National Academy of Sciences, 1994.

Gordon, Avery F. *Ghostly Matters: Haunting and the Sociological Imagination.* Minneapolis: University of Minnesota Press, 2008.

———. "The Work of Corporate Culture: Diversity Management." *Social Text* 13, no. 3 (1995): 3–30.

Gordon, Avery F., and Christopher Newfield. "Introduction." In *Mapping Multiculturalism*, edited by Avery F. Gordon and Christopher Newfield, 1–16. Minneapolis: University of Minnesota Press, 1996.

Gordon, Beate Sirota. *1945nen no Kurisumasu: Nihonkoku kenpō ni "danjo byōdō" o kaita josei no jiden.* Tokyo: Kashiwa Shobō, 1995.

———. *The Only Woman in the Room: A Memoir.* Tokyo: Kodansha, 1997.

Gotanda, Neil. "A Critique of 'Our Constitution Is Colorblind': Racial Categories and White Supremacy." *Stanford Law Review* 44 (1991): 1–68.

Grewal, Inderpal. *Transnational America: Feminisms, Diasporas, Neoliberalisms.* Durham, NC: Duke University Press, 2005.

———. " 'Women's Rights as Human Rights': Feminist Practices, Global Feminism, and Human Rights Regimes in Transnationality." *Citizenship Studies* 3, no. 3 (1999): 337–54.

Grewal, Inderpal, and Caren Kaplan, eds. *Scattered Hegemonies: Postmodernity and Transnational Feminist Practices.* Minneapolis: University of Minnesota Press, 1994.

Gupta, Akhil, and James Ferguson, eds. *Culture, Power, Place: Explorations in Critical Anthropology.* Durham, NC: Duke University Press, 1997.

Hane, Mikiso. *Peasants, Rebels, and Outcastes: The Underside of Modern Japan.* New York: Pantheon, 1982.

———. *Reflections on the Way to the Gallows: Rebel Women in Prewar Japan.* Berkeley: University of California Press, 1988.

Hara, Kimie. *Cold War Frontiers in the Asia Pacific: Divided Territories in the San Francisco System.* New York: Routledge, 2007.

Hardt, Michael, and Antonio Negri. *Empire.* Cambridge, MA: Harvard University Press, 2000.

Harootunian, Harry. *Overcome by Modernity: History, Culture, and Community in Interwar Japan.* Princeton, NJ: Princeton University Press, 2000.

Harris, Sheldon H. *Factories of Death: Japanese Biological Warfare 1932–45 and the American Cover-Up.* New York: Routledge, 1994.

Hartman, Saidiya V. *Scenes of Subjection: Terror, Slavery, and Self-Making in Nineteenth-Century America.* New York: Oxford University Press, 1997.

Hasegawa, Tsuyoshi. *Racing the Enemy: Stalin, Truman, and the Surrender of Japan.* Cambridge, MA: Harvard University Press, 2005.

Hayner, Priscilla B. *Unspeakable Truths: Confronting State Terror and Atrocity*. New York: Routledge, 2001.

Hein, Laura, ed. *Remembering the Bomb: The Fiftieth Anniversary in the United States and Japan*. A special issue of *Bulletin of Concerned Asian Scholars* 27, no. 2 (April–June 1995).

Henry, Nicola. "Memory of an Injustice: The 'Comfort Women' and the Legacy of the Tokyo Trial." *Asian Studies Review* 37, no. 3 (September 2013): 362–80.

Hesford, Wendy S., and Wendy Kozol. *Just Advocacy? Women's Human Rights, Transnational Feminisms, and the Politics of Representation*. New Brunswick, NJ: Rutgers University Press, 2005.

Hill Collins, Patricia. *Black Feminist Thought: Knowledge, Consciousness, and the Politics of Empowerment*. London: HarperCollins Academic, 1991.

Hirsch, Marianne. *The Generation of Postmemory: Writing and Visual Culture after the Holocaust*. New York: Columbia University Press, 2012.

Hiyane Teruo. *Kindai Okinawa no seishinshi*. Tokyo: Shakai Hyōronsha, 1996.

Horne, Gerald. *Race War: White Supremacy and the Japanese Attack on the British Empire*. New York: New York University Press, 2004.

Hoshi, Tōru. *Watashitachi ga Chūgoku de shita koto: Chūgoku Kikansha Renrakukai no hitobito*. Tokyo: Ryokufū Shuppan, 2002.

Howard, Keith, ed. *True Stories of the Korean Comfort Women: Testimonies Compiled by the Korean Council for Women Drafted for Military Sexual Slavery by Japan and the Research Association on the Women Drafted for Military Sexual Slavery by Japan*. Translated by Young Joo Lee. London: Cassell, 1995.

Hua, Julietta. *Trafficking Women's Human Rights*. Minneapolis: University of Minnesota Press, 2011.

Hwang, Junghyun. "Specters of the Cold War in America's Century: The Korean War and Transnational Politics of National Imaginaries in the 1950s." PhD diss., University of California, San Diego, 2008.

Ichibangase Yasuko. *Kyōdō tōgi sengo fujin mondaishi*. Tokyo: Domesu Shuppan, 1971.

Immerman, Richard H. *Empire for Liberty: A History of American Imperialism from Benjamin Franklin to Paul Wolfowitz*. Princeton, NJ: Princeton University Press, 2010.

Inoue, Masamichi. *Okinawa and the U.S. Military: Identity Making in the Age of Globalization*. New York: Columbia University Press, 2007.

Ishihara Masaie. *Okinawasen ni okeru Nihongun to jūmin gisei: Kyōkasho saiban (daisanji soshō kōsoshin) no shōgen "ikensho."* Tokyo: Kyōkasho Kentei Soshō o Shien suru Zenkoku Renrakukai, 1991.

Ishihara Shun. "Gunji senryō o meguru chi no jūsōteki hensei: Okinawa ni okeru <rekishi no shūdatsu>." *Soshioroji* 44, no. 1 (May 1995): 3–19.

Itagaki Ryūta. "Datsureisen to shokuminchi shihai sekinin no tsuikyū: Zoku/shokuminchi shihai sekinin o teiritsu suru tame ni." In *Rekishi to sekinin*, edited by Kim Puja and Nakano Toshio, 260–84. Tokyo: Seikyūsha, 2008.

————. "Shokuminchi sekinin o teiritsusuru tame ni." In *Keizoku suru shokuminchi-shugi: Jendā, minzoku, jinshu, kaikyū*, edited by Iwasaki Minoru et al., 294–315. Tokyo: Seikyūsha, 2005.

Itō Kimio. *"Danjo kyōdō sankaku" ga toikakeru mono: Jendai Nihon shakai to jendā/poritikusu.* Tokyo: Inpakuto Shuppankai, 2003.

Iwasaki Minoru et al., eds. *Keizoku suru shokuminchishugi: Jendā, minzoku, jinshu, kaikyū.* Tokyo: Seikyūsha, 2005.

Jacobs, Justin. "Preparing the People for Mass Clemency: The 1956 Japanese War Crimes Trials in Shenyang and Taiyuan." *China Quarterly* 205 (2011): 152–72.

Jameson, Fredric. "Marx's Purloined Letter." In *Ghostly Demarcations: A Symposium on Jacques Derrida's Specters of Marx*, edited by Michael Sprinker, 26–67. London: Verso, (1999) 2008.

Jeffords, Susan. *The Remasculinization of America: Gender and the Vietnam War.* Bloomington: Indiana University Press, 1989.

Johnson, Chalmers A. *Blowback: The Costs and Consequences of American Empire.* New York: Metropolitan Books, 2000.

————. "Japan in Search of a 'Normal' Role." *Daedalus* 121, no. 4 (fall 1992): 1–33.

————. *The Sorrows of Empire: Militarism, Secrecy, and the End of the Republic.* London: Verso, 2004.

Jose, Ricardo. "Nihon no sengo kokusai shakai e no fukki to Filipin." Translated by Nakano Satoshi. *Kōwa mondai to Ajia.* A special issue of *Nenpō Nihon gendaishi* 5 (1999): 78–84.

Junkerman, John, dir. *Nihonkoku Kenpō: Japan's Peace Constitution.* Brooklyn, NY: First Run/Icarus Films, 2005.

Kainuma Hiroshi. *"Fukushima"ron: Genshiryoku mura wa naze umareta no ka.* Tokyo: Seidosha, 2011.

Kang, Laura Hyun Yi. "Conjuring 'Comfort Women': Mediated Affiliations and Disciplined Subjects in Korean/American Transnationality." *Journal of Asian American Studies* 6, no. 1 (February 2003): 25–55.

Kaplan, Amy. *The Anarchy of Empire in the Making of U.S. Culture.* Cambridge, MA: Harvard University Press, 2002.

————. "Manifest Domesticity." *American Literature* 70, no. 3 (September 1998): 581–606.

Kearney, Reginald. *African American Views of the Japanese: Solidarity or Sedition.* Albany: State University of New York Press, 1998.

Keisen Jogakuen Heiwa Bunka Kenkyūjo, ed. *Senryō to sei: Seisaku, jittai, hyōshō.* Kyoto: Inpakuto Shuppankai, 2007.

Keller, Nora Okja. *Comfort Woman: A Novel.* New York: Penguin Books, 1997.

Kelly, John D., and Martha Kaplan. "Nation and Decolonization: Toward a New Anthropology of Nationalism." *Anthropological Theory* 1, no. 4 (2001): 419–37.

Kikuchi Keisuke. "Shokumichishihai no rekishi no saishin: Furaunsu no 'kako no kokufuku' no genzai." In *Rekishi to sekinin*, edited by Kim Puja and Nakano Toshio, 216–34. Tokyo: Seikyūsha, 2008.

Kim, Dong Choon. "Beneath the Tip of the Iceberg: Problems in Historical Clarification of the Korean War." *Korea Journal* (autumn 2002): 60–86.

———. "The Long Road toward Truth and Reconciliation: Unwavering Attempts to Achieve Justice in South Korea." *Critical Asian Studies* 42, no. 4 (November 2010): 525–52.

———. *A Social History of the Korean War.* Larkspur, CA: Tamal Vista Publications, 2000.

Kim, Elaine H. *Asian American Literature: An Introduction to the Writers and Their Social Context.* Philadelphia: Temple University Press, 1982.

Kim, Elaine H., and Chungmoo Choi. *Dangerous Women: Gender and Korean Nationalism.* New York: Routledge, 1998.

Kim, Elaine H., Hyun Yi Kang and Norma Alarcón, eds. *Writing Self, Writing Nation: Essays on Theresa Hak Kyung Cha's Dictée.* Berkeley: Third Woman Press, 1994.

Kim, Hyun Sook. "History and Memory: The 'Comfort Women' Controversy." *positions: east asia cultures critique* 5, no. 1 (spring 1997): 73–106.

Kim, Jodi. *Ends of Empire: Asian American Critique and the Cold War.* Minneapolis: University of Minnesota Press, 2010.

Kim Puja and Nakano Toshio, eds. *Rekishi to sekinin: "Ianfu" mondai to 1990 nendai.* Tokyo: Seikyūsha, 2008.

Kipp, Jacob Kipp, Lester Grau, Karl Prinslow, and Don Smith, "The Human Terrain System: A CORDS for the 21st Century." *Military Review*, September/October 2006.

Kiss, Elizabeth. "Moral Ambition within and beyond Political Constraints: Reflections on Restorative Justice." In *Truth v. Justice: The Morality of Truth Commissions*, edited by Robert I. Rotberg and Dennis Thompson, 68–98. Princeton, NJ: Princeton University Press, 2000.

Kitahara Megumi. "Chinmoku saserareta no wa dare ka: NHK bangumi kaihen mondai/terebi eizō ni okeru netsuzō." *Inpakushon* 124 (April 2001): 126–31.

Klein, Christina. *Cold War Orientalism: Asia in the Middlebrow Imagination, 1945–1961.* Berkeley: University of California Press, 2003.

Kobayashi, Yoshie. "A Path toward Gender Equality: State Feminism in Japan." PhD diss., University of Hawaii, 2002.

Kobayashi Yoshinori and Nishibe Susumu. *Hanbei to iu shuhō.* Tokyo: Shōgakkan, 2002.

Koikari, Mire. *Pedagogy of Democracy: Feminism and the Cold War in the U.S. Occupation of Japan.* Philadelphia: Temple University Press, 2010.

———. "Rethinking Gender and Power in the US Occupation of Japan, 1945–1952." *Gender and History* 11, no. 2 (July 1999): 313–35.

Komagome Takeshi. *Shokuminchiteikoku Nihon no bunka tōgō.* Tokyo: Iwanami Shoten, 1996.

Komori Yōichi, Sakamoto Yoshikazu, Yasumaru Yoshio, et al. *Rekishi kyōkasho nani ga mondai ka: Tettei kenshō Q&A.* Tokyo: Iwanami Shoten, 2001.

Komori Yōichi and Takahashi Tetsuya et al., eds. *Nashonaru/hisutorī o koete.* Tokyo: Tokyo Daigaku Shuppankai, 1998.

Koshiro, Yukiko. *Trans-Pacific Racisms and the U.S. Occupation of Japan*. New York: Columbia University Press, 1999.

Kumagai Shin'ichirō. *Naze kagai o katarunoka: Chūgoku Kikansha Renrakukai no sengoshi*. Tokyo: Iwanami Shoten, 2005.

Kurasawa Aiko. "Indoneshia no kokka kensetsu to Nihon no baishō." *Kōwa mondai to Ajia*. A special issue of *Nenpō Nihon gendaishi* 5 (1999): 35–77.

Kushner, Barak. "Pawns of Empire: Postwar Taiwan, Japan and the Dilemma of War Crimes." *Japanese Studies* 30, no. 1 (2010): 111–33.

Kuznick, Peter, and Toshiyuki Tanaka. *Genpatsu to Hiroshima:"Genshiryoku heiwa riyō" no shinsō, Iwanami bukkuretto* 819 (2011).

Kwon, Heonik. *The Other Cold War*. New York: Columbia University Press, 2010.

LaCapra, Dominick. "Representing the Holocaust: Reflections on the Historians' Debate." In *Probing the Limits of Representation: Nazism and the "Final Solution,"* edited by Saul Friedlander, 108–27. Cambridge, MA: Harvard University Press, 1992.

Lattimore, Eleanor. "Pacific Ocean or American Lake?" *Far Eastern Survey* (November 7, 1945): 313–16.

Lee, Ivy. "Toward Reconciliation: The Nishimatsu Settlements for Chinese Forced Labor in World War Two." *The Asia-Pacific Journal* 32–6–10, August 9, 2010.

Lee, JeeYeun. "Toward a Queer Korean American Diasporic History." In *Queer in Asian America*, edited by David L. Eng and Alice Y. Hom, 185–209. Philadelphia, PA: Temple University Press, 1998.

Lee, Robert G. *Orientals: Asian Americans in Popular Culture*. Philadelphia, PA: Temple University Press, 1999.

Lee, Wen Ho, and Helen Zia. *My Country versus Me: The First-Hand Account by the Los Alamos Scientist Who Was Falsely Accused of Being a Spy*. New York: Hyperion, 2001.

Liao, Ping-hui. "Rewriting Taiwanese National History: The February 28 Incident As Spectacle." *Public Culture* 5 (winter 1993): 281–96.

Lipsitz, George. "'Frantic to Join . . . the Japanese Army': Black Soldiers and Civilians Confront the Asia-Pacific War." In *Perilous Memories: Asia-Pacific War(s)*, edited by Takashi Fujitani, Geoffrey M. White, and Lisa Yoneyama, 347–77. Durham, NC: Duke University Press, 2001.

———. "Learning from New Orleans: The Social Warrant of Hostile Privatism and Competitive Consumer Citizenship." *Cultural Anthropology* 21, no. 3 (August 2006): 451–68.

———. *Rainbow at Midnight: Labor and Culture in the 1940s*. Urbana: University of Illinois Press, 1994.

Lowe, Lisa. *Immigrant Acts: On Asian American Cultural Politics*. Durham, NC: Duke University Press, 1996.

———. "The Intimacies of Four Continents." In *Haunted by Empire: Geographies of Intimacy in North American History*, edited by Ann L. Stoler, 191–212. Durham, NC: Duke University Press, 2006.

———. *The Intimacies of Four Continents*. Durham, NC: Duke University Press, 2015.

Lu, Catherine. "Colonialism as Structural Injustice: Historical Responsibility and Contemporary Redress." *The Journal of Political Philosophy* 19, no. 3 (2011): 261–81.

Lye, Colleen. *America's Asia: Racial Form and American Literature, 1893–1945.* Princeton, NJ: Princeton University Press, 2005.

Mamdani, Mahmood. *Good Muslim, Bad Muslim: America, the Cold War, and the Roots of Terror.* New York: Pantheon Books, 2004.

Matsui Yayori. "Naze sabaku ka, dō sabaku ka: 'Josei Kokusai Senpan Hōtei' ga mezasu mono." *Sekai* 682 (December 2000): 108–15.

May, Elaine Tyler. *Homeward Bound: American Families in the Cold War Era.* New York: Basic Books, 1988.

Mbembe, Achille. "Necropolitics." Translated by Libby Meintjes. *Public Culture* 15, no. 1 (2003): 11–40.

McAlister, Melani. *Epic Encounters: Culture, Media, and U.S. Interests in the Middle East, 1945.* Berkeley: University of California Press, 2001.

McCormack, Gavan. *Client State: Japan in the American Embrace.* London: Verso, 2007.

Media no Kiki o Uttaeru Shimin Nettowāku, ed. *Bangumi wa naze kaizan sareta ka: "NHK/ETV jiken" no shinsō.* Tokyo: Ichiyōsha, 2006.

Meyerowitz, Joanne. "Sex, Gender, and the Cold War Language of Reform." In *Rethinking Cold War Culture,* edited by Peter J. Kuznick and James Gilbert, 106–23. Washington, DC: Smithsonian Institution, 2001.

Miki, Roy. *Redress: Inside the Japanese Canadian Call for Justice.* Vancouver: Raincoast Books, 2004.

Min, Pyong Gap. "Korean 'Comfort Women': The Intersection of Colonial Power, Gender, and Class." *Gender & Society,* 17, no. 6 (December 2003): 938–57.

Minear, Richard H. *Victor's Justice.* Princeton, NJ: Princeton University Press, 1971.

Minow, Martha. *Between Vengeance and Forgiveness: Facing History after Genocide and Mass Violence.* Boston: Beacon Press, 1998.

Minzoku Sabetsu to Tatakau Renraku Kyōgikai, ed. *Zainichi Kankoku Chōsenjin no hoshō/jinken hō: Zainchi kyū-shokuminchi shusshinsha ni kansuru sengo hoshō oyobi jinken hoshō hō seitei o mezashite.* Osaka: Akashi Shoten, 1991.

Mitsui, Hideko. "The Politics of National Atonement and Narrations of War." *Inter-Asia Cultural Studies,* 9, no. 1 (2008): 47–61.

Miyagi Kimiko. "Gunji senryō to seibōryoku: mondai no shozai." In *Okinawa no senryō to Nihon no fukkō: Shokuminchishugi wa ikani keizoku shitaka,* edited by Nakano Toshio et al., 31–41. Tokyo: Seikyūsha, 2006.

Mizuno Naoki. "Zainichi Chōsenjin/Taiwanjin sanseiken 'teishi' jōkō no seiritsu: Zainichi Chōsenjin sanseiken mondai no rekishiteki kentō (1)." *Sekai Jinken Mondai Kenkyū Sentā kenkyū kiyō* 1 (March 1996): 43–65.

Mohanty, Chandra Talpade. "Under Western Eyes: Feminist Scholarship and Colonial Discourses." *boundary 2* 12, no. 3/13, no. 1 (spring/fall 1984): 338–58. Republished in *Feminist Review* 30 (1988): 65–88.

Molasky, Michael S. *The American Occupation of Japan and Okinawa: Literature and Memory.* London: Routledge, 1999.

Moon, Katharine H. S. *Sex among Allies: Military Prostitution in U.S.-Korea Relations.* New York: Columbia University Press, 1997.

Moon, Seungsook. "Regulating Desire, Managing the Empire: U.S. Military Prostitution in South Korea, 1945–1970." In *Over There: Living with the U.S. Military Empire from World War Two to the Present*, edited by Maria Höhn and Seungsook Moon, 39–77. Durham: Duke University Press, 2010.

Moraga, Cherríe, and Gloria Anzaldúa, eds. *This Bridge Called My Back: Writings by Radical Women of Color*. New York: Kitchen Table, 1981, 1983.

Morris, Errol, dir. *The Fog of War: Eleven Lessons from the Life of Robert S. McNamara*. New York, NY: Sony Pictures Classics, 2003.

Morris-Suzuki, Tessa. "Guarding the Borders of Japan: Occupation, Korean War and Frontier Controls." *The Asia-Pacific Journal* 9, issue 8, no. 3, February 21, 2011.

———. *The Past within Us: Media, Memory, History*. London: Verso, 2005.

Motohama Hidehiko. "Kaisetsu." In Ōshiro Tatsuhiro, *Kakuteru pātī*, 305–17. Tokyo: Iwanami Shoten, 2011.

Nagahara Keiji. *"Jiyūshugi shikan" hihan: Jikokushi ninshiki ni tsuite kangaeru, Iwanami bukkuretto*, 505 (2000).

Nagata Kōzō. *NHK, Tetsu no chinmoku wa dare no tame ni*. Tokyo: Kashiwa Shobō, 2010.

Nakano Toshio. "Higashiajia de 'sengo' o toukoto: Shokuminchishugi no keizoku o hasoku suru mondai kōsei towa." In *Keizoku suru shokuminchishugi: Jendā, minzoku, jinshu, kaikyū*, edited by Iwasaki Minoru et al., 12–21. Tokyo: Seikyūsha, 2005.

Nakano Toshio et al., eds. *Okinawa no senryō to Nihon no fukkō: Shokuminchishugi wa ikani keizoku shitaka*. Tokyo: Seikyūsha, 2006.

Nanumu no Ie Rekishikan Kōenkai, ed. *Nanumu no Ie Rekishikan: Handobukku*. Tokyo: Kashiwa Shobō, 2002.

Namihira Tsuneo. "Ōshiro Tatsuhiro no bungaku ni miru Okinawajin no sengo." *Gendai shisō* 29, no. 9 (July 2001): 124–53.

Nashel, Jonathan. "The Road to Vietnam: Modernization Theory in Fact and Fiction." In *Cold War Constructions: The Political Culture of United States Imperialism, 1945–1966*, edited by Christian G. Appy, 132–54. Amherst: University of Massachusetts Press, 2000.

National Air and Space Museum. "The Crossroads: The End of World War II, the Atomic Bomb, and the Origins of the Cold War, First Script." Washington, DC: National Air and Space Museum, 1994, mimeograph.

Network of Concerned Anthropologists, ed. *The Counter-Counterinsurgency Manual: Or, Notes on Demilitarizing American Society*. Chicago: Prickly Paradigm Press, 2009.

Ngai, Mae M. *Impossible Subjects: Illegal Aliens and the Making of Modern America*. Princeton, NJ: Princeton University Press, 2004.

Nihon Chōsen Kenkyūsho. *Nichi-Chō-Chū sangoku jinmin rentai no rekishi to riron*. Tokyo: Nihon Chōsen Kenkyūsho, 1964.

Nihon no Zento to Rekishi Kyōkasho o Kangaeru Wakate Giin no Kai, ed. *Rekishi kyōkasho e no gimon: Wakate kokkai giin ni yoru rekishi kyōkasho mondai no sōkatsu*. Tokyo: Tentensha, 1997.

Nishi Kiyoko. *Senryōka no Nihon fujin seisaku: Sono rekishi to shōgen*. Tokyo: Domesu Shuppan, 1985.

Nishino Rumiko. *Jūgun ianfu: Moto heishitachi no shōgen*. Tokyo: Akashi Shoten, 1992.

———. "NHK ni nani ga okita no ka: Josei Kokusai Senpan Hōtei o meguru bangumi kaihen sōdō." *Tsukuru* 31, no. 4: (May 2001): 110–17.

Nishio Kanji. "Hachigatsu jūgonichi izen no Nihonjin, igo no Nihonjin." *Seiron* 298 (June 1997): 49–58.

———. "Rekishi to minzoku e no sekinin (1): Danjo kyōdō sankaku to 'jūgun ianfu' ni tsūtei suru yamai." *Seiron* 394 (March 2005): 128–40.

Noda Masaaki. *Sensō to zaiseki*. Tokyo: Iwanami Shoten, 1998.

Norman, E. H., and John W. Dower. *Origins of the Modern Japanese State: Selected Writings of E. H. Norman*. New York: Pantheon Books, 1975.

Nosaka Akiyuki. *Amerika hijiki, Hotaru no haka*. Tokyo: Bungei Shunjū, (1968) 1988.

———. "American Hijiki." Translated by Jay Rubin. In *Contemporary Japanese Literature: An Anthology of Fiction, Film, and Other Writing Since 1945*, edited by Howard Hibbett, 436–62. New York: Knopf, 1977.

Novick, Peter. *That Noble Dream: The "Objectivity Question" and the American Historical Profession*. New York: Cambridge University Press, 1988.

Nyugen, Mimi T. *The Gift of Freedom: War, Debt, and Other Refugee Passages*. Durham, NC: Duke University Press, 2013.

Obama, Barack. *The Audacity of Hope: Thoughts on Reclaiming the American Dream*. New York: Crown, 2006.

Oguma Eiji and Ueno Yōko. *<Iyashi> no nashonarizumu: kusano ne hoshuundō no jisshō kenkyū*. Tokyo: Keiō Gijyuku Daigaku Shuppankai, 2003.

Ohno, Takushi. *War Reparations and Peace Settlement*. Manila: Solidaridad, 1986.

Okabe Makio et al., eds. *Chūgoku shinryaku no shōgensha tachi: "Ninzai" no kiroku o yomu*. Tokyo: Iwanami Shoten, 2010.

Okihiro, Gary Y. *Margins and Mainstreams: Asians in American History and Culture*. Seattle: University of Washington Press, 1994.

Okinawa Kenritsu Toshokan Shiryō Henshūshitsu, ed. *Okinawa kenshi, shiryōhen 2: Okinawasen 2 (genbunhen)*, 3–147. Okinawa: Okinawaken Kyōiku Iinkai, 1996.

Ōshiro Tatsuhiro. "Chosha no oboegaki 9: Ugoku jikan to ugokanai jikan." In *Ōshiro Tatsuhiro Zenshū*, vol. 9, 467–70. Tokyo: Bensei Shuppan, 2002.

———. "The Cocktail Party." In *Two Postwar Novellas*. Translated by Steve Rabson, 35–80. Berkeley, CA: Center for Japanese Studies, 1989.

———. *Kakuteru pātī*. In *Kakuteru pātī*. Tokyo: Iwanami Shoten, (1967) 2011.

Palumbo-Liu, David. *Asian/American: Historical Crossings of Racial Frontier*. Stanford, CA: Stanford University Press, 1999.

Park, Soyang. "Silence, Subaltern Speech and the Intellectual in South Korea: The Politics of Emergent Speech in the Case of Former Sexual Slaves." *Journal for Cultural Research* 9, no. 2 (April 2005): 169–206.

Park, You-me. "Comforting the Nation: 'Comfort Women,' the Politics of Apology and the Workings of Gender." *Interventions* 2, no. 2 (2000): 199–211.

Patterson, Orlando. *Slavery and Social Death: A Comparative Study*. Cambridge, MA: Harvard University Press, 1982.

Pharr, Susan J. *Political Women in Japan: The Search for a Place in Political Life*. Berkeley: University of California Press, 1981.

———. "Politics of Women's Rights." In *Democratizing Japan: The Allied Occupation*, edited by Robert E. Ward and Yoshikazu Sakamoto, 221–52. Honolulu: University of Hawaii Press, 1987.

Pilzer, Joshua D. *Hearts of Pine: Songs in the Lives of Three Korean Survivors of the Japanese "Comfort Women."* New York: Oxford University Press, 2012.

Price, David H. *Anthropological Intelligence: The Deployment and Neglect of American Anthropology in the Second World War*. Durham, NC: Duke University Press, 2008.

———. *Threatening Anthropology: McCarthyism and the FBI's Surveillance of Activist Anthropologists*. Duke University Press, 2004.

Price, John. *Orienting Canada: Race, Empire, and the Transpacific*. Vancouver: UBC Press, 2011.

Pyŏn, Yŏng-ju, dir. *The Murmuring/Najŭn moksori 1*. Seoul: Korean Film Council, (1995) 2005.

———. *Habitual Sadness/Najŭn moksori 2*. Seoul: Korean Film Council, (1997) 2005.

Rabson, Steve. "Introduction." In *Two Postwar Novellas*. Translated by Steve Rabson, 1–31. Berkeley, CA: Center for Japanese Studies, 1989.

Radway, Janice. "What's in a Name? Presidential Address to the American Studies Association, November 20, 1998." *American Quarterly* 51, no. 1 (1999): 1–32.

Rafael, Vicente L. "Colonial Domesticity: White Women and United States Rule in the Philippines." *American Literature* 67 (December 1995): 639–66.

Rancière, Jacques. "Overlegitimation." Translated by Kristin Ross. *Social Text* 10, no. 2 (1992): 252–57.

———. "Who Is the Subject of the Rights of Man?" *South Atlantic Quarterly* 2/3 (spring 2004): 297–310.

Reddy, Chandan. *Freedom with Violence: Race, Sexuality, and the US State*. Durham, NC: Duke University Press, 2011.

Rotberg, Robert, and Dennis Thompson, eds. *Truth v. Justice: The Morality of Truth Commissions*. Princeton, NJ: Princeton University Press, 2000.

Rothberg, Michael. *Multidirectional Memory: Remembering the Holocaust in the Age of Decolonization*. Stanford, CA: Stanford University Press, 2009.

Rowe, John Carlos, ed. *Post-nationalist American Studies*. Berkeley: University of California Press, 2000.

Rowman, Rory. "A New Nomos of Post-Nomos? Multipolarity, Space, and Constituent Power." In *Spatiality, Sovereignty and Carl Schmitt: Geographies of the Nomos*, edited by Stephen Legg, 143–62. London: Routledge, 2011.

Russo, Ann. "The Intersections of Feminism and Imperialism in the United States." *International Feminist Journal of Politics* 8, no. 4 (December 2006): 557–80.

Saitō Takao. "Futatabi 'teikoku' o shikō suru shakai to senji kenryokusha e no masumedia no kutsujū: 21seiki no 'Hakkō Jiken' dewa nai no ka." In *Bangumi wa naze kaizan sareta ka: "NHK/ETV jiken" no shinsō*, edited by Media no Kiki o Uttaeru Shimin Nettowāku, 296–32. Tokyo: Ichiyōsha, 2006.

Sakagami Kaori. "Seisaku genba de mita NHK bangumi kaihen no genjitsu." *Tsukuru* 32, no. 1/2 (January/February 2002): 98–107.

Sakai, Naoki. *Kibō to kenpō: Nihonkoku kenpō no hatsuwa shutai to ōtō.* Tokyo: Ibunsha, 2008.

———. "Kindai no hihan: Chūzetsu shita tōki: Posutomodan no shomondai." *Gendai shisō* 15, no. 15 (1987): 184–207.

———. "On Romantic Love and Military Violence: Transpacific Imperialism and U.S.-Japan Complicity." In *Militarized Currents: Toward a Decolonized Future in Asia and the Pacific*, edited by Setsu Shigematsu and Keith L. Camacho 205–21. Minneapolis: University of Minnesota Press, 2010.

———. "You Asians, On the Historical Role of the West and Asia Binary." *South Atlantic Quarterly* 99, no. 4 (2000): 789–817.

Sakai, Naoki, and Hyon Joo Yoo, eds. *The Trans-Pacific Imagination: Rethinking Boundary, Culture and Society*. Singapore: World Scientific Publishing, 2012.

Santner, Eric L. "History beyond the Pleasure Principle: Some Thoughts on the Representation of Trauma." In *Probing the Limits of Representation: Nazism and the "Final Solution,"* edited by Saul Friedlander, 143–54. Cambridge, MA: Harvard University Press, 1992.

Sasaki Yōko. *Sōryokusen to josei heishi.* Tokyo: Seikyūsha, 2001.

Satō Manabu, Komori Yōichi, Kang Sang-jung, et al. "Taiwa no kairo o tozashita rekishikan o dō kokufuku suru ka? Hikarete iku 'kokumin'/ 'hikokumin' no kyōkaisen" *Sekai* 645 (May 1997): 185–99.

Scheper-Hughes, Nancy, and Philippe I. Bourgois, eds. *Violence in War and Peace.* Malden, MA: Wiley-Blackwell, 2004.

Schlund-Vials, Cathy J. *War, Genocide, and Justice: Cambodian American Memory Work.* Minneapolis: University of Minnesota Press, 2012.

Schmitt, Carl. *The Nomos of the Earth in the International Law of the Jus Publicum Europaeum.* New York: Telos Press, (1950) 2003.

———. *Theory of the Partisan: Intermediate Commentary on the Concept of the Political.* New York: Telos Press, (1975) 2007.

Shah, Nayan. *Contagious Divides: Epidemics and Race in San Francisco's Chinatown.* Berkeley: University of California Press, 2001.

Shamsul, A. B. "Producing Knowledge of Southeast Asia: A Malaysian View." In *The Inter-Asia Cultural Studies Reader*, edited by Kuan-Hsing Chen and Beng H. Chua, 140–60. London: Routledge, 2007.

Sherwin, Martin. *A World Destroyed: The Atomic Bomb and the Grand Alliance.* New York: Knopf, 1975.

Shibusawa, Naoko. *America's Geisha Ally: Reimagining the Japanese Enemy.* Cambridge, MA: Harvard University Press, 2006.

Shigematsu, Setsu, and Keith L. Camacho, eds. *Militarized Currents: Toward a Decolonized Future in Asia and the Pacific.* Minneapolis: University of Minnesota Press, 2010.

Shimabuku, Annmaria. "Transpacific Colonialism: An Intimate View of Transnational Activism in Okinawa." *CR: The New Centennial Review* 12, no. 1 (2012): 131–58.

Shimoji Yoshio. "The Futenma Base and the U.S.-Japan Controversy: An Okinawan Perspective." *The Asia-Pacific Journal*, 18–5–10, May 3, 2010.

Shin, Gi-Wook, Soon-Won Park, and Daqing Yang, eds. *Rethinking Historical Injustice and Reconciliation in Northeast Asia: The Korean Experience.* New York: Routledge, 2007.

Shinjō Ikuo. "Okinawa senryō to gei shintai seijisei: Shokuminchi no dansei sekush-uariti." In *Okinawa no senryō to Nihon no fukkō: Shokuminchishugi wa ikani keizoku shitaka,* edited by Nakano Toshio et al., 85–107. Tokyo: Seikyūsha, 2006.

Silverberg, Miriam. "Remembering Pearl Harbor, Forgetting Charlie Chaplin, and the Case of the Disappearing Western Woman: A Picture Story." *positions: east asia culture critique* 1, no. 1 (spring 1993): 24–76.

Simpson, Caroline Chung. *An Absent Presence: Japanese Americans in Postwar American Culture, 1945–1960.* Durham, NC: Duke University Press, 2001.

Smith, Robert J., and Ella Lury Wiswell. *Women of Suye Mura.* Chicago: University of Chicago Press, 1989.

Soh, C. Sarah. *The Comfort Women: Sexual Violence and Postcolonial Memory in Korea and Japan.* Chicago: University of Chicago Press, 2008.

Spivak, Gayatri Chakravorty. "Can the Subaltern Speak?" (1988). In *Colonial Discourse and Post-Colonial Theory: A Reader,* edited by Patrick Williams and Laura Chrisman, 66–111. New York: Columbia University Press, 1994.

———. "Three Women's Texts and a Critique of Imperialism." In *"Race," Writing and Difference,* edited by Henry Louis Gates Jr, 262–80. Chicago: University of Chicago Press, (1985) 1986.

Steiner, Kurt. "The Occupation and the Reform of the Japanese Civil Code." In *Democratizing Japan: The Allied Occupation,* edited by Robert E. Ward and Yoshikazu Sakamoto, 188–220. Honolulu: University of Hawaii Press, 1987.

Streeby, Shelley. *American Sensations: Class, Empire, and the Production of Popular Culture.* Berkeley: University of California, 2002.

Suh, Hee-Kyung. "TRCK's Verification Process for Mass Civilian Killings during the Korean War." *Critical Asian Studies* 42, no. 4 (November 2010): 553–88.

Suh, Jae-Jung. "Truth and Reconciliation in South Korea: Confronting War, Colonialism, and Intervention in the Asia Pacific." *Critical Asian Studies* 42, no. 4 (November 2010): 503–24.

Sun Ge. "Shikō no shūkan: Tōkyō saiban to sengo Higashiajia." Translated by Satō Ken. *Posuto Higashiajia,* 192–200. Tokyo: Sakuhinsha, 2006.

Tadiar, Neferti Xina M. *Fantasy-Production: Sexual Economies and Other Philippine Consequences for the New World Order.* Hong Kong: Hong Kong University Press, 2004/2005.

Takahashi Shirō. "Feminisuto ni yugamerareru kaisei kyōiku kihonhō: Sore hodo aikokushin ga okirai ka." *Seiron* 366 (January 2003): 320–29.

Takaki, Ronald. *Strangers from a Different Shore: A History of Asian Americans.* New York: Penguin Books, 1989.

Takemae, Eiji. *The Allied Occupation of Japan.* New York: Continuum, 2002.

Takeuchi Yoshimi. "Kindai no chōkoku" (1959). In *Kindai no chōkoku,* edited by Kawakami Tetustarō et al., 273–341. Tokyo: Toyamabō, (1979) 2010.

Takubo Tadae, "Hitsuyō na 'hauebā' no shikō," *Seiron* 316 (December 1998): 236–40.

Tanaka, Toshiyuki, Timothy L. H. McCormack, and Gerry J. Simpson, eds. *Beyond Victor's Justice? The Tokyo War Crimes Trial Revisited.* Leiden: Martinus Nijhoff Publishers, 2011.

Tanaka, Yuki. *Japan's Comfort Women: Sexual Slavery and Prostitution during World War II and the US Occupation.* London: Routledge, 2002.

Teaiwa, Teresia K. "bikinis and other s/pacific n/oceans." *Contemporary Pacific* 6, no. 1 (1994): 87–109.

Teitel, Ruti G. *Transitional Justice.* Oxford: Oxford University Press, 2000.

Thompson, John B. *Studies in the Theory of Ideology.* Berkeley: University of California Press, 1984.

Tōkyō Saiban Handobukku Henshū Iinnkai, ed. *Tōkyō saiban handobukku.* Tokyo: Aoki Shoten, 1999.

Tomiyama Ichirō. " 'Chiiki kenkyū' to iu arīna: Sengo Okinawa kenkyū o megutte." *Chiiki kenkyū ronshū* 2, no. 1 (March 1999): 7–17.

―――. *Kindai Nihon shakai to Okinawajin: Nihonjin ni naru to iu koto.* Tokyo: Nihon Keizai Hyōronsha, 2006.

Toriyama Atsushi. " 'Okinawa no jichi' e no katsubō: Sengo shoki seitō kankei shiryō o chūshin ni miru seiji ishiki." *Okinawa kenshi kenkyū kiyō* 4 (March 1997): 61–80.

―――. "Okinawa's 'Postwar': Some Observations on the Formation of American Military Bases in the Aftermath of Terrestrial Warfare." Translated by David Buist. In *The Inter-Asia Cultural Studies Reader*, edited by Kuan-Hsing Chen and Beng H. Chua, 267–88. London: Routledge, 2007.

Totani, Yuma. *The Tokyo War Crimes Trial: The Pursuit of Justice in the Wake of World War II.* Cambridge, MA: Harvard University Asia Center, 2008.

Toyoda Maho. *Senryōka no josei rōdō kaikaku: Hogo to byōdō o megutte.* Tokyo: Keisō Shobō, 2007.

Toyoda Masayuki. "Chūgoku no tainichi senpan shori seisaku: Genbatsushugi kara 'kandai seisaku' e." *Shien* 69 (2009): 15–45.

Tozzer, Alfred M. "The Okinawas: A Japanese Minority Group, Summary Statement (Second Edition)." *Okinawan Studies* 1, Office of Strategic Services, Honolulu, Hawaii, March 16, 1944.

―――. *The Okinawas of the Loo Choo Islands: A Japanese Minority Group.* Honolulu: Office of Strategic Services, Research and Analysis Branch, 1944. Republished in *Okinawa kenshi, shiryōhen 2: Okinawasen 2 (genbunhen)*, edited by Okinawa Kenritsu Toshokan Shiryō Henshūshitsu, 3–147. Okinawa: Okinawaken Kyōiku Iinkai, 1996.

Tsurumi Kazuko and Ichii Saburō, eds. *Shisō no bōken: Shakai to henka no atarashii paradaimu.* Tokyo: Chikuma Shobō, 1974.

Uemura, Chikako. "Nihon ni okeru senryō seisaku to josei kaihō: Rōdōshō fujin shōnenkyoku no seiritsu katei o chūshin toshite." *Joseigaku kenkyū* 2 (1992): 5–28.

Ueno Chizuko. *Kindai kazoku no seiritsu to shūen.* Tokyo: Iwanami Shoten, 1994.

U.S. Army and Marine Corps. *The U.S. Army/Marine Corps Counterinsurgency Field Manual: U.S. Army Field Manual No. 3–24, Marine Corps Warfighting Publication No. 3–33.5.* Chicago: University of Chicago Press, 2007.

U.S. Navy Office of the Chief of Naval Operations. *Civil Affairs Handbook—Ryukyu (Loochoo) Islands.* OpNav 13–3, Washington, DC (1944).

U.S. Senate Committee on Rules and Administration. *Hearing: The Smithsonian Institution Management Guidelines for the Future.* May 11 and 18, 1995.

Utsumi Aiko. "Korean 'Imperial Soldiers': Remembering Colonialism and Crimes against Allied POWs." In *Perilous Memories: Asia-Pacific War(s),* edited by Takashi Fujitani, Geoffrey M. White, and Lisa Yoneyama, 199–217. Durham, NC: Duke University Press, 2001.

———. *Nihongun no horyo seisaku.* Tokyo: Aoki Shoten, 2005.

———. *Sengo hoshō kara kangaeru Nihon to Ajia.* Tokyo: Yamakawa Shuppansha, 2002.

Utsumi Aiko and Murai Yoshinori. *Chōsenjin bc kyū senpan no kiroku.* Tokyo: Keisō Shobō, 1982.

———. *Sekidōka no Chōsenjin hanran.* Tokyo: Keisō Shobō, 1980.

VAWW-NET Japan, ed. *Abakareta shinjitsu: NHK bangumi kaizan jiken, Josei Kokusai Senpan Hōtei to seijikainyū.* Tokyo: Gendaishokan, 2010.

———. *Josei Kokusai Senpan Hōtei no zenkiroku I, Nihongun seidoreisei o sabaku: 2002nen Josei Kokusai Senpan Hōtei no kiroku.* vol. 5. Tokyo: Ryokufū Shuppan, 2002.

———. *Kesareta sabaki: NHK bangumi kaihen to seiji kainyū jiken.* Tokyo: Gaifūsha, 2005.

———. *Senpan saiban to seibōryoku, Nihongun seidoreisei o sabaku: 2002nen Josei Kokusai Senpan Hōtei no kiroku,* vol. 1. Tokyo: Ryokufū Shuppan, 2000.

Video Juku, dir. *Breaking the History of Silence: The Women's International War Crimes Tribunal for the Trial of Japanese Military Sexual Slavery.* Tokyo: Video Juku; VAWW-NET Japan, 2006.

———. *"Josei Kokusai Senpan Hōtei no kiroku": Chinmoku no rekishi o yabutte.* Tokyo: Video Juku; VAWW-NET Japan, 2001.

Villa-Vicencio, Charles, and Erik Doxtader, eds. *The Provocations of Amnesty: Memory, Justice, and Impunity.* Trenton, NJ: Africa World Press, 2003.

Volpp, Leti. "Feminism versus Multiculturalism." *Columbia Law Review* 101 (June 2001): 1181–218.

———. "(Mis)identifying Culture: Asian Women and the 'Cultural Defense.'" *Harvard Women's Law Journal* 17 (1994): 57–101.

Von Eschen, Penny M. *Race against Empire: Black Americans and Anticolonialism, 1937–1957.* Ithaca, NY: Cornell University Press, 1997.

Walker, Samuel. "History, Collective Memory, and the Decision to Use the Bomb." *Diplomatic History* 19, no. 2 (spring 1995): 319–28.

Ward, Robert E., and Yoshikazu Sakamoto, eds. *Democratizing Japan: The Allied Occupation.* Honolulu: University of Hawaii Press, 1987.

White, Geoffrey M. "Memory Wars: The Politics of Remembering the Asia/Pacific War." *AsiaPacific Issues* 21 (July 1995): 1–8.

———. "Remembering Guadalcanal: National Identity and Transnational Memory Making." *Public Culture* 7 (spring 1995): 529–55.

White, Hayden. "The Value of Narrativity in the Representation of Reality," and "Narrativization of Real Events." In *On Narrative*, edited by W. J. T. Mitchell, 1–23, 249–54. Chicago: University of Chicago Press, 1981.

Williams, Randall. *The Divided World: Human Rights and Its Violence*. Minneapolis: University of Minnesota Press, 2010.

Williams, William Appleman. *The Tragedy of American Diplomacy*. New York: World Publishing, 1959.

Yamatani Eriko and Yagi Hidetsugu. "<Han feminizumu taidan> kokka, shakai kihan, kazoku no kaitai ni zeikin o tsukauna!" *Seiron* 366 (January 2003): 294–307.

Yang, Daqing. "The Malleable and the Contested: The Nanjing Massacre in Postwar China and Japan." In *Perilous Memories: Asia-Pacific War(s)*, edited by Takashi Fujitani, Geoffrey M. White, and Lisa Yoneyama, 50–86. Durham, NC: Duke University Press, 2001.

Yang, Hyunah. "Finding the 'Map of Memory': Testimony of the Japanese Military Sexual Slavery Survivors." *positions: east asia cultures critique* 16, no. 1 (2008): 79–107.

Yoneyama, Lisa. *Bōryoku, sensō, ridoresu: Tabunkashugi no poritikusu*. Tokyo: Iwanami Shoten, 2003.

———. "Complicit Amnesia: The Smithsonian 'Atom Bomb Exhibit' Controversy in Japan and the U.S." Honolulu, Hawai'i: East-West Center, 1995.

———. "Habits of Knowing Cultural Differences: *Chrysanthemum and the Sword* in U.S. Liberal Multiculturalism." *Topoi* 18 (1999): 71–80.

———. "Hihanteki feminizumu no keifu kara miru Nihon senryō." *Shisō* 955 (November 2003): 60–84.

———. Hihanteki feminizumu to Nihongun seidoreisei: Ajia/Amerika kara miru josei no jinken rejīmu no kansei." In *Rekishi to sekinin:"Ianfu" mondai to 1990 nendai*, edited by Kim Puja and Nakano Toshio et al., 235–49. Tokyo: Seikyūsha, 2008.

———. *Hiroshima Traces: Time, Space and the Dialectics of Memory*. Berkeley: University of California Press, 1999.

———. "Ken'etsu, kaizan, netsuzō: Towarenakatta senji seibōryoku." In *Kesareta sabaki: nhk bangumi kaihen to seiji kainyū jiken*, edited by vaww-net Japan, 250–72. Tokyo: Gaifūsha, 2005.

———. "Kesareta sabaki to feminizumu." In *Abakareta shinjitsu: nhk bangumi kaizan jiken, Josei Kokusai Senpan Hōtei to seijikainyū*, edited vaww-net Japan, 106–34. Gendaishokan, 2010.

———. "Kokki kokka ni hantai suru koto ni tsujite." In *"Hinomaru, Kimigayo" o koete*, edited by Ishida Hidetaka, Satoshi Ukai, Hiroko Sakamoto, and Osamu Nishitani, 53–59. Tokyo: Iwanami Shoten, 1999.

———. "Liberation under Siege: U.S. Military Occupation and Japanese Women's Enfranchisement." *American Quarterly* 57, no. 3 (September 2005): 885–910.

———. "Media no kōkyōsei to hyōshō no bōryoku." *Sekai* 690 (July 2001): 209–19.

———. "Nihon shokuminchishugi no rekishi kioku to Amerika: *Yōko monogatari* o megutte." In *Higashi Ajia rekishi ninshiki ronsō no metahisutorī: Kannichi, rentai 21 no kokoromi*, edited by Komori Yōichi et al., 267–84. Tokyo: Seikyūsha, 2008.

———. "Politicizing Justice: Post-Cold War Redress and the Truth and Reconciliation Commission." *Critical Asian Studies* 42, no. 4 (November 2010): 525–52.

———. "Sensō no katari to posuto-reisen no masukyuriniti." In *Iwanami kōza: Ajia/ Taiheiyō sensō* 1, "Naze, ima, Ajia/Taiheiyō sensō ka," edited by Tessa Morris-Suzuki et al., 317–56. Tokyo: Iwanami Shoten, 2005.

———. "Traveling Memories, Contagious Justice: Americanization of Japanese War Crimes at the End of Post-Cold War." *Journal of Asian American Studies* 6, no. 1 (February 2003): 57–93.

Yoshida, Takashi. *The Making of the "Rape of Nanking": History and Memory in Japan, China, and the United States*. New York: Oxford University Press, 2006.

Yoshida Toshimi. "Sanpunkan no sakeme: Hōmurareta mou hitotsu no koe o megutte." In *Bangumi wa naze kaizan sareta ka: "NHK/ETV jiken" no shinsō*, edited by Media no Kiki o Uttaeru Shimin Nettowāku, 335–45. Tokyo: Ichiyōsha, 2006.

Yoshihara, Mari. *Embracing the East: White Women and American Orientalism*. New York: Oxford University Press, 2003.

Yui Daizaburō. *Nichibei sensōkan no sōkoku: Masatsu no shinsō shinri*. Tokyo: Iwanami Shoten, 1995.

Yun Chung-Ok. "In Memory of Yayori Matsui." *Inter-Asia Cultural Studies* 4, no. 2 (2003): 190–92.

Žižek, Slavoj. "Carl Schmitt in the Age of Post-Politics." In *The Challenge of Carl Schmitt*, edited by Chantal Mouffe, 18–37. New York: Verso, 1999.

———. *The Sublime Object of Ideology*. New York: Verso, 1989.

Zolo, Danilo. *Victors' Justice: From Nuremberg to Baghdad*. London: Verso, 2009.

INDEX

Abe Shinzō, 124, 129, 174, 212, 256n2, 262–63n42

Ablemann, Nancy, 274n45

Afghanistan, 11, 21, 81, 84, 105

Agamben, Giorgio, 15, 78, 79, 103, 143, 267n73

Aisin-Gioro Puyi, 132

Alarcón, Norma, 252n56, 259n27

Alexander, M. Jacqui, 248n11

Allied powers, viii, x, 31, 37, 72, 81, 102, 114, 126, 138, 156, 159, 198, 232n36, 272n31

Alperovitz, Gar, 276n12

"The American Century," 229n9

"American Lake," 46, 241n19

"Amerika Hijiki," 117, 118; reactionary male psyche in, 118. *See also* revisionism (Japan)

amnesia: historical, 75, 82, 91, 105, 148, 152, 179, 184, 188–91, 205; coproduction of, 192

amnesty, 11, 75, 133, 148; gift of, 135. *See also* forgiveness

Anghie, Antony, 241n17, 254n60

anthropology: Cold War formations and, 21, 46, 58–59, 62, 63, 67, 89, 162, 234n48, 273n39; militarization of 46, 64–65, 208; political unconscious of, 23–24, 209; self-scrutiny of, 37, 46, 208–9, 281–81n10; transwar connectivity of, 37, 89, 245n37. *See also* area studies; Human Terrain System

"anticolonial empire," 225n2

anticommunism, ix, 30, 31, 45, 50, 62, 96, 159, 192, 198, 254n62

antinuclearism, 178, 196, 213

antiracism, 30, 48, 69, 136, 156, 166, 200, 213; war and, 19, 89. *See also* race

apology, 3, 74, 115, 134, 205, 237n42; contrition, 133, 135; forgiveness, 125–26, 134; Japan, 26–27, 28, 29, 112, 115, 124–25, 129–30, 135, 146, 154, 172, 189, 260–61n33; state-sponsored, 1, 11, 14, 38, 121, 135, 148, 175, 203. *See also* forgiveness

Appy, Christian G., 18

Arai Shinichi, 31

Arai Toshio, 247n49

area studies: Cold War formations and, 37, 59, 62, 63, 106, 162; critique of, 243n28, 29; transwar connectivity of, 46, 62, 66

Arendt, Hannah, 78, 203, 204, 281n4

Article 9 (Peace Clause): 114, 119, 143, 257n11, 268n79; abnormality of, 145; as "stumbling block" to remilitarization, 145–46. *See also* sovereignty

Article 24, 97

Asian/American: 38, 147; Cold War and, 152, 161, 162, 165, 169, 269n8; (un)assimilability, 163–64, 165, 169; Japanese colonialism and, 149,165–69, 170; masculinity, 135, 258n22, 258–59n23; "male hysteria," 136, 141; redress activism of, 149, 150, 152, 157, 173; transnationality of, 161, 269n9; war memories, 116, 151, 160, 162–70. *See also* transborder redress culture

Asian Centre for Women's Human Rights (ASCENT), 122

global feminism, 166, 230n20, 259n27. *See also* transnational feminism

"good war" narrative, 17, 20–21, 22, 83, 169, 194, 197, 209. *See also* World War II

Gordon, Avery F., 49, 136, 241n13, 265n62

Gordon, Beate Sirota, 21, 22, 97, 105, 234n49, 251n41, 254–55n66

Gotanda, Neil, 265n62

governmentality, 21, 51, 52, 82, 92, 104, 107, 232n20, 234n48, 259–60n27

Grew, Joseph C., 88

Grewal, Inderpal, 230n20, 259n27

Guam, 44, 208

"guilt reckoning" (*ninzai*), 74, 131, 132, 133–35. *See also* leniency policy

Gupta, Akhil, 243n31

Gusterson, Hugh, 281n10

Habitual Sadness (1997), 281n3

Hakkō Jiken (1918), 129, 263n43

Hara, Kimie, 228n6

Hardt, Michael, 238n82

Hartman, Saidiya, 232n38

Harwit, Martin, 181, 182, 185, 193

Hata Ikuhiko, 127

Hatch, Orrin, 155–56

Hatoyama Yukio, 43, 44, 45, 47, 239n3

hauntology, 240n12

Hawai'i, 20, 64, 191

Hayner, Priscilla B., 225n1

healing, 125, 126, 260n31

Henoko Beach, 44, 175, 208

heteronormativity, 27, 28, 48, 98, 113, 114, 121,229n10, 258n22, 274n45. *See also* domesticity; racism

Hinomaru and "Kimigayo" legislation, 142, 206

Hirohito (Shōwa tennō), 30, 92, 93f2.1, 126, 197

Hiroshima, 5, 170, 177

Hiroshima and Nagasaki, *see* atomic bombing

historical materialism, 113, 114

Hague Regulations (1907), 101, 102

Hiyane Teruo, 246n46

Honda Masakazu, 128

Honda, Mike, 153, 154, 164, 168

Horne, Gerald, 19, 266n65

House of Sharing (Nanum Jip), 203, 281n2, 281n3

House Resolution 121 (H. Res. 121), 13, 38, 148, 154, 173

Human Relations Area Files (HRAF), 66

human rights, 8, 32, 150, 229; anticolonial struggles and, 275n57; asymmetries, 9–10; biopolitics of, 78; international criminal justice and, 123, 150; regime, 10, 12, 201, 230n20, 259–60n27; universalism, 10, 36, 130. *See also* women's human rights

Human Terrain System, 208–9, 281n9. *See also* anthropology

humanism, 9–11, 15, 17, 32, 36, 120, 126, 131, 156, 175, 206, 229–30n13, 230n19, 258n22, 259n25

humanity, *see* humanism

Hurricane Katrina, 207

Hwang Geum Joo v. Japan, 161, 162, 272n31, 272n38, 273n40

Immigration and Nationality Act (1965), 149

Imperialism, 1, 6, 16, 20, 23, 29, 30, 35, 36, 67, 77, 85, 137, 142, 151, 193, 201, 225n2, 238–39n82; governmentality of, 67, 99, 106, 232n38, 240n10, 259–60n27; military-security, 37, 225–26n4; rivalry of, 20, 36, 68, 138, 163; violence of, ix, 8, 37, 52, 61, 148, 149, 151, 166–68, 172, 190. *See also* interimperial connection

impunity, 16, 30, 138, 204, 205; culture of, 31, 125–26, 169, 173

IMTFE *see* International Military Tribunal for the Far East

In re World War II Era Japanese Forced Labor, 157, 160, 271n21, 272n35

In the Name of the Emperor (1997), 197–200

incommensurability, 17, 35, 80, 134, 135, 165–66, 206. *See also* justice

Lutz, Catherine, 281n10
Lye, Colleen, 19, 234n48, 266n65

MacArthur, Douglas, 21, 31, 37, 81, 84, 86, 90, 98; Hirohito and, 92, 93f2.1; wife of, 100, 101. *See also* Supreme Commander for the Allied Powers (SCAP)
Magee, John, 197, 198
Malaysia, 228n3
Mamdani, Mahmood, 209, 245n40
Manhattan Project, 213
Mao Tse-tung, 72
Marcos, Ferdinand, 212
Mariana Islands, 60, 63, 66, 241–42n19. *See also* Pacific Islands
Marshall Islands, 63, 65, 66, 212, 241–42n19. *See also* Pacific Islands
Matsui Yayori, 236n65, 260n27, 281n5
May, Elaine Tyler, 98, 251n47
Mbembe, Achille, 34, 141, 144, 267n75
McAlister, Melani, 18, 85, 99
McCormack, Gavan, 46, 141, 145, 225n3
McNamara, Robert S., 232n36
Mekiki-net, 263n42
Men and Women's Collaborative Participation (*danjo kyōdō sankaku*), 113
"Mexican-American," 56, 57
Micronesia, 2, 63, 64, 66, 103
Miki, Roy, 275n56
militarization, 24, 27, 53, 64, 97, 126, 130, 178, 192, 207, 208, 236n63, 263n46
"the military normal," 281n10
Min, Pyong Gap, 229n10
Minear, Richard H., 232n37, 237n69
Minow, Martha, 230n21
miracle, 133
Mishima Yukio, 143
Mitsubishi Heavy Industry, 173
Mitsubishi Materials Corp. et al. v. Superior Court of Orange Co., 159, 271n20, 271n27, 272n33
Mitsui O.S.K. Line Ltd., 173–74
Mitsui, Hideko, 260n33
Miyagi, Kimiko, 55, 242n23
Mizuno, Naoki, 254n62
modernity: belated, 20, 232–33n38; colonial, 8, 21, 28, 30, 48, 97; humanism

and 9–10; imperial, 20, 67; liberalism and, 143; terror and, 144; racialized 195, 231–32n33, 252–53n56
modernization theory, 62, 63, 95; "functional equivalents," 63
Mohanty, Chandra Talpade, 253n56
Molasky, Michael S., 242n22, 242n23
Morimura, Seiichi, 237n71
Morris-Suzuki, Tessa, 103, 254n62, 259n23
multiculturalism: Cold War, 175, 234n48; Canada, 275n56; Japan, 48, 57, 140; "liberal racism" and, 136, 265n62; nationalism and, 172; United States, 141, 152, 163. *See also* politics of recognition
Murayama Tomiichi, 240n6
Murdock, George Peter, 65, 66, 208, 209, 244n32, 245n38
Murmuring (1995), *The*, 281n3

Nagata Kōzō, 261n39
Nakagawa Shōichi, 262n42
Nakano Toshio, 30, 237n68
Namihira Tsuneo, 67, 68, 242n20
Nanjing Massacre, 32, 188, 189, 197, 198, 199, 200, 237n72. See also *In the Name of the Emperor*
Nashel, Jonathan, 18
national allegories, 54
National History, 192, 196, 200, 267n77; Japan, 111, 116, 136, 137, 150, 190, 194, 200, 275n2; South Korea, 229n10; United States, 163–64, 165, 169, 173, 175, 178, 179, 192, 194, 195–96. *See also* nationalism
National Police Reserve, 145. *See also* Japan Self-Defense Forces
National Research Council-Pacific Science Board (NRC-PSB), 58, 63, 65
National Standards for United States History, 207, 279–80n39
nationalism, 5, 19, 31, 57, 58, 69, 97, 178, 191, 243n30, 246n46; complicity of, 146, 152, 191–92, 200, 225–26n4, 235–36n61, 267n77; as heteropatriarchal, 54, 55, 111, 114, 118–19, 150, 258–59n23; Japanese, 107, 111, 139,

Treaty of Peace between the Union of Burma and Japan (1955), 227n3
Truman, Harry, 159, 160, 189, 196
Truth and Reconciliation Commissions, 1, 11, 13, 15, 75, 121, 231n25, 233n39

uranium, 213
United States Civil Administration of the Ryukyu Islands (USCAR), 246n41
United States-Japan Security Treaty (1960), 31, 45, 81, 175, 239n2, 256n2; as Japan's lifeline, 141
U.S. Army/Marine Corps Counterinsurgency Field Manual, 281n10
Ueno Chizuko, 258n21
Ukai Satoshi, 121
"un-American," 188, 193, 200
unconditional surrender, 199
unforgivability, 133, 134
United Kingdom, 29
"unjust enrichment," 158
(un)redressability, vii, 14, 15, 16, 133, 134, 172, 201, 205, 206, 210; anticolonial, antiracist critique of, 25, 27–30, 31–32, 34–36, 76, 156, 160, 237n73, 267n75, 270–71n18; asymmetries of, 160, 271n19; Cold War/cold war formations and ix, 36, 37, 112, 139, 156, 213; colonial injustice and, 3, 5, 14, 16, 29, 159; Orientalist explanation of, 162; nuclear violence and 197; space of exception and, 55, 204. See also impunity; war crimes
USA Patriot Act, 207
Utsumi Aiko, 32, 226n8, 235n59, 270n18

vengeance, 204
Vichy regime, 4
victor's exoneration, 31
"victor's justice," 16, 31, 81, 138, 232n37
Video Juku, 255nEpigraph
Vietnam, Democratic Republic of, 22
violence, viii-ix; asymmetry of, 56; Cold War and, xi, 5, 22–23, 51, 52, 72, 163; carceral, 55, 204, 232n33; (il)legibility of, viii, 15, 52, 164, 179, 205; intercon-nectedness of, 5, 72; longue durée of, 8, 13; postviolence and, 14, 36, 46, 121; transferability of, 52. See also human rights; Japanese military comfort system; war crimes
Violence against Women in War-Network, Japan (VAWW-NET), 122, 128
Violence in War and Peace, 23, 235n54
Volpp, Leti, 9, 101, 230n20, 252–53n56, 273n39
"voluntary affiliation," 24
Von Eschen, Penny M., 99, 251n48

Walker, J. Samuel, 276n12
War Claims Fund, 270n14
war crimes, 2, 26, 33, 102, 133; gender and sexual violence as, 26, 122–23, 127, 131; United States and, 15, 16, 31, 122, 156, 232n36, 233n39. See also war crimes (Japan)
war crimes (Japan), viii, 2, 16, 31–32, 36, 73–74, 76, 126, 127, 131–32, 139, 142, 150, 154, 157–62, 197–98, 213; "Americanization" of, 152, 157, 169, 175; "Asian/Americanization" of 146, 149–53, 161, 200; B and C class, 227n8; impunity of, 138; as non-justiciable, 161, 162; unforgivability of, 134. See also Japanese military comfort system; war crimes
war crimes trials, 11; former Yugoslavia, 123. See also International Military Tribunal for the Far East (IMTFE); Women's Tribunal
war memories, 74, 116, 151, 162–70
"war on terror," 107, 208, 210
Watkins, Yoko Kawashima, 170
White, Geoffrey, 275n1
Will, George F., 81, 83–84
Williams, Randall, 8, 275n57
Williams, Williams Appleman, 225n2
women of color feminism, 248n11, 253n56
women of color, 105, 124
"women warriors," 86, 87, 88
women's human rights, 9, 10, 26, 105, 123, 127, 130, 150; 230n20, 259–60n27. See also human rights

Women's International War Crimes Tribunal on Japan's Military Sexual Slavery (Women's Tribunal), 28, 111, 122–24, 126–7, 134, 135, 140, 204, 206–7, 231n25, 255nEpigraph, 259n27, 260n27
World War II, x, xi, 1, 5; as "good war," 20, 21, 22, 83, 140, 169, 209. *See also* Asia-Pacific War

Yagi Hidetsugu, 121
Yamatani Eriko, 121
Yang, Daqing, 237n71

Yang, Hyunah, 260n31
Yasumaru Yoshio, 117, 118
Yuen Ching-lin, 111, 255nEpigraph
Yui Daizaburō, 276n2
Yun Chŏng-ok, 26, 28, 259–60n27

zainichi Korean, 103, 106, 238n74, 240n11
Zhou Enlai, 74, 131, 132–35, 264n49
Žižek, Slavoj, 13, 136
Zolo, Danilo, 33, 35, 238n76, 253n60
Zschernig v. Miller, 271n21